Chalkis Aitolias I
The prehistoric periods

Chalkis Aitolias I
The prehistoric periods

Edited by *Søren Dietz & Ioannis Moschos*

 Monographs of the Danish Institute at Athens,
Volume 7

This book is dedicated to the memory of Consul General Erik Gösta Georg Enbom (1895-1986).

Although born in Sweden Enbom spent most of his life in Europe and the Mediterranean. His intimate acquaintance with Greece made him an obvious member of the first Swedish Red Cross expedition to a starving Greece during the Second World War in 1942. For the rest of his life he lived in Athens and served in many years as a Danish Consul General in Piraeus representing first of all the Danish shipyard and engine factory Burmeister and Wain.

Enbom's interest in Classical archaeology derived from his acquaintance with another participant in the Red Cross expedition, the Uppsala professor Axel W. Persson. In 1982 Enbom established Consul General Gösta Enboms foundation which took full effect at his death on January 3 1986. Its prime purpose is to support Danish field archaeology in the Mediterranian and especially in Greece. Since the establishment the foundation has supported a broad series of archaeological activities especially in Greece and Tunisia. The Chalkis project in Aitolia (1995-2001) is the first excavation entirely sponsored by Enbom's foundation.

Athens, September 2005
Søren Dietz

Monographs of the Danish Institute at Athens
Volume 7

General Editor: Erik Hallager
Graphic design: Lone Simonsen & Erik Hallager
Printed at Clemenstrykkeriet, Århus

Printed in Denmark on permanent paper
conforming to ANSI Z 39.48-1992

The publication was sponsored by:
Nordea Danmark-fonden
Hielmstierne-Rosencroneske Stiftelse
The Eleni Nakou Foundation
The Consul General Gösta Enbom's foundation

ISBN: 87 7288 866 0
ISSN: 1397 1433

Distributed by:
AARHUS UNIVERSITY PRESS
Langelandsgade 177
DK-8200 Århus N
Fax (+45) 8942 5380

73 Lime Walk
Headington, Oxford OX3 7AD
Fax (+44) 865 750 079

Box 511
Oakvill, Conn. 06779
Fax (+1) 203 945 94 9468

Cover illustration:
Front: Drawing by Kaj Strand Petersen (from diary).
Back: Aghia Triada. Area II, west of Aghia Triada
from south. (Photo: Henrik Frost).

Contents

9   Preface
Søren Dietz, Lazaros Kolonas, Ioannis Moschos and *Sanne Houby-Nielsen*

13   Acknowledgments
14   List of illustrations
19   Abbreviations
20   Bibliography
35   The systematic approach and the numbering system

37   Part I
      The Bronze Age periods at Aghia Triada

      Chapter 1
38   Studies in the Bronze Age of Aghia Triada. A summary
      Søren Dietz and *Ioannis Moschos*
38   A definition of Early Helladic I
48   A definition of MHIIIB/LHIA
52   A definition of LHIB
55   A definition of Late Helladic III
61   Flint and obsidian from the Bronze Age deposits – a note
63   The faunal remains from the Bronze Age deposits of Aghia Triada
       Pernille Bangsgaard Jensen

      Chapter 2
64   Catalogue of contexts and finds from Aghia Triada (Area I and the area west of Aghia Triada (Area II)
      Søren Dietz
64   Classification of Pottery
69   Pottery – catalogue of contexts and finds
110   Catalogue of flint and obsidian
114   List of concordance

      Part II
116   The neolithic remains at Pangali

117   The site of Pangali, Mt. Varassova in Aitolia and the Late Neolithic Ib phase in the Aegean: social transformations and changing ideology
      Theofanis Mavridis and *Lasse Sørensen*
117   Introduction
      Theofanis Mavridis

118 The Pottery
Theofanis Mavridis

140 The chipped stone assemblage and the bone material
Lasse Sørensen

162 The animal bones from Pangali
Pernille Bangsgaard Jensen

Appendix 1
171 Shellfish in the stratigraphical context of Final Neolithic and Bronze Age supplemented by ^{14}C dating.
Kaj Strand Petersen

Appendix 2
178 The animal bones from Aghia Triada
Pernille Bangsgaard Jensen

Appendix 3
196 Radiocarbon dates on shellfish from Chalkis, Aitolias.
Jan Heinemeier

199 Summary
Søren Dietz and *Ioannis Moschos*

202 Plates

Preface

Søren Dietz, Lazaros Kolonas, Ioannis Moschos and Sanne Houby-Nielsen

The site of Chalkis placed "hard by the sea" was mentioned first by Homer as one of the five cities in the Aitolian coastland which took part in the Trojan War. Later on, in the 5th century B.C. Thucydides informs us that Chalkis was originally a Corinthian possession, among the chain of strongholds (apoikiai) founded along the important sea route from the home city to the colonies in Sicily and Southern Italy. In the middle of the 5th century B.C. the town fell to the Athenians and remained an Athenian possession during the Peloponnesian war.

Ancient Chalkis was identified by travellers in the 18th century who more or less agreed on the general position of the site on the evidence of the ancient historical sources. Travellers who actually visited the site shared the opinion that ancient Chalkis was the fortified site placed on a plateau on the east side of Mount Varassova, and it was not until 1916 that the Greek archaeologist

Fig. 1. Photo of the village of KatoVasiliki between the mountains Varassova (left) and Klokova (right). Seen from the mountains behind Patra at Voundeni (FPR, 245, fig. 4).

Fig. 2. A view inland from the summit of Aghia Triada.

Fig. 3. The mound of Aghia Triada from East (FPR, 257, fig. 7).

Konstantinos Rhomaios suggested that the coastal site of Aghia Triada east of the present-day village of Kato Vasiliki should more probably be identified as the ancient city.[1]

The 30 metre high sandstone mound of Aghia Triada is situated on the coast between the two substantial mountains of Varassova (915 m above sea level) and Klokova (1039 m above sea level) close to the small village of Kato Vasiliki further west (Fig. 1). To day the inhabitants, as they have probably always done, live partly as fishers in the gulf of Patras and partly as farmers in the well-watered and fertile valley behind the Aghia Triada itself (Fig. 2). The name of the hill derives from the 8th cent. AD basilica (with later additions) placed on a plateau on top of the mound, sur-

---

[1] For Chalkis in Ancient Written Sources and Modern Travel Accounts see Sanne Houby-Nielsen in *FPR*, 238-254.

Fig. 4. Map showing the position of Aghia Triada and Pangali (FPR, 236, fig. 2).

rounded by a substantial and still rather well preserved Byzantine fortification wall.

The mound stands on a shallow, alluvial plain bordering the sea (Fig. 3). The area on the eastern side, with little soil above bedrock, is quite different from the plain on the west side, towards the village. Geological surveys and drillings in this area indicated that a small bay had existed here in antiquity and that the low level surface, approximately 1 metre above sea level, actually rests on deposits produced during the last thousands of years. A narrow stream draining the plain in the interior into the sea is still seen between the mound and the village. It is supposed that the harbour of Chalkis

mentioned by Thucydides was situated along the borders of the lagoon.

Today the ancient remains on the mound of Aghia Triada are dominated by the above mentioned three-aisled Byzantine basilica and the fortification wall around the upper plateau. Byzantine activities on the hill have caused considerable damage and destruction to previous layers of occupation especially of the habitation which once existed on the upper plateau in Antiquity. On the top of the mound only very few insignificantly preserved levels situated directly on the bedrock were found during the excavations. Surface collections on the other hand confirmed that habitations once existed

Fig. 5. The site Pangali with the upper and lower terraces to the left and Mt. Varassova to the right. Patras and the Gulf of Patras is visible in the background. Photo: L. Sørensen.

there. On the terraces below the Byzantine wall the situation was much better, especially on the level middle terrace on the north east side of the mound where considerable areas occupied especially during the Archaic period and in Hellenistic times were found. As will appear from this first final publication important layers from the early part of the Early Helladic period were located in addition. In contrast to the conditions on the mound itself the level plain west of the mound near the suggested ancient harbour of Chalkis gave much better possibilities for detecting undisturbed levels of pre-Byzantine date. In the trenches opened, covering approximately 100 sq. metres, a stratigraphy of habitation strata from, first of all Archaic times, with well-preserved architecture, with interruptions to the Early Bronze Age were excavated down to a level of 3.5 to 4 metres below surface.

In contrast to the situation on Aghia Triada, not much had been disturbed since antiquity on the place called Pangali on the east slope of Mount Varassova (Fig. 4). Towards north and south the terrace is framed by substantial fortification walls probably of the fourth century B.C. constructed from ashlars made of local limestone, quarried at the site (Fig. 5). Surveys on the terrace carried out in 1995 disclosed substantial square buildings near the northern enceinte but remains of human activities were scanty and all of late classical date. The conclusion to be drawn was, that the site of Pangali in late classical antiquity had been a place of refuge for inhabitants of the valley in troubled times.

During the survey we located in the southern part of the plateau and above the sea thanks to considerable concentrations of sherds and flint/obsidian on the surface a substantial Final Neolithic site laid out in connection with a shelter. In 1996 a trial excavation in a small trench, 2x2 metres was carried out. The results of the field project at the Neolithic site at Pangali as well as the cultural context and chronological horizon of the material from Pangali are presented in this volume by Theofanis Mavridis and Lasse Sørensen.

The present volume is the first in a series of publications dealing with the results of the field work in Chalkis Aitolias 1995-2001. In preparation are the following successive volumes: Chalkis Aitolias II: The Archaic Periods by Sanne Houby-Nielsen. Chalkis Aitolias III: The Classical and Hellenistic Periods at Aghia Triada and the fortification at Pangali by Elizabeth Bollen, Søren Dietz, Lazaros Kolonas and Mette Mouritzen. Chalkis Aitolias IV: The Remains of the Byzantine Period at Aghia Triada.

Acknowledgments

The Chalkis Aitolias project is indebted to the inhabitants of the village of Kato Vasiliki for hospitality during the seven years of field work in Chalkis. Our thanks also go to the mayor of Gavrolimni who put at our disposal as workshop and store rooms the ancient school of Aghia Triada close to the site. Thanks also go to the Ephoria in Patras and the present Ephor Dr. Michalis Petropoulos.

Drawings for the various chapters were made by respectively Søren Dietz, Theofanis Mavridis and Lasse Sørensen; in addition a few drawing were made by Anne Hooton and Ann Thomas. Inking of the original pottery drawings was done by Irini Gkion. During the campaigns in Chalkis Aitolias photographs were taken by Mr. Henrik Frost. (Fig. 6).

The editors would like to thank all the enthusiastic students and younger scholars who have taken part in the excavations during the years and especially the highly qualified technicians, who took part in the work during all or major parts of the years in Chalkis: Apostolis Zarkadoulas, Spiros Pittas, Dimitris Evangeliou, Avgerinos Anastasopoulos and Eugenios Tsamis. Special thanks also go to the surveyor Charalambos Marinopoulos and conservator Leonidas Pavlatos for their excellent contributions to the project.

Consul General Gösta Enboms Foundation generously sponsored the field project and the subsequent studies of the excavated material. We are most grateful to the foundation for an excellent cooperation over the years.

This publication was sponsored by Nordea Danmark Fonden, Den Hielmstierne-Rosencroneske Stiftelse, Consul General Gösta Enboms Foundation and The Eleni Nakou Foundation.

The editors are greatly indebted to Professor Richard Tomlinson of Birmingham for his correction of the English text and his helpful suggestions.

Fig. 6. The excavation team. Campaign 1997.

List of illustrations

List of Figures:

Fig. 1   Photo of the village of KatoVasiliki between the mountains Varassova (left) and Klokova (right). Seen from the mountains behind Patra at Voundeni (FPR, 245, fig. 4).

Fig. 2   A view inland from the summit of Aghia Triada.

Fig. 3   The mound of Aghia Triada from East (FPR, 257, fig. 7).

Fig. 4   Map showing the position of Aghia Triada and Pangali (FPR, 236, fig. 2).

Fig. 5   The site Pangali with the upper and lower terraces to the left and Mt. Varassova to the right. Patras and the Gulf of Patras is visible in the background. Photo: L. Sørensen.

Fig. 6   The excavation team. Campaign 1997.

Fig. 7   Map of the mound of Aghia Triada and the area west of the hill with contours and grid system (Charalambos Marinopoulos). Areas I and II are shown on Fig. 8.

Fig. 8   Trench and structure numbers in Areas I (8a) and II (8b) (only numbers mentioned in the text are shown).

Fig. 9   Plan showing measurements of structures on Pangali and the position of the Final Neolithic site.

Fig. 10   Aghia Triada. Statistical survey (a and b) of EHI pottery classes (Tx43 and Tx20).

Fig. 11   Types of pottery from the EHI period. Early phase. 1:4.

Fig. 12   Types of pottery from the EHI period. Late phase. 1:4.

Fig. 13   Types of pottery from the EHI period. Various. 1:4.

Fig. 14   Statistical survey of MHIIIB/LHIA pottery classes from stratified layers in Area II (K27 to K29 and Tx72).

Fig. 15   Types of pottery from the MHIIIB/LHIA period. 1:4.

Fig. 16   Types of pottery from the MH period and the LHIB period. 1:4.

Fig. 17   Area II. Statistical survey of LHIII pottery classes from stratified layers (K27 to K29 and Tx72).

Fig. 18   Types of pottery from the LHIII period. 1:4.

Fig. 19   Diagrams showing the distribution of domesticated mammals from respectively the EHI periods and the MH/LH periods.

Fig. 20   Aghia Triada. F15/4/SW. Catalogue no. 20, sherd with vertical MP bands.

Fig. 21   Aghia Triada, Area I. Section Tx20, SE and analytical plan og strata excavated in Tx20. 1:50.

Fig. 22   Aghia Triada, Area I. Catalogue no. 26 (MT-unburnished).

Fig. 23   Aghia Triada, Area I. Catalogue no. 39 (CT-unburnished).

Fig. 24   Aghia Triada, Area I. Strap handles in CT-unburnished (Tx43/3a).

Fig. 25   Aghia Triada, Area I. Catalogue no. 75 (MT-Red burnished).

Fig. 26   Aghia Triada, Area I. Catalogue no. 98 (CT-unburnished, "Terrazzo-ware").

Fig. 27   Aghia Triada, Area I. Catalogue no. 100 (CT-unburnished).

Fig. 28   Aghia Triada, Area I. Catalogue no. 105 (KW-sand-tempered).

Fig. 29   Aghia Triada, Area I. MT-unburnished, horizontal lug handle (Tx20/4b).

Fig. 30   Aghia Triada, Area I. Two sherds from Tx20/4b. Vertical strap handle (CT-unburnished, "Terrazzo-ware") and a MT-unburnished sherd with plastic list and finger marks.

Fig. 31   Aghia Triada, Area I. CT-handle/body sherd and a MT-unburnished base. Tx20/4b.

Fig. 32   Aghia Triada, Area I. Vertical strap handle. Black burnished (MT-sand-tempered). Tx20/4b.

Fig. 33   Aghia Triada, Area I. Section through trenches N26 and N27. 1:50.

Fig. 34   Aghia Triada, Area II. Plan showing trench numbers and sections drawn in the area west of Aghia Triada. 1:100.

Fig. 35   Aghia Triada, Area II. Section Tx70/Tx71/Tx72. 1:100.

Fig. 36   Aghia Triada, Area II. Analytical plan showing strata excavated in trench Tx70. 1:50.

Fig. 37   Aghia Triada, Area II. Analytical plan I showing excavated strata measured in the deep sounding in trench Tx72. 1:50.

Fig. 38   Aghia Triada, Area II. Analytical plan II showing excavated strata in the deep sounding in Tx72. 1:50.

Fig. 39   Aghia Triada, Area II. Catalogue no. 134. Bowl with wish-bone handle.

Fig. 40   Aghia Triada, Area II. Loom-weight F98-3024 from Tx70/5.

Fig. 41   Aghia Triada, Area II. Catalogue no. 149. Cup with lustrous paint.

Fig. 42   Aghia Triada, Area II. Catalogue no. 150. Cup with lustrous paint.

Fig. 43   Aghia Triada, Area II. Catalogue no. 156. Strap handle from closed shaped jar. MP.

Fig. 44   Aghia Triada, Area II. Catalogue no. 158 (upper left) (FT). Catalogue no. 160 (lower) (MT). Catalogue 161 (upper right) (MT)

Fig. 45   Aghia Triada, Area II. Catalogue no. 159 (MT).

Fig. 46   Aghia Triada, Area II. Catalogue no. 163 (lower) (KW). Catalogue no. 164 (upper) (CT).

Fig. 47   Aghia Triada, Area II. Catalogue no. 168 (MT/MP).

Fig. 48   Aghia Triada, Area II. Catalogue no. 177 (MT/MP) (lower). Various: base of goblet (upper) (MT/MP) (bag no. 1841).

Fig. 49   Aghia Triada, Area II. Double conical bead (MT) (F98-3511).

Fig. 50   Aghia Triada, Area II. Catalogue no. 186 (upper and lower side).

Fig. 51   Aghia Triada, Area II. Prehistoric architectural remains from trenches K27-K29 (TRP, 183, fig. 9).

Fig. 52   Aghia Triada, Area II. Rear part of Mycenaean idol (horse?).

Fig. 53   Aghia Triada, Area II. Sherds from K28/9 2p. Catalogue nos. 197 (lower), 198 (upper left), 199 (upper right).

Fig. 54   Aghia Triada, Area II. K29, NE section.

Fig. 55   Aghia Triada, Area II. K29 Analytical plan of S-section. 1:50.

Fig. 56   Aghia Triada, Area II. K29. Analytical plan of SW section. 1:50.

Fig. 57   Aghia Triada, Area II. K29. Plan indicating the position of the sections and soundings. 1:100.

Fig. 58   Aghia Triada, Area II. K29. The structure ARJ.

Fig. 59   Aghia Triada, Area II. K29. The pebble floor ARM.

Fig. 60   Aghia Triada, Area II. K29. Pyramidal loom-weight F01-3015.

Fig. 61   Aghia Triada, Area II. K29/ARK. Catalogue no. 233a (F01-3025).

Fig. 62   Aghia Triada, Area II. K29/9b 1p. Catalogue no. 239. Triangular handle.

Fig. 63   Flint and obsidian from EH I levels at Aghia Triada. Photos by Lasse Sørensen.

Fig. 64   Pangali. The trench excavated.

Fig. 65a-e Pangali. Pottery - statistics.

Fig. 66   Pangali. Burnished wares.

Fig. 67   Pangali. Incised wares.

Fig. 68a-c Pangali. Jars and pithoi.

Fig. 69a-c Pangali. Lugs and handles.

Fig. 70a-b Pangali. Ring bases.

Fig. 71   Pangali. Spindle whorls.

Fig. 72   Map with selected Late and Final Neolithic sites in the Aegean and the Aegean obsidian sources with the primary and secondary distribution areas indicated. Partly after Torrence 1986; Broodbank 1999; Runnels & Murray 2001. L. Sørensen and K. Langsted.

Fig. 73   Pangali. The different types of raw materials. Front row: Marble. Second row: Radiolarite. Third row: Flint. Fourth row: Obsidian. Photo: L. Sørensen.

Fig. 74   Pangali. The frequency and weight of the different raw materials. L. Sørensen and C. Casati.

Fig. 75   The difference between the conceptual scheme and the chaîne opératoire. L. Sørensen and K. Langsted.

Fig. 76   Schematic illustration of a generalized reduction sequence, with the three main phases in the chaîne opératoire outlined in the article. L. Sørensen and C. Casati.

Fig. 77   Pangali. The different production strategies according to each raw material. L. Sørensen and C. Casati.

Fig. 78   Pangali. The different phases in the chaîne operatoire. L. Sørensen and C. Casati.

Fig. 79   Pangali. Generalized reduction sequence for radiolarite, flint and marble, indicating the different phases identified at Pangali. L. Sørensen & C. Casati.

Fig. 80   Pangali. The different tool types identified. L. Sørensen and C. Casati.

Fig. 81   Pangali. Flint technological observations L. Sørensen and C. Casati.

Fig. 82 Generalized reduction sequences for the obsidian assemblage indicating the different stages of the obsidian exchange. L. Sørensen and K. Langsted.

Fig. 83 Pangali. The different point types identified. L. Sørensen & K. Langsted.

Fig. 84 Pangali. The amount of unfinished points. L. Sørensen & K. Langsted.

Fig. 85 Pangali. The amount of sheep, goats, pigs and cows on comparable Final Neolithic cave and open air sites. L. Sørensen (graphics). Partly after Halstead 1996.

Fig. 86★ The amount of obsidian found at selected Late and Final Neolithic sites in Greece. Partly after Perlés 1990a, table 4. L. Sørensen.

Fig. 87★ Selected Late and Final Neolithic sites with their percentage of obsidian found at the sites compared with the distance to Melos, indicating two different fall off patterns. K. Langsted and L. Sørensen.

Fig. 88 The tiny *Columbella rustica* which might have been used as charms in the Late Neolithic (Bag no. 10/07/96).

Fig. 89 *Hexaples trunculus*, one of the finds from Late Neolithic with special hole on the last whorl possibly chipped off for extraction of the colour yielding hypobranchial glan (Bag no. 19/07/96).

Fig. 90 The large *Patella caerulea* recorded from the Late Neolithic Pangali material. (Bag no. 17/07/96).

Fig. 91 Limpets used as pendant at the National Archaeological Museum in Athens.

Fig. 92 Cormorant chick?"hiding" among the Patella shells in the shore region on the island of Colonsay in the Hebrides. Here many of the Limpets (*Patella vulgata*) are seen with hole in the topmost part.

Fig. 93 Air photo over the Chalkis area with Aghia Triada (HT) east of the small fishing town of Kato Vassiliki (K.V.) with the former Bay (F.B.) in between. The area is situated between the mountains Varassova (V) and Klokova (KL). R.C. stands for rocky coast and S.B. sandy beach.

Fig. 94a-b Catalogue of shellfish from Pangali and Aghia Triada.

Fig. 95 Plot of the probability distributions in the calibrated ages of the series of marine shells and one terrestrial charcoal sample.

★ Full captions with figures

List of plates

Pl. 1 Aghia Triada. Survey 1995. Selected finds and pottery from F15/AAC-3/NW. 1:3.

Pl. 2 Aghia Triada. Pottery from F15/AAC-3/SW and F15/AAC-4/SW. 1:3.

Pl. 3 Aghia Triada, Area I. Pottery from Tx43/3, 3a and 3c. 1:3.

Pl. 4 Aghia Triada, Area I. Pottery from Tx43/3d. 1:3.

Pl. 5 Aghia Triada, Area I. Pottery from Tx43/4. 1:3.

Pl. 6 Aghia Triada, Area I. Pottery from Tx43/4b. 1:3.

Pl. 7 Aghia Triada, Area I. Pottery from Tx43/4b (continued) and Tx43/5. 1:3.

Pl. 8 Aghia Triada, Area I. Pottery from Tx20/3, Tx20/4 and Tx20/4b. 1:3.

Pl. 9 Aghia Triada, Area I. Pottery from N26 and N27. 1:3.

Pl. 10 Aghia Triada, Area II. Pottery from Tx70/5. 1:3.

Pl. 11 Aghia Triada, Area II. Pottery from Tx70/5a, Tx70/6 and Tx71/7. 1:3.

Pl. 12 Aghia Triada, Area II. Pottery from Tx72/ARA/1, Tx72/ARA/2 and Tx72/11. 1:3.

Pl. 13 Aghia Triada, Area II. Pottery from Tx72/12 and Tx72/13. 1:3.

Pl. 14 Aghia Triada, Area II. Pottery from K27/6a and b, K28/9 2p, K28 AQZ/3 and K28/AQJ/2. 1:3.

Pl. 15 Aghia Triada, Area II. Pottery from K29/7b 1p, K29/7e 2p and K29/7e 3p. 1:3.

Pl. 16 Aghia Triada, Area II. Pottery from K29/8e 2p, K29/8e 3p, K29/ARK, K29/9b 1p and K29/9b 2p. 1:3.

Pl. 17 Aghia Triada, Area II. Pottery from K29/10b, K29/ARM 1N, K29/11b 1p, K29/11b pit, K29/11b 3p and K29/11b 6p. 1:3.

Pl. 18★ Drawings of selected flaked-tools from EHI. Drawing by Lasse Sørensen.

Pl. 19★ Drawings of selected blades and flakes from EHI. Drawing by Lasse Sørensen.

Pl. 20★ Drawings of selected tools, blades and flakes from MHIII, LHIB and LHIII. Drawing by Lasse Sørensen.

Pl. 21 Pangali. Fine burnished and smoothed wares. Open shapes. 1:3.

Pl. 22 Pangali. Fine burnished and smoothed

wares. Open shapes (18-20) and open mouthed closed shapes (21-24). Open shapes with asymmetrical rim (25-28). 1:3.

Pl. 23 Pangali. Incised ware. 1:3.

Pl. 24 Pangali. Closed and open mouthed shapes. 1:3.

Pl. 25 Pangali. Coarse wares. 1:3.

Pl. 26 Pangali. Lug and handles (63-82) and fine burnished ware with plastic decoration (83-84).

Pl. 27 Pangali. Bases. 1:3.

Pl. 28 Pangali. Motifs of incised ware. 1:3.

Pl. 29 Pangali. Various clay items. 1:3.

Pl. 30★ Pangali. Drawings of small flake and blade cores. C. Casati (graphic) and L. Sørensen (drawing).

Pl. 31★ Pangali. Drawings of selected larger flake cores. C. Casati (graphic) and L. Sørensen (drawing).

Pl. 32★ Pangali. Drawings of selected microblades and blades from Pangali. C. Casati (graphics) and L. Sørensen (drawings).

Pl. 33★ Pangali. Drawings of selected obsidian blades. C. Casati (graphic) and L. Sørensen (drawing).

Pl. 34★ Pangali. Drawings of selected artifacts. C. Casati (graphic) and L. Sørensen (drawings).

Pl.35★ Pangali. Drawings of selected scrapers. C. Casati (graphic) and L. Sørensen (drawings).

Pl. 36★ Pangali. Drawings of selected scrapers. C. Casati (graphic) and L. Sørensen (drawings).

Pl. 37★ Pangali. Drawings of selected obsidian artifacts. C. Casati (graphic) and L. Sørensen (drawings).

Pl. 38★ Pangali. Drawings of selected points. C. Casati (graphic) and L. Sørensen (drawings).

Pl. 39★ Pangali. Drawings of selected preformed points. C. Casati (graphic) and L. Sørensen (drawings).

Pl. 40★ Pangali. Drawings of bone tools. Graphic by C. Casati . Drawings by L. Sørensen and Anne Hooton.

Pl. 41 Pangali. Drawing of a socketed antler beam with a shaft hole. Graphic by C. Casati. Drawings by L. Sørensen and Anne Hooton.

Pl. 42 Pangali. Drawing of a larger chisel tool with rounded ends. Graphic by C. Casati. Drawings by L. Sørensen and Anne Hooton.

★ Full caption with plates

Tables on pages 166-170

Table 1 Pangali. The distribution of faunal remains.

Table 2 Pangali. The distribution of fused and non-fused bones for domesticated pig.

Table 3 Pangali. Measurements for the pig bones (in mm).

Table 4 Pangali. The distribution of fused and non-fused bones for cattle.

Table 5 Pangali. The distribution of fused and non-fused bones for sheep/goat.

Table 6 Pangali. Measurements for the sheep bones (in mm).

Table 7 Pangali. Measurements for the goat bones (in mm).

Table 8 Pangali. Measurements for the wild pig bones (in mm).

Table 9 Pangali. The distribution of fused and non-fused bones for roe deer.

Table 10 Pangali. Measurements for the roe deer bones (in mm).

Table 11 Pangali. Measurements for the red fox bones (in mm).

Table 12 Pangali. Measurements for the wild cat bones (in mm).

Table 13 Pangali. Measurements for the hare bones (in mm).

Tables on pages 185-195

Table 1 The distribution of faunal remains found at Aghia Triada.

Table 2 Mandibles from domesticated pig, Sus domesticus.

Table 3 The distribution of fused and non-fused bones for domesticated pig, Sus domesticus.

Table 4 The distribution of fused and non-fused bones for cattle, Bos Taurus.

Table 5 The distribution of fused and non-fused bones for, Equus sp.

Table 6 The distribution of fused and non-fused bones for sheep/goat, Ovis/Capra sp.

Table 7 Mandibles from sheep/goat, Ovis/Capra sp.

Table 8 The distribution of fused and non-fused bones for goat, Capra hircus.

Table 9 The distribution of fused and non-fused bones for sheep, Ovis aries.

Table 10 The distribution of fused and non-fused bones for dog, Canis familiaris.

Table 11 The distribution of faunal material found at Aghia Triada, from the EHI period.

Table 12   The distribution of faunal material found at
            Aghia Triada, from the MH and LH
            periods.
Table 13   Measurements for the pig, *Sus s. domesti-
            cus* bones (in mm).
Table 14   Measurements for the cattle, *Bos taurus*
            bones (in mm).
Table 15   Measurements for the horse/donkey.
Table 16   Measurements for the goat, *Capra hircus*
            bones (in mm).
Table 17   Measurements for the sheep, *Ovis aries*
            bones (in mm).
Table 18   Measurements for the dog.
Table 19   Measurements for the red deer.
Table 20   Measurements for the fox.
Table 21   Measurements for the beech marten.
Table 22   Measurements for the hare.
Table 23   Measurements for the chicken.

Abbreviations

Date:

EH   Early Helladic
FN   Final Neolithic
MH   Middle Helladic
LH   Late Helladic
LN   Late Neolithic

Bibliographical abbreviations

FPR   First preliminary Report.
Surveys and Excavations in Chalkis, Aetolias, 1995-1996. First preliminary report. Edited by Søren Dietz, Lazaros Kolonas, Ioannis Moschos & Sanne Houby-Nielsen. *PDIA* II, Athens 1998, 232-317.

MDIA   Monographs of the Danish Institute at Athens.

Nikopolis
Nikopolis. Foundation and destruction. Nikopolis and northwestern Greece. The archaeological evidence for the destructions, the foundation of Nikopolis and the Synoicism, MDIA, Athens 2001.

PDIA   *Proceedings of the Danish Institute at Athens.*

Periphery 1
Η περιφέρεια του Μυκηναϊκου Κοσμου. Α' Διεθνές Διεπιστημονικό Συμπόσιο, Λαμία 25-29 Σεπτεμβρίου 1994, Lamia 1999.

Periphery 2
2nd International Interdisciplinary Colloquium, The periphery of the Mycenaean World, 26-30 September, Lamia 1999, N. Kyparissi-Apostolika & M. Papakonstantinou (eds.), Athens 2003.

SPR   Second preliminary report.
The Greek-Danish Excavations in Aetolian Chalkis 1997-1998. Second Preliminary Report. Edited by Søren Dietz, Lazaros Kolonas, Sanne Houby-Nielsen & Ioannis Moschos. *PDIA* IV, Athens 2000, 219-307.

TPR   Third Preliminary Report.
Greek-Danish Excavations at Aetolian Chalkis 1999-2001. Third preliminary report. Edited by Søren Dietz, Lazaros Kolonas, Sanne Houby-Nielsen, Ioannis Moschos & Jonas Eiring. *PDIA* IV, Athens 2004, 167-258.

Abbreviations of measurements★

D   Diameter
H   Hight
Th   Thickness
W   Width

★ All measurements of finds are, unless otherwise stated, given in cm.

Other abbreviations

STR   Stratum
TR   Trench

Bibliography

Alexopoulou, G. 1992
'Οδός Γερμανού 148/152',
ArchDelt 47, Chron B1, 135.

Alram-Stern E. 2004a
*Die Ägäische Frühzeit 2. Serie. Die
Ägäische Frühbronzezeit. For-
schungsbericht 1975-2002*, 2. Band,
Teil 1, Wien.

Alram-Stern, E. 2004b
*Die Ägäische Frühzeit 2. Serie. Die
Ägäische Frühbronzezeit. For-
schungsbericht 1975-2002*, 2. Band,
Teil 2, Wien.

Andreou, H. & I. Andreou 1999
'Η Κοιλάδα του Γορμού στό
Πωγώνι της Ηπείρου, κέντρο
ζωής και ανάπτωξη κατά την
πρώιμη εποχή του Σιδήρου,' in
Periphery 1, 77-90.

Andrefski, W. 1998
Lithics, Cambridge.

Agouridis, C. 1997
'Sea routes and navigation in the
third Millennium Aegean', *OJA* 16,
1-20.

Aslanis, I. 1998
'Η πρώτη εμφάνιση οχυπώσεων
σε προϊστορικούς οικισμούς του
Αιγαιακού χώρου', in *Κέα–Κύθ-
νος: Ιστορία και Αρχαιολογία*,
A.G. Medoni & A.I, Mazarakis
(eds.), Athens, 111-2.

Aslanis, I. 2003
'Η «αφανής» Χαλκολιθική εποχή
στην Ελλάδα: Μια άλλη μεθοδο-
λογική Προσέγγιση', in *The prehistoric research in Greece and its

perspectives: theoretical and methodological considerations*, Thessaloniki, 37-46.

Bailey, D. 2001
Balkan Prehistory, London/New
York.

Bailey, G. N. 1997a
*Klithi: Palaeolithic settlement and
quaternary environments in northwest
Greece. Vol. 1: Excavations and intra-
site analysis at Klithi*, Cambridge.

Bailey, G. N. 1997b
*Klithi: Palaeolithic settlement and
Quaternary environments in north-
west Greece. Vol. 2: Klithi in its
local and regional setting*,
Cambridge.

Baker, J. & D. Brothwell 1980
Animal diseases in archaeology,
London.

Bangsgaard, P. 2001
'Animal Bones from the Barbar
Well', in *Islamic Remains in
Bahrain*, Karen Frifelt (ed.), (Jut-
land Archaeological Society Pub-
lications, 37), Højbjerg, 183-200.

Basilogambrou, A.P. 1998
'Πρωτοελλαδικό νεκροταφείο στο
Καλαμάκι Ελαιοχωρίου-Λουσι-
κών Αχαΐας', in *Πρακτικά του
Ε'Διεθνούς Συνεδρίου Πελοποννησιακών Σπουδών, Άργος-Ναύ-
πλιον. Τόμος Α.*, Athens, 366-99.

Becker, C. 1986
*Kastanas. Ausgrabungen in einem
Siedlungshügel der Bronze- und
Eisenzeit Makedoniens 1975-1979.

Die Tierknochenfunde (Prähistorische Archäologie in Südosteuropa,
Band 5)*, Berlin.

Becker, C. 1991
'Die Tierknochenfunde von den
Platia Magoula Zarkou – neue
Untersuchungen zu Haustier-
haltung, Jagd und Rohstoffver-
wendung im neolitisch-bronzezeit-
lichen Thessalien', *PZ* 66, 14-78.

Belmont, J. & C. Renfrew 1964
'Two prehistoric sites on
Mykonos', *AJA* 68, 395-400.

Benton, S. 1931-32
'The Ionian Islands', *BSA* 32, 213-
46.

Benton, S. 1947
'Hagios Nikolaos near Astakos in
Akarnania', *BSA* 42, 170-83.

Binford, L. 1981
*Bones. Ancient men and modern
myths*, New York.

Blackman, D. 1997
'Archaeology in Greece 1996-97',
AR 43, 1-125.

Blackman, D. 1998
'Archaeology in Greece 1997-9',
AR 44, 1-128.

Blegen, C.W. 1921
*Korakou, a prehistoric settlement
near Corinth*, Boston/ New York.

Blegen, C.W. 1928
*Zygouries. A prehistoric settlement
in the valley of Cleonae*,
Cambridge Mass.

Blegen, C.W. 1937
Prosymna, Cambridge Mass.

Boessneck, J. 1960
'Zu den Tierknochenfunden aus der präkeramischen Schicht der Argissa-Magula', *Germania* 38, 336-40.

Boessneck J., H-H. Müller & M. Teichert 1964
'Osteologische Unterscheidungs-merkmale zwischen Schaf (*Ovis aries* Linné) und Ziege (*Capra hircus* Linné)', *Kühn-Archiv 78. band, heft,* Berlin.

Bronk Ramsey, C. 1995
'Radiocarbon calibration and analysis of stratigraphy: The OXCAL Program', *Radiocarbon* 37, 2, 425-30.

Broodbank, C. 1999
'Kythera Survey: preliminary report on the 1998 season', *BSA* 94, 191-214.

Broodbank, C. 2000
'Perspectives on an EBA island centre: an analysis of pottery from Kavos Daskalio (Keros) in the Cyclades', *OJA* 19, 4, 323-42.

Buchholz, H.-G. 1962
'Der Pfeilglätter aus dem VI. Schacht-grab von Mykene und die helladi-schen Pfeilspitzen', *JdI* 77, 1-58.

Bökönyi, S. 1989
'Animal remains', in *A Neolithic settlement in Thessaly, Greece, 6400-5600 B.C,* N. Gimbutas *et al.* (eds.) (Los Angeles, Monumenta Archaeologica vol. 14), 315-32.

Bökönyi, S. & D. J. Jánoossy 1986
'Faunal remains', in *Excavations at Sitagroi. A prehistoric village in Northeast Greece,* Renfrew C. *et al.* (eds.), vol.1 (Monumenta Archaeologica vol. 13), Los Angeles, 63-132.

Capelle, W. 1933
Marc Aurel Selbstbetrachtungen, Leipzig.

Carter, T. & Ydo M. 1996
'The chipped and ground stone', in *The Laconia Survey, Vol.II, The archaeological data,* W. Cavanagh, J. Crouwel, R.W.V. Catling & G. Shipley (eds.), London, 141-82.

Carter, T. 2003
'The chipped and ground stone', in *The Asea Valley Survey. An Arcadian mountain valley from the palaeolithic period until modern times,* J. Forsén & B. Forsén (eds.), Stockholm, 23-38.

Caskey, J.L. & E.G. 1960
'The earliest settlements at Eutresis. Supplementary excavations, 1958', *Hesperia* 29, 126-67.

Catling H.W. & E.A. Catling 1981
'Barbarian' pottery from the Myce-naean settlement at the Menelaion, Sparta', *BSA* 76, 71-82.

Cazis, M. 1998
'Excavations at Pangali 1996', *FPR,* 280.

Chapman, J. 1982
'The secondary products revolution and the limitations of the Neo-lithic', *BICS* 19, 107-22.

Chapman, J. 2000
'Pit digging and structured deposi-tion in the Neolithic and Copper Age', *PPS* 66, 61-87.

Chatziotou M., G. Stratouli & E. Kotzambopoulou 1989 (1995)
'Η σπηλιά της Δράκαινας. Πρόσ-φατη έρευνα στον Πόρο Κεφαλο-νιάς (1992-93)', *AAA* 22, 31-60.

Cherry, J.F. 1988
'Pastoralism and the role of animals in the pre- and proto- historic eco-nomies of the Aegean pastoral eco-nomies in Classical Antiquity', in *Cambridge Philological Society Supplementary,* 14, Whittaker (ed.), Cambridge, 6-34.

Cherry, J. F. 1990
'The first colonization of the Medi-terranean islands: a review of recent research', *MA* 3, 145-221.

Cherry, J. F & Torrence, R. 1982
'The earliest prehistory of Melos', in *An island polity: the archaeology of exploitation in Melos,* A. C. Renfrew & M. Wagstaff (eds.), Cambridge, 24-34.

Cherry J. F., J.L. Davis, & E. Mantzourani 1991
Landscape archaeology as long-term history. Northern Keos in the Cycladic Islands, Los Angeles.

Chrysafi, A. 1994
'Κρήνη Πατρών. Περιφέρεια Ζωι-τάδας (οικόπεδο Γεωργίου Γαλα-νού)', *ArchDelt* 49, B' Chron., 234-6.

Christmann, E. 1996
Die deutschen Ausgrabungen auf der Pevkakia-Magula in Thessalien II. Die frühe Bronzezeit, (BAM 29), Bonn.

Coldstream, J.N. & G.L. Huxley 1972
Kythera. Excavations and Studies, London.

Coleman, J. 1977
Keos I: Kephala. A late Neolithic settlement and cemetery, Princeton.

Coleman J. 1992
'Greece, the Aegean and Cyprus', in *Chronologies in old world archaeology,* Ehrich (ed.), Chicago, 247-88.

Coy J. 1977
'Shells', in *Keos* I: *Kephala. A late Neolithic settlement and cemetery*, J. Coleman (ed.), Princeton, 132-3.

Cullen, T. 1985
A measure of interaction among Neolithic communities. Design elements of Greek Urfirnis pottery, Ph.D.diss., Indiana University.

Cullen, T. 2001
Aegean prehistory. A review. Boston.

Davares, C. 1970
'Νέοι διπλοί πρζέκεις εκ της ΣΤ' Αρχαιολογικής περιφερείς', *AAA* 3,3, 311-3.

Davidson, A. 2002
Mediterranean seafood, Prospect Books, Great Britain.

Davidson, A. 2003
North Atlantic seafood, Prospect Books, Great Britain.

Davis, J. L. 1992
'Review of Aegean prehistory 1: the islands of the Aegean', *AJA* 96, 699-756.

Davis J. L., S.E. Alcock, J. Bennet, Y.G. Lolos & C.W. Shelmerdine 1997
'The Pylos regional archaeological project. Part I: Overview and the archaeological survey', *Hesperia* 66, 391-94.

Day, P. & D. Wilson 2002
'Landscapes of memory, craft and power in pre-palatial and proto-palatial Knossos', in *Labyrinth revisited, rethinking Minoan archaeology*, Y. Hamilakis (ed.), Oxford, 143-66.

Deger-Jalkotzy, S. & M. Zavadil 2003
LHIIIC chronology and synchro-

nisms, proceedings of the international workshop, Vienna.

Delamotte, M. & E. Vardala-Theodorou 2001
Shells from the Greek Seas, The Goulandris Natural History Museum, Kifissia.

Demoule, J.P. & C. Perles 1993
'The Greek Neolithic: A new review', *JWP* 7, 4, 355-416.

Diamant, S. 1974
The later village farming stage in southern Greece, Ph.D. diss., University of Pennsylvania.

Dietz, S. 1980
The Middle Helladic cemetery. The Middle Helladic and Early Mycenaean deposits. Asine II, 1. Results of the excavations east of the Acropolis 1970-1974, Stockholm.

Dietz, S. 1991
The Argolid at the transition to the Mycenaean Age. Studies in the chronology and cultural development in the Shaft Grave Period, Copenhagen.

Dietz, S. & L. Kolonas 1998
'Preface', in *FPR*, 234-6.

Dobres, M.A. 2000
Technology and social agency, Oxford.

Dor, L., J. Jannoray & H. van Effenterre 1964
Kirrha: Études de préhistoire phocidienne, Paris.

Doumas, C. G. & V. La Rosa 1997
Πολιόχνη και η πρώιμη εποχή του χαλκού στο Βόρειο Αιγάιο/ Poliochni e l´Antica Etá del Bronzo nell`Egeo Settentrionale, Athens.

Douzougli, A. 1998
Άρια Αργολίδος, Athens.

Dousougli-Zachos, A. 1987
'Makrovouni-Kefalari Magoula-Talioti: Bemerkungen zu den Stufen EHI und II in der Argolis', *PZ* 62, 164-220.

Dousougli, A. & K. Zachos 2002
'L' Archéologie des zones montagneuses: Modèlles et interconnexions dans le Nèolithique de l' Èpire et de l' Albanie méridionale', in *L' Albanie dans l'Europe Prehistorique*, Touchais G. & J. Renard (eds.) (BCH suppl. 42), Paris, 111-43.

Döhl, H. 1973
'Iria. Die Ergebnisse der Ausgrabungen 1939', *Tiryns VI*, 127-94.

Dörpfeld, W. 1927
Alt Ithaca. I-II, München.

Driesch, A von den 1979
A guide to the measurement of animal bones from archaeological sites, Harvard University, Peabody Museum of Archaeology and Ethnology Bulletin 1.

Driesch, A. von den & J. Boessneck 1990
'Die Tierreste von der mykenischen Burg Tiryns bei Nauplion/ Peloponnes', *Tiryns* XI, 87-164.

Efstratiou, N. 1985
Agios Petros: a neolithic site in the northern Sporades (B.A.R. Supplementa 241), Oxford.

Elster, E.S. 2003
'Bone tools and other artifacts', in *Prehistoric Sitagroi. Excavations in Northeast Greece, 1968-1970. Volume 2: The final report*, Elster E.S. & C. Renfrew (eds.), Los Angeles, 31-79.

Evans, J. D. 1964
'Excavations in the neolithic settlement of Knossos, 1957-1960 Part I', *BSA* 59, 132-240.

Evans, J.D. & C. Renfrew 1968
Excavations at Saliagos near Antiparos, London.

Felsch, R. C. S. 1988
Samos. Band II. *Das Kastro Tigani. Die spätneolithische und chalkolithische Siedlung*, Bonn.

Fischer A., P. Vemming Hansen & P. Rasmussen 1984
'Macro and micro wear traces on lithic projectile points', *Journal of Danish Archaeology* 3, 19-46.

Forsén, J. 1996a
' The Early Helladic Period', in Wells & Runnels 1996, 75-120.

Forsén, J. 1996b
'Prehistoric Asea revisited', *Op.Ath.* 21, 41-72.

Forsén, J. & B. Forsén 2003
The Asea Valley Survey. An Arcadian mountain valley from the palaeolitic period until modern times. (Acta Instituti Atheniensis Regni Sueciae, Series In 4°, LI), Stockholm.

Fossey, J.M. 1969
'The prehistoric settlement by Lake Vouliagmeni, Perachora', *BSA* 64, 53-69.

Fossey, J.M. 1978
'Finds of the Early Helladic period', in *Excavations at the Barbouna area at Asine* II, I. Hägg & R. Hägg (eds.), Uppsala, 11-52.

Fotiadis, M. 1987
'Regional prehistoric research in West Macedonia, Greece: the first season', AAA Meeting, New York, 7.

French, D.H. 1972
Notes on prehistoric pottery groups from central Greece, Athens (privately distributed).

Frödin O. & A.W. Persson 1938
Asine. Results of the Swedish Excavations, 1922-1930, Stockholm.

Funke, P. 2001
'Acheloos' homeland. New historical – archaeological research on the ancient Polis Stratos', in *Nikopolis*, 189-203.

Gadolou, A. 2000
Η Αχαΐα στους πρώιμους ιστορικούς χρόνους. Κεραμεική παραγωγή και έθιμα ταφής, PhD Thesis, University of Athens.

Galanidou, N. 2002
'The chipped stone industry of Ftelia: an introduction', in *The Neolithic settlement at Ftelia, Mykonos*, A. Sampson (ed.), Rhodes, 317-32.

Gallis, K. 1992
Άτλας προϊστορικών οικισμών της ανατολικής Θεσσαλικής πεδιάδας, Larisa.

Gercke, P. u. W. u. & G. Hiesel 1976
'Tiryns-Stadt 1971, Graben H', *Tiryns* VIII, Mainz, 5-40.

Giannouli, E. G. 1990
'Η προϊστορική πανίδα της Θερμής Β', *Makedonika* 17, 262-78.

Giannouli, E. G. 1992
'Η Νεολική Θέρμη: Τα δεδομένα από τα οστά των ζώων (ανασκαφική περίοδος 1989)', *Makedonika* 18, 413-26.

Goldman, H. 1931
Excavations at Eutresis in Boeotia, Cambridge Mass.

Grammenos, D. V. *et al.* 1992
'Ανασκαφή ωεολιθικόν οικισμού Θέρμης, ανασκαφηκή περίοδος 1989', *Makedonika* 28, 381-501.

Graziadio, G. 1998
'Trade circuits and trade-routes in the Shaft Grave period', *SMEA* 40,1, 29-76.

Graziadio, G. 1999
'L'adozione della *wishbone handle* nell'Egeo: un aspetto trascurato dei rapporti cipro-egei', in *Επί πόντον πλαζόμενοι, Simposio italiano di Studi Egei*, V. La Rosa, D. Palermo & L. Vagnetti (eds.), Rome.

Greenfield, H.J. 1988
'The origins of wool and milk production in the Old World: a zooarchaeological perspective from the Central Balkans', *Current Anthropology* 4, 573-93.

Greenfield, H.J. & K. Fowler 2003
'Megalo Nisi Galanis and the secondary products revolution in Macedonia', in *Zooarchaeology in Greece, recent advances*, E. Kotjabopoulou, Y. Hamilakis, P. Halstead, C. Gamble & P. Elefanti (eds.) (BSA Studies 10), London, 133-43.

Gropengiesser, H. 1987
'Siphnos, Kap Agios Sostis: keramische prähistorische Zeugnisse aus dem Gruben - und Hüttenrevier 2', *AM* 102, 1-54.

Halstead, P. 1990a
'Waste not - want not: traditional responses to crop failure in Greece', *Rural History* 1, 2, 147-64.

Halstead, P. 1990b
'Present to past in the Pindhos: diversification and specialization in mountain economies', *Rivista di studi Liguri*, A 56, 1-4, 61- 80.

Halstead, P. 1995
'From sharing to hoarding: the Neolithic foundations of Aegean Bronze Age society', in *Politeia*, R.

Laffineur & W.D. Niemeier (eds.), Liège, 11-21.

Halstead, P. 1996
'Pastoralism or household herding? Problems of scale and specialization in early Greek animal husbandry', *WorldArch* 28,1, 20-42.

Halstead, P. 1999
Neolithic society in Greece, Sheffield.

Halstead, P. 1999
'Neighbours from Hell? The household in neolithic Greece', in *Neolithic society in Greece,* P. Halstead (ed.), Sheffield, 77-95.

Halstead, P. 2000
'Land use in postglacial Greece: cultural causes and environmental effects', in *Landscape and land use in post-glacial Greece,* P. Halstead & C. Frederick (eds.), Sheffield, 111- 28.

Halstead, P. & P. Collins 2002
'Sorting the sheep from the goats: morphological distinctions between the mandibles and mandibular teeth of adult *Ovis* and *Capra*', *JAS* 29, 545-53.

Hamilakis, I. 2003
'The sacred geography of hunting: wild animals, social power and gender in early farming societies', in *Zooarchaeology in Greece, recent advances,* E. Kotjabopoulou, Y. Hamilakis, P. Halstead, C. Gamble & P. Elefanti (eds.) (*BSA studies* 10), London, 239-48.

Hanschmann, E. 1976
'Die frühe und beginnende mittlere Bronzezeit: Die frühhelladische Kultur Mittel- und Südgriechenlands und ihre Chronologie', in *Die deutschen Ausgrabungen auf der Argissa-Magula in Thessalien III: Die frühe und beginnende*

mittlere Bronzezeit I-II, E. Hanschmann & V. Milojcic (eds.), (*BAM* 13-14), Bonn, 155-84.

Hekman, J. 1994
'Chalandriani on Syros: an early Bronze Age cemetery in the Cyclades', *ArchEph* 133, 47-74.

Hellström, P. 1987
'Small Finds', in *Paradeisos. A late neolithic settlement in Aegean Thrace,* P. Hellström (ed.), Stockholm, 83-8.

Heurtley, W.A. 1926-27
'A prehistoric site in W. Macedonia and the Dorian invasion', *BSA*, 28, 158-94.

Heurtley, W.A. & R.W. Hutchinson 1925/26
'Report of the excavations of the Toumba and tables of Vardaroftsa, Macedonia', *BSA*, 27, 1- 66.

Hillson, P. 1986
Teeth, Cambridge.

Hodder, I. 1974
'Regression analysis of some trade and marketing patterns', *WorldArch* 6, 172-89.

Hodder, I. 1978
'Some effects of distance on patterns of human interaction', in *The spatial organisation of culture,* I. Hodder (ed.), London, 155-78.

Hodder, I. 1982
'Toward a contextual approach to prehistoric exchange', in *Contexts for prehistoric exchange,* J.E. Ericson & T.K. Earle (eds.), New York, 199-211.

Hodder, I. 1990
The domestication of Europe: structure and contingency in neolithic societies, Oxford.

Hodder, I. & C. Orton 1976
Spatial analysis in archaeology, Cambridge.

Holmberg, E. 1944
The Swedish Excavations at Asea in Arcadia, Lund & Leipzig.

Hood, S. 1982
Excavations in Chios 1938-1955. Prehistoric Emporio and Ayio Gala, II (BSA Suppl. Vol. 16), London.

Hope Simpson, R. & O.T.P.K. Dickinson 1979
A Gazetteer of Aegean Civilization in the Bronze Age, Vol 1: *The Mainland and the Islands,* SIMA 52, Göteborg.

Houby-Nielsen, S. & I. Moschos 1998
'Surveys and architectural measurings at Aghia Triada and Pangali 1995', in FPR, 255-8.

Houby-Nielsen, S & I. Moschos 2004
'Excavations on the Hill of Aghia Triada', in TPR, 175-88.

Hourmouziadis, G. 1972
'Excavation in Prodromos by Karditsa', *ArchDelt* 27, Chron, 394-6.

Hourmouziadis, G. 1975
'Dimini', *ArchDelt* 30, Chron, 179-82.

Hughen, K.A. 2004
'Marine radiocarbon age calibration', 0-26 Cal Kyr BP, *Radiocarbon* 46, 3, 1059-86.

Iakovidis, S. 1969-70
Περατή, Vols. Α, Β, Γ, Athens.

Immerwahr, S. 1971
The Athenian Agora. XIII. The Neolithic and Bronze Ages, Princeton.

Inizan, M. L., M. Reduron-Ballinger, H. Rocheand & J. Tixier 1999
Technology and terminology of knapped stone, Préhistoire de la Pierre Taillée, Tome 5, Nanterre: CREP.

Jacobsen, T.W. 1969
'Excavations at Porto Cheli and vicinity. Preliminary report II. The Franchthi Cave 1967-68', *Hesperia* 38, 343-81.

Jacobsen, T.W. 1973
'Excavations in the Franchthi Cave, 1969-1971, Part I', *Hesperia* 42, 45-88.

Jacobsen, T.W. 1976
'17.000 years of Greek Prehistory', *Scientific American* 234, 6, 76-88.

Jacobsen T.W & W.R. Farrand 1987
Franchthi Cave and Paralia. Maps, plans and sections. Excavations at Franchthi Cave, fasc. 1, Bloomington/Indianapolis.

Jameson M.H., C.N. Runnels & T.H. van Andel 1994
A Greek countryside. The southern Argolid from prehistory to present day, Stanford.

Jensen, H. J. 1994
Flint tools and plant working. Hidden traces of Stone Age technology, Aarhus.

Johnson, M. 1996
'The Neolithic Period', in *The Berbati-Limnes Archaeological survey 1988-1990*, B. Wells & C. Runnels (eds.), Stockholm, 37-73.

Kalogirou, A. 2003
'Η κεραμική της τελικής Νεολιθικής από την ανασκαφή στο Μεγάλο Νησί Γαλάνης νομού Κοζάνης', in *The prehistoric research in Greece and its perspectives: theoretical and methodological considerations*, Thessaloniki, 99-106.

Kanta, A. 1998
'Relations between Crete, the Aegean and the Near East in the Late Bronze Age, an overview', in *Eastern Mediterranean, Cyprus-Dodecanese - Crete, 16th-6th cent. B.C.*, N.C. Stampolidis, A. Karetsou & A. Kanta (eds.), Herakleion.

Karali, L. 1993
'Marine shells and terrestrial molluscs from the Skoteini Cave', in *Skoteini Tharrrounion*, A. Sampson (ed.), Athens, 370-8.

Karali, L. 2002
'Ftelia on Myconos: The molluscan material', in *The Neolithic settlement at Ftelia, Mykonos*, A. Sampson (ed.), Rhodes, 201-20.

Karali L. & F. Mavridis (in press)
'Excavations at the Lion's cave, Hymettos, Athens, Greece', *Aegean Society of Japan*.

Karali L., F. Mavridis & L. Kormazopoulou (in press)
'Ανασκαφή σπηλαίου Λεονταρίου Υμηττού Αττικής, κοινότητας Γλυκών Νερών: Πρώτη ανασκαφική περίοδος', *ArchDelt*, 2003.

Karali L., F. Mavridis & L. Kormazopoulou 2005
'Cultural landscapes during the late and final Neolithic of the Aegean. A case study from Leontari Cave, Mt. Hymettos, Athens. Greece', *Antiquity* 79, 303.

Karamitrou-Mentesidi, G. 2003
'Μυκηναϊκά Αιανής-Ελιμιώτιδας και Άνω Μακεδονίας', in *Periphery* 2, 167-90.

Karampatsoli, A. 1997
'The Lithic material from the Cave', in *Το σπήλαιο των Λιμνών στα Καστριά Καλαβρύτων*, A. Sampson (ed.), Athens, 485-504, 550-2.

Kardulias P. N & C.N. Runnels 1995
'The lithic artifacts: flaked stone and other non flaked lithics', in *Artifact and assemblage. The finds from a regional survey of the southern Argolid I: The Prehistoric and Early Iron Age pottery and the lithic artifacts*, C.N. Runnels, D. J. Pullen & S. Langdon (eds), Stanford, 74-139.

Katsipanou, B. 2001
Le peuplement humain en Etoloacarnanie prehistorique: des origines à l'Helladique Moyen, Université de Paris I, Sorbonne.

Keller, D.A. 1982
'Final Neolithic pottery from Plakari, Karystos', in *Studies in South Attica*, P. Spitaels (ed.) (Misc. Graeca 5), Gent, 47-67.

Kilikoglou V., E. Kiriatze, A. Philippa-Touchais, G. Touchais & I.K. Whitbread 2002
'The evidence of chemical and petrographic analyses', in *Metron. Measuring the Aegean Bronze Age, 9th international Aegean Conference*, K. Foster & R. Laffineur (eds.), New Haven, Connecticut, 18-21.

Knapp, A.B. 1985
'Production and exchange in the Aegean and eastern Mediterranean: an overview', in *Prehistoric production and exchange*, A.B. Knapp & T. Stech (eds.), Los Angeles, 1-12.

Kolonas, L. 2006
Βούντενη. Ένα Ακμαίο Μυκηναϊκό Κέντρο της Αχαΐας, Athens.

Kopaka, K., P. Drosinou, & G. Christodoulakos 1996
'Γαύδος: επιφανειακή έρευνα', *Kritiki Estia* 5, 242-4.

Korres, G.S. 1979
Αρχαιολογικαί διατριβαί επί θεμάτων της Εποχής του Χαλκού, Athens.

Kotjabopoulou E. & K. Trantalidou 1993
'Faunal analysis of the Skoteini Cave', in *Skoteini Tharrounion*, A. Sampson (ed.), Athens, 393-434.

Koumouzelis, M. 1979
The Early and Middle Helladic periods in Elis, Michigan.

Koutsoukou, A. 1992
An archaeological survey in NW Andros, Cyclades, PhD dissertation, University of Edinburgh.

Kozlowski, J. K., M. Kaczanowska & M. Pawlikowski 1996
'Chipped-stone industries from Neolithic levels at Lerna', *Hesperia*, 65, 295-372.

Kunze, E. 1931
Orchomenos II. Die Neolithische Keramik, München.

Kunze, E. 1934
Orchomenos III. Die Keramik der frühen Bronzezeit, München.

Kyparissi-Apostolika, N. 1999
'The Neolithic use of Theopetra Cave in Thessaly', in *Neolithic Society in Greece*, P. Halstead (ed.) (Sheffield studies in Aegean Archaeology), 142-51.

Lambert, N. 1969
'Grotte de Kitsos (Laurion)', *BCH* 93, 956-66.

Lambert, N. 1981
La grotte préhistorique de Kitsos (Attique) I, II, Paris.

Lang, F. 2001
'The dimensions of the material topography', in *Nikopolis*, 205-21.

Lavezzi, J. C. 1978
'Prehistoric investigations at Corinth', *Hesperia* 47, 402-51.

Lemmonier, P. 1986
'The study of material culture today: towards an anthropology of technical systems', *JAnthArch* 5, 147-86.

Leroy-Prost C. 1981
'L'industrie osseuse de Kitsos', in *La grotte préhistorique de Kitsos (Attique)* I, N. Lambert (ed.), Paris, 241-74.

Lindblom, M. 2001
Marks and makers. Appearance, distribution and function of Middle Helladic and Late Helladic manufacturers, SIMA 127, Jonsered.

Lolos, V. 1987
The Late Helladic I pottery of the southwestern Peloponnesos and its local characteristics, Vol. I-II. Göteborg.

Mackenzie, D. 1904
'The successive settlements at Phylakopi in their Aegeo-Cretan relations', in *Excavations at Phylakopi in Melos* (The Society for the Promotion of Hellenic Studies. Supplementary Paper 4), London, 238-72.

Maran, J. 1992
Kiapha Thiti. Ergebnisse der Ausgrabungen II 2, Marburg.

Maran, J. 1992
Die deutschen Ausgrabungen auf der Pevkakia–Magula in Thessalien III. Die mittlere Bronzezeit, BAM 30/31, Bonn.

Maran, J. 1998
Kulturwandel auf dem griechischen Festland und den Kykladen im späten 3. Jahrtausend v.Chr. I-II (Universitätsforschungen zu prähistorischen Archäologie, Band 53), Bonn.

Marangou, L. 1993
'Μινόα Αμόργου', *Ergon*, 92-9.

Marinatos, S.N. 1933,
'Αι εν Κεφαλληνία ανασκαφαί Goekoop Z', *ArchEph*, 68-100.

Mastrokostas, E.I. 1967,
'Ανασκαφή του Τείχους Δυμαίων', *Prakt*, 121-36.

Matsas, D. 1991
'Samothrace and the northeastern Aegean: the Minoan connection', *Studia Troica* 1, 159-179.

Mavridis, F. 2000
'The Final Neolithic pottery from the excavation at Pangali in 1996', in *SPR*, 277-89.

Mavridis, F. 2002
'Interpreting distance and difference: inter-cultural contacts, symbolic meanings and the character of the Cycladic expansion in the Aegean during the EBA', in *World islands in prehistory*, W.H. Waldren & J. A. Ensenyat (eds.) (*BAR* Int. series 1095), Oxford, 255-66.

Mavridis, F. in press
'Neolithic decorated pottery with painted and burnished decoration of the late neolithic from the cave of Gioura, Sporadhes', in *Excavations at the cave of Gioura, N. Sporadhes*, A. Sampson (ed.).

Mavridis, F. & H.A. Alisøy 1998
'A catalogue of selected finds', in *FPR*, 272-9.

Meindl, G. & C.O. Lovejoy 1985
'Ectocranial suture closure. A revised method for the determination of skeletal age at death based on the lateral anterior sutures', *AJPA* 68. 57-66.

Melas, E. M. 1985
The Islands of Karpathos, Saros, Kasos in the Neolithic and Bronze Age (SIMA 67), Göteborg.

Milojcic, V. 1954
'Vorbericht über die Versuchsgrabung an der Otzaki-Magula bei Larisa', *AA* 1954, 1-28.

Milojcic, V. 1955
'Vorbericht über die Ausgrabungen auf der Otzaki-Magula 1954', *AA* 1955, 157-82.

Milojcic, V., J. Boessneck & M. Hopf 1976
Die deutschen Ausgrabungen auf Magulen im Larisa in Thessalien 1966. Agia Sofia Magula. Karagyös Magula. Bunar Baschi. (Beiträge zur ur- und frühgeschichtlichen Archäologie des Mittelmeer-Kulturraumes 15), Bonn.

Mitchell-Jones, A.J. 1999
The Atlas of European mammals (Societas Europaea Mammalogica, Poyser Natural History), London.

Moschos, I. 2000
'Prehistoric tumuli at Portes in Achaea, first preliminary report', *PDIA* 3, 9-49.

Moschos, I. 2006 (in print)
'Regional styles and the LH IIIC at western Archaea according to new cemeteries' material', in *Late Helladic IIIC Chronology and Synchronisms* II: *LH IIIC middle, Proceedings of the international workshop held at the Austrian Academy of Sciences at Vienna, October 29th and 30th, 2004*, S.

Deger-Jalkotzy & N. Zavadil (eds.), Wien.

Moschos, I. & S. Houby-Nielsen 1998
'Surveys and architectural measurings at Aghia Triada and Pangali 1995', *FPR*, 255-8.

Moundrea-Agrafioti, H-A. 1981
La Thessalie du Sud-Est au Néolithique: Outillage Lithique et Osseux, PhD thesis. University of Paris X.

Moundrea-Agrafioti, H-A. 1996
'Tools', in *Neolithic culture in Greece*, G.A. Papathanassopoulos (ed.), Athens, 103-6.

Mountjoy, P.A. 1976
'Late Helladic III B1 pottery dating the construction of the South House at Mycenae', *BSA* 71, 77-111.

Mountjoy, P.A. 1986
Mycenaean decorated pottery: a guide to identification, SIMA 73, Göteborg.

Mountjoy, P.A. 1990
'Regional Mycenaean pottery', *BSA* 85, 245-70.

Mountjoy, P.A. 1999
Regional Mycenaean decorated pottery, Vols. I-II. Rahdem/Westf., Leidorf.

Mylona, D. 2003
'Archaeological fish remains in Greece: general trends of the re search and a gazetteer of sites', in *Zooarchaeology in Greece: recent advances*, E. Kotjabopoulou, Y. Hamilakis, P. Halstead, C. Gamble & P. Elefanti (eds.) (*BSA Studies* 9), London, 193-200.

Müller, K. 1938
Die Urfirniskeramik, Tiryns VI, München.

Nakou, G. 1995
'The cutting edge: A new look at early Aegean metallurgy', *JMA* 8, 2, 1-32.

Noe-Nygaard, N. 1987
'Taphonomy in archaeology with special emphasis on man as a bias ing factor', *Journal of Danish Archaeology* 6, 7-52.

Noodle, B. 1974
'Ages of epiphysial closure in feral and domesticated goats and ages of dental eruption', *JAS* 1, 195-204.

Orton C., P. Tyers & A. Vince 1993
Pottery in archaeology, Cambridge.

Papadopoulos, Th.J. 1979
Mycenaean Achaea, SIMA 55, Göteborg.

Papadopoulos, Th.J. 1985
'Relations between Achaea and Cyprus in the Late Bronze Age', in *Πρακτικά του Δευτέρου Διεθνούς Κρητολογικού Συνεδρίου*, Th. Papadopoulos & S.A. Hadjistilli (eds.), Nicosia, 141-8.

Papadopoulos, Th. & L. Kontorli-Papadopoulou 2003
Προϊστορική Αρχαιολογία Δυτικής Ελλάδας και Ιονίων Νήσων, Ioannina.

Papapostolou, I.A. 1997
'Οι νεώτερες έρευνες στο μέγαρο Β του Θέρμου', *Δωδώνη* 26,1, 327-46.

Papapostolou, I.A. 2003
'Το τέλος της Μυκηναϊκής Εποχή στον Θέρμο', *Periphery* 2, 135-46.

Papathanasopoulos, G. (ed.) 1996
Νεολιθικός πολιτισμός στην Ελλάδα, Athens.

Papazoglou-Manioudaki, L. 1993
'Εισηγμένη κεραμική στους

Μυκηναϊκούς τάφους της
Πάτρας', in Wace & Blegen.
*Pottery as evidence for trade in the
Aegean Bronze Age 1939-1989,* C.
Zerner, P. Zerner & J. Winder
(eds.), Amsterdam, 209-15.

Papazoglou-Manioudaki, L. 1998
*Ο Μυκηναϊκός Οικισμός του
Αιγίου και η Πρώιμη Μυκηναϊκή
εποχή στην Αχαϊα,* PhD thesis,
University of Athens.

Papazoglou-Manioudaki, L. 1999
'Πήλινα και χάλκινα της
Πρώιμης Μυκηναϊκής Εποχής
από την Αχαϊα', in *Perifery 1,*
269-84.

Pappa M. & M. Besios 1999
'The Makriyalos project: rescue
excavations at the Neolithic site of
Makriyalos, Pieria, northern
Greece', in *Neolithic Society in
Greece,* P. Halstead (ed.), Sheffield,
108-20.

Payne, S. 1972
'Partial recovery and sample bias:
the results of some sieving experi-
ments', in *Papers in Economic Prehistory,* S. Higgs (ed.), Cambridge,
49-63.

Payne, S. 1973
'Kill-off patterns in sheep and goats:
The mandibles from Asvan Kale',
AnatSt 23, 281-303.

Payne, S. 1975
'Partial recovery and sample bias',
in *Archaeozoological studies,*
Papers of the Archaeozoological
Conference 1974, A.T. Clason
(ed.), Amsterdam, 7-17.

Payne, S. 1985
'Morphological distinctions be
tween the mandibular teeth of
young sheep, *Ovis,* and goat,
Capra', *JAS* 12, 139-47.

Perdrizet, P. 1908
*Fouilles de Delphes V.1. Monu-
ments Figurés. Petits Bronzes,
Terres-cuites, Antiquités diverses,*
Paris.

Perlès, C. 1973
'The chipped stone industries', in
Excavations in the Franchthi Cave,
1969-1971, Part I, T. Jacobsen
(ed.), *Hesperia* 42, 72-82.

Perlès, C. 1981
'Les Industries Lithiques de la
Grotte de Kitsos', in *La grotte pré-
historique de Kitsos (Attique)* I, N.
Lambert (ed.), 129-222, Paris.

Perlés, C. 1987
*Les industries lithiques taillées de
Franchthi (Argolide, Gréce). Tome
I: Présentation générale et industri-
es paléolithiques. Excavations at
Franchthi Cave, Greece,* Bloom-
ington/Indianapolis.

Perlès, C. 1989
'La néolithisation de la Gréce', in
*Néolithisations: Proche et Moyen
Orient, Méditerranée orientale,
Nord de l' Afrique, Europe méri-
dionale, Chine, Amérique du sud,*
in O. Aurenche & J. Cauvin (eds.)
(*BAR,* Int. Series. 516), Oxford,
109-27.

Perlès, C. 1990a
'L´outillage de pierre taillèe néolithique en Gréce: approvisionnement
et exploitation des matières premiè-
res', *BCH* 67, 1-42.

Perlès, C. 1990b
*Les industries lithiques taillées de
Franchthi. Vol. II, Les industries du
Mésolithique et du Néolithique
initial. Excavations at Franchthi
Cave,* fasc. 5, Bloomington/-
Indianapolis.

Perlès, C. 1992a
'Systems of exchange and organiza-

tion of production in neolithic
Greece', *JMA* 5, 2, 115-64.

Perlès, C. 1992b
'In search of lithic strategies: a cognitive approach to prehistoric chipped stone assemblages', in *Repre-
sentations in archaeology,* J. C.
Gardin & C. Peebles (eds.), Bloom-
ington, 223-47.

Perlès, C. 1993
'Les industries lithiques Taillees de
Tharrounia', in *Skoteini Tharrounion,* A. Sampson (ed.), Athens,
448-95.

Perlès, C. 2001
The Early Neolithic in Greece,
Cambridge.

Perlès, C. & K.D. Vitelli 1999
'Craft specialization', in Halstead
1999, 96-107.

Pelegrin, J. 1984
'Approche technologique expéri-
mentale de la mise en forme de
nucléus pour le débitage systémati-
que par pression', in *Prehistoire de
la pierre talliée 2, Economie du
débitage laminaire,* J. Tixier (ed.),
Paris, 93-103.

Pelegrin, J. 1988
'Débitage expérimental par pres-
sion: du plus petit au plus grand', in
Technologie préhistorique, J.
Tixier (ed.), Valbonne, 37-53.

Petersen, K.S. 2000
'Geological investigations in the
area of Aghia Triada', in *SPR,* 269-
75.

Petersen, K.S. 2004
'Shellfish from the excavations at
Aetolian Chalkis', in *TPR,* 215-27.

Petersen, K.S. & E. Hoch 2005
'Holocene marine fauna and shore-

line studies in the Sisimiut area', *Meddelelser om Grønland*, 209-21.

Phelps, W. 2004
The neolithic pottery sequence in southern Greece (*BAR* International Series 1259), Oxford.

Philippa-Touchais, A. 2002
'Apercu des céramiques mésohelladiques à décor peint de l'Aspis d'Argos', *BCH* 126, 1, Études, 1-40.

Philippa-Touchais, A. 2003
'Apercu des céramiques mésohelladiques à décor peint de l'Aspis d'Argos. II. La céramique á peinture lustrée', *BCH* 127, 1-47.

Phoca-Cosmetatou, N. 2002
'The faunal remains from Ftelia: a preliminary report', in *The neolithic settlement at Ftelia, Mykonos*, A. Sampson (ed.), Rhodes, 221-6.

Pirazzoli, P.A. 1976
'Sea level variations in north west Mediterranean during Roman times', *Science* 29, 194, 519-21.

Protonotariou-Deilaki, E. 1980
Οι τύμβοι του Άργους, Athens.

Prummel, W. & H. J. Frisch 1986
'A guide for the distinction of species, sex and body side in the bones of sheep and goat', *JAS* 13, 567-77.

Pullen, D.J. 1985
Social organization in Early Bronze Age Greece: a multi-dimensional approach, PhD diss., Indiana University.

Pullen, D.J. 1986
'The Early Bronze Age settlement on Tzoungiza Hill, ancient Nemea', in *Early Helladic architecture and urbanization*, R. Hägg & D. Konsola (eds.), (*SIMA* 76), Göteborg, 73-8.

Pullen, D.J. 1988
'The earlier phases of the Early Bronze Age at Tzoungiza hill, ancient Nemea', Greece, *AJA* 92, 252.

Pullen, D.J. 1990
'The Early Bronze Age village on the Tsoungiza hill, ancient Nemea, Greece', in *L´Habitat égéen préhistorique*, P. Darcque & R. Treuil (eds.) (*BCH* Suppl. 19), 331-46.

Pullen, D.J. 1995
'The pottery of the Neolithic, Early Helladic I, and Early Helladic II periods', in *Artifacts and assemblage: the finds from regional survey of the southern Argolid, Greece, I: The Prehistoric and Early Iron Age pottery and the lithic aspects*, C. N. Runnels, D.J. Pullen & S. Langdon (eds.), Stanford, 6-42.

Pullen, D.J. 2000
'The prehistoric remains of the Acropolis of Haleieis. A final report', *Hesperia* 69, 133-87.

Randsborg, K. 2003
Kepallénia (*Acta Archaeologica suplementa*), Copenhagen.

Reese, D.S. 1987
'Palaikastro Shells and Bronze-Age Purple-dye production', *BSA* 82, 201-6.

Reimer, P.J. & F.G. McCormac 2002
'Marine radiocarbon reservoir corrections for the Mediterranean and Aegean Seas', *Radiocarbon* 44, 159-66.

Reimer, P.J. *et al.* 2004
'IntCal04 terrestrial radiocarbon age calibration, 0-26 Cal Kyr BP.', *Radiocarbon* 46, 3, 1029-58.

Reitz, E. & E. Wing 1999
Zooarchaeology, Cambridge.

Renard, J. 1989
Le site Néolithique et Helladique Ancien de Kouphououno (Laconie) (*Aegaeum* 4), Liége.

Renfrew, C. 1969
'The autonomy of the south-east European Copper Age', *PPS* 35, 12-47.

Renfrew, C. 1972
The emergence of civilization: the Cyclades and the Aegean in the 3rd millenium B.C, London.

Renfrew, C. 1973
'Trade and craft specialisation', in *Neolithic Greece*, D.R. Theocharis (ed.), Athens, 179-200.

Renfrew, C. 1975
'Trade as action at a distance: questions of integration and communication', in *Ancient civilization and trade*, J.A. Sabloff & C.C. Lamberg-Karlovsky (eds.), Albuquerque, 3-60.

Renfrew, C. 1977
'Alternative models for exchange and spatial distribution', in *Exchange systems in prehistory*, T. K. Earle & J.E. Ericson (eds.), New York, 71-90.

Renfrew, C. 1982
'Bronze age Melos', in *An islands polity: the archaeology of exploitation on Melos*, C. Renfrew & J.M. Wagstaff (eds.), Cambridge, 35-44.

Renfrew, C. 1989
'Introduction: the transition from the Neolithic to the EBA in the Aegean', in *Archaeometry*, I. Maniatis (ed.), Amsterdam, 677-8.

Renfrew C., J.E. Dixon & J.R. Cann 1965
'Obsidian in the Aegean', *BSA* 60, 225-47.

Renfrew C., J.E. Dixon & J. R. Cann 1966
'Obsidian and early cultural contact in the Near East', *PPS* 30-72.

Renfrew C., J. E. Dixon & J.R. Cann 1968
'Further analysis of Near Eastern obsidian', *PPS* 319-31.

Renfrew C., M. Gimbutas & E. Elster 1986
Excavations at Sitagroi. A prehistoric village in northeast Greece, Vol. 1 (*Institute of Archaeology, Monumenta Archaeologica* 13), Los Angeles.

Renfrew C. & A. Aspinall 1987
'Aegean obsidian and Franchthi Cave', in *Les industries lithiques taillées de Franchthi (Argolide, Gréce). Tome I: Présentation générale et industries paléolithiques. Excavations at Franchthi Cave, Greece,* C. Pèrles (ed.), Bloomington/Indianapolis, 257-70.

Rhomaios, K.A. 1915
'Εκ του προϊστορικου Θέρμου', *ArchDelt* 1, 225-79.

Ridley C. & K. A. Wardle 1979
'Rescue excavations at Servia, 1971-1973', *BSA* 74, 185-226.

Ridley, C., K.A. Wardle & C.A. Mould 2000
Servia I. Anglo-Hellenic rescue excavations 1971-73 (BSA Suppl. Vol. 32), Oxford and North Hampton.

Rodden, R. 1962
'Excavations at the Early Neolithic site at Nea Nicomedeia, Greek Macedonia', *PPS* 28, 267-88.

Rodden, R. 1964
'Recent discoveries from prehistoric Macedonia', *BalkSt* 5, 109-24.

Rodden, J. R. & K. A. Wardle 1996
Nea Nikomedeia I. The Excavation of an Early Neolithic village in Northern Greece 1961-1964 (BSA Suppl. Vol. 25), Oxford and North Hampton.

Rohlfs, G. 1963
Antikes Knöchelspiel im einstigen Gross Griechenland. Eine vergleichende historisch-linguistisch Studie, Tübingen.

Runnels, C. 1985
'The Bronze-Age flaked-stone industries from Lerna: a preliminary report', *Hesperia* 54, 357-91.

Runnels, C. 1996
'The stone artifacts from the neolithic period', in *The Berbati-Limnes archaeological survey 1988-1990,* B. Wells & C. Runnels (eds.), Stockholm, 40-3.

Runnels, C. 1995
'Review of Aegean prehistory VII: The Stone Age of Greece from the paleolithic to the advent of the neolithic', *AJA* 99, 4, 699-728.

Runnels, C.N., & T.H. van Andel 1987
'The evolution of settlement in the southern Argolid, Greece. An economic explanation', *Hesperia* 56, 303-34.

Runnels, C. & T.H. van Andel 1988
'Trade and the origins of agriculture in the Eastern Mediterranean', *JMA* 1,1, 83-109.

Runnels, C.N., D. J. Pullen & S. Langdon (eds.) 1995
Artifact and assemblage. The finds from a regional survey of the southern Argolid I: The prehistoric and Early Iron Age pottery and the lithic artifacts, Stanford.

Runnels C & P. Murray 2001
Greece before history, Stanford.

Rutter, J. 1979
'The last Mycenaeans at Corinth', *Hesperia* 48, 348-92.

Rutter, J.B. 1989
'A Ceramic Definition of Late Helladic I from Tzoungiza', *Hydra* 6, 1-19.

Rutter, J.B. 1990
'Pottery groups from Tzoungiza of the end of the Middle Bronze Age', *Hesperia* 59, 359-458

Rutter, J.B. 1993
'Review of Aegean prehistory II: The prepalatial Bronze Age of the southern and central Greek mainland', *AJA* 97, 745-97.

Rutter, J.B. & S.H. 1976
The transition to Mycenaean. A stratified Middle Helladic II to Late Helladic IIA pottery sequence from Aghios Stephanos in Laconia, Los Angeles.

Rye, O. 1981
Pottery technology, Washington.

Sampson, A. 1980
'Το σπήλαιο Νέστορος', in *Ανασκαφαί ανά την Πυλίαν,* G. Korres (ed.), *Prakt,* 175-87.

Sampson, A. 1981
Η Νεολιθική και η Πρωτοελλαδική Ι στην Εύροια, Athens.

Sampson, A. 1985
Μάνικα Ι. Μια Πρωτοελλαδική πόλη στη Χαλκίδα, Athens.

Sampson, A. 1987
Η Νεολιθική περίοδος στα Δωδεκάννησα, Athens.

Sampson, A. 1988
Η Νεολιθική κατοίκηση στο Γιαλί της Νισύρου, Athens.

Sampson, A. 1989
'Some chronological problems of the end of the neolithic and the EBA', in *Archaeometry*, I. Maniatis (ed.), Amsterdam, 709-18.

Sampson, A. 1992
'Late neolithic remains at Tharrounia, Euboea: a model for the seasonal use of settlements and caves', *BSA* 87, 61-101.

Sampson, A. 1993
Σκοτεινή Θαρρουνίων, Athens.

Sampson, A. 1996
'Excavation in the cave of Cyclope', In *Die Agäische Frühzeit*, E. Alram-Stern (ed.), Wien, 507-20.

Sampson, A. 1997
Το σπήλαιο των Λιμνών στα Καστριά Καλαβρύτων, Athens.

Sampson, A. 1998
'The Neolithic and Mesolithic occupation of the cave of Cyclope, Youra, Alonnessos, Greece', *BSA* 93, 1-22.

Sampson, A. 2000
'Το σπήλαιο του Σαρακηνού και η σπηλαιο-κατοίκηση στην περιοχή της Κωπαίδας', *in Συμπόσιο Βοιωτικών Μελετών,* 133-55.

Sampson, A. 2002
The neolithic settlement at Ftelia, Mykonos, Rhodes.

Sampson, A., G. Facorellis & I. Maniatis 1998
'New evidence for the cave occupation during the late neolithic period in Greece', in *Actes du Colloque "C14 et Archeologie",* Liége, 279-86.

Saranti, E. 2004
'A prehistoric settlement at Chania-Gavrolimni in Aetolia', in TPR, 229-36.

Schmid, E. 1972
Atlas of animal bones, for prehistorians, archaeologists and quaternary geologists, Amsterdam.

Seder, M. 1999
'Animal domestication in the Zeros: a review of past and current research', *Paleorient* 25,1, 11-25.

Shackleton, N.J. 1968
'The mollusca, the crustacea, the echnodermata', Appendix IX, in *Excavations at Saliagos near Antiparos,* J. Evans & C. Renfrew (eds.), London, 68-9, 122-38.

Shackleton N.J & T.H. van Andel 1980
'Prehistoric shell assemblages from Franchthi Cave and evolution of the adjacent coastal zone', *Nature* 288, 357-9.

Schiffer, M. B. 1987
Formation processes of the archaeological record, Salt Lake City.

Schneider G., H. Knoll, H. Gallis & J.P. Demoule 1990
'Production and distribution of coarse and fine pottery from neolithic Thessaly, Greece', in *International Symposium of Archaeometry 1990, 27th Symposium*, M. Pernicka & G. Wagner (eds.), Basel, 513-22.

Sherratt, A. 1981
'Plough and pastoralism: aspects of the secondary products revolution', in *Patterns of the past, studies in honour of D. Clarke,* I. Hodder G. Issac & N. Hammond (eds.), Cambridge, 261-305.

Sherratt, A. 1982
'The secondary products revolution of animals in the Old World', *WA* 15, 1, 90-104.

Siedentopf, H. 1971
'Frühhelladische Siedlungsschichten auf der Unterburg von Tiryns', *Tiryns* V, 77-85, Frankfurt a.M.

Siedentopf, H. 1991
Mattbcmaltc Keramik der Mittleren Bronzezeit, Alt-Ägina VII,2, Mainz.

Silver, I. A. 1971
'The aging of domestic animals', in *Science in Archaeology*, D. Brothwell & E. Higgs (eds.), London, 283-302.

Skourtopoulou, K. 1999
'The chipped stone from Makriyalos: a preliminary report', in *Neolithic society in Greece*, P. Halstead (ed.), Sheffield, 121-7.

Snyder, L. M. & W.E. Klippel 2003
'From Lerna to Kastro: further thoughts on dogs as food in ancient Greece', in *Zooarchaeology in Greece, recent advances,* E. Kotjabopoulou, I. Hamilakis, P. Halstead, C.Gamble & P. Elefanti (eds) (*BSA Studies* 9), London, 221-31.

Sotirakopoulou, P. 1990
'The earliest history of Akrotiri: the late Neolithic and early Bronze Age phases', in *Thera and the Aegean World* III, 3: *Chronology*, D. A. Hardy & C. Renfrew (eds.), London, 41-7.

Sotiriadis, G. 1908
'Ανασκαφαί εν Αιτωλία και Ακαρνανία', *Prakt,* 95-100.

Souyoudzoglou-Haywood, C. 1999
The Ionian Islands in the Bronze Age and Early Iron Age 3000-800 BC, Liverpool.

Spencer, N. 1995
A Gazetteer of Archaeological Sites in Lesbos (BAR Int. Ser. 623), Oxford.

Spyropoulos, A. 1996
'Πίθος', in *Neolithic culture in Greece*, G. Papathanasopoulos (ed.), Athens, 274.

Stamoudi, A. 2003
'Ταράτσα - Αγ. Παρασκευή. Εναία πολιτισμική προσέγγιση μέσα από μια αποσπασματική ματιά σε μια προϊστορική θέση της περιοχής της Λαμίας', in *Periphery 2*, 263-80.

Stavropoulou-Gatsi, M. 1980
'Πρωτογεωμετρικό νεκροταφείο Αιτωλίας', *ArchDelt* 35, A. Mel., 102-30.

Stavropoulou-Gatsi, M. 1998
'Οικισμός της Εποχής του Χαλκού στην "Παγώνα" της Πάτρας', in *Πρακτικά του Ε'Διεθνούς Συνεδρίου Πελοποννησιακών Σπουδών*, Vol. A', Athens, 514-33.

Stavropoulou-Gatsi, M. 2001
'Οικισμός της εποχής του Χαλκού στην "Παγώνα" της Πάτρας', in *Forschungen in der Peloponnes. Akten des Symposions anlässlich der Feier, 100 Jahre Österreichisches Archäologisches Institut Athen*, Athen 5.3.-7.3.1998, Athens, 29-38.

Stavropoulou-Gatsi M. & V. Karageorghis 2003
'Imitations of Late Bronze Age Cypriote ceramics from Patras-Pagona', *RDAC*, 95-102.

Stratouli, G. 1997
'Bone and antler artefacts from the cave of Lakes', in *Το σπήλαιο των Λιμνών στα Καστριά Καλαβρύτων*, A. Sampson (ed.), Athens, 550-2.

Stratouli, G. 1998
Knochen Artefakte aus dem Neolithikum und Chalkolithikum Nordgriechenlands, Bonn.

Stratouli, G. 2000
'Neolithic bone and antler artifacts from *Theopetra Cave*, western Thessaly: Tracing the use of the cave', in *Theopetra Cave. Twelve years of excavation and research 1987-1998*, N. Kyparissi-Apostolika (ed.), Athens, 307-28.

Stuiver, M. & H.A. Polach 1977
'Reporting of 14C data', *Radiocarbon* 19, 3, 355-63.

Stuiver, M. & T.F. Braziunas 1993
'Modeling atmospheric 14C influences and 14C ages of marine samples to 10,000 BC.', *Radiocarbon*, 35, 1, 137-90.

Säflund, G. 1965
Excavations at Berbati, 1936-1937, Stockholm.

Sørensen, L. 2004
'The cave of Hagios Nikolaos near Kato Vasiliki in Aetolia: flint-technological observations', in TPR, 237-58.

Theocharis, D. 1951
'Ανασκαφή εν Παλαιά Κοκκινιά Πειραιώς', *Prakt*, 105-13.

Torrence, R. 1986
Production and exchange of stone tools. Prehistoric obsidian in the Aegean, Cambridge.

Torrence, R. 1991
'The chipped stone', in *Landscape archaeology as long term history. Northern Keos in the Cycladic islands*, J. Cherry, D. Cherry & E. Mantzourani (eds.), Los Angeles, 173-95.

Treuil, R. 1983
Le Néolithique et le Bronze Ancien Egéeen: Les Problémes Stratigraphiques et Chronologuiqùes, Les Techniqùes, Les Hommes, Paris.

Tringham, R. 2003
'Flaked stone', in *Prehistoric Sitagroi: excavations in northeast Greece, 1968-1970, vol. 2: the final report*, E.S. Elster & C. Renfrew (eds.), (*Monumenta Archaeologica* 20), Los Angeles, 81-126.

Vitelli, K. 1989
'Were pots first made for food? doubts from Franchthi', *WA* 21, 1, 17-29.

Vitelli, K. 1993a
'Power to the potters', *JMA* 6, 2, 247-57.

Vitelli, K. 1993b
Franchthi neolithic pottery I. Classification and ceramic phases 1 and 2. Fasc.8, Bloomington/ Indianapolis.

Vitelli, K. 1999
Franchthi neolithic pottery, Vol.2, Fasc.10, Bloomington/Indianapolis.

Vokotopoulou, I. 1986
Βίτσα. Τα Νεκροταφεία μιας Μολωσσικής Πόλης, Vols. A-B, Athens.

Wace, A.J.B. & M.S. Thompson 1912
Prehistoric Thessaly, Cambridge.

Wace, A.J.B. & C.W. Blegen 1916-1918
'The Pre-Mycenaean pottery of the mainland', *BSA* 22, 175-89.

Walter, H. & F. Felten 1981
Die vorgeschichtliche Stadt. Alt-Ägina III,1, Wien.

Wardle, K.A. 1972
The Greek Bronze Age west of the Pindus: a study of the period ca.

3.000-1.000 B.C. in Epirus, Aetolo-Akarnania, the Ionian Islands and Albania, with reference to the Aegean, Adriatic and Balkan regions, University of London, (Unpublished Ph.D.-thesis).

Wardle, K.A. 1977
'Cultural groups of the Late Bronze and Early Iron Age in north west Greece', Godišnjak Knjiga 15, Sarajevo, 153-99.

Wardle, K.A. & D. Wardle 2003
'Prehistoric Thermon: pottery of the Late Bronze and Early Iron Age', in Periphery 2, 147-56.

Watson, A. 1984
'Chipped stone artifacts from Servia in Greek Macedonia', JFA,10, 120-3.

Weinberg, S. 1962
'Excavations at prehistoric Elateia, 1959', Hesperia 31, 172-96.

Weinberg, S. S. 1970
The Stone Age in the Aegean. Cambridge Ancient History I, Part 1, Cambridge, 557-672.

Weisshaar, H-J. 1981
'Ausgraungen in Tiryns, 1978, 1979: Bericht zur frühhelladischen Keramik', AA 96, 220-56.

Weisshaar, H.-J. 1982
'Ausgrabungen in Tiryns, 1980: Bericht zur frühhelladischen Keramik', AA 97, 440-66.

Weisshaar, H.-J. 1983,
'Bericht zur frühhelladischen Keramik: Ausgrabungen in Tiryns 1981', AA 98, 329-58.

Weisshaar, H.J. 1989
Die deutschen Ausgrabungen auf der Pevkakia-Magula in Thessalien. Das späte Neolithicum und das Chalcolithicum, Bonn.

Weisshaar, H.-J. 1990
'Die Keramik von Talioti', Tiryns Forschungen und Berichte Band XI, Mainz, 1-34.

Wells, B. with C. Runnels 1996
The Berbati-Limnes Archaeological survey 1988-1990, Stockholm.

West, B. & X. B. Zhou 1988
'Did chickens go north? New evidence for domestication', JAS 15, 515-33.

Whitehead P.J., P. M-L Bauchot, J-C Hureau, J. Nielsen, & E. Tortonese 1984,
Fishes of the north-eastern Atlantic and the Mediterranean, vol. I, Paris.

Wickens, J. 1986
The archaeology and history of cave use in Attica, Greece from prehistoric through late Roman times, Ph.D thesis, Indiana University.

Wiencke, M. H. 2000
Lerna. A preclassical site in the Argolid Vol. IV: the architecture, stratification, and pottery of Lerna III, Princeton New Jersey.

Williams-Thorpe, O. 1995
'Obsidian in the Mediterranean and the Near East: A provenancing success story', Archaeometry 37, 2, 217-48.

Wohlmayr, W. 2000
Schachtgräberzeitliche Keramik aus Ägina. Österreichische Forschungen zur Ägäischen Bronzezeit, Akten der Tagung am Institut für Klassische Archäologie der Universität Wien 2-3, Mai 1998 (Wiener Forschungen zur Archäologie 3), Wien, 127-36.

Yannouli, E. 2003
'Non-domestic carnivores in Greek prehistory: a review', in Zoo

archaeology in Greece, E. Kotjabopoulou, Y. Hamilakis, P. Halstead, C. Gamble & P. Elefanti P. (eds.) (BSA studies 10), London, 175-92.

Zapheiropoulos, N. 1958
'Ανασκαφή εω Φαραίς', Prakt, 167-76.

Zachos, C. 1987
Ayios Dhimitrios, a prehistoric settlement in the southwestern Peloponnesos: The Neolithic and Early Helladic Periods, PhD diss., Boston University.

Zachos, K. 1990
'The neolithic period in Naxos. In Cycladic culture. Naxos in the third millennium BC', in Η Νάξος στην Τρίτη χιλιετία π.Χ., L. Marangou (ed.), Athens, 29-38.

Zachos, K. 1999
'Zas Cave on Naxos and the role of caves in the Aegean late neolithic', in Neolithic society in Greece, P. Halstead (ed.), Sheffield, 153-63.

Zeder, M. 1999
'Animal domestication in the Zagros: A review of past and current research' Paleorient 25, 2, 11-25.

Zerner, C. 1978
The beginning of the Middle Helladic period at Lerna, PhD diss., University of Cincinnati.

Zerner, C. 1988
'Middle Helladic and Late Helladic I pottery from Lerna', Hydra 2, 58-74.

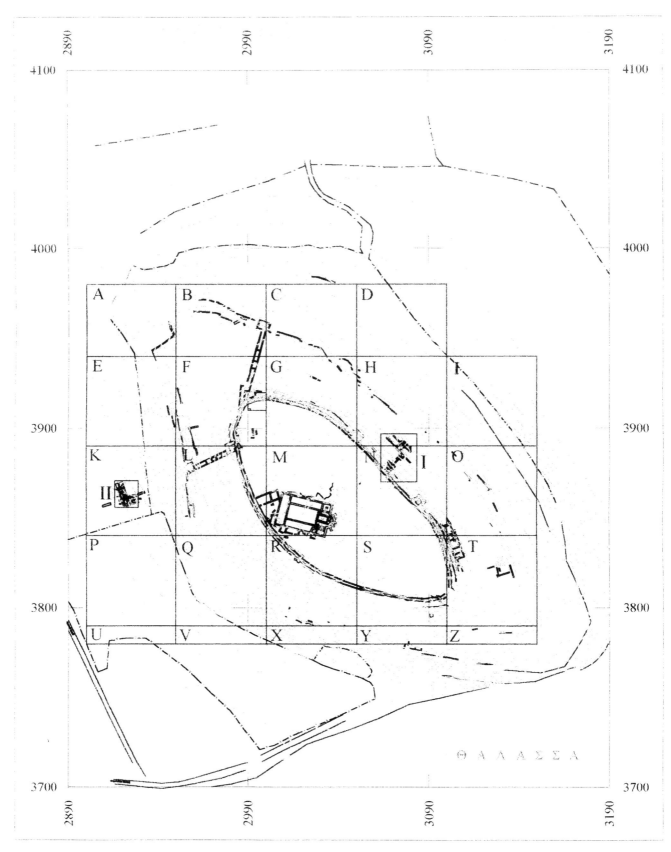

Fig. 7. Map of the mound of Aghia Triada and the area west of the hill with contours and grid system (Charalambos Marinopoulos). Areas I and II are shown on Fig. 8a-b.

The systematic approach and the numbering system

The field project in and around Aghia Triada developed in the following stages (for a more detailed treatment, see the preliminary reports):

1995: Surveys conducted on the mound of Aghia Triada. Measurement of remains visible on the surface continued every year until 2001.

1996: Excavations on the acropolis of Aghia Triada, concentrated in the North West corner. First year of geological survey which aimed towards the definition of the ancient coast line and the determination of the ancient harbour. The geological survey and studies of the shell fish continued, with interruptions, until 2000.

1997: Cleaning of the middle terrace on the East side of the Aghia Triada and start of excavations. Extensive trial trenches (among others Tx 20 below) opened on the mound of Aghia Triada.

1998: Continued excavations on the middle terrace and further trial trenches (Tx 43 below). Trial trenches opened in the area west of the Aghia Triada (among others Tx 70, 71 and 72 below) in order to investigate the shores of the small bay shown by the geological survey to exist on this side of the hill.

1999: Continued excavations on the mound of Aghia Triada and opening of trenches K 26 to K 28 in the area West of Aghia Triada.

2000: Continued excavations on the hill of Aghia Triada and in the area west of the mound. Trench K 29 was opened in this last mentioned area.

2001: Final excavations in the area West of Aghia Triada.

At Pangali work was carried out during two seasons

1995: Surveys conducted on the East slope of Varasssova, the terrace of Pangali.

1996: Trial excavations at the Final Neolithic site of Pangali (see Mavridis and Sørensen below).

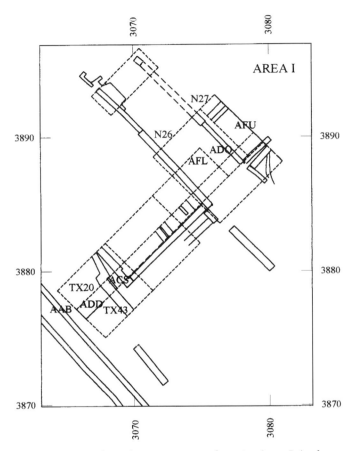

Fig. 8a. Trench and structure numbers in Area I (only numbers mentioned in the text are shown).

(Fig. 7) Before excavation on Aghia Triada started in 1996, the area was divided in a N–S/E–W grid system with squares measuring 10x10 metres and labelled with capital letters A, B, C, …Z.[2] Regular trenches laid out on Aghia Triada were first given a capital letter referring to the square in which it was placed and a running number (Arabic numerals) (F15, N 26 etc.). The many trial trenches

---

[2] FPR, 282, fig. 15.

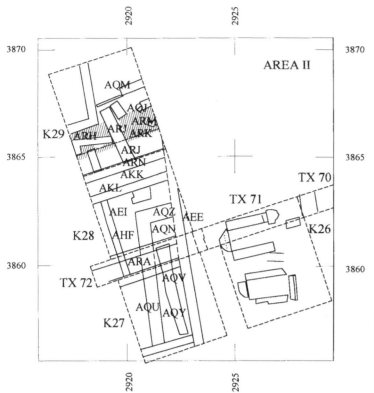

Fig. 8b. Trench and structure numbers in Area II (only numbers mentioned in the text are shown).

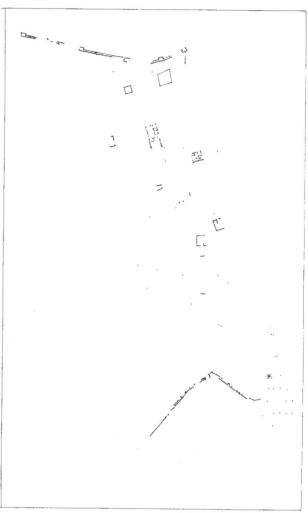

Fig. 9. Plan showing measurements of structures on Pangali and the position of the Final Neolithic site (★).

opened in order to locate preserved deposits got running numbers (Arabic numerals) proceeded by Tx (Tx43, Tx20 etc.). Strata in trenches or trial trenches are marked with a slash and a running number: N26/2, K29/3 ..... Tx43/4b etc. Other numbers used in the registration are as follows:

Structure: For instance walls, pits, floors, fire places etc. are numbered with three capital letters: AAA, AAB, ... AKL etc.

Strata in structures: are marked with a slash and a running number: AAA/2, AAB/4 etc. (Figs. 8a and b).

Finds: are specific objects selected for special reasons: – of importance for dating structures – of specific value (coins, sculpture, terracottas, obsidian, iron nails etc.) – of significance for the determination of function (spindle whorls, charcoal, etc.). Finds cited either within structures: AAA-3 or within strata: F-1087 etc.

(Fig. 9) shows the measurements of structures on Pangali and the position of the Final Neolithic site.

Part I

The Bronze Age periods at Aghia Triada

Chapter 1

Studies in the Bronze Age of Aghia Triada. A summary

By Søren Dietz & Ioannis Moschos

A definition of Early Helladic I

Introduction

The phase EHI was first briefly defined by Wace and Blegen in 1918.[3] The definition was based on stratigraphy where EHI represented the lowest layer in Blegen's excavations in Korakou and Zygouries, succeeded by a much more substantial EHII horizon with sauceboats etc. From his stratigraphical observations in Korakou it was possible to define the pottery of the EHI as first of all characterized by the surface treatment of pottery (Group AI) as unslipped, buff, red or black and smoothly polished with marks of the burnishing instrument distinctly visible. The relations to other waregroups were, however, not stated and the contextual definition of the horizon is not clear. No vases with raised base were found from this early group. The material was badly preserved and it was only possible to restore one complete bowl.[4] According to Weisshaar, the slipped version, Group II should be dated to EHII in present day terminology.[5] Stratigraphical excavated material from north eastern Peloponnese came to light in Kephalari-magula where ("a pre-sauceboat phase") EHI was found below an EHII stratum. In addition important surface material was recovered from the Talioti valley behind Asine.[6]

In her 1931 report of the excavations in Eutresis in Boeotia, Hetty Goldman attributed both her "First meter of deposit" and her "Second meter of deposit" to the period EHI. In Eutresis the EHI layers are preceded by two Neolithic horizons and succeeded by EHII layers. Even if the general stratigraphical observations were substantiated, Goldman's attribution and definitions have been revised, following a re-excavation by J.L. and E.C. Caskey in 1958.[7] There are some disagreements concerning terminology and the chronological attribution to EHI. Weisshaar 1990 for instance considered only Eutresis III-IV to be EHI (=Goldman's "First meter of deposit"), while Eutresis V is considered to be EHII (=Goldman's "Second meter of deposit"). Maran 1998 among many others includes Eutresis V in his EH I phase (see also below).

The period and its characteristic local variations of pottery waregroups have now been identified in greater parts of Southern Greece in Boeotia, Attica, Euboia, the Argolid, Arcadia, Kythera, Messenia and Elis. Not yet, however, with safety in Achaia[8] and Aitolia/Akarnania.[9]

---

[3] Wace & Blegen 1916-18, 176f.

[4] For a fairly detailed comparison between EH I in Korakou/Zygouries and Talioti in the Argolid, see Weisshaar 1990, 13f.

[5] Weisshaar 1990, 13. Blegen 1921, 4ff.

[6] Douzougli 1987 and Weisshaar 1990.

[7] Caskey & Caskey 1960.

[8] The EHI material from Teichos Dymaion defined by Mastrokostas 1967,126, should probably be dated in EHII. Basilogambrou 1998 consider the tombs from the cemetery of Kalamaki Elaiochoriou to be EH I in dating (based on comparisons with Manika I).

[9] Good surveys in Dousougli 1987, 165ff., Weisshaar 1990, 13f. and more recently in Maran 1998, 8ff, Wiencke 2000, 631f. and Alram-Stern 2004a, 156-7.

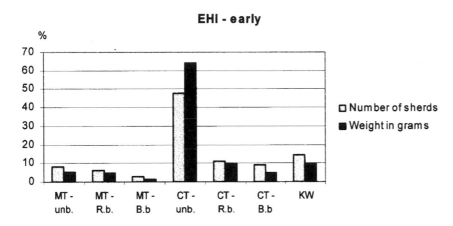

EHI - early

EHI-early	MT-unb.	MT-R.b.	MT-B.b.	CT-unb.	CT-R.b.	CT-B.b.	KW	Total
No	64	50	24	385	91	72	117	803
Weight	800	750	250	9800	1450	700	1500	15250

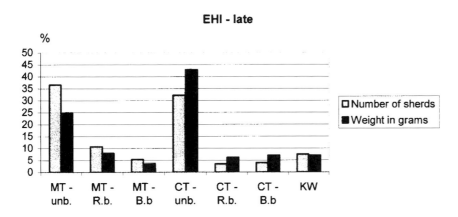

EHI - late

EHI-late	MT-unb.	MT-R.b.	MT-B.b.	CT-unb.	CT-R.b.	CT-B.b.	KW	Total
No	629	186	92	553	59	70	128	1717
Weight	5400	1750	800	9300	1350	1550	1550	21700

Fig. 10. Aghia Triada. Statistical survey (a and b) of EHI pottery classes (Tx43 and Tx20).

EHI – Early Phase

The deposits

We have isolated three deposits as representatives for an earlier phase of EHI (Tx43/4b, Tx43/5 and Tx20/4b). Fig. 10 indicates the relative frequency of various pottery waregroups. It is most significant that almost 2/3 of the pottery according to weight, almost 1/2 according to number is classified in the group of CT-unburnished. The explanation is clearly that the deposit derives from the surround-

ings of a fireplace (ADD-3) where coarse tempered pottery for storage and kitchen ware is expected to be found. Within the group of MT wares, three times as many are red burnished as black burnished counting number of sherds, twice as many by weight. In the group of CT wares there is only slightly more red burnished than black burnished by numbers, approximately twice as many by weight; 17.5 % are red burnished by number, 14.4 % by weight – 12 % by numbers are black burnished, 7.2 % by weight. Thus 29.5 % by number, 21.6 % by weight of all sherds are burnished. We

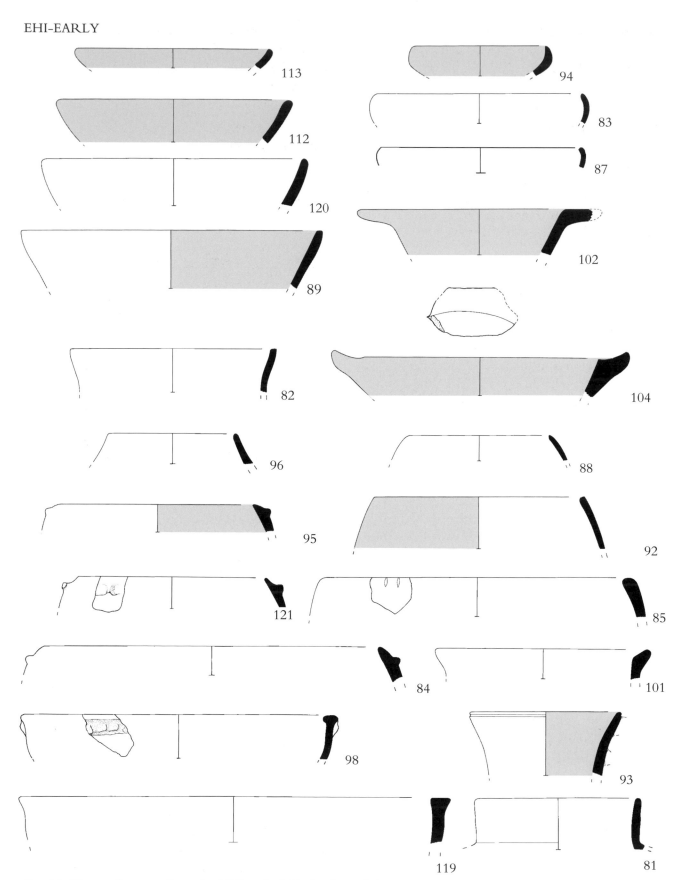

Fig. 11 Types of pottery from the EHI period. Early phase. 1:4.

should like to emphasize that parallel grooves are often found where burnished slip is registered, a feature often found on EH pottery if not always described in detail.[10]

Shapes and decorations

Open shapes (Fig. 11)

Open bowls (20 –28 cm estimated diameter) with rounded rim and often with red burnish on in-and outside are the most characteristic pottery shapes in the deposits (Fig. 11 nos.112, 113 and 120). These "Kalottenschale" are either rather shallow (no. 113) or deeper (no. 120).[11] A related type of deep bowl (Fig. 11 no. 89) has outwards thickened rim, flattened on the top and red burnish on inside with clear traces of burnishing tool – or a prepared surface? (broad parallel horizontal shallow grooves).[12]

Less common in the earlier layers are the open small bowls with inturned rim. The small shallow bowl no. 94 has a rather unusual section with pointed inturned rim.[13] A more usual type has a thinner wall than the "Kalottenschale" and inturned thin or slightly thickened rim (nos. 83 and 87). This type is common in the Argolid and Boeoetia.[14]

The red burnished bowl, catalogue no. 102 is related to the EHI type of bowl with broad, flat rim set off from the body at a sharp angle placed on a large pedestal ("Fruitstand"). On the usual type the rim is convex and the bowl itself concave approaching the rim in a clay bevel. In the Argolid, the rim often has incised decoration.[15] „Fruitstands" are first of all present in EHI in Southern Greece even if its general distribution is much larger[16] (see also catalogue no. 66 from EHI-late phase, below p. 43)

Basins with thickened rim. T-rim bowl no. 98 – as for the raised band with tactile decoration, see also below p. 42.[17]

The large and deep coarse tempered basin no. 119 (D.46 cm) might be compared with coarse ware open jars or deep basins with flattened and thickened rims from Eutresis III.[18] While the open rounded bowl with concave ridge-handle on the

rim (no. 104) probably has almost the same section as another piece from Eutresis[19] but without the lugs. The sherd from Eutresis is said to derive from the lower filling of the chasm but is probably intrusive from later deposits.

Closed shapes (Fig. 11)

The hole mouth jar (no. 96) is probably of Final Neolithic date, Phelps Period IV, late phase contemporary with the Grotta/Pelos culture in the Cyclades.[20]

Hemispherical hole mouth jars are the most

---

[10] Zachos 1987, 169f. Wace & Blegen 1916-18, Class Ib. Caskey & Caskey 1960, 139-40, Weisshaar 1990; Dousougli 1987 *et al.* The traces of the burnishing tool are not always described in detail and not usually as parallel grooves as seen in Chalkis Aitolias.

[11] Dousougli 1987, 178, fig. 7,1-2. Dousougli distinguishes "Kalottenförmige Schalen" (AIa) from „Schalen mit einziehendem Rand" (AIb). This distinction is followed in this treatment. Contra Weisshaar 1990 who includes bowls with inturned rims in the terminology "Kalottenschale". Caskey & Caskey 1960, figs. 7, IV,1 and IV,3, fig. 4, III,3 (Red slipped ware). For the same shapes in Thessaly see Hanschmann 1976, Gattung A1 (Kalottenschale (Gattung A1) in use during all periods of the EB in Argissa Magula. Fossey 1969, 67 and fig. 3, 12-13 (phase x).

[12] For shape comp. Fossey 1969, fig. 3, 18-22 (phase x) with flat rim see p. 57: "Bowls with round lips .... are much more frequent than those with flat ones".

[13] comp. Dousougli 1987, Abb. 7,5-7 for a similar size, rim/shoulder, the bowl, however, is deeper. Except for no. 7, these bowls from Makrovouni, according to Dousougli, should be dated in EHII, Dousougli 1987 cit. 216.

[14] Talioti, Weisshaar 1990, Taf. 18,6 and 9. Makrovouni, Douzougli 1987, fig. 8,23. Perachora phase y, Fossey 1969, fig. 5,7 and 9. Eutresis, Caskey & Caskey 1960, fig. 7,IV,2.

[15] Weisshaar 1990, Taf. 2-3 and Taf. 18,9. Dousougli 1987, fig. 12, 42-45. A quite close parallel from Ayios Dhimitrios period IIa (Zachos 1987, 130/81, fig. 51). Also Hanschmann 1976, Taf. 7,1 (Graben 2/3/FThI=early EHII). According to Zachos 1987 „the incised decoration on the rims and the vertical handles should be considered a northeastern Peloponnesian feature" (cit. p. 278).

[16] Weisshaar 1990, 191. Also Zachos 1987, 186 ff with catalogue of "Fruitstands".

[17] According to Zachos 1987 T-rim bowls are not found until EHII.

[18] Caskey & Caskey 1960, 142 (III.11-12), fig. 4.

[19] Caskey & Caskey 1960, 140 (III.9), pl. 47.

[20] Phelps 1975, fig. 59 passim (Alepotrypa), 339.

usual type of closed shaped vessels. On Fig. 11 six pieces are depicted, representing various aspects of the closed shaped jar. Nos. 95, 121 and 84 have pointed rim and a raised band with tactile decoration shortly below the rim; the decorations are of the types with very closely overlapping disks and with fingerprints.[21] The rim diameter varies between 20 cm (95 and 121) and 36 cm for the large jar no. 84. No. 121 is a sand-tempered kitchen ware fabric, the large jar no. 84 an MT-unburnished fabric and no. 95 a MT hard sandy fabric, slipped and burnished black on the inside.

The three bowls nos. 88, 92 and 85 are without raised bands. The small jar no. 88 with a pointed rim, medium tempered in a non-local fabric, is probably an import. No. 92 has a rounded, slightly thickened rim and is black burnished on the outside, while finally no. 85 has a pronounced thickened and rounded rim with incised ovals or "potter's marks". The type is also found in EHII.[22]

Hole-mouth jars with incurved rim were almost globular and probably had flat bases.

Coarse bowls with incurved rim are among the most common groups of EHI vessels.[23] They are only exceptionally burnished, as in the present deposits. The type continues in the earlier phases of EHII in Lerna (Lerna III, Early phase A) and in early EHII layers in Tiryns and is probably in use as a general type to the end of the EHII period.[24]

Closed jars with funnel shaped neck and thin rim, no. 93 is red slipped (unburnished) on the outside and black burnished on the inside. The neck is rather high and narrow and thus seems to equivalent to EHII jars with carinated shoulder from Makrovouni rather than the more open late EHI types from Kephalari.[25] The shape, however, is also found in Perachora phases x and y and this together with the characteristic red slipped surface does not seem to exclude a dating in EHI.[26]

The jar with almost cylindrical neck, thin rim and carinated shoulder (no. 81) does not seem to be found in the Talioti horizon in the Argolid, but is most common in Perachora in both phase x and y.[27] In Chalkis the neck is somewhat higher.

The small coarse tempered jar with thickened and carinated, out-turned rim no. 101 is somewhat similar in shape to open bowl "Fruitstands" from Talioti.[28] The vessel from the Argolid, however, is fine tempered, red slipped and more open than our jar from Chalkis.

A definition of EHI – late phase

The deposits

There are more deposits isolated as characteristic of a late phase of EHI than from the earlier phase. The number of the deposits, however, is of no great importance as such, since it mainly reflects, on the one hand the procedures of excavation, on the other hand the fact that these deposits might have been more or less redeposited. It is thus of some importance that, talking about an earlier and a later horizon, we are not dealing with two contexts *in situ* – only the early phase, the lower levels, could be considered a deposit in its original position.

Twice as many sherds were counted deriving from the late phase than from the early (1717 against 803); by weight the material from the early phase makes up approximately 70% of that of the later (15.250 kg against 21.700 kg) (Fig. 10). The plain, unburnished ware groups constitute by far the majority of the pottery (almost 70 % by both number and weight), but it is significant that the amount of MT pottery approximately equals the amount of CT – in contrast to the clear predominance of CT in the earlier layer. This probably derives from two different depositional situations. Within the group of MT wares, the red burnished

[21] Weisshaar 1983 type b1 and c.

[22] For nos. 88 and 92 on Euboia see Sampson 1981, fig. 15. Also from Limnes, Kastria (Phase IV). Katsarou in Sampson 1997, nos. 651-652, p. 281, figs. 78 and 80. In general Wiencke 2000, 625ff (P603) with parallels.

[23] Dousougli 1987, 189, 103-105 and fig. 19. Fossey 1969, fig. 3, 1-3 (phase x), fig. 5, 3-7 (phase y).

[24] Wiencke 2000, 549-550. Weisshaar 1983, 336-338.

[25] Dousougli 1987, 87-92, fig. 17 (Makrovouni), 157, fig. 26 (Kephalari).

[26] Dousougli 1987, 218.

[27] Fossey 1969, fig. 2,9 and fig. 4,17.

[28] Weisshaar 1990, pl. 2, 2.

make up twice as many, by both number and weight, as black burnished (10.8/5.4 % - 8/3.7 %), within the coarse ware group, red and black burnished wares almost equal each other (3.5/4.0 % - 6.2/7.1 %). In total, red burnished make up 14.3 % by number, 14.2 % by weight; the same proportions for black burnished are 9.4 % and 10.8 %, thus 23.7 % by number and 25 % by weight were burnished. Kitchen ware constitutes a less significant part of the pottery in the late phase than in the earlier. The reason for these slight differences is hardly a chronological development, rather different depositional conditions.

Shapes and decoration (Figs. 12-13)

Bowls with inturned, pointed rim nos. 41, 27 and 51 are medium tempered, red burnished and probably flat based.[29] The two first are rather shallow. Estimated diameters at rim between 14 and 25 cm. The open bowl with inturned rim is related to the previously mentioned piece from Makrovouni in the Argolid with thick, matt tile red slip considered to be of (probably) EHI date by Dousougli.[30] The hemispherical shape of the bodies differs from the more straight sided bowls from EHII.[31] For the deep bowl no. 51 see Palaiá Kokkiniá in Attica.[32] The open „Kalottenschalen" with rounded rim (nos. 55 and 49) are larger than the above mentioned bowls, 30 and 32 cm in estimated diameter of rim. No. 55 is red burnished on the inside. The large open bowl no. 71 with flat rim has a parallel in Perachora phase x.[33] For the bowl no. 48 (Pl. 4) with notches on the rim – compare Talioti.[34]

Large open shallow bowls with inturned, carinated rim (nos. 56, 68 and 53) with estimated diameter respectively 34 cm, 30 cm and 40 cm. The bowls are rather thin walled and produced in a medium tempered fabric, one is red, the other is black (no. 56 with reddish brown rather dark surface). Carinated rim sections appear (for the first time?) in Eutresis Group V; the bowls from Boeotia, however, are deeper.[35] Similar shapes are found in Ayios Dhimitrios, Period IIa where the bowls are shallow but much smaller.[36] Catalogue no. 66, a kitchenware fabric, related in general to "Talioti" shapes described by

Weisshaar as open bowls, with outturned carinated rim with the off-set from the body more or less angular. In the Argolid the bowls are usually sand-tempered (as no. 66) with a reddish, sometimes burnished, slip. The rim often has incised decoration. It is likely that our bowl, like the example from the Argolid, rested on a high base ("Fruitstands").[37] Catalogue no. 60 (Pl. 4) is also likely to be the rim of a "fruitstand".

Closed shapes

Deep bowls with incurved rim as nos. 34 and 44 are related to the types from the early phase (above note 22). Both have a black burnished slip on in- and outside. The type does not seem to be present in Ayios Dhimitrios.

The fragment of a globular jar with broad outturned, slightly thickened neck no. 50 has a rather good parallel in a jar from the EHI horizon in Kephalari-Magula in the Argolid.[38]

No. 64 is probably the spout of a coarse ware jug (?) The neck is familiar with jugs from Ayios Dhimitrios phase IIa, where the diameter of the rim, however, is larger.[39]

Bases, handles and decoration (Fig.13)

The two pedestal bases nos. 45 and 79 are both from "Fruitstands". The first is unusual small com-

---

[29] Caskey & Caskey 1960, fig. 7, IV.3.

[30] 1987, fig. 7, 7. Comp. Also Caskey & Caskey 1960, IV.2 (red slipped).

[31] Comp. for instance Weisshaar 1981, 223 "kleinen Schüsseln mit abgesetztem Rand" Tp. II (mit einziehendem Rand).

[32] Theocharis 1951, fig. 18.

[33] Fossey 1969, 58, fig. 3,21.

[34] Weisshaar 1990, pl. 10,11 – on a close shaped jar, however.

[35] Caskey & Caskey 1960, fig. 7, V.1-3.

[36] Zachos 1987, fig. 40.

[37] Weisshaar 1990, 5, pls. 2-3. Ayios Dhimitrios, Zachos 1987, figs 51-52. In Ayios Dhimitrios there is no decoration on the rim. See also above no. 102 from the early phase of EHI.

[38] Dousougli 1987, fig. 26, 157.

[39] Zachos 1987, fig. 63.

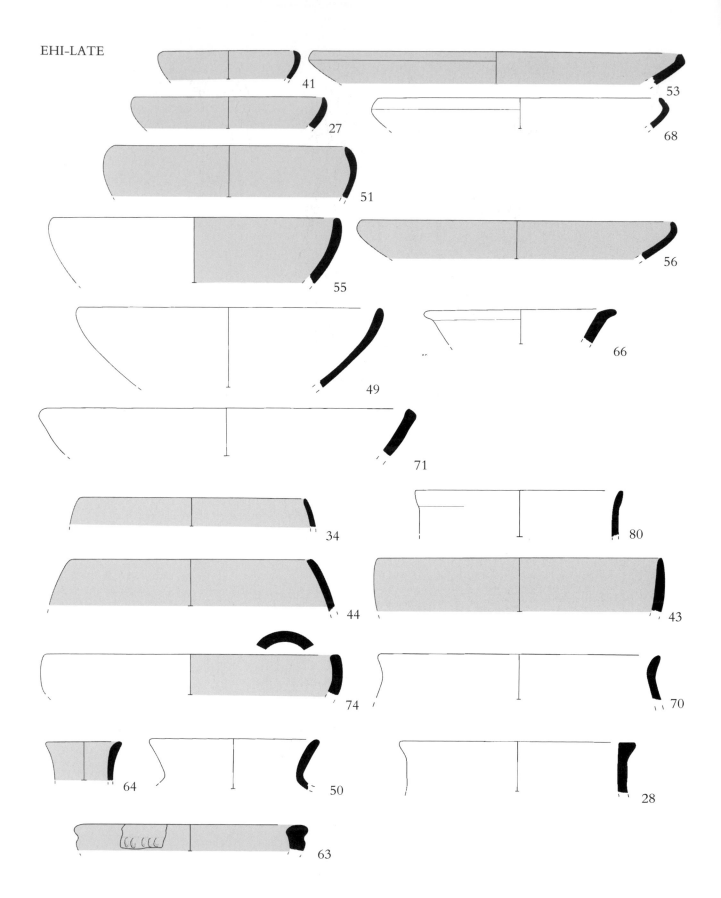

Fig. 12. Types of pottery from the EHI period. Late phase. 1:4.

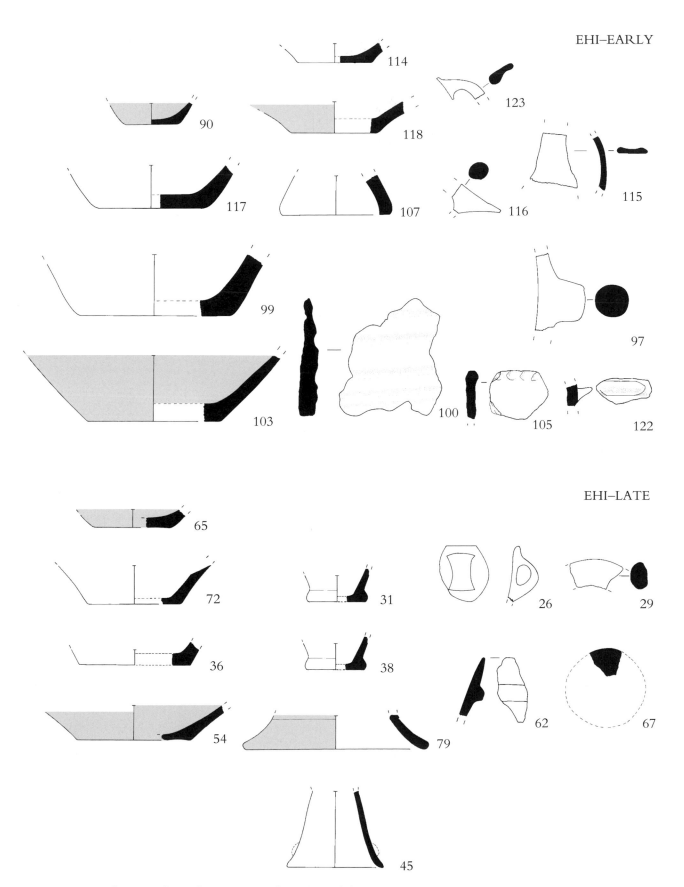

Fig. 13. Types of pottery from the EHI period. Various. 1:4.

pared to the types present in the Peloponnese. The fabric and the very pale brown matt slip indicates that the piece has been imported. More usual is the other stand with an incised line on the stem which compares well with pedestals from Ayios Dhimitrios in Triphylia and Kephalari–Magula and Talioti in the Argolid.[40]

Raised bands are found on coarse and medium tempered jars, basins, pithoi etc. They are undoubtly decorative elements, but do have at the same time practical functions as did handles and lugs.[41]

Summary EH I. Chronology and foreign relations.

Due to the many activities on the mound of Aghia Triada from the Bronze Age onwards and especially the construction of the substantial Byzantine fortification systems surrounding the Basilica of Aghia Triada on the top, most contexts from the Prehistoric periods have been scattered and mixed up with material from later periods. As for the Early Bronze Age itself, sherds have been found all over the mound partly during the surveys conducted the first years of the archaeological activities and partly from the trenches opened inside the Byzantine fortification itself. The material found should be dated to either EHI or EHII (catalogue numbers 8, 17 and 18. See also FPR). Nothing has been found which can be safely attributed to the EH III period.

Of specific interest is a preserved context from the EHI period which has been isolated on the slope below the Byzantine fortification wall. The deposit rests on the bedrock and the superposed strata mainly contain material from the Archaic habitation on the hill. Based on stratigraphical observations the deposit has been divided into two chronological phases, an earlier with material found, more or less in situ, around and above a fireplace based on the bedrock, and a later phase placed on top of the first one but consisting of material which might to some extent have been re-deposited.

In the early phase of EHI approximately 30 % of the sherd material was burnished. Traces of the burnishing instrument are usually visible but the burnish itself often peels of and is usually not very lustrous. Red burnish is more usual than black burnish (in the proportion 3/2 in number 2/1 by weight).

"Kalottenschale" and larger bowls of the same general open shape with thin, rounded or flat rims are very common. They are produced in medium (often sand-) tempered fabrics often with a surface covered by a red burnish directly on the surface or on a thin slip. Red burnish was clearly preferred on open shapes, black burnish on closed. Cups and bowls with inturned rim are likewise found in considerable quantities. All cups and bowls had flat bases, no raised bases are found in the lower stratum. (no. 107 on Fig. 13 is of FN date)

One sherd with outturned flat rim, coarse tempered fabric with red burnish on in- and outside, was considered to derive from a so-called "fruit stand" with a high pedestal base. A coarse tempered and red burnished basin of unusual shape with a trapezoidal extension at the rim probably has a parallel in Eutresis in Boeotia. Among other large basins produced in medium tempered fabrics, one has a raised band with finger imprints right below a T-rim. All plastic/incised decorations in this phase are made with simple finger- or nail impressions. A huge basin with flat rim is of a distinct local type.

Final Neolithic elements are most unusual in these context; one hole-mouth jar and the ring base no. 107 (Fig. 13) might be of this early date. A most common closed shape is a clearly local type of hole-mouth jar with a thin or (more unusual) thickened rim and sometimes a raised band with finger imprints near the rim. These jars are produced in medium tempered fabrics and sometimes black burnished on in- or outside. Finally the deposit includes the funnel neck and a cylindrical neck of globular jars

In the late phase of EHI approximately 25 % of the sherd material is burnished. The technique of burnishing is as in the earlier phase. In the group

---

[40] Zachos 1987, fig. 37, 9. Dousougli 1987, fig. 27, 167. Weisshaar 1990, pl. 5.
[41] See Wiencke 2000, 619.

of medium tempered wares the red burnished is twice as usual as the black burnished, but in the coarse ware group the two types of burnishing are equal. In total the black burnished makes up around 2/3 of the red burnished – approximately as in the early phase.

The most usual open shape is the cup or bowl with inturned thin rim and red burnished on in- and outside. In contrast to the early phase, the "Kalottenschale" are less common and appear only in the large bowl version. In addition shallow plates with incurved, carinated rim are now, for the first time, added to the inventory. One rather typical rim of a "fruit stand" and two pedestal bases were found among the shapes in the late phase.

As in the early phase, hole-mouth jars with black burnish on in-and outside are found, but not as commonly. Various types of rather open jars with or without black burnish are found in the later phase and an open jar with thick, flat rim, as in the early phase but smaller. Jars with funnel neck and T-rim bowl with "knickwand" (no. 63 on Fig. 12) and raised band with bands of closely overlapping disks (Weisshaar b1) are found. Finally the neck of a jug has been registrered.

It should be emphasized that flat bases are the most usual but that raised bases, in contrast to the early phase, are also found.

Compared to other assemblages of EH I pottery the local tradition in Chalkis Aitolias seems, on the one hand, to show very characteristic features of the period, on the other hand, some shapes and specific details seem to be missing. The surface treatment with a thin, reddish or brown, often slightly burnished slip fits the standard definition well and so does the majority of the cups and bowls. On the other hand, the flat bowls with outturned, flattened or carinated rim (it is not clear whether they are always supplied with a pedestal base) found in abundance in North East Peloponnese and in Triphylia, are not present in Chalkis Aitolias.[42] The incised decorations on the flat rims are specific for the north east Peloponnese. Missing are also bowls with horizontal, tubular projections, "spoons"[43] and matt impressions below the base.

As for the chronological significance of the pottery, it is of importance to point out that the fol-lowing characteristic features are absent from the deposits: - there are no rolled rim bowls – pattern burnish is not found – neither is pattern painted pottery – and there are no sauceboats. The absence of these features might indicate that the deposits, from a chronological point of view, should be placed between the Final neolithic and the EHII or the "sauceboat phase" to use the expression of Angelika Dousougli. Rolled rims are found on pottery from Eutresis group III "the only secure stratigraphic evidence for the rolled rim bowls in southern Mainland Greece …".[44] This confirms that our EHI–early phase is contemporary with Eutresis group IV,[45] also indicated by the similari-ties between the shallow bowls. The similarities between the shallow plates with carinated section in the EHI-late phase in Chalkis and the bowls of Eutresis group V indicate that these two phases are contemporary. The presence of a T-rim bowl with "knickwand" probably indicates that this phase might overlap the EHII in the Argolid[46] in the very early part of Lerna III phase A.[47] Zachos con-sidered Ayios Dhimitrios IIa to be a transitional phase between EHI and EHII, contemporary with Eutresis V and VI (=Goldmans "second meter of deposits"). There are similarities between especial-ly Chalkis Aitolias EHI – late phase and Aghios Dhimitrios IIa, but it is possible that the dating of IIa is the result of a certain mixture between the EHI horizon and EHII.[48]

Even if EHI is thus by far well understood and defined in details, it is possible to conclude that it is a chronological phase between the chalco-lithic/end of Final Neolithic and a longer and much better defined and understood EHII in Central and Southern Greece though with consid-erable local variations. It has been substantiated

---

[42] Comp. Weisshaar 1990, pl.1, 1-9 and pl. 4, 6-7. Zachos 1987, figs. 52-53.

[43] Caskey & Caskey 1960, fig. 7, IV.8 and IV.9. Dousougli 1987, fig. 26, 161.

[44] French 1972, 19.

[45] And Perachora phase y, Dousougli 1987, 212, n. 128.

[46] Weisshaar 1990, 11.

[47] Wiencke 2001, 641.

[48] Maran 1998, 17.

that the phase is not more or less contemporary with the late Chalcolithic[49] even if it is still a problem that this phase has not been defined everywhere (not in Aitolia/Akarnania and nor for instance in North Eastern Peloponnese). One of two radiocarbon dates (see Jan Heinemeier below p. 198) confirms a dating of the phase EHI-early to around 3.000 BC while the other (around 3.700 BC) indicates that there might be a Final Neolithic element in the deposit even if it has not been possible to isolate a Final Neolithic context.

A definition of MHIIIB/LHIA[50]

Introduction

Stratified material from the transitional period MHIIIB/LHIA in Aitolia has only been published sporadically.[51] More material is known from Achaia on the south coast of the gulf.[52] Of specific interest for the problems concerning the definition of the transition from MH to LHI in the provinces around the gulf of Patras are the results of the recently excavated site of Pagona in Patras situated on a shallow mound 2.4 km from the sea and 1.2 km southeast of the Kastro of Patras.[53] The rescue excavations in Pagona revealed an extensive Mycenaean habitation on the hill mainly of LHII-IIIA/B/C date terminating in a conflagration. Particularly on locality 3 (Liakopoulou Str. 6) and locality 4 (Chrisovitsiou Str. 9) important habitation layers of MH and Early Mycenaean date were recovered below the floors of the Mycenaean houses.

Only a small amount of material from the Middle Helladic period before MHIII came to light during the recent excavations in Chalkis Aitolias. A dark faced "minyan bowl" from the survey on the Aghia Triada (Catalogue no. 10, Pl. 1) derives from an early angular bowl with high swung handles. In Lerna similar bowls are dated in later Lerna VA.[54]

In the area west of the Aghia Triada stratum 5a and 6 below the LHIB stratum 5 in trial trench Tx70 contains material which might be dated somewhat earlier than MHIII. It is a very restricted material with a relatively high percentage of fine tempered fabrics, especially in stratum 5a, and some imported lustrous painted wares. Stratum 6 in addition contains a certain amount of EH material.

Of shapes in "Lustrous Paint" fabric should be mentioned two imported vessels both thin walled, fine tempered products with a red lustrous paint on a brown, slightly burnished slip. No. 154 (Fig. 16) is undoubtedly an angular cup as for instance found in Lerna where it is more related to the earlier MHI/Lerna V1 forms of angular cups than later (MHIII) forms. The general type imitates Minoan prototypes.[55] The cup from Chalkis Aitolias is larger than the parallels mentioned and the monochrome lustrous paint on the surface does not give any indications of the actual provenance. The globular shape of no. 155 (Fig. 16) is unusual. There thus seem to be indications of the presence of MHI occupation in Chalkis Aitolias even if the traces are scanty. Among the local wares from the survey should be mentioned the jars with oblique, outwards sloping flat rim (no. 151 (Fig. 16) and nos. 158 and 163 from stratum 6). The type is most characteristic for MHIII/LHIA but is not found in LHIB. Especially close to MHIII shapes is no. 151 even if the clay indicates that it is not local.

---

[49] Already Phelps 1975. See Christmann 1996, 260 and Maran 1998, 8.

[50] The terminology is used because the material excavated seems to be contemporary with the period MHIIIB/LHIA in the Argolid. See also summary below.

[51] See in general Wardle 1972.

[52] In general Papazoglou-Manioudaki 1998. For instance from Odos Polychroniadou 8 in Aigion cit. 28ff and Odos Smirnis 145 in Patras, cit. 121 ff.

[53] Stavropoulou-Gatsi 1998 and 2001. The authors are most obliged to Mrs. Stavropoulou-Gatsi for useful information concerning the excavations at Pagona. For general surveys of the area during the period MHIII/LHI see also Papadopoulos 1978-1979 and Moschos 2000.

[54] Zerner 1978, BE429/1+5, p. 140.

[55] Earlier cups from Lerna: Zerner 1978, D591, fig. 6, 17 and p. 79 (Lerna VA) and Zerner 1988, fig. 24, 4 (MHI). The later cups are lower, for instance Zerner 1988, fig. 27, 2. The type is also found in Aspis, Argos, Philippa-Touchais 2003, 10ff. where the early types are likewise dated to Lerna V1/MHI imitating MMIA/B (Philippa-Touchais 11, notes 39-40).

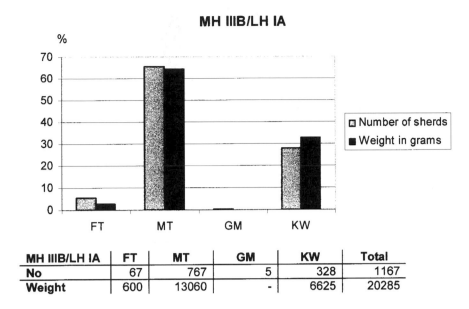

MH IIIB/LH IA

Fig. 14. Statistical survey of MHIIIB/LHIA pottery classes from stratified layers in the area II, West of Aghia Triada (K27 to K29 and Tx72).

MH IIIB/LH IA	FT	MT	GM	KW	Total
No	67	767	5	328	1167
Weight	600	13060	-	6625	20285

The MHIIIB/LHIA deposits

Material from the MHIIIB/LHIA period appeared in the lower layers in the area west of the Aghia Triada (Fig. 14). In contrast to the deposits from the EHI period on the mound, the MHIII deposits contain an element of Fine Tempered sherds even if the percentage is not as impressive as in the Argolid. More than 50 % of the fine tempered sherds are wheel-made. 2/3 of the material is produced in medium tempered ware groups; the majority of the rest is kitchen ware. Grey Minyan is present but unusual. In addition to the MHIIIB/LHIA material from the area west of the Aghia Triada, an amount of sherds from the period was found on Aghia Triada itself, from a small deposit near and below the Byzantine wall, F15/ACC-3/NW.[56]

Shapes and decorations (Fig. 15)

The deposits from the lower levels in the area west of the Aghia Triada are specific in the sense that by far the majority of the shapes are closed. Closed shapes in this period are usually produced in a very hard fabric with many lime grits (MT(2)). Approximately 8 times as many closed shapes as open shapes are produced in this ware group. In contrast the relation between open and closed shapes within the other major ware group, the

softer MT (1) without or with fewer lime grits is almost fifty-fifty. Unfortunately, it has not been possible in all deposits to draw the line between the two ware groups with certainty but it is safe to say that by far the majority is in the hard MT (2) fabric.

One characteristic group of jars changing in size between small with an estimated diameter at the rim around 10 cm to medium sized jars with a rim diameter 20 to 25 cm, has a flat oblique rim set off from the body at a right angle (catalogue nos. 175, 170, 182, 235 and 177). All pots in this group were produced in the hard MT (2) fabric (water containers?). The rather large jar no. 177 is burnished and has black matt paint on the surface.

Another significant group of local manufactures are the cups, close shaped bowls or jars with an S-shaped profile and a thin rim (nos. 174, 234, 173, 184 and 229). The diameter of the rim varies between 8 cm and around 20 cm. They are usually produced in medium tempered fabric, no. 234, however, in a very fine tempered clay with grits. The hole-mouth and the vertical pointed handle on catalogue no. 229 might indicate some rela-

---

[56] Catalogue numbers 12 to 14, Pl. 1. As for the shape of the fine tempered cup, no. 12 see Dietz 1991, fig. 19, no. 141 (MH-IIIB). Catalogue no. 20 from the mixed stratum F15/4/SW should be dated to LHIA. Compare Dietz 1980, fig. 46 and 47 (no. 35).

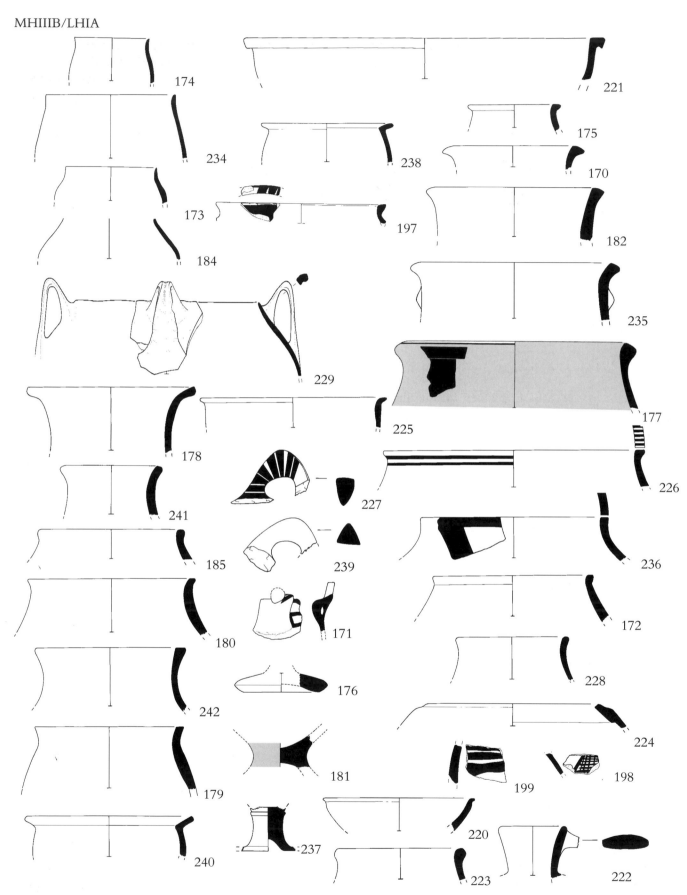

Fig. 15. Types of pottery from the MHIIIB/LHIA period. 1:4.

tionship with the semi-globular kantharoi with vertical pointed handle found in both Central Greece and the Northwestern Peloponnese.[57] The piece from Mycenae circle B should be dated in LHIB.

Small hemispherical bowls like catalogue no. 238 are found in several places.[58] The shape continues into the next phase LHI (LHIB) (no. 147 on Fig. 16)

Catalogue no. 178 is a most general shape, a cylindrical or funnel shaped neck of a stamnos or hydria with horizontal bands on the neck.[59]

Shapes of kitchen ware comprise rather small open jars, often with a flat rim. The shapes do not look standardized (as for instance in Aegina). Catalogue no. 240 has been classified as a kitchen ware jar even though the shape is more like the hemispherical bowls in fine tempered fabrics (as no. 238).

Besides the local variations of the pottery there are a few sherds of more or less canonical MHIII character. Catalogue no. 227 is as matt painted triangular, horizontal handle from a closed shaped jar. The clay is local. Similar handles were recovered from the MH layers in Pagona and Odos Polychroniadou 8 in Aigion.[60] In Pagona, the matt painted pottery published from locality 3 (or 4) is medium tempered and derives from closed shaped vessels. Shapes and the heavy style decoration are all of clear MHIIIB character in Argive terminology. At least the four sherds to the right are from jugs type AF-1, AF-2.[61] The horizontal handle probably derives from a rather large ovoid jar.

The profile of the krater catalogue no. 221 with the characteristic flat, "hawk beak rim", usually produced in local fabric, becomes very popular towards the end of the MH period and at the beginning of the LH. Parallels are found on a medium tempered "Yellow Minyan" spouted krater from the LHIA in the circle B at Mycenae,[62] in Grey Minyan from the A-circle[63] and from the same period (MHIII/LHI) in Kirrha,[64] in "Yellow Minyan" from Eutresis,[65] from Korakou[66] and Tzoungiza[67] and from Kiapha Thiti.[68] A much smaller jar from a MHIIIB grave in the West Cemetery of Eleusis also shows the same section.[69] The matt painted sherd no. 198 probably

derives from the upper part of a kantharos with globular body.[70] The cross hatched triangle on the shoulder probably first appears in MHIIIA in the Argolid.[71] A close parallel is found in Argos, Aspis deriving from couche 3, corresponding to phase MHIIIB.[72] The matt painted sherd, catalogue no. 197 is probably a bowl or small krater with carination. Parallels for the hemispherical, matt painted jars with flat rims (nos. 226 and 236) are not known to us, nor the hemispherical jar (no. 172) with parallel grooves below the rim.

The matt painted sherd no. 171 derives from a cup/bowl with vertical handle with pierced, circular lug above a vertical strap handle from the rim. The same principle is seen on a cup from Argos.[73] The vertical handle with hole might be as shown on pieces from Thermon.[74]

Catalogue no. 181 is a stem for an usual goblet

[57] Thermon (Wardle 1972, fig. 69), Portes (Moschos 2000, fig. 9, no. 5. and particularly note 64), Katarraktis (Drakotrypa) (Papadopoulos 1979, fig. 48 (d)), Aigion (Papazoglou-Manioudaki 1998, 46, no. 75), Mycenae (Circle B, O-192). Dietz 1991, fig. 67, GA-2 in Fine Orange ware and Pevkakia. Dietz 1991, 214 considers the type to be of Central Greek origin.

[58] For instance in Asine. Dietz 1991, fig. 19, 145.

[59] For instance Dietz 1991, fig. 25, 14-15 (MHIIIB). Wardle 1971, fig. 53 (Thermon).

[60] Stavropoulou-Gatsi 1998, fig. 14, upper left. Papazoglou-Manioudaki 1998, 35, fig. 15, 8 (MHIII/LHI) with further parallels.

[61] Stavropoulou-Gatsi 1998, fig. 14. Ref. Dietz 1991, 175f and fig. 53.

[62] B-circle, I-104, Dietz 1991, AG-3 (fig. 56).

[63] Grave VI, 949, Dietz 1991 type BF-1 (fig. 61).

[64] Dor et al. 1960, 73 and pls. XXXII/ XXXIII.

[65] Goldman 1931, 165, fig. 23 with maximum diameter 45 cm.

[66] Davis 1979, fig. 10, 207 (LHIB).

[67] Rutter 1989, no. 13, fig. 6 (LHIA).

[68] Maran 1992, pl. 9, no. 342 (Polychrome Mainland).

[69] Mylonas 1975, 618 (pl. 101). Mylonas furthermore refers to Prosymna II, fig. 79, no. 584. See also Maran 1992, 383.

[70] Dietz 1991, 87 considers the shape to be of Central Greek origin.

[71] Dietz 1991, 159, AB-6.

[72] Philippa-Touchais 2002, 14 (no. 37), fig. 9.

[73] Protonotariou-Deilaki 1980, fig. 30, 1-4 (inv. No. 3770). Also Dietz 1991, 133 and 159 with a dating in the LHIA phase.

[74] Wardle 1972, fig. 62, 218-219.

of MHIII/LHI date[75] while no. 237 is an unusual high stem with incised rings and a hollowed base with stand ring.[76]

The jug with strap handle no. 222 is evidently imported but the exact origin is difficult to determine,[77] nor have we been able to find other samples of the small (and probably carinated) krater or bowl no. 197. Finally the jug handlewith the twisted central part no. 186 from Tx72/13 is familiar with a jug from Lerna grave BC.3 dated to LHIA even if the twisted clay band is placed on top of the handle on the Lerna piece (Caskey 1956, pl. 40; Dietz 1991, 285).

Summary

In spite of the fact that in Chalkis Aitolias pottery of MHIIIB/LHIA character is relatively abundant, the shapes of the deposits are restricted mainly to close shaped vessels. The dating of the deposits depends on parallels mainly with Argive materials from the general period MHIIIB/LHIA. Based on the present material it is not possible to define separate phases MHIIIB and LHIA in the coastal area of Aitolia.

A definition of LHIB

Introduction

Material from the LHIB period in the area is even scantier published than the pottery from MHIII.[78]

The deposits

The phase is found in one area west of the Aghia Triada mound but only in a small pocket in the rock (trial trench Tx70/5). In addition a few sherds from the top of the mound itself, from the trench 15, close to the Byzantine wall (F15/ACC-3/NW) include material which should probably be referred to LHIB (for instance the Polychrome Mainland krater catalogue no. 21).

The most significant difference between the MHIIIB/LHIA levels and the layers from trench Tx70 is that the relative amount of fine tempered fabrics has increased considerably. It should be noticed, however, that the amount of fine ware from trench Tx70/5a and /6 is quite abundant in layers earlier than MHIII. The reason for the low percentage of fine ware in MHIII/LHIA layers might be that the shapes are predominantly closed.

Shapes and decorations (Fig. 16)

Conical open bowls or basins (D: between 16 and 32 cm) with thickened lozenge rim seem to be innovations in the repertoire of shapes (nos. 140 and 143). They are produced in the local medium tempered fabric and evidently continue in modified form in the following centuries.[79] Among other local features should be mentioned the two thin-walled kraters nos. 142 and 144 and household jars as nos. 139 with flat rim. An interesting shape is the hemispherical bowl (no. 147) with a section almost as no. 238 from MHIIIB/LHIA but in Grey Minyan and probably with a (ring?) handle on the rim.

Catalogue no. 138 is a local product but probably imitates LHI kraters from the North Eastern Peloponnese and Aegina (usually Polychrome Aegina) for instance from Asine, Lerna and Korakou.[80] It should be emphasized, however, that the base is flatter and the wall more steep on no.

---

[75] For instance Dietz 1991, fig. 121, no. 183. From Aegina, Lindblom 2001, catalogue no. 124 (pl. 8), no. 363 (pl. 18) et al.

[76] For the general type see for instance Dietz 1991, fig. 25, 246 with lustrous decoration (MHIIIB). As for the flat base see a piece from Lerna phase VI, Lindblom 2001, catalogue no. 93, pl. 7.

[77] For a somewhat similar section from Asine see Dietz 1991, fig. 27, no. 269 (LHIA).

[78] see references to MHIIIB/LHIA above.

[79] LHIII below nos. 214-215 with a more detailed treatment of the type.

[80] Dietz 1991, fig. 28, no. 291 (LHIA). Zerner 1988, fig. 8, nos. 22-23 (LHI). Davis 1979, fig. 5, 47 (LHIB) (many Polychrome Aegina kraters were found in Korakou). The type is especially common in Aeginetan ware groups. Lindblom 2001 depicts 9 with pre-firing/potters marks and MP band around the base (catalogue nos. 130, 188, 236, 292, 299, 318, 293, 601 and 737). Lindblom dates them within a general frame LHI-II.

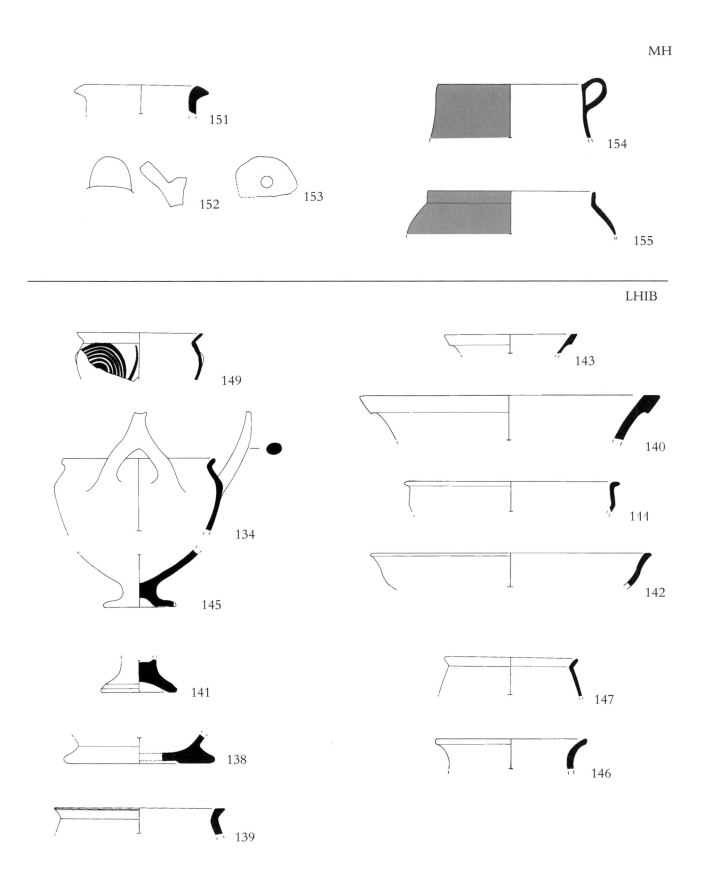

Fig. 16. Types of pottery from the MH period and the LHIB period. 1:4.

138 than on the parallels mentioned (the diameter of the rim on no. 138 must have been around 30 to 35 cm). One more piece of the general type was found on the middle terrace on Aghia Triada (catalogue no. 124, Pl. 9).

The conical base catalogue no. 141 derives from a goblet or stemmed bowl.[81]

It is not clear whether the two lustrous decorated, semi globular cups are imported or locally produced (nos. 149 and 150). The clay could be local. Shape and decoration with running tangent spirals is brought from abroad.

Deep semi globular cups (FS 211) are present in the Early Mycenaean pottery repertoire[82] but are not as usual as the straight sided (Keftiu) cups. Semi globular cups with running spiral pattern are found in the Argolid in North Eastern Peloponnesos, for instance in Argos[83] and in settlement deposits from Asine[84] dated to LHIB in the Argive chronological sequence.[85] The spiral pattern is open with a solid frame, however, and with a loop. In Laconia the type was found in Aghios Stephanos[86] but with multiple parallel bands on the rim, dots and "blob filled" in the centre of the spiral. In Messenia the cup type with spiral patterns are found in Pylos[87] and Voidokoilia.[88] Until now the LHI type has not been published from Achaea, nor in Aitolia/Akarnania before the finds from Chalkis.

Close parallels for shape and decoration with open tangent spiral without "blob fill" are found in Kythera in the area between Kastri and Kastraki.[89] The deposit is dated to LMIA.

Cups with "wishbone" handles (no. 134) have been published and studied on several occasions. In Chalkis one more piece was found by the survey on the top of the Aghia Triada mound (catalogue no. 5, Pl. 1). The carinated, hemispherical bowl has a thin outturned rim and is based on a low raised pedestal (see for instance samples from Thermon (below). The group of "wishbone" handles in general is both typologically and chronologically very much unhomogeneous.

A preliminary survey of sites with "wishbone" handles of some relevance to the Chalkis type specimen may be cited Volimidia (Lolos 1987, fig. 21); Makrysia, Profitis Ilias;[90] Pagona, Patras;[91] Chalkis, Aitolias; Graves, Astakos;[92] Thermon;[93] Pelikata, Ithaka;[94] Choirospelia (Kephali?) Levkas;[95] and Dodona.[96]

Lolos (from a Messenian point of view) considers "wishbone" handles to reflect northern ceramic influence probably deriving from "schools" in West Central Greece such as Thermon in Aetolia while Heurtley regarded them as a Macedonian creation.[97] In Thessaly "wishbone" handles are found from EH to the Iron Age in Vardaroftsa.[98] More closely connected with the handles from Pagona/Chalkis Aitolias. and Thermon, and approximately of the same age, are handles from Lianokladhi III.[99] According to Wardle, "wishbone" handles are found in Thessaly and are common in Macedonia, but do not occur south of the Corinthian Gulf.[100] Finds from Makrysia and Pagona have now altered this situation. Specimens from Orchomenos are not safely dated.[101] We should finally like to mention the

[81] Dietz 1991, fig. 21, no. 180 (MHIIIB) and fig. 27, no. 260.
[82] For a recent treatment of origin and development of the shape see Mountjoy 1999 passim.
[83] Protonotariou-Deilaki 1980, pls. 36.1 – 2, 40.1.
[84] Dietz 1980, fig. 124, no. 324.
[85] Dietz 1991, 103 ff.
[86] Rutter & Rutter 1976, no. 237.
[87] Lolos 1987, 267 (Vroulia).
[88] Korres 1979, fig. 7 - with dots.
[89] Coldstream & Huxley 1972, i.e. p. 121 and pl. 31 and fig. 41, no. 7.
[90] Lolos 1987, 334-35. figs. 613-15 (the only piece in SW Peloponnese).
[91] Stavropoulou-Gatsi 1998; Stavropoulou-Gatsi & Karageorghis 2003.
[92] Katsipanou 2001, 72 ff (Bibliography p. 73): Catalogue no. 125. Wardle 1972, fig. 34, 17-18.
[93] Rhomaios 1915, 262, fig. 28. Wardle 1977, 171. Wardle 1972, fig. 67, 235, 237. fig. 68, 236).
[94] Wardle 1977, 171 (ref. BSA 35 1934/35, 22 n. 1).
[95] Wardle 1977, 171 (ref. BSA 35 1934/35, 22 n. 1). Wardle 1972, fig.36, 43. Wardle 1972, 813-816).
[96] Wardle 1977, 171 (ref. BSA 35 1934/35, 22 n. 1). Wardle 1972, fig. 133, 668 and 669).
[97] Heurtley 1926-28, 179-188.
[98] Heurtley & Hutchinson 1926/27, 15 and pl. III.
[99] Wace & Thompson 1912, 185 and fig. 134. Maran 1992, pl. 146 (section).
[100] Wardle 1977, 171 and Wardle 1972, 79.
[101] Kunze 1934, 81, pl. XXX, 4, a-b.

similarity between the type mentioned and the well known kantharos from Mycenae Circle A, 198. This kantharos should be dated in LHIB and is considered a representative of the significant influences from Central Greece in the Argolid during the period[102] and at Pevkakia.[103]

Summary

Stratified material of LH IB date is restricted to a small group in a pit cut in the bedrock from the area West of Aghia Triada. There are some significant local shapes and in addition two more canonical semiglobular cups (FS 211), with spiral decoration in lustrous paint which are the main indications of a dating in the LH IB period. Two "wishbone" handles are found, one on the surface on the mound of Aghia Triada and one in the deposit in the area west of the mound with the upper part of a hemispherical bowl preserved. The type has a wide distribution in time and space and the present authors find it difficult to maintain that the presence of this specific type of "wishbone" handles should reflect relations with Cyprus as recently suggested by Maria Stavropoulou-Gatsi and Vasos Karageorghis.[104]

A definition of Late Helladic III

Introduction - Chalkis and the LH III period in Aetolia and Akarnania

In contrast to the case in Achaia and on the island of Kephalonia opposite the coast of Akarnania, we are not for the time being able to define the features of the LH III period in Aetolia and Akarnania, but it is certain that the regions of Aetolia and Akarnania developed a significant civilization during the period under study. A characteristic element, depending on a most limited or selective research is that, although the area in general and in particular Aetolia constituted an integral part of the Mycenean world, it is the only region where tholos tombs outnumber chamber tombs. This of course is a most preliminary result. In addition the absence of researched settlements makes the picture even more fragmentary.

Regarding the isolated plain between Varassova and Paliovouna, on the coast where Chalkis lies, a bronze double axe of mainland origin found in the wider area of Ano Vasiliki[105] was the only information we had concerning the Mycenaean presence in the region. Recently the ruins came to light of a LH I (?) and LH III settlement in Chania Gavrolimni (Saranti 2004, 229), lying on top of MH III remains, as in Chalkis. The two settlements thus probably show a parallel development. As a most preliminary proposal we might suggest that the same situation occurs on the Aitolian coast as on the coast around Patra, that a dense habitation pattern was found in areas where the plains are favorable for providing self-sufficiency. A similar picture could be suggested for the fertile area around Stamna and Agios Elias – Seremeti, where five tholos and one chamber tomb have been investigated. The only settlement information in the region comes from below the Archaic acropolis of Aghios Elias.[106] Further inland, in the plain of Stratiki,[107] recent surveys attested a Mycenaean presence. In the same region, at Palaiomanina-Mila,[108] a tholos tomb has been excavated, while at Stratos[109] a tumulus, currently submerged under the artificial lake, has not been securely dated (prehistoric). The same picture applies to the area around lake Trichonis (Thermos,[110] Lithovouni[111]), where the surveys by the Dutch School have managed to locate intense prehistoric habita-

---

[102] Dietz 1991, 154, Type AA-8, mentions parallels from Kirrha (Dor *et al.* 1964, pl. I (Inv. No. 6235 (MHIb, however).

[103] Maran Pevkakia 1992, Phase 7 (Transitional MHIII/LHI (for instance pls.116, 5-123-5 and 139-7-8).

[104] Stavropoulou-Gatsi & Karageorghis 2003.

[105] Davaras 1970, 311-2, figs. 1-2, without exact provenance and not from Kato Vasiliki as stated by Dararas.

[106] Wardle 1972, 102-103, fig. 86.

[107] Funke 2001. Lang 2001.

[108] Hope-Simpson – Dickinson 1979, 182, E 4.

[109] Sotiriadis 1908, 100.

[110] Hope-Simpson – Dickinson 1979, 103-104, B 102.

[111] Ibid 104, B 103.

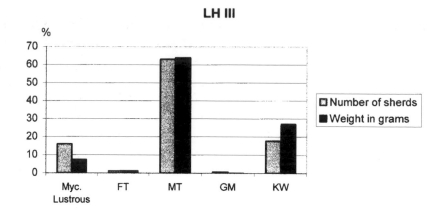

LH III	Myc. lustrous	FT	MT (CT)	GM	KW	White W.	Total
No	135	11	530	6	149	7	838
Weight	550	100	4700	-	2000	-	7350

Fig. 17. Area II. Statistical survey of LHIII pottery classes from stratified layers (K27 to K29 and Tx72).

tion. This "inland" habitation supports the assumption that Aitolia and Akarnania, on the periphery of the Mycenaean world, was well populated during the Mycenaean period. In contrast on the coast of Epirus, where there is no substantial Mycenaean presence, the few sites attested seem to be commercial stations on the route to the Adriatic. Equally unclear is the picture concerning the coast of Akarnania, the most important site being Loutraki on the Ambracian gulf, where two tholos tombs have been excavated.[112] Surface finds in Thyrreion[113] indicate Mycenaean presence here too. The report of a Mycenaean settlement in ancient Palairos[114] has not been confirmed by recent surveys. LH III sherds have been found in the fill of the caves at Graves[115] and Agios Nikolaos[116] near Astakos.

Known Mycenaean sites along the coast around Chalkis are Naupaktos, Kryoneri,[117] Kalydon[118] and Pleuron.[119] The lack of excavation data, though, does not allow any connection with ancient Chalkis. A Mycenaean treasure of bronze objects, found in Psorolithi,[120] Kalydon, cannot be connected to a habitation site, as shown by the geomorphology of the region.

The deposit

Stratified LH III layers are found primarily in the area West of Aghia Triada (Area II) where they are situated in a well defined horizon of approximately 30 cm between 2.20 and 1.90 above sea level. The LH III horizons are often mixed with material from the superposed strata of the archaic period and only a few levels are contexts without intrusions. Among these, four have been selected for a statistical evaluation of the deposits (Fig. 17). The amount of material is rather small with only 838 sherds counted weighing slightly more than 7 kg. What especially distinguishes the LH III layers from the preceding horizons of the LH IB period is the substantial amount of lustrous decorated Mycenaean Fine ware sherds making up to 16 % according to numbers, 7.5 % measured by weight. The medium tempered groups make up the majority while kitchen ware fabrics constituted another substantial group. The clay is more finely tempered than previously and the hard burned fabric MT (2) so characteristic of the ware groups in the transitional layers, MH III/LH I, almost disap-

[112] For the bibliography see Moschos 2000, 24, note 7.
[113] Moschos 2000, 24, note 7.
[114] Hope-Simpson & Dickinson 1979, 183, E 8.
[115] Hope-Simpson & Dickinson 1979, E 6.
[116] Hope-Simpson & Dickinson 1979, E 7.
[117] Hope-Simpson & Dickinson 1979, 103, B 99.
[118] Hope-Simpson & Dickinson 1979, B100.
[119] Hope-Simpson & Dickinson 1979, 181, E1.
[120] Hope-Simpson & Dickinson 1979, B101.

pears. What might be surprising is the very modest amount of simple Fine ware only represented by 1.3 % (number and weight) indicating that the simple Fine ware products of the early Mycenaean period are being replaced by Mycenaean lustrous painted wares during the mature Mycenaean age. In the LH III horizons the majority of the pottery is wheel-made.

Shapes and decoration (Fig. 18)

Open Shapes

Cups

Catalogue no. 212 is probably a deep semi-globular cup (FS 215?) of LH IIIC date, although the flat everted rim is not convenient for drinking cups, perhaps an indication that it was spouted. The two examples with linear decoration (210, 213) are of a type widely distributed in Western Greece during the LH IIIC Middle and Late.

Catalogue no. 210 is probably from a spouted cup (FS 249), with an exact parallel at Lakkithra, Kephalonia[121], wrongly dated to LH IIIC Early, instead of LH IIIC Late or Submycenaean.

Other cups: Catalogue nos. 16 (Pl. 2), 192 (Pl. 14) and 211 (Pl. 15).

Goblets

Catalogue nos. 206 and 207.

Stemmed bowls

Catalogue no. 203.

Skyphoi

Catalogue no. 209.

Bowls

Local MT bowls with lozenge shaped rims derive from LH III deposits in K28 (no. 208, Pl. 14) and K29 (nos. 214 and 215). Lozenge shaped rim

probably survives from MH yellow Minyan ware.[122] It is known at Thermon, where it occurs on an amphora of wheel-turned matt-painted ware.[123] Mountjoy refers to a Middle Helladic influence in a lozenge shaped angular rim of a LH IIIA jug from Krisa, Phocis.[124] It has also been found at Iria[125] and is known from a huge cylindrical jar from the Potter's Shop at Zygouries[126], in a bowl from Chios[127] and from LH IIIC context at Corinth.[128]

Other bowls: Catalogue nos. 204 and 219 ("White Ware")

Basins

This rare shape is represented by three specimens (1 (Pl. 1), 166, and 218).

Catalogue no. 1 is probably a vessel of FS 294 type as indicated by the heavy inclination of the belly, which is not applied to kraters. It also seems too big to be assigned to the shallow bowl FS 295. The flat horizontal rim is borrowed from a krater shape, but in general rim shapes on basins are found in many varieties. No traces of strap handles survived. Quite exceptional is the decoration on the rim and in a reserved zone below the rim as here, while linear, monochrome and unpainted vases are more common. A good parallel to this is found in a local style LH IIIA2 vase from Delphi.[129] Isolated wavy line motifs below the rim are also present on a small fragment of a probably shallow bowl (FS 295) or a basin (FS 294) from Thermon.[130] A LH IIIC linear local example found at dromos of Th.T. 2 at Agios Ilias—Marathia, has horizontal loop handles and joining semi-circles on

[121] Souyoudzoglou-Haywood 1999, pl. 4: A 1313.
[122] cf. French 1972, fig. 21:29, from Kalami-Boeotia.
[123] Wardle 1972, 72, 330, fig. 52:173.
[124] Mountjoy 1990, 254, fig. 255.
[125] Döhl 1973, Abb. 13, taf. 66:B28.
[126] Blegen 1928, 163-164, fig. 159.
[127] Hood 1982, 601, fig. 270:2815.
[128] Rutter 1979.
[129] Perdizet 1908, fig. 88. cf. Mountjoy 1999, 762, fig. 295:80.
[130] Wardle 1972, 70, 328, fig. 50:156.

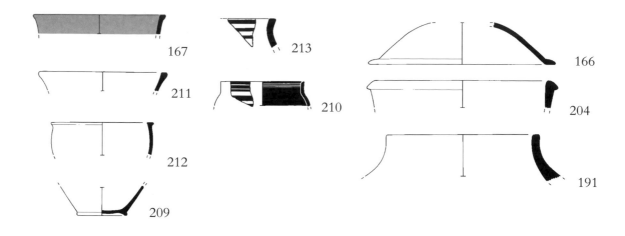

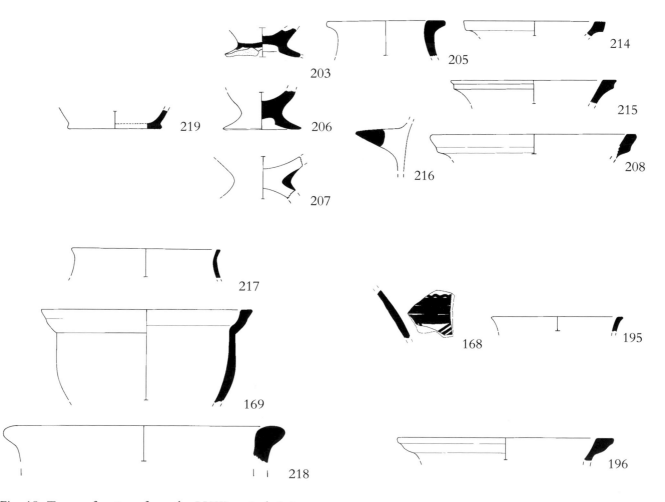

Fig. 18. Types of pottery from the LHIII period. 1:4.

rim.[131] A LH IIIC Early fragment with monochrome interior and wavy line below rim is in the Nauplion Study Collection.[132]

No. 166 is probably a small example of a basin (FS 294) or a lid. It has a rounded body with flat rim and it is quite shallow. Two LH IIIC similar shapes come from Athens, Fountain House.[133] No. 218 is a KW large basin which probably finds an exact parallel in a LH IIIB1 coarse ware vase from Mycenae.[134]

Cooking ware

Catalogue no. 169 with rounded body and an elegant rim suitable for a lid. Angular tall rims have been found in coarse ware LH III B1 construction level of the South House at Mycenae.[135]

Catalogue no. 185 (Pl. 14) is probably the most common LH III C cooking jar with one handle and an ovoid body, usually made on a fast wheel but also found handmade, as in Chios.[136]

Closed shapes

Catalogue nos. 191 and 194 (Pl. 14) are closed jars.

Catalogue no. 193 (Pl. 14) is an open jar.

Catalogue no. 168 (see comments below). The decoration has a close parallel on a handmade bowl sherd from Thermos,[137] identified as local geometric and also in handmade jar fragments, probably of the same shape as our specimen.[138]

Catalogue no. 194 is large and it could be a tripod.[139]

As for the horizontal, triangular handle no. 216 a parallel is found in the LBA tumulus C at Paliopyrgos, Epirus.[140]

Excurs: Catalogue no. 168 and the 'South' matt-painted ware.

The introduction and production of the Iron Age matt-painted pottery in Aetolia, which was recognized as 'Northwest matt-painted Ware' by Heurtley[141] or due to its specific and particular characteristics as 'Local Geometric' by Rhomaios[142] and Wardle,[143] has been associated with the period following the LH IIIB/C destruc-

tion of the prehistoric settlement of Thermos.[144] Certainly, LH IIIC pottery was not, according to Wardle, safely attested in the newly excavated destruction level[145] and the 'Local Geometric' was neither found in the destruction level nor in earlier levels from before the destruction horizon.

What we know for certain is that the "Local Geometric" is related to the construction and the use of Megaron B, as has been shown by the recent excavations where Mycenaean pottery was absent.[146] The Protogeometric matt painted ware from the Aetolian coasts never reached Thermos. Both the levels in Thermos and the pottery from the Aitolian coast have been dated to the Early Iron Age.

The main and still unanswered question, directly associated with the appearance of the 'Local Geometric' at Thermos, is exactly when the destruction of the prehistoric settlement took place and if it was contemporary with the introduction of the 'Northwest matt-painted Ware'. Is it accidental that LH IIIC pottery has not yet been safely located neither in nor over the destruction level?

Characteristic imported pottery of the LH IIIC, belonging to the advanced phases of the period, is known from the older excavations at Thermos, but we have no information on the stratigraphical

[131] Wardle 1972, 99, 101, 362, fig. 85:392. Mountjoy 1999, 805, fig. 321:39.

[132] Mountjoy 1999, 153, fig. 196:3.

[133] Mountjoy 1999, figs 214:383, 224:500.

[134] Mountjoy 1976, 95, fig. 10:106.

[135] Mountjoy 1976, 95, fig. 10:115, 118.

[136] Hood 1982, 617, fig. 280:2956. For a discussion on the shape, see Iakovidis 1969-1970, vol. 2, 227-228.

[137] Wardle 1972, fig. 78:351.

[138] Wardle 1972, fig. 80, 319, 321.

[139] Döhl 1973, 174, Abb. 20, taf. 75:1-3(A34).

[140] Andreou & Andreou 1999, fig. 37.

[141] 'North Greek matt-painted pottery' in Heurtley 1926-1927, 186-187. Also known as 'Bouboushti ware', 'Macedonian matt-painted' and 'Dorian ware'.

[142] Rhomaios 1915, 263-265.

[143] Wardle 1972, 80-83. Wardle 1977, 173, 176. Wardle & Wardle 2003, 150-51.

[144] Papapostolou 2003, 137-138.

[145] Wardle & Wardle 2003, 150.

[146] Papapostolou 2003, 138.

situation. This pottery included vases imported from Western Achaia, belonging to the typical local style of the LH IIIC Middle/Late phases. The material from Thermos, according to the latest study of the Mycenaean Achaean pottery[147] and contrary to P. Mountjoy's opinion[148], seems to belong partly to late LH IIIC Middle and partly to early LH IIIC Late . This means that contacts with Western Achaia probably stopped during the LH IIIC Late, a few years before the Submycenaean period. In Western Achaia this period is marked by a second destruction of Teichos Dymaion,[149] without any direct influence on the population pattern in the wider region.

Among the imported Achaean vessels at Thermos is a pictorial krater with warriors,[150] produced by a craftsman with a rich pictorial production deriving from the flourishing Vounteni workshop of the LH IIIC Late phase.[151] Contacts with Thermos have also been substantiated at the Vounteni cemetery by the presence in the dromos of chamber tomb 18 of a handmade cut–away neck jar with ovoid body and pointed base, which finds an exact parallel in Thermon's local undecorated pottery.[152] A second similar jar was also found in the Patras region, in front of the blocked entrance of Ch.T. A at Krini-Zoetada,[153] which is possibly to be associated with the last burials in the chamber and to be dated in LH IIIC Late. A further identical jar had been found years ago at Metaxata, but lacked attention as it was wrongly restored when published.[154] This jar deviates from local coarse wares of Kephalonia and appears to be imported, if not a very good local imitation of the shape. It probably belongs to the latest use of the tomb (LH IIIC Late or somewhat later). The influence from the pottery in Thermos and Aetolia in general on Western Achaia pottery production probably continues in the Protogeometric period as indicated by a kantharos found in a pithos burial context at Drepanon near Patras.[155]

The finding of 'Local Geometric' or better 'South' matt-painted Ware in a close LH IIIC Late context in Chalkis on the Aitolian coast towards the Peloponnese, thus revises and expands the time-span of its presence in the Southern part of the mainland. Furthermore and contrary to what we hitherto believed, it attests the existence of this kind of pottery in the region well before the Protogeometric Period. It was even incorporated in the everyday activities of the inhabitants and is included in the utilitarian pottery, a conclusion that could not be drawn previously from the Protogeometric cemeteries of Kalydon[156] and Stamnà[157], where only cups have been found.

From Western Macedonia this type of wares is known from the 14th century B.C.[158] and coexists with the continuously increasing Mycenean pottery of the LH IIIA-C period. With the new Chalkis data, the introduction and production of the 'Northwest matt-painted Ware' in the Southernmost part of the mainland does not seem to be significantly later than the introduction of the type in Epirus,[159] to which the pottery from Aetolia[160] is obviously related. A common Aitolian and Vitsa group has recently been published from Phthiotis,[161] which we think should be dated to the LH IIIC period onwards, rather than in Early LH, as suggested by Stamoudi (2003, 266-7). Although sufficient evidence is still lacking, it seems reasonable to presume that a homogeneous matt-painted group of pottery with local characteristics existed in the Southern part of the Mainland, from Phthiotis to Aetolia and even

---

[147] Moschos 2006, in print.
[148] Mountjoy 1999, 798.
[149] Papadopoulos 1978-79, 24.
[150] Wardle & Wardle 2003, 150, fig. 3.
[151] Kolonas 2006, in print.
[152] Wardle 1972, 335, fig. 58:215. Wardle 1977, 171.
[153] Chrysaphi 1994, 234.
[154] Marinatos 1933, fig. 32:B4. After the destructive earthquake in 1953 it remained for a long time among the piles of sherds in the warehouses of the Argostoli Museum, (Argostoli Museun, no 1689).
[155] Gadolou 2000, 429, fig. 80.
[156] Stavropoulou-Gatsi 1980, 111, fig. 6, pl. 37d.
[157] Recent unpublished finds.
[158] Karamitrou-Mentesidi 2003, 171, note 32.
[159] Mid 12th century B.C., Papapostolou 1997, 224-225 with bibliography. According to Vokotopoulou 1986, 265 the presence of this ware in Epirus cannot be dated before the end of the 12th cent.
[160] It has more resemblances to the Vitsa pottery, which is not prehistoric. Vokotopoulou 1986, 246.
[161] Stamoudi 2003, figs. 2-4, 8.

Northwards to Vitsa. These local elements were established during the LH IIIC Late with a clear influence from usual lustrous decorated Mycenaean pottery. The ware continued to be produced until the Geometric period.

The Chalkis pottery, although fragmentary and small in quantity, presents the particular local characteristics found not only in Thermos but also on pieces from Protogeometric tombs along the Aitolian coastline (Kalydon and Stamná).

In sum, the local characteristics combine a mixture of elements from the ware of Western Macedonia and decorations on LH IIIC Middle/ Late pottery in Western Achaea creating a Western Mainland Koine, in which Pthiotis and Phocis are included (e.g. hatched and stacked triangles, hatched lozenges, fringes). We meet these symbiotic features somewhat later in the Vitsa pottery. Having almost fully developed its local characteristics before LH IIIC Late, its production continued at Thermos without clear external influences, while it continues along the coastline most probably until the end of the Protogeometric period. This "inland ware" was thus already manufactured at several settlements near the coastline at the time when Protogeometric civilization was introduced. The pottery of this type reflects the presence of an original population which first becomes visible towards the end of the Mycenean period and clearly before the Submycenaean and which survives at least till the end of the Protogeometric period. In Thermos the tradition continues in a strange isolation which does not allow contacts with the introducers of Iron Age along the Southern Aitolian coastline, but was rather directed towards North and the regions of Epirus. There, the Aetolian matt-painted ware finds more resemblances to the pottery of Vitsa, which, although geographically isolated, includes imported Protogeometric pottery.

Summary

Thus the LH IIIC phase at Chalkis should be contemporary with the LH IIIC Late and Early Submycenaean period in Western Achaea

(Moschos 2006, in print), to judge from the pottery with which comparisons are possible, even if the material from Achaea mainly derives from tombs and thus mainly consists of closed shaped vessels. The Chalkis pottery is clearly included in the so-called 'Western Mainland Koine'. The presence of the "White Ware" reveals contacts and relations even beyond Western Achaia, where this ware is unknown at present. Contacts with Phocis and Kephalonia, have already been mentioned.

Chalkis' late phase is slightly earlier than Phase I (Submycenaean and Protogeometric) of the Northwest matt-painted Ware, known from Platanies–Boubousti,[162] from the Korytsa area and from Vitsa.[163] The 'Aetolian' matt-painted Ware is found for the first time in Aitolia in LH IIIC closed contexts and in association with pottery of well known local characteristics.

Flint and obsidian from the Bronze Age deposits – a note

A catalogue of flint and obsidian found in the Bronze Age levels at Aghia Triada and in the area west of the mound is given below p. 110 with Plates 18 to 20 and Figs. 65, a-d. When compared with the chert/obsidian material from the Final Neolithic levels in Pangali (see Sørensen below p. 140) it is first of all striking that the amount is considerably smaller even if the area excavated is somewhat larger. On the other hand one should keep in mind that Pangali is a one-period site where all material collected is included in the statistical evaluation, while the stratigraphical situation on the Aghia Triada and in the trenches west of the mound is much more complicated and that, as a result, much chert and obsidian deriving from the Bronze Age levels is mixed up in later contexts. In addition it should be noted that the soil from Pangali was dry sieved which was not the case in Aghia Triada. The information is thus selective and rather fragmentary. As can be seen it is nevertheless possible to outline some trends in a general pattern.

---

[162] Heurtley 1926-27, 158-194.
[163] Vokotopoulou 1986, 255 *passim*.

In this brief note we use the same distinctions as has been used for the Final Neolithic material from Pangali i.e. raw material divides into the reddish brown radiolarite local material of excellent quality, local flint, marble and obsidian imported from Melos. As for the treatment of the raw material and the type of tools we are likewise in general referring to the material from Pangali.

As for the EHI-early period only material from the safe layers in Tx43 is included in the catalogue. Two blades with retouche in radiolarite are found in the levels, three flakes in local flint and as many as 11 blade fragments and three flake fragments in obsidian. Only one piece of marble was recorded. Among the obsidian blades some fragments of sickles were recorded (Pl. 18)

More chert and obsidian was recorded from the layers containing EHI-late material. Like the early phase only finds from Tx43 are included in the catalogue. As in the earlier layers there are two blades of radiolarite, while seven flakes were included in the catalogue. Of the local flint there are two blades and four flakes and of marble five flakes. As in the earlier layers obsidian makes up by far the most important group with nine blades and nine flakes registrered. Of tools identified, three pieces are probably sickle blades, two in obsidian and one in local flint (Pl. 18, 1, 2 and 7), one end scraper in radiolarite and one probable scraper in obsidian (Pl. 18, 8 and 13), one perforator in white marble (Pl. 18, 9). In addition should be mentioned the presence of two of the very characteristic crested blades in obsidian (Pl. 19, 13 and 18, 3).

In summary it is possible to say with some certainty that the raw material used in the EHI horizons is mainly obsidian while the local radiolarite and flint dominating in the Final Neolithic layers were less abundantly represented. There are significantly fewer tools in the early Bronze Age levels and there are no arrow heads/points present whether tanged or with hollow base which is a most characteristic feature in the final Neolithic assemblage. It should finally be mentioned that obsidian, in contrast to the situation in the MH and LH layers, seems to be quite usual in the deep EH (EHII ?) horizons in the area West of Aghia Triada (catalogue numbers 71 to 74).

In the MH and LH layers the situation evidently changes radically. In MHIIIB/LHIA layers in the area west of the mound there is still some obsidian present for instance the crested blade from Tx70/5a (catalogue no. 36, Pl. 20, 10) and from the lower strata in Tx72 (strata 11-13. see catalogue nos. 44-49). Radiolite seems to be the preferred raw material for stone implements in the Middle Bronze Age levels. From the small deposit of LHIB date in Tx50/5, 27 lithics are preserved. Of these 19 are flakes in radiolarite, 6 pieces are of marble and 2 in local flint. No obsidian is found in this layer. Finally no obsidian was found in the LHIIIC layers (mainly from trench K29). The majority of flakes and blades in these strata is produced by radioralite and local flint.

Only few analyses of the lithic industries in Bronze Age levels from Central and Southern Greece have been published. A most useful preliminary summary of the flake-stone industries from the Early and Middle Helladic levels in Lerna, published some years ago by Curtis Runnels, could be used for comparison.[164] It should be noted, however, that the Lerna material is much larger and that the periods treated cover Lerna III to V, thus not exactly the phases present in Chalkis Aitolias. It is significant, however, that obsidian, probably from Melos, by far outnumbers chert among the raw material used.[165] As in Chalkis, the advanced technique of pressure flaking is used quite abundantly for blades. In contrast to Lerna, no obsidian cores were found in Chalkis probably indicating that obsidian was rarer in Chalkis than in the Argolid and that the cores for that reason had been totally exhausted. In Lerna some 10 % of the lithics could be classified as tools, more commonly in obsidian than in chert. Runnels was able to distinquish 13 principal tools types in obsidian; in Chalkis we were only able to identify sickle blades and end scrapers.[166] In Lerna very few arrowheads were found and it is thus hardly surprising that none were found in Chalkis Aitolias.

---

[164] Runnels 1985.

[165] Runnels 1985, 359. 94.2 % in Lerna III.

[166] A crested blade from Lerna IV, very much like ours Pl. 19, 12 is depicted in Runnels 1985, fig. 8, D.

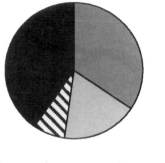
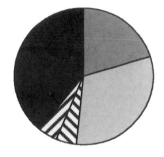

□pig □cattle ◩goat ■sheep/goat   □pig □cattle ◩goat ▨sheep ■sheep/goat

Fig. 19. Diagrams showing the distribution of domesticated mammals from respectively the EHI periods (left) and the MH/LH periods (right).

In the Middle Bronze Age as in Lerna IV the sample of lithics is considerably smaller than in Lerna III and the amount of obsidian from Melos much smaller.[167] As has been pointed out the same tendency is seen in the material from Chalkis. Finally it should be noted that during the Late Helladic the use of flaked stone tools in all materials declined even if obsidian arrowheads are excellent in execution found in the Shaft Graves of Mycenae.[168] It is thus in accordance with the general pattern that the flaked-stone industry in LHIII from Chalkis is less advanced and that no obsidian was found in the layers.

The faunal remains from the Bronze Age deposits at Aghia Triada

By *Pernille Bangsgaard Jensen*

A number of bones were found *in loci* that could be dated to the Early Helladic I (144 fragments and 969.6 grams) and the Middle-Late Helladic period (157 fragments and 1422,4 grams) (Fig. 19). The material is very limited from both periods, and therefore a number of statistical avenues are not possible and furthermore the material can not be considered as being representative of the period at Aghia Triada. However, it is perhaps still worth

mentioning a number of interesting facts concerning the distribution of animal bones from these limited areas.

In both periods the goat/sheep group appears to be the main domesticated animal (48% in EHI and 46% in MH-LH of the identified material). In the EHI period sheep are completely absent, whereas sheep and goat are represented by equal amount of fragments in MH-LH period, but due to the amount of material this could simply be a coincidence. Pig and cattle appear to change positions during this time, where pig is the more predominant of the two in the EHI period (34% of the identified material and cattle 18% of the identified material), while in the late phase cattle predominate (30% of the identified material and pig 19% of the identified materials) (Fig. 19).

This could be an actual change in the importance of these two species. However, it could also be due to a difference in excavation area between the two periods. The faunal material dated to the EHI period is primarily from the eastern side of the site close to the city wall (Tx20 and 43), whereas the faunal material dated to the MH-LH period is primarily from the western side of the site (Tx71-72).

---

[167] Runnels 1985, 381.
[168] Runnels 1985, 358 and Buchholz 1962.

Chapter 2

Catalogue of context and finds from Aghia Triada (Area I) and the area west of Aghia Triada (Area II)

By Søren Dietz

Abbreviations

CT: Coarse Tempered
F .... indicate Find number: i.e. F96-210 indicate find number 210 from the campaign 1996
FT: Fine Tempered
KW: Kitchen Ware
MP: Matt Painted
MT: Medium Tempered
GM: Grey Minyan

Classification of pottery

Note: In this study FT has been defined as Fine Tempered fabrics strictly, that is fine tempered clay with or without few and small visible grits. In this sense Fine Tempered fabrics are not found for instance in the Early Helladic horizons.

The Early Helladic period

The most important EH deposits were found on the top of the hill of Aghia Triada (Area I) and especially in the trial trenches Tx43 and Tx20 with good stratification (Fig. 8a and below p.72ff.) As has been summarized in chapter 1 (p. 38) the deposits should be dated to EHI. In addition EH material has been found in the lower strata in the areas excavated West of the Aghia Triada mound towards the village of Kato Vasiliki. All material was preserved for further study. It should be emphasized that EH materials have been found in most places on the hill – on the surface and in mixed excavation strata. In the present study I have selected stratigraphically isolated, chronologically homogeneous assemblages – contexts – and a few important mixed deposits.

The sherds from the pottery assemblages on the Aghia Triada mound and the flat area towards Kato Vasiliki are heavily covered with lime, firmly fixed to the surface of the sherds. Usually it has been possible to remove this cover only partly without damaging the surface. This fact influences to a certain degree the classification and the results obtained.

The pottery has been classified primarily according to ware groups. A rather simple terminology has been chosen: Medium tempered (MT), Coarse tempered (CT) and Kitchen Ware (KW). The terminology semi-coarse or coarse could quite as well have been used. In a very few instances fine tempered (FT) fabrics have been found, in all of which the fabric deviates from the local and the pottery has been considered imports. Because of the lime cover it has not been possible with any certainty to distinguish systematically between open and closed shapes.

The distinction between burnished and unburnished is usually very clear. Parallel grooves on the surface of burnished pottery, deriving from a burnisher, are characteristic.[169] Usually the not very shiny burnish has been added on top of a rather thin slip, though examples of a high polish on a rich slip have also been found. Burnish is used in both medium and coarse tempered ware groups. It has not been possible usually and with certainty to distinguish between burnish on unslipped/smoothed surface[170] and burnish on a slipped sur-

---

[169] See also Zachos 1987, 169f (Ayios Dhimitrios). Wace & Blegen 1916/18 class Ib. Caskey & Caskey 1960, 139-140.
[170] Blegen 1921 and 1928 group AI.

face (Blegen AII). In the catalogue I have distinguished between Red burnished and Black burnished. The different colours of course depend on firing conditions but the choice of colour is probably conscious. Black burnished fabrics are often more coarse in the clay temper (with larger grits) and show thicker walls than Red burnished. Red burnished are usually open shapes of good quality. The burnish is often added on both sides in- and outside, but always on the inside. Thus Red burnished is predominantly the "table ware" of the deposit.

The local ware groups

Standard description

(The size of grits is usually included in the catalogue. The measurements in brackets are always the max. size of measured grits).

MT: Medium tempered wares are usually reddish yellow (5YR 6/8 or 5YR 7/8 more unusually 7.5YR 7/8) or more red (2.5YR 5/8, 2.5YR 6/8, 2.5YR 7/8). The fabric is rather soft, often sandy[171] with white lime inclusions (diagnostic for local fabrics), black/red and brown stone grits (max. 3 mm). Silver mica is usual. In a few instances the surface has been deliberately covered with a white lime cover. Shapes are open bowls and plates with more or less inturned rim (thin or rounded) or close shaped jars and vessels with thick wall (above 12mm). The wares are handmade, but sometimes a slow wheel seems to have been used.

CT: Coarse tempered fabrics are usually reddish yellow (5YR 6/8) or red (2.5YR 5/8) with white lime and/or black/brown/red stone inclusions. The grits might measure between 4 and 11 mm. A specific group has been named Terrazzo Ware with large stone inclusions, with the flat facet towards the surface creating the illusion of a terrazzo floor (below Fig. 26). Silver mica is usual. Coarse tempered fabrics with walls 27 mm or more are used for large storage jars/pithoi with horizontal plastic bevels, flat bases and large strap handles (typical in Tx43/4b).

KW: Kitchen ware has been distinguished as a hard, flaking fabric with (sometimes) large stone and lime inclusions (7mm) and smoothed surface. Shapes are small jars. Another fabric is a very hard, sand-tempered version of MT.

Shapes: (see also chapters above p. 38ff.).[172]

The Middle Helladic and Early Mycenaean periods

Middle Helladic and Early Mycenaean material was mainly excavated in the lower strata west of the Aghia Triada (Area II) (for stratigraphical analyses, see below). In addition sherds from late MH/early LH came to light among the surface finds from Aghia Triada and in a deposit which evidently went below the Byzantine wall on the mound (F15). As mentioned below all pottery from Aghia Triada and surroundings has a lime encrustation on the surface which is very difficult to clean without damaging the surface. This fact influences the classification to some degree. Thus in many cases it has been difficult to estimate whether a sherd derives from an open or a closed shaped jar, if the profile could not be made out and the study of the surfaces is less detailed than could be wished.

Compared to the EH pottery above there are substantial differences. The clay used for EH pottery is usually more red than that used in the transitional period between MH and LH and later in LH. Evidently different sources for clay have been used. First of all these strata contain quite an amount of local genuine Fine tempered fabrics (FT), never found among the older materials. Probably more than half of the FT wares are

---

[171] Comp. Weisshaar 1990 for Talioti.
[172] The terminology, characteristic features (rim, handle etc.) usually follows Wiencke 2000, 529ff and Fossey 1978, 45-49.

wheel-made. Genuine coarse ware (CT) has only been isolated in a few instances. This does not mean that sherds with quite large grits are not found, but that storage jars are very unusual, evidently due to the character of the deposits. Quite large jars, however, are also produced in Medium tempered fabrics (MT). MT ware groups are by far the most usual clay to be used in MH/LHI in Chalkis Aitolias (see below). Most coarse tempered fabrics have been included in the Kitchen Ware group which makes it somewhat unhomogeneous. By far the majority classified as Kitchen Ware, however, does consist of rather small pots. Grey Minyan (GM) is very unusual, but is found.

The local ware groups

Standard description[173]

FT (Fine tempered)

Biscuits: Very fine fabrics with none or very few small (0.5mm) inclusions: very small white lime grits or (red/brown) stones. Silver mica is found. Colours: Yellowish red (5YR 5/8), reddish yellow (5YR 6/6, 5YR 6/8, 5YR 7/6, 5YR 7/8, 7.5YR 7/6). Light red (2.5YR 7/8). Pink: (7.5YR 8/4) The surface is unburnished, smoothed (FT(1)) or burnished (FT(2)). The unburnished variant is the more usual; on average less than 20% of the FT wares are burnished. Colours (FT(1)): Reddish yellow (7.5YR 7/6, 5YR 7/6). Very pale brown (10YR 7/4, 10YR 8/4). Pink (7.5YR 8/4). Shapes: See chapters above p. 48f. Decoration: MP is present on Fine ware. Comments: More than half seems to be wheel-made.

MT (Medium tempered).

It should be emphasized that the line between FT and MT is sometimes difficult to draw. The distinction primarily relates to the amount and size of grits. Based on the grits, a sherd would thus be classified as MT even if the clay is rather fine. *Biscuits*: Fine to medium fine clay with lime (rather diagnostic), black/brown/grey stone inclu-

sions, grits between 1 and 3 mm – and silver mica. Voids are often seen on the surface. Colours: Red (2.5YR 6/8). Reddish yellow (5YR 6/6, 5YR 6/8, 5YR 7/6, 5YR 7/8, 7.5YR 7/6, 7.5YR 6/6). Reddish brown (5YR 5/4). Weak red (2.5YR 6/4, 2.5YR 5/4). Surface: The usually matt surface is smoothed or slipped. Colours: Reddish yellow (5YR 7/6, 5YR 7/8, 7.5YR 6/6, 7.5YR 8/6). Light red: (2.5YR 7/6). Light brown: (7.5YR 6/4) or pink: (7.5YR 7/4, 7.5YR 8/3). Finally a monochrome matt black cover is sometimes seen on the surface. Shapes: See chapters above p. 48ff. Decoration: MP is found in several cases, though as the surface is usually badly corroded, it is normally not possible to identify a pattern. Comments: Usually handmade.

MT – a note on variations!

Especially in TR72/11 and TR72/12 it is possible to distinguish between two groups of MT fabrics. A rather soft variant (MT (1)) and a hard variant (MT(2)). The levels mentioned should date to MH III/LHI A (see chapters' above). In later periods the distinction between the two groups is not so pronounced and it has not been possible to draw the distinction in the statistics. In the two trenches mentioned a distinction could be defined as follows:

MT(1)

Biscuits: Usually yellowish red (5YR 5/6) to reddish yellow (5YR 6/7 5YR 6/8) soft fabric with rather few visible grits, not usually white (lime). Silver mica is rather characteristic. Surface: 1) either without slip or 2) with slip, usually reddish yellow (7.5YR 7/6) to very pale brown (10YR 8/4) - a "Yellow Minyan" surface is usual. Some are burnished. Shapes: There are approximately twice as many open shapes as closed shapes. Decoration: MP is found. Comments: Some are clearly wheel-made.

---

[173] As far as possible according to Dietz 1991.

MT(2)

Biscuits: Usually reddish yellow (7.5YR 6/6), hard fabric with white (lime) grits. Surface: either 1) unslipped or 2) slipped often with a "Yellow Minyan" colour surface – very pale brown (10YR 8/3) – never burnished, however. Shapes: There are approximately 8 times as many closed shapes as open shapes in this group. Decoration: MP. Comments: Excellent hard fabric.

Summary. The two fabrics could be distinguished: 1) by the soft fabric, with few lime grits and a hard fabric with many lime grits 2) by a surface, never burnished on the hard fabric and 3) by shapes with a clear dominance of closed shapes within the hard fabric (MT(2)) and the contrary in the soft (MT(1)). MP is found in both ware groups and kantharoi are produced in both fabrics. Larger containers are usually produced in a thick walled version (wall between 9 and 13 mm) of MT(2) (without many lime grits, however).

KW (Kitchen ware)

Biscuits: The Kitchen ware can be either dark, black/brown: Dark reddish grey (2.5YR 4/1), very dark grey (10YR 3/1) or light: Red (2.5YR 6/8), reddish yellow (7.5YR 7/6), yellowish red (5YR 5/6, 5YR 5/8) . Often with a dark core and more red margin. White (lime) inclusions or brown/black/grey stone grits (between 1 and 9 mm) or straw tempered. Often flaking with brown stone inclusions. Always very hard fabric. Surface: Can be either black, brown or red: Red (2.5YR 6/8) or red (2.5YR 5/6), reddish yellow (5YR 6/6). The surface is sometimes burnished. Shapes: Usually rather small cooking jars. Decoration: None. Comments: Always handmade.

GM (Grey Minyan).

Grey Minyan has a hard fabric, wheel-made wares are found. Another variant (not the canonical) is more soft and handmade, with the same clay, however.

Non-local ware groups

Lustrous painted (Tx70/5/5a)

Biscuit: Reddish yellow (7.5YR 7/6). Fine tempered. Very small inclusions and voids. Surface: Very pale brown (10YR 8/3), burnished slip. Shape: Cups or small kraters. Decoration: Black or red, lustrous paint. Comments: Imported.

Lustrous painted (K27/6a-b)

Biscuits: Margin: Red (2.5YR 6/8). Brown core. Quartz grits. Surface: Red (2.5YR 6/8) covered with monochrome black, lustrous paint. Shape: Large open. Wall 13 mm. Decoration: None Comments: Imported.

White on lustrous (/burnished) dark (Tx72/12)

Biscuits: 1) Reddish yellow (5YR 6/6, 5YR 6/8) – light brown (7.5YR 6/4) or 2) Red (2.5YR 6/8), fine "sandwich" – very hard fabric. Surface: The surface is black and probably burnished, not very lustrous. Sometimes the black zone is just a band on which the white is added. Shapes: closed. Decoration: fat white = Very pale brown (10YR 8/3). Comments: Imported.

LHIII pottery

LHIII ceramic material in context was found only in the area West of Aghia Triada (Area II). Finds on the hill including finds from the LHII and LHIIIC periods are all stray finds from the survey (see below).

All LHIII layers contain quite a lot of Mycenaean fine ware sherds – all very tiny. All are wheel-made with lustrous paint. The surface is usually badly preserved and patterns are difficult to identify. Many sherds are painted with a monochrome, lustrous black paint. Monochrome deep bowls are identified in most layers.

The layers also contain Medium tempered ware groups with colours as described above (MHIII/LHI). The clay however is more fine tempered. Some are burnished. Kantharoi with high swung handles are identified in MT burnished. It is characteristic that the hard, unburnished fabric MT(2) is relatively less frequent than in earlier layers (MHIII/LHI). The most significant difference between the LHIII layers and the earlier deposits is that approximately 50% of the pottery within all ware groups is wheel-made.

KW (Kitchen Ware) is usually as follows:
Biscuit: Black with white stone grits (1mm). Surface: can be red (2.5YR 6/8), more dark on inside – red (2.5YR 5/6). Shapes: Small jars. Decoration: None. Comments: At least 50% wheel-made.

GM (Grey Minyan) in a light grey colour is found in a few cases.

Mycenaean "White" ware is described as follows:
Biscuit: Very pale brown (10YR 8/3) homogeneous fine fabric. Surface: Very pale brown (10YR 8/3), smoothed. Shapes: Bowls. Decoration: None. Comments: May be wheel-made.

Note! Statistical evaluations are suggested only when the stratum treated is considered to be homogeneous – which means with none or relatively few earlier/later intrusions. In the groupings the abbreviations refer to the standard description of ware groups. Deviations from the standard description have been noted.

Pottery – catalogue of context and finds

Aghia Triada Area I

Survey 1995. Selected Finds:[174]

1. 3770/3100 (Pl. 1)
Biscuit: Yellow (10YR 7-8/6) well fired, slightly porous fabric, with light red coring and some small black grits. Surface: Thin matt black slip and lower wall out. Shape: Flat everted rim to belly of krater/bowl. D 25. Decoration: Painted radial stripes on top of rim and a wavy horizontal band in reserved area below rim on outside. Comments: FPR, 261 no. 18. fig. 9, 18. Date: LHIIIC.

2. 3910/3010 (Pl. 1)
Biscuit: Very pale brown (10YR 7/4) fine, slightly porous fabric. Surface: Waxy surface with worn brownish black slip out. Shape: Base of a mug. Decoration: None. Comments: FPR, 259,3. fig. 9, 3. Date: LHIIIC to G(?).

3. AAI (Pl. 1)
Biscuit: Brownish yellow (10YR 6/6) porous, semi-coarse fabric with mica. Surface: "Yellow Minyan". Shape: Handle with part of wall of kantharos with tripartite strap handle. Decoration: None. Comments: FPR, 263,2. fig. 10, 2. Date: MHIII/LHI.

4. AAI (Pl. 1)
Biscuit: Light red (2.5 6/8) semi-coarse fabric with grey core. Few mica and small white inclusions. Surface: Matt with voids. Shape: Fragment of circular handle with part of wall of large basin. D (handle) 2. Decoration: None. Comments: FPR, 263,5. fig. 10, 5. Date: MH.

5. AAD (Pl. 1)
Biscuit: Brownish yellow (10YR 6/6) gritty, slightly porous fabric, with small pale inclusions. Surface: Smoothed. Shape: Fragment of a wishbone handle. Decoration: None. Comments: FPR, 265,20. fig. 10, 20. Date: LHI.

6. AAD (Pl. 1)
Biscuit: Reddish yellow (7.5 7/6) well fired, semi-fine fabric, porous with mica and white and grey inclusions. Surface: Smoothed. Shape: Body fragment of close shaped vessel. Decoration: Outside: Matt painted, dark brown decoration with series of oblique lines. Comments: FPR, 16. fig.10, 16. Date: MHIIIB.

7. AAD (Pl. 1)
Biscuit: Yellowish red (5YR 5/6) well fired, fine, porous fabric. Surface: Pink (7.5YR 6-7/4) burnished. Shape: Stemmed foot (broken at edge) and part of belly of a goblet. D (stem) 4. Decoration: None. Comments: FPR, 265,21. fig. 10, 21. Date: MHIII/LHI.

8. AAI (Pl. 1)

Biscuit: Red (2.5YR 5/8) coarse fabric with white and dark inclusions. Surface: Smoothed. Shape: Flaring T-rim of large bowl. D (app.) 45. Decoration: Raised band with series of discs below rim. Comments: FPR, 264,6. fig. 10, 6. Date: EHII.

9. 3050/4061 (Pl. 1)
Biscuit: Dark greyish brown (2.5YR 4/2) core. Margins: Yellowish brown (10YR 5/4) to Red (2.5YR 5/8) fabric with pale oatmeal inclusions. Surface: -. Shape: Probably a figurine. Decoration: None. Comments: FPR, 266,25. fig. 10, 25. Date: EH (suggested).

10. ABS (Pl. 1)
Biscuit: Grey, flaky fabric with white inclusions and voids (misfired). Surface: Smoothed, light olive brown (2.5Y 5/3) with visible mica. D 21. Shape: Rim and root of vertical handle of bowl. Decoration: None. Comments: Handmade. FPR, 268,17. fig. 11, 17. Date: MH.

11. AAO (Pl. 1)
Biscuit: Very pale brown (10YR 7/4) fine fabric with large (3mm) angular, black inclusions. Surface: Pale yellow (2.5Y 8/4). Shape: Rim to shoulder of jar with slightly thickened outturned rim. D 14 (app.). Decoration: None. Comments: Handmade. FPR, 23. fig. 11, 23. Date: MHIII.

F15

F15/AAC-3/NW (22.07.96)

The Deposit: Found in a soil with charcoal and stones (ACC-3) east of ABV (FPR, 287f.). The layer rested on bedrock and probably continued below the wall ABV. 30 sherds all MHIII/LHI

STATISTICS:	No.	Weight
FT ("Yellow Minyan")	3	50 gr
MT (2 with MP)	4	50 gr
CT/KW	18	200 gr
GM (1 vertical handle)		

12. FT (Pl. 1)
Biscuit: Pink (7.5YR 8/4). Fine, soft fabric. Surface: Very pale brown slip (10YR 8/4). Shape: Cup with slightly concave, thin rim D 11. Decoration: Black MP. Two parallel, horizontal bands on outside and a band on the inside. Comments: Handmade. FPR, 289, 8. fig. 25, 8. F96-210.

13. MT (Pl. 1)
Biscuit: Reddish yellow (5YR 7/8) fine fabric with small red inclusions. Surface: Pale yellow (2.5YR 8/3), matt, slightly burnished slip ("yellow Minyan"). Shape: Two-handled kantharos with rim, slightly concave on the inside. D 10. Decoration: None. Comments: wheel-made (?). FPR, 289, 9. fig. 25, 9. F96-209.

---

[174] Coordinates and structure numbers refer to FPR, fig. 8.

Fig. 20. Aghia Triada. F15/4/SW. Catalogue no. 20, sherd with vertical MP bands.

14. KW (Pl. 1)
Biscuit: Black/brown, very hard fabric with black and white (lime)grits (2mm). Surface: Gray. Shape: Rim of jar. D 14. Decoration: None. Comments: Traces of slow wheel.

F15/AAC-3/SW

The deposit: Mixed stratum inside the Byzantine wall (FPR, 295)

15. FT (Mycenaean) (Pl. 2)
Biscuit: Reddish yellow (5YR 7/8) medium fine fabric with quite a few white (lime) inclusions. Surface: Very pale brown (10YR 8/3) matt slip. Shape: Mycenaean alabastron. D 12. Decoration: Black/brown lustrous paint. Running spirals. Comments: Handmade. FPR, 295, no. 5. fig. 28, 5. Date: LHI/IIA.

16. FT (Mycenaean) (Pl. 2)
Biscuit: Pink (5YR 8/4), fine fabric. Surface: –. Shape: Body sherd of a cup. Decoration: Red (2.5YR 5/6) paint on inside with red (2.5YR 6/8) horizontal line. Black/reddish brown lustrous paint on outside. Comments: wheel-made. FPR, 297, no. 7. fig. 28, 7. Date: LHIIIC.

17. CT (Pl. 2)
Biscuit: Red (10YR 5/8) coarse fabric with white inclusions. Surface: Smoothed. Shape: T-rim of bowl. D (app.) 30. Decoration: Raised band below rim. Comments: Handmade. FPR, 297, no. 8. fig. 28, 8. Date: EHII.

18. CT (Pl. 2)
Biscuit: Red (10YR 7/6) coarse fabric with black and white

inclusions. Surface: –. Shape: T-rim bowl. D 30. Decoration: None. Comments: Handmade. FPR, 297, no. 11. fig. 28, 11. Date: EH.

F15/AAC-4/SW

The Deposit: EH (?)/MH/LH stratum with a few A/C intrusions ? (FPR, 297)

19. FT (Pl. 2)
Biscuit: Reddish yellow (7.5YR 7/6) fine tempered fabric. Surface: Thick, burnished slip in the same colour ("Yellow Minyan"). Shape: Everted rim of kantharos or cup. D 12. Decoration: None. Comments: Handmade ? FPR, 297, no. 12. fig. 28, 12.

20. MT (Fig. 20)
Biscuit: Reddish yellow (5YR 6/8) fabric with white inclusions and silver mica. Surface: Very pale yellow (more creamy than 2.5YR 8/2) slip on outside. Shape: Closed shaped jar. Decoration: Very pale brown vertical bands (10YR 7/4), changing to red (when colour is worn). Comments: Handmade (probably). FPR, 297, no. 13. fig. 28, 13. Date: LHIA.

21. Polychrome Mainland (Pl. 2)
Biscuit: Gray core between Reddish yellow (5YR 7/6). White inclusions. Surface: –. Shape: Large krater with out falling, thickened rim. D (app.) 40. Decoration: Traces of red (2.5YR 5/8) colour on rim and inside. Traces of horizontal bands in "lustrous", very pale brown (10YR 8/3) paint. Comments: wheel-made. FPR, 297, no. 14. fig. 28, 14.

22. Empty number

23. MT (Pl. 2)
Biscuit: Reddish yellow (5YR 6/8) fabric with white inclusions and silver mica. Surface: Smoothed and burnished. Shape: Rim of jar with thin, everted rim and vertical strap handle. D 15. Decoration: Traces of MP at strap handle and below the rim. Comments: Handmade. FPR, 297, no. 16. fig. 28 and 29. Date: MHIII/LHI.

24. MT (Pl. 2)
Biscuit: Light reddish brown (5YR 6/4) core. Surface: Yellow (10YR 7/6) slip on outside. Shape: Flat, disc shape base from a bowl (?). D 8. Decoration: None. Comments: FPR, 297, no. 17. fig. 28.

Tx 43 and Tx 20

The Deposit: Tx 20 (Fig. 8a) is a 1 metre broad trench next to Tx 43 at the west side laid out in 5.78 metre towards north-east, from the Byzantine wall AAB to the wall ACS. The trench was excavated the year before Tx 43. Section and the excavation strata are shown on Fig. 21. The surface layer

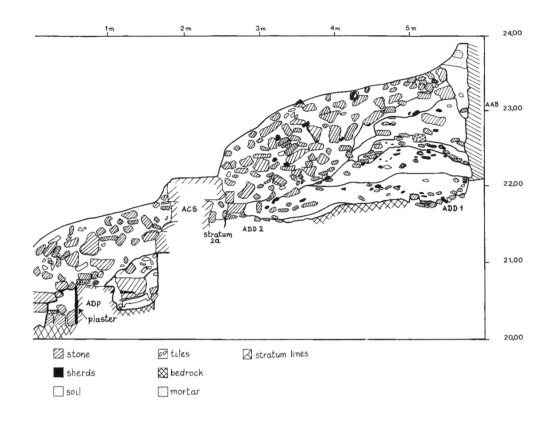

stone ◫ tiles ◨ stratum lines

■ sherds ⬚ bedrock

☐ soil ⬚ mortar

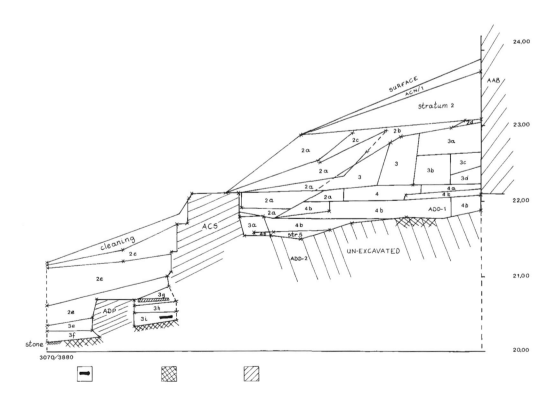

Fig. 21. Aghia Triada, Area I. Section Tx20, SE and analytical plan of strata excavated in Tx20. 1:50.

is greyish brown with many roots, lots of mortar and rubble from AAB. STR 2 contained no mortar but many sherds from various periods (STR 2d should be included in STR 3).

The prehistoric levels begin with STR 3. The thickness of the levels near AAB is approximately 1.25 m. The deposit slopes down towards north. STR 3 is defined as an olive brown (2.5Y 4/4) fat clayish soil with few small stones, sherds, flint and obsidian. STR 3a/3b colour and contents as STR 3, more sherds were found in 3b than in 3a, some charcoal. STR 3c more sandy than the former strata, stones (15 cm). Colour: Dark yellowish brown (10YR 4/4). STR 3d. Colour as 3a/b, some charcoal, shells and bones. STR 4. Colour: Light olive brown (2.5Y 5/6) sandy soil with small pebbles, sherds and charcoal. STR 4a. Colour: Light olive brown (2.5Y 5/6), sandy soil with small pebbles, few sherds, bones and shells. STR 4b. Colour: Light olive brown (2.5Y 5/6) sandy soil with stones, stone flakes, sherds and charcoal. In the bottom of STR 4 a circular structure, ADD-1 was found considered to be a fireplace with flat sand stones, lots of charcoal. The surrounding soil was olive brown (2.5Y 4/3). Some burnt bones, flint and sherds were found in ADD-1 (FPR, 237, fig. 21). STR 5 is a small pit in the northern part of the trench towards the wall ACS. Colour: Light olive brown (2.5Y 5/6) with small pieces of charcoal, small stones and pebbles (probably just a lower stratum of 4b). STR 4b continues below the Byzantine wall AAB.

Tx 43 (Stratum description according to Tx 20) The trench is placed on the middle terrace as a prolongation of trenches Tx 41/42 towards south (Figs. 8a and 21). The trench is placed next to trench Tx 20 towards the Byzantine wall AAB and measures 2x5.8 m. The upper layer STR 2 is a mixed fill with stones fallen from the Byzantine wall ABB, mortar, lots of tiles and a few sherds. The prehistoric layers are found in strata 3 to 4 and measure up to 1.5 meters towards the Byzantine wall AAB; further north the layer slopes down towards bedrock. STR 3 probably has been redeposited in connection with the construction of the Byzantine wall while original strata begin at STR 4.

Fig. 22. Aghia Triada, Area I. Catalogue no. 26 (MT-unburnished).

Tx43

Tx43/3 (Bag no. 1259 (01.07.98)

STATISTICS:	No.	Weight
Intrusions:		
Archaic: (some with black glaze)	20	250 gr
Mycenaean (?): small pieces	20	100 gr
MT- unburnished	88	500 gr
MT-Red burnished[175]	5	50 gr
MT-Black burnished	10	100 gr
CT-unburnished	82	800 gr
CT-Red burnished	3	50 gr
CT-Black burnished	15	250 gr

Shapes

25. MT-unburnished (Pl. 3)
Biscuit: Core: grey. Margins: Reddish yellow (5YR 6/8), very hard fabric with small white grits. Surface: idem (margin), smoothed. Shape: Large open bowl with rounded rim. D 28. Decoration: None. Comments: Handmade.

---

[175] One marked exception from standard description: Biscuit: Brown (7.5YR 5/4) hard, sandy fabric with many small white inclusions – a few white stones (4 mm) Surface: Black surface. Comments: Handmade.

26. MT-unburnished (Pl. 3 and Fig. 22)
Biscuit: Reddish yellow (5YR 7/8) with mainly black grits (2/3 mm). Surface: idem. Smoothed. Parallel, incised lines on inside from production. Shape: Small jar with thin rim and band shaped (strap) handle. D 20. Decoration: None. Comments: Handmade.

27. MT-Red burnished (Pl. 3)
Biscuit: Reddish yellow (5YR 6/8), sandy fabric with black and white stone inclusions. Surface: Light red (2.5YR 6/6) slipped, burnished on in-and outside. Shape: Bowl with inturned, pointed rim. D 20. Decoration: None. Comments: Handmade.

28. CT-unburnished (Pl. 3)
Biscuit: Reddish yellow (5YR 6/8) with white and black stone grits (4mm). Surface: Smoothed. Shape: Jar with a high, vertical, flattened rim. D 25. Decoration: None. Comments: Handmade.

29. Horizontal handles in CT-unburnished (drawing) (Pl. 3)

Various

Several smaller parts of rims – not drawn.

Tx43/3a

(Bag nos. 1260 (01.07.98), 1262 (01.07.98), 1263 (01.07.98), 1264 (02.07.98))[176]

STATISTICS:	No.	Weight
Intrusions:		
Black glaze (Archaic/Classical + Corinthian)	41	500 gr
MT-unburnished	152	1.200 gr
MT-Red burnished	14	200 gr
MT-Black burnished	8	100 gr
CT-unburnished	148	1.900 gr
CT-Red burnished	18	300 gr
CT-Black burnished	16	250 gr
KW- Kitchen ware	34	400 gr

Shapes

30. MT-unburnished (Pl. 3)
Biscuit: Very pale brown (10YR 8/4) with white (lime), black and reddish yellow (5YR 6/8) inclusions. Surface: idem (margin). Shape: Hemispherical (?) jar with cylindrical collar and pointed rim D 12. Decoration: None. Comments: Handmade – not local fabric.

31. MT-unburnished (Pl. 3)
Biscuit: Core: black. Margins: Light red (2.5YR 7/8) with small, white grits. One black stone (4mm). Surface: idem. Smoothed. Shape: Flat bottom (basin ?) with marked foot D 7. Decoration: None. Comments: Handmade.

Fig. 23. Aghia Triada, Area I. Catalogue no. 39 (CT-unburnished).

32. MT-unburnished (Pl. 3)
Biscuit: Light red (2.5YR 6/8) with black and grey grits. Surface: idem. Smoothed. Shape: Small jar with vertical collar and pointed rim. D 16. Decoration. –. Comments: Handmade.

33. MT- (Pl. 3)
Biscuit: Core: black, hard. Margins: Red (10YR 5/8) hard fabric with very small white inclusions + one white (one black) stone inclusion (4mm). Surface: idem. Inside probably Red burnished. Shape: Small jar with rim slightly thickened on outside. D 20. Decoration: One band in black burnished on outside – perhaps other bands. Comments: Handmade.

34. MT-Black (dark) burnished (Pl. 3)
Biscuit: Reddish brown (5YR 5/4) rather fine fabric, but with a few larger white stone grits (4mm). Surface: Reddish brown (5YR 4/4) burnished in- and out. Shape: Closed shaped jar with incurving, pointed rim. D 24. Decoration: None. Comments: Handmade.

35. CT-unburnished (Pl. 3)
Biscuit: Core: Black. Margin: Reddish yellow (5YR 7/8) white (lime) and black/red stone inclusions (5mm). Surface: Smoothed. Colour: idem (margin). Shape: Jar with vertical, rounded rim. D 34. Decoration: None. Comments: Handmade.

36. CT-unburnished (or KW) (Pl. 3)
Biscuit: Light red (2.5YR 6/8) with many stone inclusions (7 mm). Surface: Smoothed. Shape: Flat base. D 12. Decoration: None. Comments: Handmade.

37. CT-unburnished (Pl. 3)
Biscuit/surface: as no. 36. Shape: Ring base. D 11.

38. CT-unburnished (Pl. 3)
Biscuit: Red (2.5YR 5/8) with many white stone grits

[176] Note to Bag no. 1435 (06.07.98): Insignificant material, 11 sherds, all EH.

Fig. 24. Aghia Triada, Area I. Strap handle in CT-unburnished (Tx43/3a).

(5mm)(a few pieces of mother of pearl). Surface: idem. Smoothed. Shape: Ring base. D 10. Decoration: None. Comments: Handmade.

39. CT-unburnished (Pl. 3 and Fig. 23)
Biscuit: Light red (2.5YR 6/6) with white grits (4mm). Surface: Yellowish brown (10YR 5/4). Smoothed . Shape: ?. Decoration: Raised band with grooves. Comments: Handmade.

Various

- One more base – not well preserved
- Two vertical handles with circular section.
- One vertical strap handle in CT-unburnished (Fig. 24).
- One thin rim of a shallow bowl. MT-unburnished. D 30?

Tx43/3c

(Bag nos. 1273 (02.07.98), 1275 (02.07.98), 1608 (06.07.98))

STATISTICS:
Intrusions: 2FT sherds probably from Archaic cups

	No.	Weight
MT-unburnished	51	400 gr
MT-Red burnished	28	250 gr
MT-Black burnished	12	100 gr
CT-unburnished	17	300 gr
CT-Red burnished	4	100 gr
CT-Black burnished	2	50 gr
KW - Kitchen ware	13	100 gr

Shapes

40. MT-Red burnished (Pl. 3)
Biscuit: Red (2.5YR 5/8) hard fabric with small grits (1mm). Surface: In- and outside covered with red (10R 4/8) burnished slip. Shape: Open bowl with inturned, thickened and pointed, hooked rim. D 20. Decoration: None. Comments: Handmade.

41. MT-Red burnished (Pl. 3)
Biscuit: Red (2.5YR 5/8) fabric with black and white grits (2mm). Surface: Red slipped, burnished (2.5YR 5/8) on in- and outside. Shape: Small bowl with inturned thickened and pointed, hooked rim. D 14. Decoration: None. Comments: Handmade.

42. CT-unburnished (Pl. 3)
Biscuit: Black, flaking with black stone grits (3mm). Surface: Light red (2.5YR 6/8) smoothed. Shape: Large bowl with splaying, rounded rim. D 32. Decoration: None. Comments: Handmade.

43. CT-Black burnished (Pl. 3)
Biscuit: Core: Black. Margin: Reddish yellow (5YR 7/8). Small lime grits and larger stone (5mm), a few silver mica. Surface: Smoothed, in- and outside covered with a black, burnished slip. Shape: Jar with vertical slightly inturned rim. D 30. Decoration: None. Comments: Handmade.

44. CT-Black burnished (Pl. 3)
Biscuit: Reddish yellow (5YR 6/8) rather fine tempered clay with grey/black stone grits (5mm). Surface: In-and outside covered with black burnished slip. Shape: Closed shaped hemispherical jar with incurved, rounded rim. D 26. Decoration. –. Comments: Handmade.

45. CT- (imports) (Pl. 3)
Biscuit: Reddish yellow (5YR 6/8) very hard fabric with many small, white grits and a few black grits. A few larger stone grits (4mm). Surface: The Reddish Yellow (5YR 6/6) surface has been covered with a very pale brown (10YR 8/3) matt slip (fragmentarily preserved) on in-and outside. Shape: Conical pedestal from a small "fruitstand". D 10. Decoration: Traces of a boss. Comments: Probably imported.

46. KW (Pl. 3)
Biscuit: Hard, black flaking fabric with large stone inclusions (5mm). Surface: Smoothed. On inside reddish yellow, outside black. Shape: Small hemispherical jar with vertical, slightly inturned, pointed rim. D 18. Decoration: None. Comments: Handmade.

Various

- Further two-three thin rims (KW+MT black burnished)
- 1 CT jar, black inside, smoothed on outside
- 2 MT Red burnished bowls with incurved rim
- 3 strap handles. 1CT and 2 MT
- 1 flat base

- One horizontal handle with oval section

See also Catalogue of flint/obsidian (TR 43/3c)

Tx43/3d

(Bag nos. 1429 (03.07.98), 1431 (06.07.98), 1609 (06.07.98))

STATISTICS: | No. | Weight
Intrusions: Archaic–1 rim sherd of a cup
Two Mycenaean plain sherds (?)

	No.	Weight
MT-unburnished	139	1.000 gr
MT-Red burnished	60	500 gr
MT-Black burnished	18	150 gr
CT-unburnished	79	1.550 gr
CT-Red burnished	9	400 gr
CT-Black burnished	7	300 gr
KW (MT)	3	50 gr
KW (CT)	3	100 gr
Five lumps of Reddish yellow clay, could be from wall plaster?	5	300 gr

Shapes

47. FT (Pl. 4)
Biscuit: pale yellow (2.5YR 8/4) fine clay with few small brown/red grits. Surface: Smoothed covered with monochrome yellowish red (5YR 5/6) matt paint. Shape: Pedestal base. Decoration: Monochrome paint. D 6. Comments: Probably handmade with parallel, horizontal incisions from slow wheel on the outside – no traces on inside. The fabric is not Chalkidian neither is the paint.

48. MT-unburnished (Pl. 4)
Biscuit: Reddish yellow (7.5YR 7/8) fabric with small white (lime) grits. Surface: Smoothed. Shape: Open bowl with rounded, "jagged" rim. D 34. Decoration: None. Comments: Handmade but with clear horizontal zones on inside. Slow wheel ?

49. MT-unburnished (Pl. 4)
Biscuit: Red (2.5YR 6/8) hard, sandy fabric with small white (lime) and grey grits. Surface: Smoothed. Shape: Large bowl with splaying, thickened, rounded rim. D 32. Decoration: None. Comments: Handmade.

50. MT-unburnished (Pl. 4)
Biscuit: Reddish yellow (7.5YR 7/6) rather fine tempered, sandy clay with white and black stone grits (3mm). Surface: Smoothed. Shape: Fragment of a globular jar with broad outturned, slightly thickened neck. D 18. Decoration: None. Comments: Handmade.

51. MT-Red burnished (Pl. 4)
Biscuit: Red (2.5YR 6/8) with hard, rather sandy fabric with small white (lime) grits dominating (1.5mm) – a few black/brown grits. Surface: Red (10R 5/8) burnished slip. Specially well preserved on the inside, but also traces on the outside. Shape: Large bowl with thickened, incurving, pointed rim. D 25. Decoration. –. Comments: Handmade.

52. MT-Red burnished (Pl. 4)
Biscuit: Red (2.5YR 6/8) fine, sandy fabric with small brown/black and white (lime) grits. Surface: Reddish yellow (7.5YR 7/8) smoothed with thick, burnished red (10YR 5/8) slip (in and out). Shape: Shallow bowl with pointed, slightly inturned rim. D 20 (app.). Decoration: None. Comments: Handmade. Traces of horizontal, incised lines/grooves on inside.

53. MT-Red burnished (Pl. 4)
Biscuit: Reddish yellow (5YR 6/8) with small (1mm) white (lime) grits. Surface: Covered with red (2.5YR 5/8) burnished slip (in and out). Shape: Flat bowl with thickened, narrowly carinated rim. D 40 (app). Decoration: None. Comments: Handmade.

54. MT-Red burnished (Pl. 4)
Biscuit: Reddish yellow (5YR 6/8) with small white grits (2mm). Surface: Red (10YR 5/6) burnished slip on in – and outside. Shape: Open (bowl) – base with recessed bottom. D.10. Decoration: None. Comments: Handmade.

55. MT-Red/brown burnished (Pl. 4)
Biscuit: Reddish yellow (5YR 6/8) rather sandy fabric with small (1mm) white (lime) grits. Surface: Traces of reddish brown (5YR 5/3) burnished slip on inside. Shape: Bowl with slightly thickened, plain tapered, slightly inturned rim. D 30. Decoration: None. Comments: Handmade.

56. MT-Black burnished (Pl. 4)
Biscuit: Reddish yellow (5YR 6/8) with hard, sandy fabric with white, small grits (1mm). One larger grit stone (5mm). Surface: Reddish brown (5YR 5/4) burnished slip best preserved on inside. Shape: Flat bowl with thickened, pointed, hooked rim. D 34. Decoration: None. Comments: Handmade.

57. MT-Black burnished (Pl. 4)
Biscuit: Reddish yellow (5YR 6/8) fabric with small, white (lime) grits. Surface: Covered with black, burnished slip (in and out). Shape: Bowl with hooked, pointed rim. D 20. Decoration: None. Comments: Handmade.

58. MT-Black/brown burnished (Pl. 4)
Biscuit: Reddish yellow (5YR 6/8) rather sandy fabric with small white (lime) inclusions (1mm). Surface: Traces of reddish brown (5YR 5/3) burnished slip on outside. Shape: Bowl with slightly thickened, plain tapered, slightly inturned rim. D 34. Decoration: None. Comments: Handmade.

59. MT-Black/brown burnished (Pl. 4)
Biscuit: Reddish yellow (5YR 6/8) sandy fabric with many small white (lime) grits (1mm). Surface: Reddish yellow (7.5YR 6/89 with white grits and voids. Brownish yellow slip (slightly burnished) on inside. Shape: Jar with thickened, slightly inturned rim. D 40. Decoration: None. Comments: Handmade but parallel, horizontal incised grooves on inside.

60. CT-unburnished (Pl. 4)
Biscuit: Red (2.5YR 5/6) coarse fabric with white and black grits (3mm). Surface: Red (2.5YR 5/8) smoothed with a thin slip (?). Shape: Flat splaying rim of a "Fruchtschale" (?) D 26. Decoration: None. Comments: Handmade. Unusual fabric.

61. CT-unburnished (Pl. 4)
Biscuit: Core: Black. Margins: Reddish yellow (5YR 7/8) fabric with many white (stone) grits (3mm) (one lime grit).

Surface: Smoothed. Shape: Large bowl with thickened, rounded rim. D 28. Decoration: None. Comments: Handmade. The black core is not usual in Chalkis.

62. CT-unburnished (Pl. 4)
Biscuit: Red (2.5YR 5/8) fabric with white, grey grits (5mm). Surface: Smoothed. Shape: Jar (?) side with high plastic fillet (– imprints/finger grooves) – thin rim. Decoration: see above. Comments: Handmade.

63. CT-Red burnished (Pl. 4)
Biscuit: Red (2.5YR 5/8) fabric with many white (lime) grits and some grey stones (4mm). Surface: Red (10YR 5/6) burnished slip on in- and outside. Shape: Bowl with thickened T-rim and "Knickwand". D 25. Decoration: Raised band with finger impressions below rim. Comments: Handmade.

64. CT – Black burnished (Pl. 4)
Biscuit: Black coarse tempered flaking fabric with stone grits (3mm), Surface: Black slipped, slightly burnished on in- and outside. Shape: spout of a coarse ware jug with inwards thickened, rounded rim. D 8. Decoration: None. Comments: Handmade. Rather unusual fabric.

65. CT-Black burnished (Pl. 4)
Biscuit: Black with white grits (5mm). Surface: Black burnished slip, especially preserved on inside. Shape: Base with recessed bottom. D 8. Decoration: None. Comments: Handmade.

66. KW– unburnished (Pl. 4)
Biscuit: Strong brown (7.5YR 5/6) rather coarse, sand-tempered, flaking fabric with many small and larger stone grits (3mm). Surface: Smoothed. Shape: Flat splaying rounded rim of a "Fruchtschale". D 20. Decoration: None. Comments: Handmade. Rather unusual fabric.

67. KW (Pl. 4)
Biscuit: Strong brown (7.5YR 5/6) coarse tempered, flaking fabric with many small and larger stone grits (3mm). Surface: Smoothed. Shape: Circular plate. D 9/ H 1.2. Decoration: None.

Various
- two ring bases
- two flat bases
- one vertical, flat oval handle
- one vertical rounded handle
- one vertical strap handle
- several smaller jars/cups/bowls with thin incurved rims

See also catalogue of flint and obsidian (below p. 110)

Tx43/4

(Bag nos. 1436 (06.07.98), 1603 (07.07.98))

STATISTICS:

	No.	Weight:
Intrusions: Ten small FT sherds are of later date, three might be Mycenaean. Two small sherds are probably Archaic.		
MT-unburnished	151	1.700 gr
MT-Red burnished	46	500 gr
MT-Black burnished	33	250 gr
CT-unburnished	130	2.400 gr
CT-Red burnished	24	500 gr
CT-Black burnished	27	650 gr
KW-sand-tempered	12	200 gr

Shapes

68. MT-unburnished (Pl. 5)
Biscuit: Reddish yellow (more red than 5YR 6/8), homogeneous sandy fabric with many white (lime) grits (1mm) and a few black grits. Surface: idem. Smoothed. Shape: Large bowl or plate with narrowly carinated, rounded rim. D 30. Decoration: None. Comments: Handmade.

69. MT-unburnished (Pl. 5)
Biscuit: Reddish yellow (more red than 5YR 6/8), homogeneous fabric with white (lime) grits and a few silver mica grits–voids. A few larger grits (5mm). Surface: Smoothed. Shape: Close shaped hemispherical jar with inturned rounded rim. D 30. Decoration: None. Comments: Handmade.

70. MT-unburnished (Pl. 5)
Biscuit: Reddish yellow (5YR 6/8) rather fine, sandy fabric with a few, small white (lime) grits (1mm). Surface: Smoothed. Shape: Closed shaped jar with concave collar and out-turned, pointed rim. D 30. Decoration: None. Comments: Handmade.

71. MT-unburnished (Pl. 5)
Biscuit: Reddish yellow (5YR 7/8) rather fine, sandy fabric with a few smaller white (lime) grits. Surface: Smoothed. Shape: Large bowl with splayed, thick flat rim. D 40. Decoration: None. Comments: Handmade.

72. MT-unburnished (Pl. 5)
Biscuit: Margins: Light red (2.5YR 6/8) fabric with white (lime) and black inclusions (2mm). Core: Darker. Surface: Smoothed. Shape: Flat bottom of open vessel. D 10. Decoration: None. Comments: Handmade.

73. MT-Red burnished (Pl. 5)
Biscuit: Reddish yellow (5YR 7/6) rather sandy, soft fabric with white (lime) and black grits (3mm) and lots of silver mica. Surface: Reddish yellow (5YR 6/6) slipped and burnished – in and out. Horizontally flattened bands where the burnished surface is registered. Shape: Bowl with inturned, pointed rim. D 19. Decoration: None. Comments: Handmade.

74. MT-Red burnished (Pl. 5)
Biscuit: Reddish yellow (more red than 5YR 6/8), homogeneous fabric with white (lime) inclusions. Surface: idem (on outside). On the inside light red (10YR 6/6) burnished (hor-

Fig. 25. Aghia Triada, Area I. Catalogue no. 75 (MT-Red burnished).

izontal lines from burnishing). Shape: Open vessel. D 32. Decoration: Black paint on rim. Comments: Handmade.

75. MT-Red burnished (Pl. 5 and Fig. 25)
Biscuit: Reddish yellow (5YR 6/8) with white (lime) and black grits (3mm) and a few silver mica grits. Surface: idem. On inside Reddish yellow (5YR 6/6) burnished with horizontal, flat zones where the burnishing is placed. Shape: Wall from an open jar. Decoration: Raised band with U-shaped grooves. Comments: Handmade.

76. MT-Red burnished (Pl. 5)
Biscuit: Light red (2.5YR 6/8) rather fine, sandy fabric with a few smaller white (lime) grits. Surface: Red (10R 5/6) slightly burnished slip. Shape: Asymmetrical strap handle. Decoration: None. Comments: Handmade.

77. CT-unburnished (Pl. 5)
Biscuit: Core: Black. Margins: Reddish yellow (7.5YR 7/6). Large, white/light brown stone grits (10mm). Surface: Smoothed. Shape: Small jar with vertical, pointed rim. D 18. Decoration. –. Comments: Handmade.

78. CT-unburnished (Pl. 5)
Biscuit: Reddish yellow (5YR 6/8) with large stone grits (light brown/brown) (11mm). Surface: Smoothed – colour idem. Shape: Large hemispherical basin with thickened, pointed rim. D 32. Decoration: None. Comments: Handmade.

79. CT-Red burnished (Pl. 5)
Biscuit: Gray/brown with white (lime) grits and stones (4mm) brown and black rather coarse ware. Surface: Red (2.5YR 4/6) slipped, burnished (only out ?). Shape: Pedestal base of a "fruitstand". D 20. Decoration: None. Comments: Handmade.

80. KW (Pl. 5)
Biscuit: Core: Black, very hard. Margins: Yellowish red (5YR 5/6). Small white grits – one large white stone (5mm). Surface: idem (margin). Shape: Jar with vertical thickened

rim. D 22. Decoration: None. Comments: Handmade. Cooking ware.

Various
- Vertical handle with oval section (MT)
- Vertical handle with oval section (Coarse–sand-tempered, grits (3mm), very hard)
- Thickened rim of a square basin
- Flat bowl with thick, incurved rim

See also catalogue of flint/obsidian (Tx 43/STR 4).

Tx43/4b

(Bag nos. 1437 (06.07.98), 1604 (07.07.98), 1606 (07.07.98), 1610 (08.07.98), 1612 (08.07.98), 1703 (10.07.98))

Stratigraphical comments: Bag no. 1612: A majority of large "kitchen equipment" – found close to fireplace (ADD-1). Bag no. 1612: Series of large sherds (pithoi-coarse kitchen equipment). Wall thickness 2,7 cm. Decoration: Horizontal plastic bevels. Flat bases and large strap handles.

STATISTICS:	No.	Weight:
Later intrusions are very few:		
LHIII: 7 and Archaic-Hellenistic: 7		
MT-unburnished	62	800 gr
MT-Red burnished	39	650 gr
MT-Black burnished	16	200 gr
CT-unburnished	303	7.450 gr
CT-Red burnished	88	1.350 gr
CT-Black burnished	72	700 gr
KW-sand-tempered	46	750 gr
NB! Coarse tempered clay with straw tempering and large grits probably derive from a fireplace	5	600 gr

Shapes

81. MT-unburnished (Pl. 6)
Biscuit: Black rather fine, hard fired fabric with white/black/brown grits (2mm). Surface: Smoothed. Reddish yellow (5YR 6/6). Shape: Globular jar with vertical high neck and carination at the transition to the rounded rim. D 18. Decoration: None. Comments: Handmade.

82. MT-unburnished (Pl. 6)
Biscuit: Core: black. Margin: Red (2.5YR 6/8) rather fine tempered. Grits (some white)(2mm). Surface: Well smoothed. Shape: Jar with thickened, rounded rim. D 32. Decoration: Incisions at rim. Comments: Handmade.

83. MT- unburnished (Pl. 6)
Biscuit: Light red (2.5YR 7/8) hard fabric with small white

grits and a few larger grits (3mm). Surface: Smoothed. Shape: Bowl with inturned, pointed rim. D 22. Decoration: None. Comments: Handmade.

84. MT-unburnished (Pl. 6)
Biscuit: Reddish yellow (5YR 7/8), sandy fabric, rather fine tempered but with white (lime) grits and red/grey (3mm). Surface: Smoothed. Shape: Jar with incurving, pointed rim. D 36. Decoration: Raised horizontal band or fillet (Weisshaar tp. b1). Comments: Handmade.

85. MT-unburnished (Pl. 6)
Biscuit: Core: black. Margin: Red (2.5YR 6/8) rather fine tempered. Grits (some white) (2mm). Surface: Well smoothed. Shape: Jar with thickened, rounded rim. D 32. Decoration: Incisions at rim. Comments: Handmade.

86. MT-unburnished (Pl. 6)
Biscuit: Light red (2.5YR 6/8) with small stone grits (2mm). Surface: Smoothed. Shape: Bowl with slightly outturned vertical, rounded rim. D 32. Decoration: None. Comments: Handmade.

87. MT-unburnished (Pl. 6)
Bowl with inturned, rounded rim. D 22.

88. MT-unburnished (Pl. 6)
Biscuit: Black, very hard fabric with a few small, white grits. Surface: Smoothed, black surface. Shape: Hemispherical jar with incurved, pointed rim. D 15. Decoration: None. Comments: Handmade. Unusual fabric and shape.

89. MT-Red burnished (Pl. 6)
Biscuit: Core: black. Margin: Reddish yellow (5YR 6/8) hard fabric, white/grey grits. Surface: Traces of red (Light red 2.5YR 6/8) on inside. Shape: Bowl, slightly thickened outside wall and flat rim. D 32. Decoration: None. Comments: Parallel horizontal grooves on inside.

90. MT-Red burnished (Pl. 6)
Biscuit: Reddish yellow (5YR 6/8), rather fine clay with small white grits, a few larger (3mm). Surface: Red (10YR 5/6) burnished slip. Shape: Flat bottom, open vessel. D 6. Decoration: None. Comments: Handmade.

91. MT-Red burnished (Pl. 6)
Biscuit: Red (2.5YR 6/8) rather fine, hard fabric with white (lime) grits (2mm). Surface: Red (10YR 4/6) thick well burnished slip on in- and outside. Shape: Open bowl with splaying, rounded rim. D 25. Decoration: None. Comments: Handmade. Excellent product.

92. MT-Black burnished (Pl. 6)
Biscuit: Black with hard, fine fabric. White/brown grits (2mm). Surface: Black burnished on outside. Shape: Hemispherical jar with incurving thickened rounded rim. D 22. Decoration: None. Comments: Handmade.

93. MT-Black burnished (Pl. 6)
Biscuit: Red (2.5YR 6/8) rather fine, hard fabric with small white grits (2mm). Surface: Light red (2.5YR 7/6) unburnished slip on outside. Black burnished on inside. Shape: Jar with funnel shaped neck. D 16. Decoration: None.

Fig. 26. Aghia Triada, Area I. Catalogue no. 98 (CT-unburnished, "Terrazzo-ware").

Comments: Handmade. Rather unusual fabric and shape. Import?

94. MT- Black burnished (Pl. 6)
Biscuit: Red (2.5YR 6/8) hard fabric rather fine tempered with many white and grey grits (2mm). Surface: Black burnished on outside. Smoothed and burnished on inside. Shape: Bowl with inturned, pointed rim. D 14. Decoration: None. Comments: Handmade.

95. MT-Black burnished (Pl. 6)
Biscuit: Core: black. Margins: Red (2.5YR 6/8) very hard, sandy fabric with small white (lime) and grey/black grits (1mm). Surface: Black burnished slip on inside. Shape: Small hemispherical jar with incurving, pointed rim (hole mouth jar). D. 20. Decoration: Raised band with tactile decoration. Comments: Handmade.

96. CT-unburnished (Pl. 7)
Biscuit: Black with white/brown stone inclusions (4mm)Surface: Smoothed on outside. Inside with parallel incisions from an instrument (a "comb"). Shape: Small hole mouth jar with concave collar and pointed rim. D 14. Decoration: None. Comments: Handmade - but "combed" on inside. Late Neolithic.

97. CT-unburnished (Pl. 7)
Biscuit: Reddish yellow (5YR 6/8) coarse, hard fabric with large grits, white (lime) and grey (4mm). Surface: Smoothed. Inside: black. Outside: Reddish yellow.Shape: Wall of a pithos—with knob. Decoration: None. Comments: Handmade.

98. CT-unburnished (Pl. 7 and Fig. 26)
Biscuit: Black with white stone grits (5mm) and a few black grits. Surface: Smoothed. Terrazzo ware. Shape: Bowl with T-rim. D 34. Decoration: Raised band below rim. Comments: Handmade.

99. CT-unburnished (Pl. 7)
Biscuit: Yellowish red (5YR 5/8) coarse fabric. White/black

Fig. 27. Aghia Triada, Area I. Catalogue no. 100 (CT-unburnished).

Fig 28. Aghia Triada, Area I. Catalogue no. 105 (KW-sand-tempered).

grits (5mm). Surface: Smoothed. Shape: Flat bottom of a large basin. D 16. Decoration: None. Comments: Handmade.

100. CT-unburnished (Pl. 7 and Fig. 27)
Biscuit: Reddish yellow (5YR 6/8) rather fine tempered fabric with stone grits, mainly white (3mm) and straw. Surface: Smoothed on outside. Back unworked. Shape: Plate of clay (5 joining pieces). Groove on inside probably indicates horizontal position (see drawing Pl. 7). Decoration: Grooves on outside. Comments: Handmade coarse.

101. CT-unburnished (Pl. 7)
Biscuit: Red (2.5YR 5/8) very hard fabric with many smaller stones and a few larger grits (3mm). Surface: Smoothed. Shape: Bowl or jar with everted, thickened rim. D 22. Decoration: None. Comments: Handmade.

102. CT-Red burnished (Pl. 7)
Biscuit: Light red (2.5YR 6/8) fabric with white/and a few black grits (4mm). Surface: Light red (10YR 6/6) red burnished – in and out. Shape: Bowl with everted flat collar (probably from a "fruitstand"). D (inside) 26. Decoration: None. Comments: Handmade but with parallel lines/grooves on inside – slow wheel.

103. CT-Red burnished (Pl. 7)
Biscuit: Red (2.5YR 5/8) coarse fabric with white (stone) grits (3mm). Surface: Red (10R 5/6) burnished slip, in and out. Shape: Flat bottom of a large bowl. D 14. Decoration: None. Comments: Handmade.

104. CT-Red burnished (Pl. 7)
Biscuit: Reddish yellow (5YR 6/8) rather fine, sandy fabric with white and black grits (3mm). Surface: Red (2.5YR 5/6) burnished slip (in-and-out). Shape: Large basin with lug handle (a flat trapezoidal extension) at rim. D (app.) 26. Decoration: None. Comments: Handmade.

105. KW-sand-tempered (Pl. 7 and Fig. 28)
Biscuit: Yellowish (5YR 5/6) very hard, dense fabric, sand-tempered with many small white (lime) grits. Very few larger grits. Surface: Finely smoothed. Shape: Closed shape (?) ... body sherd. Decoration: Slightly raised band with finger grooves. Comments: Handmade.

Various
- Dark burnished square basin (?)
- One MT-black burnished sherd with incurved rim
- Three bowls with pointed rim
- One basin
- MT-unburnished pointed rim
- CT vertical strap handle
- Vertical strap handle. MT-Red burnished
- Vertical handle–oval section (CT/KW- sand-tempered)
- One CT-unburnished horizontal handle with oval section
- CT-horizontal, oval handle
- Horizontal handle-oval section (CT/KW- sand-tempered)
- One CT-unburnished with a knob
- One base of a large jar (base: 2,8 cm thick)
- Base CT

See also Catalogue of flint/obsidian (Tx 43/STR 4b)

Tx43/5

(Bag no. 1616 (08.07.98)

STATISTICS:	No.	Weight:
No later intrusions		
MT-unburnished	2	

MT-Red burnished	1	
MT-Black burnished	2	
CT-unburnished	7	150 gr
CT-Red burnished	3	100 gr

Shapes

106. MT-unburnished (Pl. 7)
Biscuit: Light red (2.5YR 6/8) hard fabric with white stone grits (2mm). Surface: Smoothed. Shape: Hemispherical jar with incurved mouth and rounded rim. D 16. Decoration: None. Comments: Handmade.

107. CT-unburnished (Pl. 7)
Biscuit: Light red (2.5YR 6/8) with fine, white grits and larger grits (typical coarse w.). Surface. Smoothed. Inside with parallel, incised lines. Shape: Ring base. D 12. Decoration: Comments: Handmade. LN.

Tx 20

Tx20/3

(Bag nos.180 (04.07.97), 225 (03.07.97)[177]

STATISTICS:	No.	Weight
Intrusions: 1 Mycenaean sherd		
MT-unburnished	37	500 gr
MT-Red burnished	16	100 gr
MT-Black burnished	4	50 gr
CT-unburnished	28	1.050 gr
KW (MT, sand-tempered)	32	200 gr
"White Ware"	4	50 gr

Shapes

108. MT-unburnished (Pl. 8)
Biscuit: Reddish yellow (5YR 7/6) rather fine, soft fabric with a few white lime grits, black and red stones (2mm). Surface: idem smoothed. Shape: Jar with everted collar and rounded rim. D 24. Decoration: None. Comments: Handmade. Could be imported, not typical local clay.

109. MT-unburnished (Pl. 8)
Biscuit: Light red (2.5YR 6/8) rather soft, sandy fabric with white and black inclusions (2mm). Surface: idem smoothed. Shape: Hemispherical jar with incurved, rounded rim. D 24. Decoration: None. Comments: Handmade.

110. MT-unburnished (Pl. 8)
Biscuit: Core: Black. Margin: Light red (10YR 6/8), rather fine fabric with white (lime) grits. Surface: Smoothed. Shape: Small, shallow bowl with thickened, hooked rim. D 20. Decoration: None. Comments: Handmade.

111. CT-unburnished (Pl. 8)
Biscuit: Very pale brown (10YR 8/3) coarse tempered fabric

with large red/brown grits (5mm). Surface: Smoothed. Shape: Sherd with an incipient horizontal handle and raised band. Decoration: Plastic, horizontal rib. Comments: Light, unusual fabric – not local.

Various

- 2 CT vertical oval handles
- Sherd with a plastic line

Flint and obsidian (Tx20/3):
F97-4007: Obsidian
F97-4008: Flint
F97-4009: Obsidian
(04.07.97: 1 bag of flint)

Tx20/3a

(Bag no. 188 (04.07.97))
Insignificant material, no intrusions (nothing drawn).

---

[177] Tx 20 notes on various selected strata (see Fig. 21):
Tx20/2. Bag no. 78 (30.06.97). Mixed Layer

STATISTICS:	No.	Weight
Classical/Hellenistic	64	850 gr
EH:	43	1100 gr

CT – Red burnished/one Black burnished
MT sand-tempered/"Terrazzo ware"
One T-rim basin/
MH/LH:
One handle from a kantharos
Tx20/2a. Bag no. 131 (01.07.97)
Classical/Hellenistic
Tx20/2a. Bag no. 262 (07.07.97)
One prehistoric sherd - the rest (900 gr) are Archaic/Classical
Tx20/2a. Bag no.187. (03.07.97)
Archaic/Classical - 6 Prehistoric sherds
Tx20/2a. Bag no. 206. (03.07.97/
1 Prehistoric Sherd - the rest are Archaic/Classical
Tx20/2b. Bag no. 146. (02.07.97). Mixed stratum.

STATISTICS:	No.	Weight
Handmade EH	49	500 gr
Later sherds	9	

Tx20/3h (NE). Bag no. 871. (22.07.97)
Classical/Hellenistic
Tx20/3 (NE). Bag. no. 873. (22.07.97)
Classical/Hellenistic
Tx20/3g (NE). Bag no.: 880. (22.07.97)
Classical/Hellenistic
Tx20/3i (NE). Bag No. 927. (23.07.97)
Classical/Hellenistic

STATISTICS:	No.	Weight
MT-unburnished	1	-
MT-Red burnished	2	-
MT-Black burnished	1	-
CT-unburnished (one "Terrazzo ware")	12	200 gr

Various

- One sherd (MT) with list (rib)
- Fragment of horizontal handle (MT). sand-tempered, white lime grits
- Sand-tempered disc ?
- Flat base

Flint and obsidian:
(04.07.97: 1 bag of flint)

Tx20/3b

(Bag no. 300 (07.07.97)
Insignificant material, no later intrusions (nothing drawn).

STATISTICS:	No.	Weight
MT-unburnished	3	50 gr
MT-Red burnished	2	-
(One sherds with white lime cover on inside)		
MT-Black burnished	3	-
CT-unburnished	3	100 gr
KW (MT–sand-tempered)	4	50 gr

Various

F97-4011 (Bag no. 313): wattle and daub
F97-4013 (Bag no. 314): wattle and daub

Tx20/3c

(Bag no. 299 (07.07.97))
Insignificant material, no later intrusions (nothing drawn).

STATISTICS:	No.	Weight:
MT-unburnished	1	-
MT-Red burnished	1	-
CT-unburnished	8	200 gr
CT-Black burnished	1	-
KW (MT-sand-tempered)	4	200 gr

Tx20/3d

(Bag no. 298 (07.07.97))
Insignificant material, no later intrusions (nothing drawn).

STATISTICS:	No.	Weight:
MT-Red burnished	1	-
MT-Black burnished	1	-
CT-unburnished	14	200 gr
KW (MT-sand-tempered)	5	50 gr

Various

F97-4014 (Bag no. 211): Double handle
F97-4015 (Bag no. 228): Charcoal

Tx20/4

(Bag no. 352 (08.07.97))

STATISTICS:	No.	Weight
No later intrusions		
MT-Red burnished	4	50 gr
CT-unburnished	24	350 gr
CT-Black burnished	3	50 gr
MT/KW (in these layers the usual MT is sand-tempered)	15	150 gr

Shapes

112. MT-Red burnished (Pl. 8)
Biscuit: Red (2.5YR 5/8) fine hard fabric with small white (lime) grits, silver mica and a few larger grits (2mm). Surface: Red (10R 5/6) red burnished slip on in-and outside. Shape: Bowl with splayed, rounded rim. D 28. Decoration: None. Comments: Handmade.

113. MT-Red burnished (Pl. 8)
Biscuit: Red (2.5YR 6/8) hard fabric with small white grits (1mm). Surface: Red (10YR 4/6) burnished slip on in-and outside. Shape: Shallow bowl with slightly inturned, rounded rim. D 20. Decoration: None. Comments: Handmade.

Tx20/4a

(Bag no. 307 (08.07.97))

STATISTICS:	No.	Weight
Later intrusions: One Mycenaean sherd		
MT-unburnished	6	50 gr
MT-Red burnished	7	100 gr
MT-Black burnished	2	50 gr
CT-unburnished	8	250 gr
KW (MT sand-tempered)	3	50 gr

Fig. 29. Aghia Triada, Area I. MT-unburnished, horizontal lug handle (Tx20/4b).

Various

- One part of a vertical handle (CT-unburnished)
- One rim of a bowl with thin rim

Tx20/4b

(Bag nos. 302 (09.07.97) and 492 (10.07.97))

STATISTICS:

	No.	Weight
No later intrusions		
MT–Red burnished	10	100 gr
MT–Black burnished	6	50 gr
CT–unburnished ★	75	2.200 gr
KW–sand-tempered	71	750 gr

MT-imported (?) Three pieces with black core and margins: Red yellow (5YR 6/8) very well smoothed or slipped matt surface.
★ Large sherds of pithoi. Stone grits 10mm. Some with red and black unburnished slip

Shapes

114. MT-unburnished (Pl. 8)
Biscuit: Red (2.5YR 6/8) rather sandy fabric with white (lime) and grey stone grits. Surface: Smoothed. Shape: Flat bottom. Slightly concave wall. D 8. Decoration: None. Comments: Handmade.

115. MT-unburnished (Pl. 8)
Biscuit: Red (2.5YR 6/8) rather fine, hard clay fabric with small white (lime) and black/grey stone grits (2mm). Surface: Smoothed. Shape: Strap handle with central groove. Decoration: None. Comments: Handmade.

116. MT-unburnished (Pl. 8)
Biscuit: Red (10YR 6/8) dense fabric with many small white

Fig. 30. Aghia Triada, Area I. Two sherds from Tx20/4b. Vertical strap handle (CT-unburnished, "Terrazzo-ware") and a MT-unburnished sherd with plastic list and finger marks.

(lime) (1mm) grits. Surface: Smoothed. Shape: Horizontal handle with almost circular section. The handle is fixed directly on the surface. Decoration: None. Comments: Handmade.

117. CT-unburnished (Pl. 8)
Biscuit: Red (2.5YR 5/6) very coarse tempered fabric with large grits. Surface: Reddish yellow (7.5YR 6/6) matt slip. Shape: Flat bottom of a large closed shaped jar (?). D 12. Decoration: None. Comments: Handmade.

118. CT-Black burnished (Pl. 8)
Biscuit: Red (10YR 5/8) rather coarse fabric with white (lime) (3mm) and black/grey grits. Surface: Outside: Black burnished slip. Inside: Smoothed Red. Shape: Flat base of closed shaped jar. The wall is concave. D 9 (app.). Decoration: None. Comments: Handmade.

119. KW (CT-sand-tempered) (Pl. 8)
Biscuit: Red (2.5YR 6/8) hard sand-tempered fabric with white (lime) (3mm) and grey stone grits. Surface: idem smoothed. Shape: Basin with thickened flat rim. D 46. Decoration: None. Comments: Handmade.

120. KW (MT-sand-tempered) (Pl. 8)
Biscuit: Red (2.5YR 6/8) hard sand-tempered fabric with white (lime) (2mm) and grey/black stone grits. Surface: idem. Smoothed. Shape: Open bowl with splayed, slightly inturned rim. D 28. Decoration: None. Comments: Handmade.

Fig. 32. Aghia Triada, Area I. Vertical strap handle. Black burnished (MT-sand-tempered). Tx20/4b.

dle with oval section and a MT-unburnished sherd with plastic bevel and finger imprints (Fig. 30).
- F97-4016: polished bone point.

Tx20/4b

Various other bags

Tx20/4b: Bag No. 551. (15.07.97)
    Later intrusions: Four Hellenistic sherds.
Tx20/4b: Bag No. 304. (08.07.97)
    Three sherds from same vessel. Red slipped, slightly burnished.
Tx20/4b: Bag No. 306. (08.07.97)
    CT+MT sand-tempered. CT handle/body (from ADD-1) sherd and a white lime cover on the inside. MT-unburnished base (Fig. 31).
Tx20/4b: Bag no. 492. (10.07.97)
    Vertical strap handle. MT-sand-tempered, black burnished ("Urfirnis") (Fig. 32).

N 26/N 27

The Deposit (Fig. 8a): Fig. 33 shows a section through trenches N 26 and N 27 and a schematic survey of the strata excavated. Prehistoric material was found especially with structures AFL and AFU. Both layers are fill from deposits higher up the slope and only a very selected amount of material has been treated in the catalogue (see also various below N 27, and n. 178).

Fig. 31. Aghia Triada, Area I. CT- handle/body sherd and a MT-unburnished base. Tx20/4b.

121. KW (MT-sand-tempered) (Pl. 8)
Biscuit: Red (10R 5/8) hard sand-tempered fabric with small white (lime) grits. Surface: idem. Smoothed. Shape: Hemispherical jar with incurved rim. D.20. Decoration: Raised band with finger impressed grooves. Comments: Handmade.

122. KW (MT-sand-tempered) (Pl. 8)
Biscuit: Red (10YR 5/8) hard sand-tempered, rather fine fabric with small white (lime) and silver grits. Surface: Red slipped (unburnished). Shape: Clay bevel from an open shaped vessel. Decoration: The clay bevel is fixed directly on the surface. Comments: Handmade.

123. KW (MT-sand-tempered) (Pl. 8)
Biscuit: Black, hard, dense fabric with many small white (lime) and grey stone (2mm) grits. Surface: Smoothed. Shape: Strap handle. Decoration: None. Comments: Handmade. NB! The handles are "glued" directly on the surface (cf. above no. 122.)

Various
- One MT-unburnished horizontal lug handle (Fig. 29)
- One CT-unburnished ("terrazzo ware") vertical strap han-

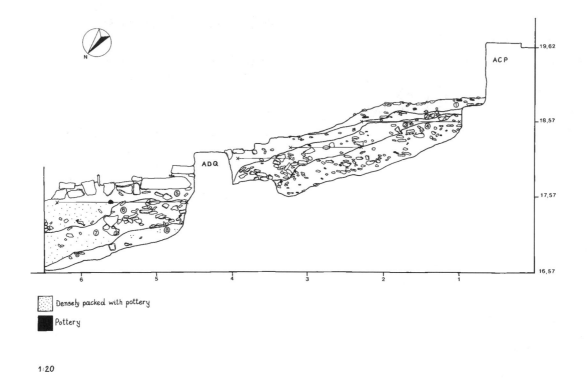

Densely packed with pottery

Pottery

1:20

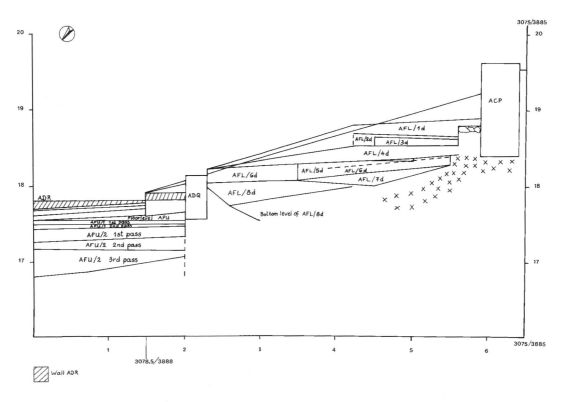

Fig. 33. Aghia Triada, Area I. Section through trenches N26 and N27. 1:50.

N26

N26/AFU/2 1st pass

(Bag no. 3360 (13.07.97))
Mainly MHIII/LHI – but also quite an amount of EH. 25 Archaic sherds.

Shapes

124. MT (Pl. 9)
Biscuit: Light red (2.5YR 6/6) fine tempered hard fabric with white (lime) inclusions (2mm) and red stone grits. Surface: Smoothed. Shape: Low pedestal base of bowl. Not entirely preserved. D 7. Decoration: Badly preserved MP. Yellowish red band (5YR 6/6) around "stem". More paintings on the body (in- and outside). Comments: Handmade. Worn with hard lime cover. MHIII/LHI.

125. CT-unburnished (Pl. 9)
Biscuit: Light reddish brown /5YR 6/4) very coarse fabric with lime grits (3mm) and black stone grits (5mm). Almost "terrazzo ware". One large concentration of lime (10x8mm) in break. Surface: Smoothed. Shape: Ring base. D 12. Decoration: None. Comments: Handmade. EH.

126. CT-unburnished (Pl. 9)
Biscuit: Core: Grey coarse fabric. Margins: Light red (2.5YR 6/8) with stone grits (5mm). Surface: Same colour. Smoothed. Shape: Large T-rim bowl/basin. D more than 40. Decoration: None. Comments: Handmade. EH.

127. MT (Pl. 9)
Biscuit: Core: Gray. Margin: Reddish yellow (5YR 7/6) hard fabric with red and white (lime) grits (5mm). Surface: Same colour. Smoothed. Shape: Triangular handle. Decoration: None. Comments: Handmade. Probably MH/LHI.

128. FT (Pl. 9)
Biscuit: Reddish yellow (5YR 7/6) fine hard fabric. No visible grits. Surface: Smoothed. Black burnished on outside(?). Shape: Bowl with inturned thin rim. D 14. Decoration: None. Comments: Handmade. FT is very unusual in EHI.

Various

- Two stems (bowl/goblet)(MH/LH)
- One ring-base (MH/LH)
- Vertical strap handle

N 27

Various (N27)

All strata from N27 AFU are fill - mixed EH/MH/ARCH[178].

N27/AFU/1 2nd pass

(Bag no. 3470 (22.07.99))
Mixture of Archaic and EH.

Shapes

129. CT-unburnished/burnished (?) (Pl. 9)
Biscuit: Core: Gray. Margins: Light red (10R 6/6) with white stone inclusions (5mm). Silver mica grits. Surface: Smoothed. Slightly red burnished. Shape: Knob on the wall of a vessel. Decoration: None. Comments: Handmade.

130. MT-unburnished (Pl. 9)
Biscuit: Core: Greyish/brown. Margins: Light red 82.5YR 6/8). Black and red stone inclusions (3mm). Surface: Smoothed. Shape: T-rim bowl. D 25. Decoration: None. Comments: Handmade.

Various

- One body fragment/handle (EH)

N27/AFU/2 3rd pass

(Bag No. 3490 (28.07.99))
EH – Mainly CT sherds/+MT sand-tempered; MH. One sherd. MP on creamy white. 10 to 15 Archaic sherds.

Shapes

131. CT-unburnished (Pl. 9)
Biscuit: Core: Grey. Margins: Light red (5YR 6/8) hard fabric with many stone grits (5mm). "Terrazzo Ware". Surface: Smoothed. Shape: Conical ring base and part of body. D 10. Decoration: None. Comments: Handmade. EH (I?).

132. MT-unburnished (Pl. 9)
Biscuit: Core: Grey. Margins: Light red (2.5YR 6/8) hard fabric with white/black stone grits (2mm). Surface: Smoothed. Shape: Jar with outturned rim. D 25. Decoration: None. Comments: Handmade. EH.

---

[178] **N27/AFU2** 2nd pass. Bag No. 3474. (26.07.99). Mixture of Arch./EH and MH (MP + GM).
N27/AFU2 3rd pass. Bag No. 3480. (26.07.99) Mixed Prehistoric/Archaic.
N27/AFU2 3rd pass. Bag No. 3481. (27.07.99) Mixed stratum containing: EH: - Strap handle - CT-unburnished - No Red/Black burnished. MH: (majority) - MP. Two sherds with strap handle - CT. Horizontal handle with triangular section - MT. Goblet stems – three pieces
N27/AFU 3rd pass. Bag No. 3364. (23.07.99) Mixed Archaic/BA.

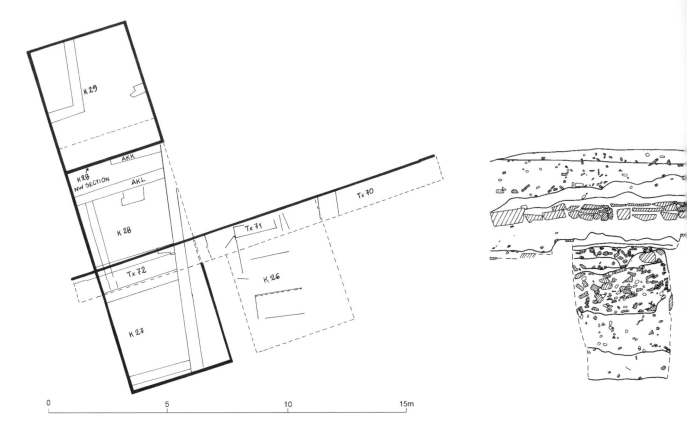

Fig. 34. Aghia Triada, Area II. Plan showing trench numbers and sections drawn in the area West of Aghia Triada.

133. CT-unburnished (Pl. 9)
Biscuit: Core: Black/grey. Margins: Light red (2.5YR 6/8) very hard fabric with many stone grits (11mm) and lime grits. Surface: Smoothed. Shape: Round bottom of a large pithos(?). Decoration: None. Comments: Handmade.

Aghia Triada Area II

Excavations were conducted in the years 1998 to 2001 in the level area west of the Aghia Triada (Area II) towards the stream and the present village of Kato Vasiliki (Fig. 8b). Fig. 34 shows the trench number system and indicates the sections drawn in the area. See also back cover.

Tx70/Tx71/Tx72

The Deposit: Fig. 35 (heights above sea level) shows the section drawn of the southern side of the 1 metre broad, 15 metre long trial trench opened in the area. The upper strata are first of all

Archaic, but even some later material has been found. The layers are described as follows:

Tx70 (Analytical plan on Fig. 36). The upper levels (strata 1 to 4) mainly contain pottery from Archaic, Classical and Hellenistic periods. Lime/mortar and some Byzantine material were found in the uppermost layers.

The prehistoric deposits are found in an approximately 0.8 metre deep pit in the bedrock. Larger stones were found in STR 5 and even more stones in STR 5a. Soil colour, light olive brown (2.5Y 5/4). Some charcoal is found in the two levels.

Tx72 In this trench excavations were carried out in a 3.5 to 4 metre deep sounding down to the ground water level (sea level=0). An analytical plan I is seen on Fig. 37. The strata are described as follows:
STR 1: Surface soil with a lot of white (lime) stones, some tiles, sherds, shells and a few bones. Colour: Dusky red (2.5YR 4/3).
STR 2: A light clayish more dense (compact) soil

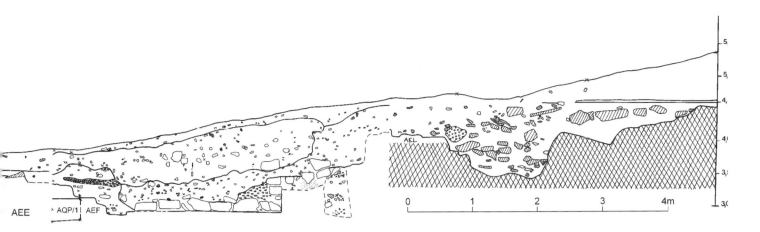

Fig. 35. Aghia Triada, Area II. Section Tx70/Tx71/Tx72.

with sherds, tiles, shells and some bones. Colour: Red (2.5YR 6/6-5/6).

STR 3: Character as STR 2. Colour: Light olive brown (2.5Y 5/3-5/4).

STR 4: Clayish, crumbly(?) soil with many tiny sherd fragments, some pieces of charcoal and concentrations of yellow soil. Colour: Light olive brown /olive brown (2.5Y 5/4-4/4).

STR 5: Sandy moist soil with lots of small sherds and many medium sized stones. Colour: Light olive brown (2.5Y 5/4). Floor level?

STR 6: Dark, crumbly soil with lots of small, packed with large-medium, irregular stones. Colour: Brown-Dark yellowish brown (10YR 4/3-4/4).

STR 6a: Against wall AEI, yellowish, sandy soil with small pieces of charcoal and small sherd fragments. Colour: Yellowish brown (10YR 5/4-5/6)

STR 7: Thin layer of sandy soil without sherds and stones. In STR 6 against wall AEI. Colour: Light yellowish brown (2.5Y 6/4).

STR 8: Very hard, dry clayish soil with small sherd fragments. Colour: Very dark greyish brown (10YR 3/2).

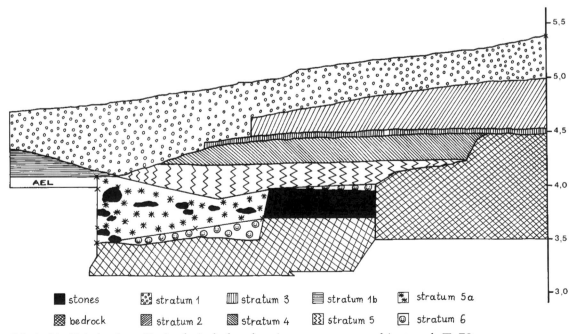

Fig. 36. Aghia Triada, Area II. Analytical plan showing strata excavated in trench Tx70.

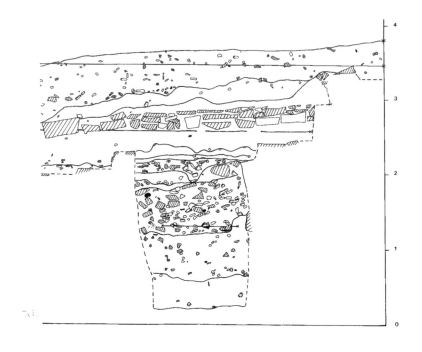

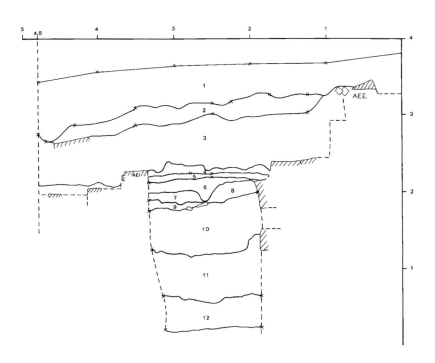

Fig. 37. Aghia Triada, Area II. Analytical plan I showing excavated strata measured in the deep sounding in trench Tx72. 1:50.

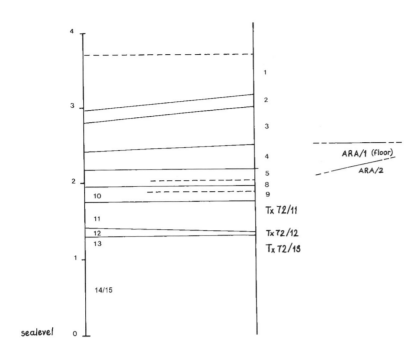

STR 9: As STR 8 but more reddish.

STR 10: Clayish crumbly soil with tiny stones, small sherds and charcoal. Colour: Light olive brown (2.5Y 5/6).

STR 11: Clayish, compact soil with stone filling and some sherds. Colour: Olive brown (2.5Y 4/3).

STR 12: Yellow, clayish soil with sand stone flakes, charcoal and bones.

STR 13: Soft, clayish wet soil with little pottery, sand stone flakes. Colour: Dark yellowish brown (10YR 4/4).

STR 14: Fat, clayish wet soil with pieces of charcoal, flint and obsidian. Colour: Dark yellowish brown (10YR 4/6)

STR 15: As STR 14.

The analytical plan Fig. 38 is a survey of excavation levels in the deep sounding in Tx72. The prehistoric levels are found from STR 10, lower than approximately 2 metres above present sea level. The uppermost part of this stratum, however, is rather mixed with Archaic material. Excavation stratum 11 is a Middle Helladic/LHI level without intrusions while the deeper levels contain Early Helladic material. In a slightly higher position, the structure ARA, probably a floor, mainly contains Mycenaean material, but with some Archaic intru-sions. As for the Mycenaean levels see below under trench K28.

Tx70

Tx70/5

(Bags nos. 1458 (09.07.98), 1794 (10.07.98), 1799 (10.07.98), 1800 (13.07.98), 1821 (13.07.98), 1826 (13.07.98) and 1828 (13.07.98))

STATISTICS:

(only made for Bag no. 1799) No later intrusions	No.	Weight:
FT	77	500 gr
MT/CT	64	700 gr
GM	3	
Black (lustrous?) painted	5	100 gr

Shapes

134. FT(2) (Pl. 10 and Fig. 39)
Biscuit: Reddish yellow (7.5YR 7/6). Very fine soft fabric with voids and small white stone inclusions. Surface: Reddish yellow (5YR 7/6). Slipped burnished. Decoration: Plain. Shape: Bowl with everted thin rim and wishbone handle. D 16. Comments: Probably handmade. Local fabric. F98-3025. Comp. catalogue no. 5. Pl. I.

135. FT(1) (Pl. 10)
Biscuit: Reddish yellow (5YR 7/6). Small white inclusions – one silver mica. Surface: Reddish yellow (5YR 7/6).

Fig. 39. Aghia Triada, Area II. Catalogue no. 134. Bowl with wish-bone handle.

Smoothed. Shape: Bowl with flat rim. D 30. Decoration: Plain. Comments: wheel-made.

136. FT(1) (Pl. 10)
Biscuit: High red (2.5YR 7/8). Grey core at thickened rim. No visible inclusions. Surface: idem. Smoothed. Shape: Bowl with lozenge shaped flat rim. D 16. Decoration: Plain. Comments: Handmade.

136a. FT (Pl. 10)
Biscuit: Reddish yellow (5YR 6/6). Fine tempered fabric with white and black inclusions (0.5mm). Surface: Reddish yellow (7.5YR 7/6). Shape: Flat base of a straightsided cup. Decoration: None. Comments: Handmade(?).

137. FT (1) (Fig. 40)
Biscuit: Fine tempered. Small dark inclusions (0,5mm). Powdery. Surface: Pink (7.5YR 8/4), with tinge of (5YR 8/4). Decoration: Plain. Shape: Pyramidal loom weight. Drilled hole. Comments: Handmade. F98-3024.

138. MT (Pl. 10)
Biscuit: Reddish yellow (5YR 7/6). White and red/brown inclusions. Surface: Reddish Yellow (5YR 7/6). Smoothed. Shape: Torus disc base of krater. D 16. Decoration: plain. Comments: Handmade (Further one bowl was found under this number).

139. MT (Pl. 10)
Biscuit: Reddish Yellow (7,5YR 7/6). Hard with white inclusions (one brown). Surface: idem. Smoothed. Shape: Jar with outturned thickened, flat rim. D 18. Decoration: MP. Brown band below rim. Comments: wheel-made(?).

Fig. 40. Aghia Triada, Area II. Loom-weight F98-3024 from Tx70/5.

140. MT (Pl. 10)
Biscuit: Core: Gray (5YR 6/1)/margin: Reddish brown (5YR 5/4). Numerous voids. Surface: Reddish yellow (5YR 7/6). Shape: Conical ("household") basin with lozenge shaped thick rim. D 32. Decoration: None. Comments: Handmade.

141. MT (Pl. 10)
Biscuit: Reddish yellow (7.5YR, 7/6). White stone inclusions (1mm). Surface: Reddish yellow (7.5YR 8/6). Waxy, yellow surface. Shape: Pedestalled base stem of goblet. D 4, 6. Decoration: None. Comments: Handmade.

142. MT (?) (Pl. 10)
Biscuit: Weak red (2.5YR 6/4). Surface: Reddish yellow (5YR 7/6). Shape: Basin with slightly offset rim. D 30. Decoration: None. Comments: Handmade?

143. MT (Pl. 10)
Biscuit: Weak red (2.5YR 5/4). White and dark inclusions (1mm). Many voids. Surface: Light red (2.5YR 7/6). Shape: Bowl with thickened lozenge shaped rim. D 16. Decoration: None. Comments: Comp. No. 136 (in FT).

144. MT (Pl. 10)

Biscuit: Reddish yellow (7.5YR 7/6). Numerous voids. Surface: Reddish yellow (7.5YR 7/6). "Waxy, yellow surface". Shape: Bowl with carination and protruding rim. D 24. Decoration: None. Comments: Handmade?

145. MT (Pl. 10)

Biscuit: Reddish Yellow (5YR 6/6) hard fabric. Brown and white inclusions. Irregular and elongated voids. Silver mica. Surface: Light brown (7.5YR 6/4)/Reddish yellow (7.5YR 6/6). Traces of "brown" paint on inside (reddish yellow (5YR 4/4). Shape: Pedestal base, stem and lower wall of bowl/kantharos. D 7,5. Decoration: Reddish yellow paint inside (5YR 4/4). Comments: Handmade. (five joining pieces).

146. KW (Pl. 10)

Biscuit: Core: Very dark grey (10YR 3/1). Margins: Reddish brown (5YR 4/3). Brown inclusions (4mm). Surface: Black, burnished. Shape: Jar with outturned, rounded rim. D 16. Decoration: None. Comments: Handmade?

147. GM (Pl. 10)

Biscuit: Grey, fine (rather soft). Surface: id. Shape: Small hemispherical jar with everted rim. Trace of vertical handle at rim. D 14. Decoration: Plain. Comments: Handmade.

148. "Grey Ware" (Pl. 10)

Biscuit: Pale olive (5Y 6/4). Very hard with small stone inclusions. Surface: Dark grey (5Y 4/1). Shape: Open vessel with vertical, flat rim. D 16. Decoration: Plain. Comments: wheel-made.

149. Lustrous painted (Pl. 10 and Fig. 41)

Biscuit: Reddish yellow (5YR 7/6), fine tempered fabric. White/grey inclusions (0.2mm). Numerous voids. Surface: Very pale brown (10YR 8/3-4) burnished slip on outside. Inside rough. Shape: Deep semi globular cup with everted, thin rim (FS 211). D 13. Decoration: Red (2.5YR 5/6) lustrous paint and added white. Lustrous paint on in–and outside of rim. Running open tangent spirals on body. Comments: Clear wheel traces. Slow wheel (F98-3020).

150. Lustrous painted (Pl. 10 and Fig. 42)

Biscuit: Reddish yellow (5YR 7/6), fine tempered fabric. Small voids. Surface: Very pale brown (10YR 8/3 ext.) burnished slip. Inside rough. Shape: Deep semi globular cup with everted, thin rim (FS 211). D 12. Decoration: (peeled) Red (2.5YR 5/6) and yellowish red (5YR 4/6) lustrous paint and added white. Lustrous paint on in–and outside of rim. Running open tangent spirals on body. Comments: Slow wheel (F98-3023).

Various

- One further FT rim of a plate
- Three band-shaped handles from kantharoi. One FT, slightly burnished (fabric: Reddish Yellow (7,5YR 7/8). Surface: very pale brown (10YR 8/4) (Yellow Minyan).
- One CT sherd with black paint.

Fig. 41. Aghia Triada, Area II. Catalogue no. 149. Cup with lustrous paint.

Fig. 42. Aghia Triada, Area II. Catalogue no. 150. Cup with lustrous paint.

Tx70/5a

(Bag no. 1830 (13.07.98)

STATISTICS:	No.	Weight
FT (1)	25	100 gr
FT (2)	1	
MT	35	300 gr
KW	25	350 gr

Shapes

151. MT (Pl. 11)

Biscuit: Reddish yellow (7.5YR 6/6) and grey, very hard fabric. Surface: Light brown (7.5YR 6/4). Shape: Closed shape with protruding flat outwards-sloping rim. D 14. Decoration: Traces of black paint on outside. Comments: Handmade? Hardly local!

152. MT (Pl. 11)

Biscuit: Reddish yellow (5YR 7/6). White stone inclusions

(1 mm). Surface: Reddish yellow (5YR 7/6). Shape: Flat handle (no lug). Decoration: None. Comments: Handmade?

153. KW (Pl. 11)
Biscuit: Core: Reddish brown (2.5YR 3/1). Coarse fabric. Surface: None. Shape: Lug-handle of a "household basin". Decoration: None. Comments: Handmade?

154. Lustrous painted (Pl. 11)
Biscuit: Reddish brown (5YR 5/4). Fine tempered. Surface: Light yellowish brown (10YR 6/4). Slipped and slightly burnished. Shape: Rim, body, handle of a carinated cup. D 15. Decoration: Black, lustrous paint on surface, out. Comments: wheel-made. Not local.

155. Lustrous painted (Pl. 11)
Biscuit: Reddish yellow (5YR 7/6). Fine tempered. Surface: Very pale brown slip (10YR 8/3-4). Slightly burnished. Shape: Small krater with cylindrical collar. D 18. Decoration: Traces of red, lustrous paint on rim, inside (2.5YR 5/6). The outside was totally covered with the red paint. Comments: Two other joints (rim) with well preserved colours!

Tx70/6

(Bag nos. 1831 (14.07.98), 1833 (14.07.98), 1834 (14.07.98), 1838 (14.07.98))

STATISTICS:	No.	Weight:
No later intrusions		
FT (1)	13	100 gr
FT (2)	4	
MT	125	1.800 gr
KW	49	1.300 gr
GM	1	

Shapes

156. FT(2) (Fig. 43)
Biscuit: Reddish yellow (7.5YR 7/6). Fine with small (1mm) white/black/brown inclusions. Surface: Reddish yellow (7.5YR 7/6). Burnished. Shape: Strap handle from a closed shaped jar. H 5, 5. Decoration: Black MP bands. Comments: wheel-made.

157. FT(2) (Pl. 11)
Biscuit: Reddish yellow (5YR 6/6). Surface: Pink (7.5YR 8/4). Slipped, burnished on outside. Shape: Jar with thickened flat rim. D 15. Decoration: Plain. Comments: wheel-made(?).

158. FT (Pl. 11 and Fig. 44)
Biscuit: Grey. Silver mica inclusions (5mm). Surface: Reddish yellow (7.5YR 7/6). Shape: Rim and body of a jar/jug with thickened outturned oblique, flat rim. D 14. Decoration: Plain. Comments: None.

159. MT (Fig. 45)
Biscuit: Reddish yellow (7.5YR 7/6). White inclusions

Fig. 43. Aghia Triada, Area II. Catalogue no. 156. Strap handle from closed shaped jar. MP.

(1,5mm) and voids. Surface: Pink (7.5YR 7/4 ext.). Burnished. Shape: Closed shaped jar. Decoration: Three MP bands. Comments: -.

160. MT (Fig. 44)
Biscuit: Reddish yellow (5YR 6/6). White inclusions (1mm). Surface: Reddish yellow (7.5YR 7/6). Shape: Closed vessel. Decoration: Black/brown parallel bands. MP. Comments: Handmade.

161. MT (Fig. 44)
Biscuit: Reddish yellow (5YR 7/6). White/grey inclusions (1mm). Surface: Brown matt paint looks as though it covered the entire surface. The white paint is added in a thin line just below the flaring rim. Shape: Jar/jug. Decoration: Brown and white paint (MP). Comments: -.

162. KW (Pl. 11)
Biscuit: Dark reddish grey (2.5YR 4/1). White/black inclusions (3mm). Surface: Reddish brown (5YR 5/4). Inside: bright orange. Shape: Basin with thickened outturned rim. D 38. Decoration: Plain. Comments: Handmade(?)

163. KW (Pl. 11 and Fig. 46)
Biscuit: Grey 5/1. White inclusions. Surface: Reddish yellow (7.5YR 7/6) and black. Shape: Small bowl with thickened outturned, flat oblique rim. D 10. Decoration: Plain. Comments: -.

164. CT (Pl. 11 and Fig. 46)
Biscuit: Core: Yellowish red (10YR 6/6). Margin: Yellowish red (5YR 5/8). Many white and dark inclusions. Surface: Yellowish red (5YR 5/6). Shape: Basin with vertical T-rim. D 42. Decoration: Plain. Comments: Handmade. Date: EH.

Fig. 44. Aghia Triada, Area II. Catalogue no. 158 (upper left) (FT). Catalogue no. 160 (lower) (MT). Catalogue 161 (upper right) (MT)

Tx71

The deposit: (Fig. 35)

Tx71/7

(Bag no. 1945 (:1) (17.07.98))

165. MT (Pl. 11)
Biscuit: Black with many rather large grits – white (lime and black (2mm). Surface: Black burnished on outside, smoothed on inside. Shape: Jar with everted thick round rim. D 26. Decoration: None. Comments: Handmade.

Tx72

The deposit: (above p. 86ff. and Figs. 37 and 38)

Tx72/ARA/1

(Bag nos. 4835 (21.06.01), 4836 (21.06.01), 4837 (22.06.01))

STATISTICS: Small material not classified in details or counted – contain:
- Intrusion: 1 sherd – Black glazed
- Mycenaean lustrous painted sherds (LHIII)
- Sherds with MP
- Local MT fabrics
- KW

Fig. 45. Aghia Triada, Area II. Catalogue no. 159 (MT).

Fig. 46. Aghia Triada, Area II. Catalogue no. 163 (lower) (KW). Catalogue no. 164 (upper) (CT).

Shapes

166. FT (Mycenaean) (Pl. 12)
Biscuit: Pink (7.5YR 8/4). Very fine, soft ware. Surface: Very pale brown (10YR 8/4), soft. Shape: Lid? D 20. Decoration: None. Comments: Typical Mycenaean fabric. wheel-made.

Fig. 47. Aghia Triada, Area II. Catalogue no. 168 (MT/MP).

167. FT (Mycenaean) (Pl. 12)
Biscuit: Reddish yellow (7.5YR 7/6). Surface: Pink (7.5YR 8/4). Traces of dark red (2.5YR 3/6) lustrous paint on in-and outside. Shape: Small bowl with flat everted rim. D. 14. Decoration: None. Comments: wheel-made.

168. MT (Pl. 12 and Fig. 47)
Biscuit: Red (2.5YR 6/6). Many white (lime) inclusions (local). Surface: Very pale brown (10YR 8/3) matt, creamy slip. Shape: Closed shape. Decoration: Black matt paint. Comments: Handmade. F01-2002.

Various

F01-2002
Three Mycenaean sherds (Bag no. 4836 (21.06.01))

F72/ARA/2

(Bag nos. 4839 (22.06.01), 4844 (22.06.01))

STATISTICS: Insignificant material. Not classified in details (250 gr) – contain:
- Mycenaean lustrous painted sherds (6) (LHIII)
- Local MT red fabrics
- KW

169. KW (Pl. 12)
Biscuit: Red (2.5YR 6/8). White (lime) inclusions. Surface: Same colour. Very fine and even surface. Smoothed. Shape: Cooking pot with outturned flat rim. D 22. Decoration: Plain. Comments: Mycenaean cooking vessel. wheel-made (very clear traces of wheel).

Tx72/11

(Bag nos. 1697 (13.07.98), 1841 (14.07.98), 1844 (15.07.98))

STATISTICS:	No.	Weight:
No later intrusions		
FT(1)	6	300 gr
FT(2)	3	–
FT TOTAL (INCL. 1697★)	28	400 gr
MT1	61	1.000 gr
MT2	128	3.000 gr
MT TOTAL (INCL: 1697★)	266	5.860 gr
GM (Grey Minyan)	5	
KW	119	3.200 gr
Burnt clay pieces	22	600 gr

★ In bag no. 1697 the FT/MT (1) and (2) groups were not specified.

Shapes

170. MT (Pl. 12)
Biscuit: Reddish Yellow (5YR, 6/8). Surface: idem. Unburnished. Shape: Small jar with thickened outturned oblique flat rim. D 13. Decoration: Plain. Comments: Handmade.

171. MT(1) (Pl. 12)
Biscuit: Reddish yellow (5YR, 7/8) with two visible, small grits. Surface: Reddish yellow (7.5YR, 7/6) smoothed surface. Shape: Partly preserved handle with upright ring handle on the rim. Decoration: Badly preserved MP (black). Comments: Handmade.

172. MT(1) (Pl. 12)
Biscuit: Reddish yellow (5YR, 7/8) with small, black and white grits. Surface: Reddish yellow (7.5YR, 7/8) smoothed surface. Shape: Open jar. D 19. Decoration: Parallel grooves below rim. Comments: Handmade.

173. MT (1) (Pl. 12)
Biscuit: Reddish yellow (5YR, 6/6). A few black and white grits. Very fine ware. Surface: Reddish yellow (5YR, 7/6). Smoothed surface (faint parallel lines on surface). Shape: Small jar with S-shaped section and pointed inturned rim. D 10. Decoration: Plain. Comments: Handmade or very slow wheel.

174. MT(2) (Pl. 12)
Biscuit: Reddish yellow (7.5YR, 6/6) hard fabric with brown and white small grits. Surface: Yellow (10YR, 8/6).

Smoothed surface. Visible small grits on surface. Shape: Cup with S-shaped section and pointed inturned rim. D 8. Decoration: Plain. Comments: Excellent hard ware. Handmade.

175. MT(2) (Pl. 12)
Biscuit: Reddish yellow (7.5YR, 6/6). White and brown grits. Surface: Reddish yellow (7.5YR, 7/6). Smoothed. Visible grits on surface. Shape: Cup with thickened out-turned, slightly oblique flat rim. D 10. Decoration: MP bands on rim and surface. Comments: Handmade?

176. MT(2) (Pl. 12)
Biscuit: Reddish yellow (7.5YR, 6/6). White grits (2 pieces of silver mica). Surface: Reddish yellow (7.5YR, 7/6). Smoothed. Grits visible on surface. Shape: Base of stemmed kantharos with high swung handles. D 10. Decoration: Plain. Comments: Handmade.

177. MT(2) (Pl. 12 and Fig. 48)
Biscuit: Reddish yellow (7.5YR, 7/6). Very small reddish/brown grits. Very hard fabric. Surface: Very pale brown (10YR, 8/3). Slipped on in-and outside. Burnished. Shape: Jar with thickened outturned, oblique flat rim. D 25 Decoration: MP (black). Comments: Excellent hard ware.

178. MT(2) (Pl. 12)
Biscuit: Reddish yellow (5YR, 7-6/6). White and a few black inclusions (2 mm). Surface: Very pale brown (10YR, 8/3). Slipped. Shape: Cylindrical or funnel shaped neck of a stamnos or hydria. D 18. Thick variant of MT(2). Decoration: MP (black) bands below rim on white line(?). Comments: Softer than usual MT(2).

179. KW (Pl. 12)
Biscuit: Yellowish red (5YR, 5/6). Hard fabric. Stone grits – white/brown (5 mm). Surface: Yellowish red (5YR, 5/6) smoothed, uneven surface grits visible on surface. Shape: Cooking jar with S-shaped section and flat rim. D 16. Decoration: Plain. Comments: Handmade.

180. KW (Pl. 12)
Biscuit: Grey core – margins: reddish yellow (5YR, 6/6). Many white grits/and black less than 5 mm. Surface: Reddish yellow (5YR, 6/6) smoothed. Grits visible on surface. Shape: Cooking jar with inturned collar and flat rim. D 18. Decoration: Plain. Comments: Close to no. 179 in fabric.

Various

Preliminary reg. no. 6. MT (1)
Biscuit: Reddish yellow (7.5YR, 7/6). Surface: Very pale brown (10YR, 8/3) with many grits (and grit holes - voids). Slipped and burnished. Shape: Open. Decoration: MP (black) bands. Comments: Slightly finer clay than no. 177.

Preliminary reg. no. 5. MT (2)
Biscuit: Reddish yellow (5YR, 7/6). Surface: Very pale brown (10YR, 8/4). Smoothed and slipped(?). Shape: Closed. Thick wall as no. 178. Decoration: MP decoration. Comments: Handmade?

Fig. 48. Aghia Triada, Area II. Catalogue no. 177 (MT/MP) (lower). Various - base of goblet (MT/MP) (upper).

Preliminary reg. no. 1. (Imported ware?)
Biscuit: Light brown (7.5YR, 6/4). Very hard fabric, white, small grits. Surface: Reddish yellow (7.5YR, 7/6). Shape: Closed. Decoration: Lustrous(?) black bands with white band (fat white colour). Comments: "minoanizing"?

Various

- Base of goblet (MT), MP on the stem (Bag no. 1841) (Fig. 48 (upper))
- Double conical clay bead (MT). F98-3511 (Fig. 49)

Fx72/12

(Bag nos. 1849 (15.07.98), 1856 (16.07.98))

STATISTICS: (No later intrusions)	No.	Weight:
FT	5	50 gr
MT2	65	1.350 gr
MT11	2	50 gr
K	14	425 gr
Lumps of burnt clay	7	250 gr

Fig. 49. Aghia Triada, Area II. Double conical bead (MT) (F98-3511).

Fig. 50. Aghia Triada, Area II. Catalogue no. 186 (upper and lower side).

Shapes

181. MT (1) (Pl. 13)
Biscuit: Reddish yellow (5YR 6/8). Fine fabric with white grits (also seen on surface). Surface: Reddish yellow (5YR 7/8). Burnished. Shape: Low stem of a goblet (wall 9 mm). Decoration: Plain. Comments: Handmade.

182. MT (2) (Pl. 13)
Biscuit: Grey core. Margins: Reddish yellow (5YR 6/8). White, red and black inclusions. Fine, hard fabric. Surface: Reddish yellow (5YR 6/8), smoothed. Shape: Collar of jar with outturned thickened, slightly oblique flat rim. D 18 (wall 13 mm). Decoration: Plain. Comments: Handmade.

183. MT (Pl. 13)
Biscuit: Grey core. Margins: Reddish yellow (7,5 YR 7/6). White, grey, red/brown grits. Surface: Reddish yellow (7.5YR 7/6) smoothed. Shape: Recessed bottom of a small jar (very coarse on inside) (wall: 6 mm). Decoration: Plain. Comments: Rather coarse ware without surface treatment.

184. MT(2) (Pl. 13)
Biscuit: Reddish yellow (5YR 7/6). Small grits, white and voids on surface. Surface: Pale yellow (2.5YR 8/3). Slipped, matt surface. Shape: Small, hemispherical jar with S-shaped section and pointed rim. D 10. Decoration: Plain. Comments: Fine clay–but too many grits for a FT fabric.

185. KW (Pl. 13)
Biscuit: Yellowish red (5YR 5/8). Large grits, white dominating (9 mm). Surface: Yellowish red (5YR 5/6). Sandy surface. Shape: Close shaped jar with thickened rounded everted rim. D 16. Decoration: Plain.Comments: None.

Tx72/13

(Bag nos. 1852 (15.07.98), 1853 (16.07.98), 1858 (17.07.98), 1860 (20.07.98)
Comments: The worn sherds in STR 13 look redeposited.

STATISTICS:	No.	Weight:
No later intrusions		
MT-unburnished	111	1.900 gr
MT-burnished	100	750 gr
KW	100	1.700 gr

Shapes

186. FT (imported ware) (Pl. 13 and Fig. 50)
Biscuit: Very pale brown (10YR 8/3). Very soft, fine fabric with few small black grits. Surface: idem. Shape: Vertical, band shaped strap handle with twisted pattern in centre. From a jug. Decoration: Plain. Comments: Not local fabric.

187. MT-unburnished (Pl. 13)
Biscuit: Dark grey core. Margins: Reddish yellow (5YR 6/8). White stones (not lime) are diagnostic. Surface: Reddish yellow (5YR 6/8). Well smoothed, sandy surface. White stone inclusions are visible on the surface. Shape: Everted thickened flat rim of a bowl. D 22. Decoration: Plain. Comments: Handmade.

188. KW (Pl. 13)
Biscuit: Dark grey core. Margins: Reddish yellow (5YR 6/6). Many large grits: white. (7mm)(both stone and lime inclusions). Surface: Reddish yellow (5YR 6/6). Shape: Jar with S-shaped section, straight inturned collar with pointed flat rim D. 22. Decoration: None. Comments: Handmade.

189. KW (Pl. 13)
Biscuit: Dark grey core. Margins: Reddish yellow (5YR 6/6). Surface: Reddish yellow (5YR 6/6). Shape: Large jar with straight thickened flat rim. D 28. Decoration: None. Comments: Handmade.

190. KW (Pl. 13)
Biscuit: Dark/grey (close to (2.5YR 4/1) with many stone grits, black, grey and smaller white (lime). The stones are seen clearly on the surface. Surface: Reddish yellow (5YR 6/6) well smoothed, sandy surface. Stone grits are clearly visible on

Fig. 51. Aghia Triada, Area II. Prehistoric architectural remains from trenches K27–K29 (TRP, 183, fig. 9). The structure (floor) AQV (p. 97) in K 27 is placed between AQY and the Archaic wall AEE (see p. 6 lower right). The Archaic stoneslabs AQZ in K28 (p. 98) are situated north of AQN and south of the Archaic wall AKL (TPR fig. 8) while the Archaic foundation AHF was placed on top of the Mycenaean Foundation AQY (Fig. 51).

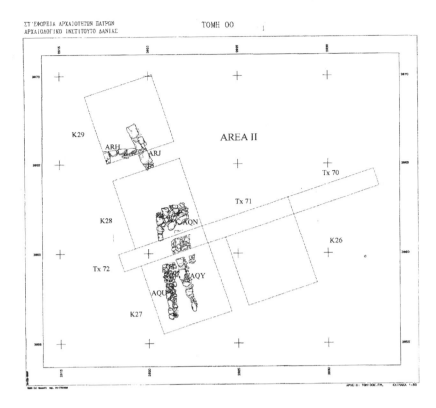

the surface. Shape: Band shaped – loop handle. Decoration: Plain. Comments: Handmade.

K27/K28 and K29.

Fig. 51 shows the foundations for architectural structures dated to the prehistoric periods.

K27/6a/b/6

(Bag nos. 4553 (19.07.00), 4554 (19.07.00), 4808 (19.06.01), 4812 (19.06.01), 4813 (19.06.01), 4817 (20.06.01))

The deposit: Stratum 6a was excavated in the centre of K27 near structure AQU (Fig. 51). The soil is fat clayish with many small sherd fragments, small concentrations of yellow soil, small stones (2 to 5 cm), traces of mud bricks, bones and small fragments of charcoal. Colour: Light olive brown (2.5Y 5/6). The level corresponds to STR 10 in section Tx72 (above Figs. 37 and 38). Stratum 6b is a slightly lighter layer in the north eastern part of the trench, between AQY and AEE, where two large, flat stones were found. The strata are excavated approximately between 2.00 and 1.90/1.80 metre (see section Figs. 37 and 38). Stratum 6b partly belongs to a structure (floor) AQV. In

trench K27 excavation stopped at level approximately 1.8 metre above sea level.

STATISTICS   No.   Weight
Comments: LHIII layer. No Intrusions.
The majority of ceramics in these contexts are wheel-made

	No.	Weight
LHIII lustrous painted	30	100 gr
FT	8	100 gr
MT(1)	52	350 gr
MT2	37	400 gr
GM	2	
KW	35	400 gr

Various

- White ware – homogeneous pale yellow, fine fabric (2.5YR 8/3) 4 sherds
- Light red fabric, white (inclusions ?) – burnished

Shapes

191. FT (Mycenaean) (Pl. 14)
Biscuit: Pale yellow (2.5YR 8/2). Fine. Surface: Same. Shape: Closed shaped jar with inturned collar, straight flat rim. D 16. Decoration: None. Comments: Wheel traces on inside.

192. FT (Pl.14)
Biscuit: Reddish yellow (5YR 6/6), fine, hard fabric. One white (lime) inclusion. Very small silver mica. Surface: Very pale brown (10YR 7/4), smoothed. Shape: Small cup(?) with

everted flat rim. D 11. Decoration: Plain. Comments: unusual fabric for Chalkis. Handmade?

193. MT(1) (Pl.14)
Biscuit: Reddish yellow (5YR 7/8). Small, black stone grits. Grey core. Surface: Reddish yellow (5YR 7/8), smoothed with small voids. Shape: Fairly open jar with inturned collar and straight flat rim. D 24. Decoration: Plain. Comments: Handmade.

194. KW (Pl. 14)
Biscuit: Black with many black stone grits (9 mm) and white stone. Surface: Black on inside. Reddish yellow (7.5YR 7/6) on outside. Well smoothed, even surface. Shape: Jar with inturned collar and thin rim. D 24. Decoration: Plain. Comments: Handmade.

195. GM (Pl. 14)
Biscuit: Homogeneous light grey. Surface: Slightly more dark. Shape: Small (with spout?) cup with everted, flat rim. D 14. Decoration: None. Comments: Handmade.

Various

196. Stone (Pl. 14)
App. dark greenish grey (Colour Chart 2, 4/1). D 21. Bowl: clear traces of grinding (steatite?).

F00-5084:
Mycenaean seal stone (fragment) (2922.704/3858.456 – level: 1.97) (Bag no. 4555).
F00-5085:
Mycenaean seal stone (intact) (2922.293/3858.298 – level: 1.92) (Bag no. 4556).
F00-5086:
Mycenaean seal stone (fragment) (same coordinate and level) (Bag no. 4557).
F01-1001:
Fragment of an idol, probably the rear part of a horse (2922.61/3858.56) (Bag no. 4821) (Fig. 52).

See also catalogue of flint/obsidian.

K28

The Deposit: (Fig. 51). The prehistoric levels were excavated between the Archaic foundations in trench K28. Between the large wall AEE and the stone slabs AQZ north of AQN (Fig. 51) the mixed layer STR 9 2p was excavated with the isolated area 9a 1p in a level between approximately 1.85 and 2.05 metre. The soil is fat clayish olive brown (2.5Y 4/4) with sherds, shells, flint, bones and quite an amount of charcoal. Level AQZ/3 is the deposit below the slabs AQZ which should thus safely be dated post LHIII or Archaic.

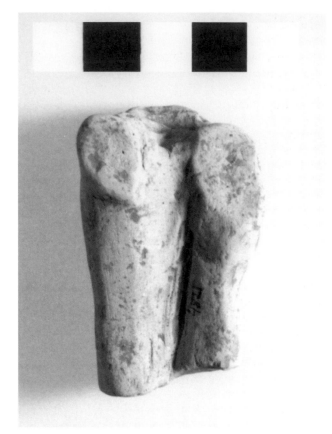

Fig. 52. Aghia Triada, Area II. Rear part of Mycenaean idol (horse?).

Similarly stratum AHF/1 was excavated below structure AHF. Stratum AQJ/2 was excavated as a sub soil to an Archaic floor(?), between the two substantial Archaic foundations AKK and AKL [179] on a rather higher level (bottom level app. 2.30). The stratigraphical situation is thus rather clear. LHIII deposits are sealed below later Archaic constructions (AQZ, AHF and AQJ) while a few MH intrusions are found only in a few instances in the lower layers (STR 9 2p) in connection probably with the construction of the Archaic wall AEE. Excavation in trench K28 stopped around level 1.8 metre above sea level.[180]

---

[179] TPR,183, fig.8.
[180] Notes: **K28/5b** (cleaning)(Bag no. 4827 (20.06.01)): Probably LHIII. **K28/5c, 1p** (Bag no. 4914 (05.07.01)): Large material covered with lime. Fine ware, KW etc. LHIII layer. **K28/6, 1p** (Bag nos. 4825 (20.06.01), 4831 (21.06.01)) MP and FT (insignificant material) LHIII.

K28/9 2p

(Bag nos. 4814 (19.06.01), 4822 (20.06.01), 4828 (21.06.01))

STATISTICS:	No.	Weight

Comments: All bags contain quite a lot of small, fine tempered, wheel-made lustrous painted LHIII sherds (badly preserved)

LHIII lustrous painted	12	50 gr
FT	3	
MT(1)	10	50 gr
MT(2)	30	150 gr
KW	22	300 gr

Shapes

197. FT (Pl. 14 and Fig. 53)
Biscuit: Reddish yellow (7.5YR 7/6). No visible inclusions. Very fine clay. Surface: Reddish yellow (7.5YR 7/6). Burnished. Shape: Small carinated krater with thickened, flat slightly oblique (inwards) rim (specific shape). D 18. Decoration: MP black on the rim and outside. No decoration. on inside. Comments: Handmade. Imported.

198. FT (Pl. 14 and Fig. 53)
Biscuit: Reddish yellow (7.5YR 7/6). More "sandy" than 197. A few white and dark inclusions. Surface: Pale yellow (2.5YR 8/2) slip, slightly burnished. Shape: Fragment of rounded bowl with inturned rim. Off-set to rim seen at the top. Decoration: MP – chessboard pattern. Comments: Handmade. Imported.

199. MT(1) (Pl. 14 and Fig. 53)
Biscuit: Reddish yellow (5YR 6/6). Black and white (lime) grits. One clearly visible on the inside (surface). Surface: Reddish yellow (5YR 6/6). Voids and grits visible on surface. Shape: Closed shape. Decoration: MP – horizontal bands. Comments: Handmade.

200. MT(1) (Pl. 14)
Biscuit: Reddish yellow (5YR 7/6) with black grits. Surface: Reddish yellow (5YR 7/6) with voids. Shape: Circular, horizontal handle of a closed shaped jar. Decoration: None. Comments: Handmade.

201. MT(2) (Pl. 14)
Biscuit: Reddish yellow (5YR 7/6) with many small grits, white (lime) and black. A few silver mica. Surface: Smoothed, reddish yellow (5YR 7/6). Voids on surface. Shape: Closed. Decoration. MP horizontal bands. Comments: Handmade.

202. "KW" (Pl. 14)
Biscuit: Black, sandy fabric with many small grains of sand, white and black grits. Surface: Reddish yellow sandy, smoothed surface. Shape: Small basin with inturned, pointed rim. D 24. Decoration: None. Comments: Not the usual coarse tempered KW. Handmade. "EH intrusion"(?).

Fig. 53. Aghia Triada, Area II. Sherds from K28/9 2p. Catalogue nos. 197 (lower), 198 (upper left), 199 (upper right).

K28/9a 1p

(Bag no. 4829 (21.06.01)

STATISTICS:	No.	Weight:
Comments:		
Insignificant material (very dirty)	31	300 gr
The context is LHIII		

Various

- LHIII lustrous painted
- One triangular, horizontal handle
- One circular, horizontal handle
- KW
- MT white ware

See also catalogue of flint/obsidian

K28/AQZ3

(Bag nos. 4842 (22.06.01), 4843 (–))
Comments: LHIII layer without intrusions

STATISTICS:	No.	Weight:
Lustrous Paint (LHIII fine ware)	38	100 gr
MT (1-2)	55	750 gr
KW	25	300 gr

Import(?): One sherd: FT, Pale yellow (2.5YR 8/3), hard fabric, wheel-made.

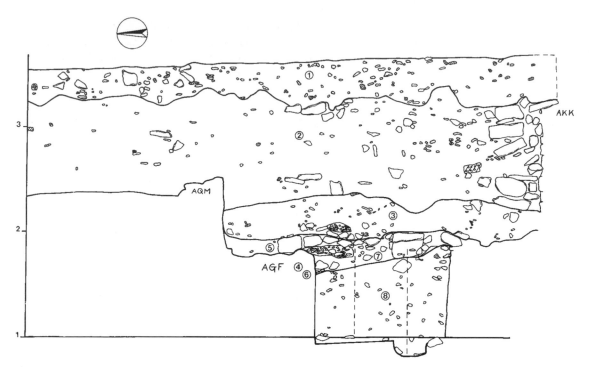

Fig. 54. Aghia Triada, Area II. K29, NE section.

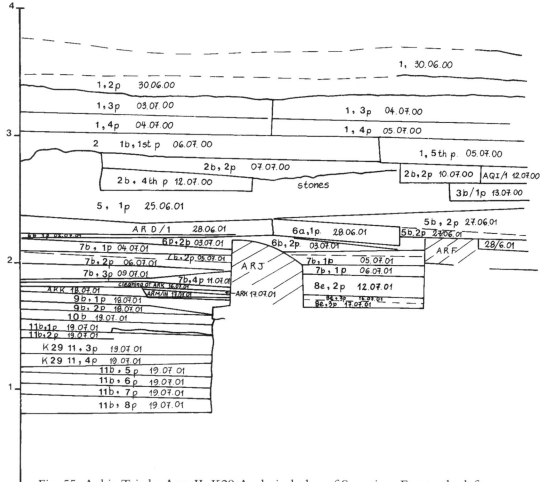

Fig. 55. Aghia Triada, Area II. K29 Analytical plan of S-section. East to the left.

Shapes

203. (Pl. 14)

Biscuit: -. Surface: -. Shape: Stem of bowl/kantharos. D – Decoration: MP on stem. Comments: F01-2003.

204. FT (Pl. 14)

Biscuit: Very pale brown (10YR 8/3) very fine clay. Surface: idem. Probably smoothed. Shape: Open bowl(?) with thickened, oblique everted rim (outwards) "hooked" rim. D 20. Decoration: None. Comments: Probably wheel-made.

205. MT (Pl. 14)

Biscuit: Reddish yellow (5YR 7/6). Very fine soft clay with white (lime) inclusions. Soft fabric. Surface: idem. Very fine surface. Smoothed. Shape: Cylindrical neck from small jar with thickened everted, flat rim. D 13. Decoration: None. Comments: wheel-made.

206. MT (1a) (Pl. 14)

Biscuit: Reddish yellow (5YR 7/8). Fine clay, smaller and not as many inclusions as no. 4–black and a few white. Surface: idem. smoothed. Shape: Low pedestal of a goblet. Decoration: None. Comments: Clearly wheel-made.

207. MT (1a) (Pl. 14)

Biscuit: Reddish yellow (5YR 7/6) with many white (lime) grits. A few silver mica grits. Surface: The original surface is modelled on hand (many fingerprints). On this surface (on the outside) a thick coat of clay (3 mm) is added. At the curve of the stem, the coat is 8 mm. No coat on the inside where many voids from stones and straw temper are seen. Shape: Fragment of a pedestal of a large goblet (only the stem is preserved). Decoration: None. Comments: Handmade.

208. MT (2) (Pl. 14)

Biscuit: Light red (2.5YR 6/8) in margin brownish/black in core. Very hard fabric with white and a few black inclusions. Surface: Reddish yellow (5YR 7/6), smoothed. Shape: Bowl with flat rim and plastic band below rim. D. app. 22. Decoration: Plastic bands below rim. Comments: wheel-made.

Various

F01-2003:

Fragment of a vessel (Bag no. 4843) (22.06.01)

K28/AQJ/2

(Bag no. 4859 (27.06.01))

Comments: All LHIII. Total 25 sherds–one closed shape, the rest are open, and all (except one) are decorated. All wheel-made.

Shapes

209. FT – Mycenaean (Pl. 14)

Biscuit: Reddish yellow (7.5YR 8/6). Very fine. Surface: Reddish yellow (7.5YR 8/6). Shape: Skyphos (bottom). D 5.5. Decoration: Monochrome, reddish brown (2.5YR 4/3). Comments: wheel-made. Traces of parallel horizontal lines are seen on both in-and outside.

210. FT–Mycenaean (Pl. 14)

Biscuit: Reddish yellow (7.5YR 7/6) fine. Surface: Yellow (10YR 8/4). Shape: cup. D 9. Decoration: Horizontal bands in zones. Lustrous paint. Comments: wheel-made.

K28 (and Tx72)/AHF/1

(Bag no. 4861 (27.06.01))

Comments: LHIII level as K28/AQJ/2. No. 98/Weight:500 gr

- Mycenaean fine ware with reddish brown, monochrome paint
- KW and medium tempered groups

K29

The Deposit: Fig. 54 shows the NE section, Fig. 55 is an analytical plan of the South section showing the deep sounding, Fig. 56 is an analytical plan of the SW section showing the deep sounding and Fig. 57 is a plan indicating the position of the sections and the deep soundings.

Fig. 54 NE section:

STR 1: Surface. Loose soil with many potsherds
STR 2: Yellowish homogeneous soil with large stones. Walls AQM and AKK
STR 3: Darker soil with some LH sherds
STR 4: Pebble layer
STR 5: Level with larger stones
STR 6: Layer with pebbles
STR 7: Dark moist soil
STR 8: Dark moist and fat clayish soil

Fig. 55 Analytical plan of the S section

The prehistoric deposits begin around 2.20 metre with stratum 7b 1p corresponding to stratum 3 in the NE section. Stratum 8e 2p and 3p and ARK are more ancient deposits found in strata below 7b 1p. EH layers begin with stratum 11.

The structure numbers from the prehistoric levels on the analytical plan are described as follows:

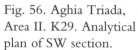

Fig. 56. Aghia Triada, Area II. K29. Analytical plan of SW section.

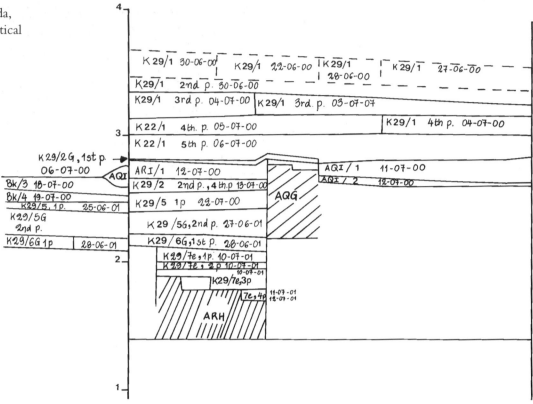

Fig. 57. Aghia Triada, Area II. K29. Plan indicating the position of the sections and soundings.

Fig. 58. Aghia Triada, Area II. K29. The structure ARJ with floor level ARM and ARK. NE section seen in the background.

ARJ: A foundation consisting of larger boulders with the level side upwards and several smaller stones (Fig. 58-59). Size, shape and level correspond to the Mycenaean foundation AQY in trenches K27, K28 and Tx72. The foundation is dated by stratum 7b 1p and rests upon stratum 9b/ 1p.

ARM: The floor is placed below floor level ARK and rests upon stratum 9b/ 1p. (Fig. 55)

ARK: Floor level consisting of pebbles with many sherds, shells and bones. Soil colour: Olive brown (2.5Y 4/3) and Very greyish brown (2.5Y 3/2). The stratum is placed below stratum 7b 4p and above the floor ARM.

ARD: ?

ARN: Dry stone foundation below ARJ. Only a few stones were excavated. Top level: 1,67-1,70.

Fig. 56 Analytical plan of the SW section

The prehistoric deposits begin around level 2.10 metre with stratum 7e/ 1p.

The structure number ARH is described as fol-

lows: Foundation wall running east-west constructed by fairly large stones with the level side upwards. The stones in the wall are smaller, however, than stones used for ARJ. In the western ter-

[181] Notes: **K29/7b** 2p (Bag nos. 4916 (05.07.01), 4920 (06.07.01)): Mixed Archaic/MH layer. MH material: Strap handles for kantharoi. Some MP material – KW of typical MH fabric. Obs! The MH material seems to be without Mycenaean intrusions. **K29/7b 3p** (Bag no. 4930 (09.07.01)): Mixed Archaic/MH. MH material: Strap handles for kantharoi. KW of typical fabrics. No MP. No Mycenaean. **K29/7b 4p** (Bag nos. 4939 (10.07.01), 4944 (11.07.01), 4953 (16.07.01)): Mixed Archaic/MH layer. Mainly MH: triangular handles with triangular section. Goblet base–KW of typical fabric. No Mycenaean. A few ARCHAIC sherds. **K29/7d 1p** (Bag nos. 4924 (06.07.01), 4927 (09.07.01): Mixed Mycenaean/Archaic level. Mycenaean material: Two bottom fragments of LHIII cylindrical cups (FS 226) with decoration (encircling parallel, horizontal bands). One horizontal handle, circular section–Mycenaean lustrous paint. Strap handle of kantharos (Late type!). Very few MH sherds (MP medium temp.). Very nice Archaic fine ware and other Archaic ware groups. **K29/7d 2p** (Bag no. 4934 (10.07.01)): Nothing but Archaic material! **K29/7e 1p** F01-3015 (Fig. 60) (Bag nos. 4936) (10.07.01), F01-3016 (Bag no. 4937)

Fig. 59. Aghia Triada, Area II. K29. The floor ARM. ARJ to the right. S. section in background.

mination there seems to be a corner turning south. Upper level: 1.91-1.94. The foundation is situated below strata 7e 3p and 4p. The lower part of the wall was not excavated. (Fig. 57).[181]

The stratigraphy in trench K29 – a note

The stratigraphy of the prehistoric horizons in trench K29 is complicated by the fact that later Archaic activities (deriving from pits) had disturbed the layers in most parts of the trench. In order to clarify the situation we should like to add the following comments to the sections shown on Figs. 55 and 56:

Fig. 55 (S section): On the left side of the foundation ARJ, the Archaic activities were substantial and Archaic material was found abundantly even down to level 1.80 (STR 7b 3p). It is characteristic that the later material was mixed first of all with

MH, only with very few LHIII sherds included. The same situation is noticed for the "floor" levels

(10.07.01). Pyramidal loom weights. (Fig.47). **K29/7e 4p** (Bag no. 4943 (11.07.01)): Mainly MH (late)/LHI (?) material but also a few LHIII monochrome sherds, flint and probably some Archaic. **K29/8b 1p** Bag no. 4974 (18.07.01)): MP sherd. Bag no. 4977 (F01-3035)(18.07.01). **K29/8e 1p** (Bag no. 4942 (10.07.01)): Mixture Archaic + MH. **K29/8e 2p** Bag No. 4947) (12.07.01): Archaic. **K29/AQF** (Bag No. 4874)(29.06.01): Mainly Archaic. **K29/ARE/1** (Bag No. 4852)(28.06.01): (?)/Archaic. **K29/ARG** (Bag No. 4900)(04.07.01): G/Archaic. **K29/Cleaning of ARK** (Bag No. 4950)(Date: 13.07.01): Archaic. **K29/ATD** (Bag No. 4931)(09.07.01): Archaic (or later?) Tiles. **K29/ARK** (cleaning) (Bag No. 4952) (16.07.01): Archaic. **K29/ARF** (cleaning) (Bag No. 4872)(28.06.01): Archaic. **K29/GRM** (Cleaning) (Bag No. 4964)(17.07.01): Archaic ? (insignificant. Material). **K29/ARK West** (cleaning) (Bag No. 4951)(13.07.01): ? (hardly Mycenaean). **K29/ATD** (Bag No. 4932)(Date: 06.07.01): Archaic. **K29/ARK** (cleaning) (Bag No. 4949)(12.07.01).

ARK and ARM where only very few LHIII sherds were counted. On the right side of the foundation ARJ on the other hand the layers 7b 1p were clearly LHIII. Part of this layer is found on top of the soil on the left side of the foundation. STR 7b 1p corresponds to STR AQJ/2 in TR K28 (p. 99). The foundation ARJ should be dated from this level to LHIIIC. The dry stone foundation ARN below ARJ (not shown on the section) is safely dated to MHIII. We suggest that the "floors" ARK and ARM should likewise be dated to MHIII even if a substantial amount of Archaic material, but very little LHIII material, was found in the deposits.

Fig. 56 (SW section): Not much LHIII material was found west of the foundation ARF. In the SW section the Archaic activities – like in the S section left of ARJ proceeds down to the MHIII deposits (from STR 7e 1p downwards) almost without LHIII material present. The foundation ARH with upper level around 1.90 above sea level is MHIII in date (perhaps connected with the above mentioned ARN).

K29/7b 1p

(Bag nos. 4858 (05.07.01), 4904 (04.07.01)):
Comments: LHIII layer

STATISTICS:	No.	Weight:
(No later intrusions)		
Mycenaean – Lustrous painted	55	300 gr
MT★	346	3.000 gr
KW	67	1.000 gr
GM	4	
Mycenaean "White Ware"	7	
★(Many are wheel-made)		

Shapes

211. FT (Pl. 15)
Biscuit: Reddish yellow (5YR 7/8). Very fine, homogeneous fabric. Surface: Reddish yellow (7.5YR 7/6) with fine slip. Monochrome reddish brown (2.5YR 5/4) lustrous paint. Shape: Small cup with outturned thickened flat rim. D 14. Decoration: None. Comments: Very clear wheel traces.

212. FT-Mycenaean (Pl. 15)
Biscuit: Light brown (7.5YR 6/4) very fine tempered. Surface: Outside: pale yellow (2.5YR 7/3) smoothed. Brown paint on the inside and on top of rim. Shape: Globular cup

Fig. 60. Aghia Triada, Area II. K29. Pyramidal loom-weight F01-3015.

with everted flat rim. D 11. Decoration: None. Comments: wheel-made.

213. FT-Mycenaean (Pl. 15)
Biscuit: Reddish yellow (5YR 7/6) very fine fabric. Surface: Reddish yellow (5YR 7/6). Shape: Cup (?) with outturned flat rim. D 10.Decoration: Lustrous black paint on horizontal bands and on rim. Comments: wheel-made

214. MT (Pl. 15)
Biscuit: Reddish yellow (5YR 6/8). Core: Grey. White (lime) inclusions are diagnostic. Surface: idem. Smoothed. Shape: Shallow bowl with a thick lozenge shaped, flat rim. D 15. Decoration: None. Comments: Probably wheel-made.

215. MT-Mycenaean (Pl. 15)
Biscuit: Light red (2.5YR 7/8). White and brown stone grits. Surface: Reddish yellow (5YR 7/6), smoothed. Voids in surface. Shape: Small bowl with thick lozenge shaped flat rim. Concavity on outside. D 18. Decoration: None. Comments: Wheel-made.

216. MT-Mycenaean (Pl. 15)
Handle with triangular section.

217. KW (Pl. 15)
Biscuit: Reddish brown (5YR 5/4) with small, white and brown inclusions. Surface: Dark grey (5YR 4/1) smoothed. Shape: Small jar with outturned flat rim. D 16. Decoration: None. Comments: Handmade.

218. KW (Pl. 15)
Biscuit: Reddish yellow (7.5 YR 7/6). Very hard fabric with small grits – silver mica. Surface: Very pale brown (10YR

8/3). Smoothed. Shape: Basin with thickened everted rim. D 30. Decoration: None. Comments: None.

219. Mycenaean "White ware" (Pl. 15)
Biscuit: Very pale brown (10YR 8/3) homogeneous, fine fabric. Surface: Very pale brown (10YR 8/3). Shape: Flat base of a bowl. D.10. Decoration: None. Comments: no visible wheel traces.

K29/7e 2p

(Bag no. 4938 (10.07.01))

STATISTICS:	No.	Weight:
FT	14	50 gr
MT1 (-2)★	43	350 gr
KW	19	300 gr

★Mainly the soft variant (MT1) silver mica is rather diagnostic.

Shapes

220. FT (Import ?) (Pl. 15)
Biscuit: Reddish yellow (5YR 5/4). Very hard fabric. One white (lime) grit. Surface: Pink (7.5YR 5/4), smoothed. Shape: Shallow bowl with thin everted rim. Groove below rim. D 16. Decoration: None. Comments: Not local fabric.

221. MT1 (Pl. 15)
Biscuit: Reddish yellow (5YR 6/8) very soft fabric. White (lime) grits, a few black and red inclusions – silver mica. Surface: idem. Smoothed. Shape: Krater with rectangular flat "hawk beak rim". D 38. Decoration: None. Comments: Handmade. The fabric is typical local!

See also catalogue of flint and obsidian.

K29/7e 3p

(Bag no. 4940 (10.07.01))

STATISTICS:	No.	Weight:
Intrusions: One probable LHIII monochrome brown – wheel-made		
FT★		
MT1-2★★	48	500 gr
KW	19	250 gr

★ Very few FT
★★ All handmade. A few sherds with hard grey fabric (not GM). MT sherds with a Pink surface/fabric – some of terrazzo type (CT).

Shapes

222. FT (Pl. 15)
Biscuit: Pink (5YR 7/4) very fine tempered clay. Surface:

Pink idem. Smoothed. Shape: Neck of jug with strap handle from rim. D 7. Decoration: None. Comments: Handmade. Not local fabric.

223. FT (as catalogue no. 222) (Pl. 15)
Biscuit: Pink (5YR 7/4) very fine tempered clay. Surface: Pink idem. Smoothed. Shape: Bowl with thickened rounded outturned rim. D. 14. Decoration: None. Comments: Not local fabric.

224. MT(1) (Pl. 15)
Biscuit: Light red (2.5YR 6/8). White (lime) grits, rather soft fabric. Surface: idem. Shape: Closed jar with thick concave rim. D 18. Decoration: None. Comments: Handmade. Local fabric.

225. MT(1) (Pl. 15)
Biscuit: Light red (2.5YR 6/8). White (lime) grits and black/red. Surface: idem. Smoothed. Shape: Bowl with thin everted rim. D 20. Decoration: None. Comments: Handmade. Local fabric.

See also catalogue of flint and obsidian.

K29/8e 2p

(Bag nos. 4945 (12.07.01), 4948 (?))

STATISTICS:	No.	Weight:
12 sherds are ARCHAIC intrusion		
MT(1)★	67	750 gr
MT(2)	5	–
KW	28	350 gr

★- White (lime) grits are diagnostic. 6 sherds with MP. 2 sherds from jugs. Vertical strap handles. Two are thick walled.

Shapes

226. MT(1) (Pl. 16)
Biscuit: Reddish yellow (5YR 7/6) soft fabric. White (lime) inclusions are diagnostic/(lots of) silver mica. Surface: idem. Smoothed. Shape: Jar with thickened outturned, flat rim. D 28. Decoration: MP lines below rim and on the rim. Comments: Handmade.

227. MT(2) (Pl. 16)
Biscuit: Reddish yellow (7.5YR 7/6) very hard fabric. Lots of white (lime) grits, also visible on the surface. A few black grits. Surface: Pale yellow (2.5YR 8/3) cover of surface. Shape: Triangular handle for a large storage jar. Decoration: MP (black). Comments: Handmade.

228. KW (Pl. 16)
Biscuit: Strong brown (7.5YR 4/4). White stone grits (less than 5 mm). Surface: idem (somewhat darker and more red on the inside). Shape: Jar with thickened slightly out falling rim. D 12. Decoration: None. Comments: Handmade.

229. KW ? (Pl. 16)

Biscuit: Fine, reddish yellow (5YR 7/6) fabric with black, red and white (lime) inclusions (2mm). Silver mica. Surface: Smoothed. Shape: Hemispherical jar with inturned, pointed rim and vertical pointed strap handles from the rim. D app. 20. Decoration: None. Comments: Local ware.

K29/ARK

(Bag nos. 4958 (16.07.01), 4959 (16.07.01))

Comments: The bags contain a mixture of Archaic, MH and very little Mycenaean material. Plain ware has been sorted out (app. 2/3 of the material) as it has not been possible to distinguish with certainty between materials from the two periods. ARCHAIC fabrics are separated by the following criteria:

1. Fine ware usually with a pale yellow/slightly green, very fine fabric.
2. Sherds painted (not MH).
3. wheel-made sherds (fast wheel).
4. Certain features – handles with a square section etc.

Shapes

(MH (diagnostic) material selected)

230. MT(1) (Pl. 16)

Biscuit: Reddish yellow (5YR 7/6). Voids and smaller inclusions – some white. Surface: idem, smoothed. Shape: Stem and base of goblet. D 8 (at base). Decoration: None. Comments: Handmade.

231. KW (Pl. 16)

Biscuit: Reddish brown (2.5YR 4/4). Grits (less than 8mm), white (stone) and black/brown. Very hard fabric. Silver mica. Surface: Light red (2.5YR 6/8). Smoothed. Shape: Triangular handle. Decoration: None. Comments: None.

232. "MT(2)"(with gold mica grits) (Pl. 16)

Biscuit: Light red (2.5YR 6/8) fabric (fine tempered) with white (lime) grits. Lots of voids indicate that larger stones and probably straw are fallen out. Silver mica and a few Gold mica grits. Surface: Smoothed with voids from out fallen stones and straw. Shape: Globular pedestalled bowl/jar. D 5 (at stem). Decoration: None. Comments: Further one piece of this fabric (see above). Gold mica indicates that it is imported.

233. (Pl. 16)

Biscuit: Fine, reddish yellow (7.5YR 7/6) fabric with black inclusions (2mm). Surface: Reddish yellow (7.5YR 7/69 burnished surface. Shape: Jar with outturned flat rim and narrow vertical, slightly oblique, strap handles and a boss. D

Fig. 61. Aghia Triada, Area II. K29/ARK. Catalogue no. 233a (F01-3025).

approx. 17. Decoration: None. Comments: Handmade. Hardly local.

233a. (Fig. 61)

Biscuit: Light red (2.5YR 6/8) fine tempered fabric with few white (lime) inclusions. Surface: Smoothed. Shape: Globular jar with part of collar. Decoration: Wavy lines in horizontal zones. Black matt/dull paint. Comments: Handmade. Not local.

Various

– F01-3020:
Bag no. 4956 (16.07.01). Jar with outturned flat rim and black MP band (15 mm) below collar (section as catalogue no. 233).
– F01-3024:
Bag no. 4958 (16.07.01). Rim.
– MT(1) Kantharoi with vertical strap handles.
– Four MP sherds – MT1 with white (lime) grits – the colour is rather lustrous, peeling.

K29/8e 3p

(Bag nos. 4961 (16.07.01), 4962 17.07.01))

STATISTICS:	No.	Weight:
Intrusions: 1 Archaic sherd		
FT	4	–
MT1/2	78	900 gr
MT1 (Thick walled MT1)	8	1.100 gr
KW	28	600 gr

Shapes

234. FT (Pl. 16)
Biscuit: Reddish yellow (7.5YR 7/6). No visible inclusions. Very hard fabric. Surface: Very pale yellow (10YR 8/4) cover on in-and outside. Small, fine white grits seen on the surface. Shape: Small rounded jar with S-shaped section and inturned, pointed rim. D 14. Decoration: None. Comments: Handmade.

235. MT(2) (Pl. 16)
Biscuit: Light red (2.5YR 6/8). White (lime) grits/silver mica. Fine, hard fabric. Surface: Pale yellow (2.5YR 8/2) slip on surface – outside. Shape: Jar with out falling oblique flat rim and traces of a vertical handle. D 22. (thickness of wall app. 10 mm). Decoration: None. Comments: Handmade.

236. MT – ? (Pl. 16)
Biscuit: Pink (7.5YR 7/4). Very fine tempered clay with few white (lime) grits. Surface: Pink idem. Smoothed. Shape: Jar with inturned straight, slightly thickened flat rim. D 20. Decoration: MP (black) – also on rim. Comments: Imported?

237. MT(1) (Pl. 16)
Biscuit: Light red (2.5YR 6/8). White (lime) grits and black/brown. Surface: idem. Smoothed. Shape: High stem of bowl with plastic band around stem. Decoration: None. Comments: Handmade.

K29/9b 1p

(Bag no. 4978)
Comments: Late MH layer

STATISTICS: No. Weight:
Intrusions: 2 pieces of LHIII date:
- one ring base (FT) and one small, horizontal handle (from alabastron) with red paint. 3 Archaic sherds

	No.	Weight:
FT	12	100 gr
MT(1)	135	1.400 gr
KW	56	900 gr

Shapes

238. FT (Pl. 16)
Biscuit: Pale yellow (5Y 8/2). Very fine tempered clay with very few, small black stone grits seen on the surface. Surface: Same. Smoothed, sandy surface. Shape: Small jar of globular shape. Everted rim. D 14. Decoration: None. Comments: Handmade.

239. MT(1) (Pl. 16 and Fig. 62)
Biscuit: Reddish yellow (5YR 6/8). White (lime) grits are diagnostic. A few black/brown grits. Surface: Same. Smoothed. Shape: Triangular, horizontal handle with triangular section from a large (storage) jar. Decoration: None. Comments: Handmade. Compare a similar handle but better preserved in K29/7e.

Fig. 62. Aghia Triada, Area II. K29/9b 1p. Catalogue no. 239. Triangular handle.

240. KW (Pl. 16)
Biscuit: Reddish yellow (5YR 6/8). White (mainly) and black stone (not lime) grits. Surface: idem. Smoothed. Shape: Globular jar with everted rim. D 18. Decoration: none. Comments: Handmade. Unsual type of KW.

241. KW (KW–"white") (Pl. 16)
Biscuit: Pale yellow (5Y 8/2). Mainly black stone grits, a few are white (stone). Surface: Pale yellow (idem). Sandy, smoothed surface. Shape: Small jar with outturned rounded rim. D 11. Decoration: None. Comments: Handmade. (specific function ?)

Various

– F01-3036:
Bag no. 4949 (18.07.01). Jar with outturned thickened, flat rim (as catalogue no. 242).
– F01-3037:
Bag no. 4980 (18.07.01). Sherds of a carinated kantharos (?), yellow burnished surface.
– F013038:
Bag no. 4981 (18.07.01). Neck of a jar with MP bands.

K29/9b 2p

(Bag no. 4984 (18.07.01)
Comments: Late MH layer. Comp. Tx72/11

STATISTICS:	No.	Weight:
FT	4	–
MT1	15	100 gr
MT2★	35	350 gr
MT (burnished) (IMPORT ?)		
KW	45	600 gr

★More MT2 than MT1 characteristic

Shapes

242. KW (Pl. 16)
Biscuit: Light red (10YR 6/8). White stone inclusions (7 mm). Surface: idem. Smoothed. Shape: Jar with out turned thickened flat rim. D 16. Decoration: None. Comments: Handmade.

Various

- F01-3039:
Bag no. 4982 (18.07.01). Clay piece, hard burned from fire place?

K29/10b

(Bag no. 4983 (18.07.01))

STATISTICS:	No.	Weight:
FT	3	–
MT1	12	200 gr
MT2★	32	250 gr
KW	32	450 gr

★ NB! "White" version comp. K29/8e 2p, no. 227

Shapes

243. KW (Pl. 17)
Biscuit: Grey core–Margin: Red (2.5YR 5/6). White stone (6mm) inclusions. Surface: Reddish brown ((5YR 5/4) smoothed. Shape: Jar with inturned thickened, everted flat rim. D 20. Decoration: None. Comments: Handmade.

244. MT(2) (Pl. 17)
Biscuit: Reddish yellow (5YR 7/6) with white (lime) grits. Surface: Reddish yellow (7.5YR 7/6) smoothed. Shape: Jar with everted thickened flat rim. D 26. Decoration: Horizontal MP bands below rim and MP on the rim. Comments: comp. No. 226 (K29/8e 2p).

K29/ARM 1N

(Bag no. 4969 (17.07.01))
Comments: Mixed deposit. Archaic: intrusions – Corinthian pale yellow ware with both green and pink biscuit. EH: see 245 and 246 + KW. MHIII: bases of goblets + KW+White ware.

Shapes

245. KW (EH) (Pl. 17)
Biscuit: Light red (10R 6/8) sandy fabric. White inclusions. Surface: idem. Smoothed. Shape: Jar with straight T-rim. D 40. Decoration: None. Comments: Handmade.

246. KW (EH) (Pl. 17)
Biscuit: Core: weak red (10YR 4/3), margins: Red (2.5YR 5/8) very hard fabric (excellent hard ware). White (stone) inclusions. Silver mica. Surface: idem. Very well smoothed. Shape: T-rim jar. D 22. Decoration: None. Comments: Much harder fabric than 245 which has a homogeneous biscuit. The dark core probably means higher temperatures.

247. MT(2) (Pl. 17)
Biscuit: Pink /7.5YR 7/4) hard fabric. White (stone/lime) grits. Surface: Smoothed. Shape: Stem of a kantharos. D 8 (at base). Decoration: None. Comments: Handmade.

Various

- F01-3027:
Bag no. 4966 (ARM/IB) (07.07.01). Part of a GM kantharos with high swung handles.
- F01-3030:
Bag no. 4970 (17.07.01). White ware (pale yellow 5Y 6/3) jug (?)

248. Deleted.

K29/11b 1p

(Bag no. 4985 (19.07.01))

STATISTICS:	No.	Weight:
Intrusions: Two insignificant FT sherds		
MT	20	150 gr
CT★	18	300 gr

★Two sherds have a slightly burnished surface

249. KW (Pl. 17)
Biscuit: Grey core. Margins: Red (10R 5/6). Surface: idem. Shape: T-rim bowl (?). D 28. Decoration: None. Comments: Handmade.

K29/11b pit

(Bag no. 4986 (19.07.01))

250. KW (CT) (Pl. 17)
Biscuit: Red (10YR 5/6) hard fabric. White stone and lime inclusion (less than 3mm). Surface: Light red (2.5YR 6/6) slightly burnished on inside. Shape: T-rim jar. D 32. Decoration: Plastic list of clay dots below rim. Comments:

Handmade. („Schüssel mit Knickwand" Weisshaar 1990 Pl. 15,9).

K29/11b 3p

(Bag no. 4992 (19.07.01))

STATISTICS:	No.	Weight:
FT★		
KW/CT	15	150 gr
KW/CT★★	4	50 gr

★ Two insignificant sherds. One with brown paint on inside (?).Biscuit: Pink (5YR 7/4)
★★ Burnished

Shapes

251. KW (Pl. 17)
Biscuit: Red (2.5YR 5/8). White (lime) grits are diagnostic–also black stone grits (less than 3mm). Surface: idem. Well smoothed. Shape: T-rim bowl. D 28. Decoration: None. Comments: Handmade.

252. KW (Pl. 17)
Biscuit: as no. 1 or black – mainly red, however. Surface: idem. Shape: One vertical strap handle. Decoration: None. Comments: Handmade.

See also catalogue of flint and obsidian.

K29/11b 4p

Bag no. 4993 (19.07.01))

STATISTICS:	No.	Weight:
KW	21	250 gr
KW★	3	-

★ Burnished

See also catalogue of flint and obsidian.

K29/11b 6p

(Bag no. 4997 (19.07.01))

STATISTICS:	No.	Weight:
KW (MT)	10	150 gr
KW (CT)	22	200 gr

Shapes

253. MT (Pl. 17)
Biscuit: Reddish yellow (5YR 6/6) very hard fabric. Silver mica. Rather small black/white grits. Surface: idem. Smoothed with horizontal "zones" on outside. Shape: Large basin with outwards thickened rim. D 50. Decoration:

None. Comments: Handmade, but slow wheel used. Not local fabric.

254. KW (Pl. 17)
Biscuit: Red (10YR 5/8) small (15mm) white (lime) grits and black. Silver mica. Surface: Red burnished on in-and outside. Shape: open. Decoration: Chess board pattern–white paint also on other pieces are found in other bags from 19.07.01. Comments: Handmade.

K29/11b 7p

Bag no. 4998) (19.07.01))

KW (CT)	4 sherds
KW (MT)	5 sherds

See also catalogue of flint and obsidian.

Catalogue of flint and obsidian[182]

Pls 18 - 20, Fig. 65, a-d

Locality and description/material

1) Tx43/2b (Bag no. 1256) (30.06.98)
   1 blade fragment with retouché/ local black flint.
2) Tx43/3 (Bag no. 1259) (01.07.98)
   1 large flake/radiolarite (hard direct precussion) + 2 small flakes/radiolarite + 1 piece of marble.
3) Tx43/3a (Bag no.1261) (01.07.98)
   1 obsidian blade with retouché in one end (pressure flaking) (sickle blade ?) Ref. Pl. 37, 1-6.
4) Tx43/3a (Bag no.1260) (01.07.98)
   1 flake/radiolarite + 3 pieces of marble.
5) Tx43/3c (Bag no. 1272) (02.07.98)(F98-2014)
   1 blade fragment/local (creamy white) flint with retouché on edge and proximal termination (sickle blade ?).
6) Tx43/3c (Bag no. 1275) (02.07.98)
   1 flake/radiolarite + 1 flake/obsidian.
7) Tx43/3c (Bag no. 1421) (02.07.98)(F98-2016)
   1 flake/obsidian (pressure flaking).
8) Tx43/3c (Bag no. 1270)(02.07.98) (F98-2012)
   1 blade fragment/radiolarite. End scraper. Ref. Pl. 36, 1.
9) Tx43/3c (Bag no. 1271) (02.07.98)
   1 blade fragment/obsidian (black shiny).
10) Tx43/3c (Bag no. 1273) (02.07.98)
   1 fragm.of a perforator/milk white marble.

---

[182] This catalogue was written in collaboration with Lasse Sørensen (L.S.). Terminology in accordance with the publication of the more extensive LN material from Pangali (below p. 140).

Fig. 63a–d. Flint and obsidian from EH I levels at Aghia Triada. Photos by Lasse Sørensen. 1:1.

11) Tx43/3c (Bag no.1274)(02.07.98) (F98-2015)
1 blade/obsidian (black shiny) (press. flaking) + 1 flake/local flint.

12) Tx43/3d (Bag no. 1430) (03.07.98)
1 blade/obsidian (grey shiny) (soft direct flaking).

13) Tx43/3d (Bag no. 1432) (06.07.98) (F98-2017)
1 one-sided, crested blade with retouché/obsidian (grey shiny). Sickle fragm. Ref. Pl. 37, 1-6.

14) Tx43/3d (Bag no. 1433) (06.07.98)
1 blade/obsidian (black shiny) (pressure flaking).

15) Tx43/3d (Bag no. 1434) (06.07.98) (F98-2018)
1 two-sided, crested blade/obsidian (grey shiny).

16) Tx43/3d (Bag no. 1431) (06.07.98)
1 flake/local dark flint + 1 flint core + 1 fragment of blade/obsidian (grey shiny). Scraper ?. Ref. Pl. 37, 7-9.

17) Tx43/4 (Bag no. 1436) (06.07.98)
1 flake/dark local flint + 1 flake/light greenish local flint + 1 flake/obsidian (grey shiny).

18) Tx43/4 (Bag no. 1437) (06.07.98)
1 raw nodule/local greenish flint

18b) Tx43/4 (Bag no. 1437)(06.07.98)
1 flake with original surface preserved/obsidian (grey shiny).

18a) Tx43/4 (Bag no. 1438) (07.07.98) (F98-2020)
1 two-sided, crested blade/obsidian (black shiny).

19) Tx43/4 (Bag no. 1439)(07.07.98) (F98-2019)
1 flake/radiolarite + 1 fragm. of blade with edge retouché/obsidian (grey shiny). Ref. Pl. 33, 13-17.

20) Tx43/4 (Bag no. 1440) (07.07.98) (F98-2021)
1 one-sided, crested blade with retouché/obsidian (grey shiny). Ref. 37, 1-6

21) Tx43/4 (BA no. 1601)(07.07.98) (F98-2022)
1 flake with original surface preserved/obsidian (grey shiny)

22) Tx43/4 (Bag no. 1602)(07.07.98)
1 flake/local flint + 1 flake/obsidian (grey shiny). Original surface preserved.

23) Tx43/4b (Bag no. 1604)(07.07.98)
1 blade/radiolarite (soft indirect percussion). Along the edge, traces of pressure percussion.

24) (23a) Tx43/4b (Bag. no. 1604) (07.07.98) Flake/marble.

25) (24)Tx43/4b (Bag no.1605) (07.07.98) (F98-2024)

1 flake/local flint + 1 flake with original surface preserved/obsidian (grey shiny) + 2 flakes/obsidian (hard direct percussion) + 4 blade fragments/obsidian (3 grey shiny, 1 black shiny).

26) (25) Tx43/4b (Bag no. 1606)(07.07.98)
Flake/local flint.

27) (26) Tx43/4b (Bag no. 1610)(08.07.98)
Blade/obsidian (black shiny).

28) Tx43/4b (Bag no. 1611)(08.07.98) (F98–2025)
1 Blade with very fine retouché /obsidian (grey matt). Sickle fragment + 1 blade with retouché and notch/obsidian (black shiny).

29) Tx43/4b (Bag no. 1612)(08.07.98)
2 flakes/local flint + 2 blades fragments/obsidian (black shiny). Sickle fragment + 2 blade fragments/obsidian (grey shiny).

30) Tx43/4b (Bag no. 1704)(10.07.98) (F98–2028)
1 blade/radiolarite with end retouché.

Tx70

31) Tx70/5 (Bag no. 1797)(10.07.98)
1 flake/radiolarite + 1 exhausted core/radiolarite.

32) Tx70/5 (Bag no. 1799)(10.07.98)
6 flakes/marble + 6 flakes/radiolarite (hard direct percussion).

33) Tx70/5 (Bag no. 1821)(13.07.98)
4 flakes/radiolarite.

34) Tx70/5 (Bag no. 1824)(13.07.98)
1 flake/radiolarite.

35) Tx70/5 (Bag no. 1826)(13.07.98)
6 flakes/radiolarite + 2 flakes/local flint.

36) Tx70/5a (Bag no. 1830)(13.07.98)
1 flake/local flint + 1 one-sided crested blade/obsidian (black shiny).

37) Tx70/5a (Bag no. 1836)(14.07.98)
1 flake/local flint.

38) Tx70/6 (Bag no. 1834)(14.07.98)
1 flake/radiolarite.

Tx71

39) Tx71/7 (Bag no. 1952)(17.07.98)
3 flakes/radiolarite.

40) Tx71/8 (Bag no. 1950)(17.07.98)
2 flakes/marble.

41) Tx71/9 (Bag no. 1954)(20.07.98)
2 flakes/radiolarite.

42) Tx71/11 (Bag no. 2163)(23.07.98)
1 flake/radiolarite + 1 flake with retouché/radiolarite.

Tx72

43) Tx72/10 (Bag no. 1696)(13.07.98)
1 one-sided, crested blade/local black flint (hard direct percussion).

44) Tx72/13 (Bag no. 1853)(16.07.98)
1 flake/radiolarite + 1 flake with traces of original surface/obsidian.

45) Tx72/13 (Bag no. 1858)(17.07.98)
1 flake with cortex/local flint + 1 flake/obsidian (black shiny).

46) Tx72/13 (Bag no. 1860)(20.07.98)
2 flakes with cortex/local flint + 1 flake/milk white flint –import + 1 small end scraper/local light brown flint. Ref. Pl. 35, 4–5 + 2 flakes, one with retouché and one with original surface preserved/obsidian (black shiny).

47) Tx 72/13 (Bag no. 2063)(20.07.98) (F98–3512)
Blade fragment with distal end preserved/obsidian (black shiny).

48) Tx72/14 (Bag no. 2062) (22.07.98)
8 flakes/radiolarite + 12 flakes/black local flint + 9 flakes/dark brown flint + 14 flakes/local light brown flint + 1 blade fragment/white flint, import + 1 blake/obsidian (black shiny).

49) Tx72/15 (Bag no. 2065) (23.07.98)
5 flakes/radiolarite + 1 flake/black local flint + 3 flakes/local dark brown flint + 2 flakes/light brown local flint + 1 flake/marble 1 flake with retouché/white flint.

K27

50) K27/6b (Bag no. 4556) (19.07.00) F00–5085
Circular stone with edges (D 2cm)/slate) (game piece?).

51) K27/6b (Bag no. 4557) (19.07.00) (F00–5086)
Circular stone, as previous, polished (D 2cm)

52) K27/6b (F00–5081) (19.07.00)
Circular stone, as previous, polished (D. 2cm) (slate).

53) K27/AQB/1 (Bag no. 3689)(27.06.00)
1 flake/radiolarite.

54) K27/AFU/2 3p. (Bag no. 3490)(28.07.99)
1 flake/radiolite (hard direct percussion).

K28

55) K28/9a 1p (Bag no. 4832) (21.06.01)
1 flake/greenish local flint (hard direct percussion) + 1 flake/radiolite with retouché.

K29

55a) K29/AQD/1 (Bag no. 4869)(28.06.01)
1 flake/dark brown local flint (hard direct percussion).

56) K29/7b 1p (Bag no. 4818)(05.07.01)
4 flakes/dark brown local flint (hard direct percussion) + 1 flake/light brown local flint (hard direct percussion) + 1 end scraper /light brown local flint (hard direct percussion).

57) K29/7b 1p (Bag no. 4906) (04.07.01)

4 flakes/dark brown local flint (hard direct percussion) + 1 flake/light brown local flint (hard direct percussion) + 1 end scraper/light brown locl flint (hard direct percussion).

58) K29/7b 2p (Bag no. 4919) (05.07.01)
2 flakes/radiolite (hard direct percussion) +1 flake/radiolite – burned.

59) K29/7b 2p (Bag no. 4923) (06.07.01)
3 flakes/radiolite + 2 flakes/dark brown local flint + 2 flakes/light brown local flint + 1 flake/marble (hard direct percussion).

60) K29/7b 3p (Bag no.4930)(09.07.01)
1 flake/dark brown local flint (hard direct percussion) + 1 flake/marble + 1 flake/radiolite with retouché.

61) K29/7b 4p (Bag no. 4944)(11.07.01)
4 flake/radiolite (hard direct percussion) + 4 flakes/radiolite + 1 flake/dark brown local flint.

62) K29/7b 4p (Bag no. 4953)(16.07.01)
1 flake/radiolite + 1 flake/marble.

63) K29/7d 1p (Bag no. 4926)(06.07.01)
2 flakes/dark brown local flint + 1 scraper/dark brown local flint + 2 flakes/marble.

64) K29/7e 2p (Bag no. 4938)(10.07.01)
2 flakes/radiolite (hard direct percussion).

65) K29/7e 3p (Bag no. 4940)(10.07.01)
1 flake/radiolite (burned).

66) K29/8b 1p (Bag no. 4974)(18.07.01)
1 flake/radiolite with cortex + 1 flake/dark brown local flint + 1 dark brown local flint (burned).

67) K29/8e 2 p (Bag no. 4945)(12.07.01)
1 flake/radiolite (hard direct percussion).

68) K29/8e 3p (Bag no. 4962)(17.07.01)
1 flake/light brown local flint with contex (hard direct percussion).

69) K29/ARM/1B (Bag no. 4965)(17.07.01)
4 flakes/light brown local flint (hard direct percussion) + 2 flakes/dark brown local flint with cortex + 1 natural flake/light brown local flint with cortex and retouché.

70) K29/9b 1p (Bag no. 4978)(18.07.01)
5 flakes/radiolite + 3 flakes/light brown local flint + 3 flakes/dark brown local with cortex nodule with retouché, possibly scraper + 1 blade fragment/obsidian (redeposited).

71) K29/10b (Bag no. 4983)(18.07.01)
2 flakes/light brown local flint (hard direct percussion) + 1 flake/creamy white – imported + 1 flake/obsidian (grey shiny) with patina suggeting redeposition.

72) K29/11b 3p (Bag no. 4992 (19.07.01))
3 flakes of obsidian + 1 small, fine flint blade + 1 flake of radiolarite.

73) K29/11b 4p (Bag no. 4993) (19.07.01))
1 flake and 1 blade of obsidian. 2 flakes of flint.

74) K29/11b 7p (Bag no. 4998) (19.07.01))
3 blades of obsidian + 5 flakes of flint.

List of concordance

Catalogue number	Bag nos.	Catalogue number	Bag nos.	Catalogue number	Bag nos.
1	3770/3100	41	1275	81	1604
2	3910/3010	42	1275	82	1604
3	AAI	43	1273	83	1604
4	AAI	44	1273	84	1604
5	AAD	45	1273	85	1604
6	AAD	46	1273	86	1606
7	AAD	47	1431	87	1610
8	AAI	48	1431	88	1610
9	3050/4061	49	1609	89	1604
10	ABS	50	1429	90	1606
11	AAO	51	1431	91	1612
12	F15/AAC–3/NW	52	1431	92	1604
13	–	53	1431	93	1612
14	–	54	1431	94	1604
15	F15/3/SW	55	1431	95	1604
16	–	56	1431	96	1437
17	–	57	1431	97	1604
18	–	58	1431	98	1610
19	F15/4/SW	59	1431	99	1612
20	–	60	1429	100	1612
21	–	61	1431	101	1703
22	–	62	1431	102	1604
23	–	63	1431	103	1612
24	–	64	1429	104	1612
25	1259	65	1431	105	1612
26	1259	66	1429	106	1616
27	1259	67	1429	107	1616
28	1259	68	1436	108	180
29	1259	69	1436	109	180
30	1260	70	1603	110	225
31	1262	71	1603	111	225
32	1264	72	1436	112	352
33	1262	73	1436	113	352
34	1264	74	1436	114	302
35	1260	75	1436	115	302
36	1260	76	1603	116	303
37	1260	77	1436	117	302
38	1262	78	1436	118	302
39	1264	79	1436	119	302
40	1273	80	1436	120	302

Catalogue number	Bag nos.	Catalogue number	Bag nos.	Catalogue number	Bag nos.
121	302	166	4835	211	4858
122	302	167	4835	212	4904
123	302	168	4836	213	4904
124	3360	169	4839	214	4858
125	3360	170	1697	215	4904
126	3360	171	1841	216	4904
127	3360	172	1841	217	4858
128	3360	173	1841	218	4904
129	3470	174	1841	219	4904
130	3470	175	1841	220	4938
131	3490	176	1841	221	4938
132	3490	177	1841	222	4940
133	3490	178	1841	223	4940
134	1828	179	1841	224	4940
135	1799	180	1841	225	4940
136	1799	181	1849	226	4945
137	1800	182	1849	227	4945
138	1799	183	1849	228	4945
139	1799	184	1849	229	4945
140	1821	185	1849	230	4959
141	1821	186	1858	231	4959
142	1821	187	1858	232	4959
143	1821	188	1852	233	4958
144	1821	189	1852	234	4961
145	1826	190	1858	235	4961
146	1821	191	4553	236	4961
147	1799	192	4817	237	4961
148	1799	193	4817	238	4978
149	1458	194	4817	239	4978
150	1794	195	4817	240	4978
151	1830	196	4817	241	4978
152	1830	197	4822	242	4984
153	1830	198	4822	243	4983
154	1830	199	4822	244	4983
155	1830	200	4822	245	4969
156	1831	201	4822	246	4969
157	1831	202	4822	247	4969
158	1834	203	4843	248	4967
159	1833	204	4842	249	4985
160	1834	205	4842	250	4986
161	1834	206	4842	251	4992
162	1831	207	4842	252	4992
163	1838	208	4842	253	4997
164	1838	209	4859		
165	1945	210	4859		

Part II

The Neolithic remains at Pangali

The site of Pangali, Mt. Varassova in Aitolia and the Late Neolithic Ib phase in the Aegean: social transformations and changing ideology

By Theofanis Mavridis[183] and Lasse Sørensen[184]

Introduction

By Theofanis Mavridis

The site of Pangali is situated on the eastern slopes of Mount Varassova, on a saddle formed by a pointed and steep ridge, N-S orientated[185] which comes to an end on the coast, at a sloping narrow saddle about 200-250 m wide and about 800m long opening into a small, natural bay.[186] The site was located during an intensive survey of the area conducted in 1995.[187] The next year, a small trial trench was opened to investigate the nature of occupation.[188] A brief account of the excavated material was presented in a preliminary report.[189]

Three levels of occupation were recovered during excavation (stratum 1: topsoil, stratum 2, strata 3 and 3a), relating to a single cultural phase. No differences were observed in reference to the material of each phase, and for this reason all sherds were studied as a single unit. In the deepest level, stratum 3, a hearth was found immediately above bedrock. It measured approximately 1.5 m. in diametre, and consisted of hard burned earth, small pieces of clay, and particles of fine gravel and charcoal (Fig. 64). Also, the material collected during the survey of the area[190] showed no typological or chronological differences compared with that from the excavation, which at an early stage of research was generally characterized as Final Neolithic.

Although the occurrence of a distinct phase at the end of the Neolithic Age had been assumed for several years it was C. Renfrew (1972) who first acknowledged and described in detail some of its characteristics. The limited evidence about this period in the Aegean islands raised difficulties in relating it to earlier and later advances. Therefore, the introduction of the term "Final Neolithic" that could cover all cultural developments and peculiarities in different parts of the Aegean was a necessity.

In Southern Greece this phase is represented by several sites, some of which belong to Phelps' "phases III and VII",[191] or to Diamant's "later village farming stage".[192] More recent studies[193] have distinguished a number of sub-phases, such as the Late Neolithic Ia, b, IIa, b, and took a necessary step for a more detailed classification of a period spanning from ca. 4500 to 3200 BC.[194] In addition, other scholars have made use of the term "Chalcolithic", after the terminology and cultural features of the Balkan Neolithic, and, in this case, it is technology, and especially metallurgy that constitutes the chief criteria for cultural classification.[195] A distinct phase is therefore generally

---

[183] Ephorate of Palaeoanthropology-Speleology, Ministry of Culture (archaeo@otenet.gr).
[184] University of Copenhagen. Saxo-Institute. Department of Archaeology and Ethnology. Vandkunsten 5. DK – 1467 Copenhagen K.
[185] Dietz & Kolonas in FPR, fig.1.
[186] Houby-Nielsen & Moschos in FPR.
[187] Mavridis & Alisøy in FPR, 272-279 and Houby-Nielsen & Moschos in FPR, 255-257.
[188] Cazis in FPR, 280, also fig.3.
[189] Mavridis 2000 in SPR.
[190] Mavridis & Alisøy in FPR.
[191] Phelps 1975.
[192] Diamant 1974.
[193] Sampson 1989. Coleman 1992.
[194] See also Renfrew 1989.
[195] See discussion in Dousougli 1998,127, and Aslanis 2003, 37-46.

Fig. 64. Pangali. The trench excavated.

accepted for the period between the second half of the 5th millennium and the entire 4th millennium B.C., which can be placed between the Late Neolithic Age and the Early Bronze Age. However, in reference to the Aegean chronological sequence it is still not clear what the term "Final Neolithic" denotes: Is it used to imply a single phase? While, in the case of adopting other, more detailed classification systems, it is similarly necessary to specify what these different phases and sub-phases exactly represent.

As a result of recent archaeological finds and a new series of absolute and related dates, what follows is a discussion about a specific phase related to an early stage of the Final Neolithic, the so called LN Ib phase.[196] Radiocarbon dates indicate that it lasted for about 400-500 years, between ca. 4.600 and 4200 BC.[197] This chronological estimation is confirmed for the case of Pangali by radiocarbon dates which recently became available (Jan Heinemeier below). This is a phase during which important innovations become evident, in all spheres of social and economic life, ideology and symbolism. The term "Late Neolithic Ib" is here adopted to imply a cultural horizon of specific characteristics. Correlations of this horizon to earlier and later phases in the Neolithic cultural sequence are a matter of further research.

The Pottery
By Theofanis Mavridis[198]

The pottery assemblage

All sherds from the trial trench were counted and studied. The weight of the Pangali pottery assemblage measured 60 kg and 862 gr (Fig. 65a), a total

---

[196] For a detailed discussion on chronological evidence, see Sampson *et al.* 1998.

[197] For approaches according to which even earlier phases are included in the early stages of the Final Neolithic, see Aslanis 2003.

[198] I would like to thank Dr. L. Kolonas and Dr. Søren Dietz for permission to study the pottery finds. Dr. Dietz for continuous support and advice and P. Fotiadi for editorial assistance.

of 2483 pieces. It is a large quantity of material coming from a 2 x 2 m trench and a deposit one metre thick, and, due to the very limited extent of the excavation, it is uncertain whether all types of shapes and wares are represented.

Beyond the various technological and typological features, a significant part of information concerning the biography; the life history of the vases cannot be extracted. A number of concealed practical and symbolic necessities led to a choice of specific shapes and wares. The operational chain in pottery production, from the selection of raw materials to the sequel of different stages of the construction of the vases, their role and the final disposal as refuse are important aspects that need to be studied for a better understanding of an archaeological context. However, for such a detailed study the aid of several scientific techniques and methods and a systematic field research are demanded.

The largest amount of the material belongs to coarse ware pottery (Fig. 65b). This category comprises all shapes with coarse surface treatment, from thin walled bowls to large pithoi. Burnished and incised wares are also adequately represented. In terms of the different parts of vases represented, body sherds are the most numerous, followed by rim sherds of incised and burnished wares. Few rim sherds of coarse vases, closed as well as open mouthed are recovered. A fair amount of lugs and

surface	5 Kg 194 gr
Stratum 1	17Kg 865 gr
Stratum 2	24Kg 078 gr
Stratum 3	13Kg 725 gr
Total	60Kg 862 gr

Fig. 65a. Weigh of Pangali pottery by strata.

handles occurred, as well as relatively few bases. Lugs and handles belong to all pottery wares, though the number of lugs of incised ware is limited (Fig. 65e). Handles and various types of lugs are characteristic of the Pangali pottery and the specific period in general. Moreover, the material of rim fragments shows that open shapes of all wares (coarse, smoothed, incised, and burnished) predominate (Fig. 65c). In reference to decorated sherds, those with incised patterns and coarse vases with plastic ridges and bands are most characteristic, while impressed and pointillè decorated sherds are limited (Fig. 65f).

The above data are indicative of wares, shapes, body parts etc. present in relation to the total population and the number of sherds into which vases of a specific type have been broken. Pottery fragmentation varies between different types and sizes of vases.

In general, the representation of shapes and wares in a context is influenced by several factors. Overall, thin walled pottery breaks more easily in

Preservation	Body		Rim		Base		Handle/lug		Rim & lug		Total
WARE											
COARSE	765	70%	182	17%	50	5%	72	7%	6	1%	1075
		47%		30%		83%		49%		32%	43%
SMOOTHED	277	79%	30	9%	7	2%	33	2%	3	1%	350
		17%		5%		12%		23%		16%	14%
BURNISHED	368	54%	273	40%	3		36	5%	7	1%	687
		22%		45%				25%		36%	28%
INCISED	71	37%	118	61%					3	2%	192
		4%		20%						16%	8%
PLASTIC	172	96%	2	1%			5	3%			179
		10%						3%			7%
TOTAL	1653	67%	605	24%	60	2%	146	6%	19	1%	2483

Fig. 65b. Body part representation /Total sherds found.

Rim / Ware	Open		Open mouthed		Closed		Total
Coarse	172	91%	12	6%	6	3%	190
		31%		27%		60%	31%
Smoothed	22	67%	8	24%	3	9%	33
		4%		18%		30%	5%
Burnished	250	92%	22	8%	1		273
		44%		48%		10%	44%
Incised	118	98%	3	2%			121
		21%				7%	20%
Total	562	91%	45	7%	10	2%	617

Fig. 65c. Representation of shapes on the basis of rim sherds found.

comparison to coarser wares and is therefore expected to come out in bigger numbers. Other significant elements for pottery preservation and frequency are the strength of items, their function, method and context of use (e.g. the care taken by the user), the cost of manufacture etc.[199] Other post-depositional factors are also important.[200] Moreover, ethno-archaeological research has investigated the role of these factors in relation to types and numbers (the life expectancies) of pottery use. For instance, it has been observed that storage vases lasted considerably longer than other types. On the other hand, pots in daily contact with fire and vessels that are regularly moved have the shortest life span. It is therefore probable that

cooking and serving vessels are over-represented in a context, while more immobile storage jars and higher value items are under-represented. The type of the site and the specific context of the finds (in our case, a hearth) are also responsible for the pottery types and wares represented. Thus, a complicated range of factors needs to be taken into consideration before jumping to any conclusions for the character of a site's occupation. Ethnographic observations are generally useful, but unless proved to reflect on the behavior of agents

[199] Orton, Tyers & Vince 1993, 207.
[200] Schiffer 1987.

handles/lugs / Wares	Strap		Tubular		Horned		Tab		Ledge		Knob		Mastoid		Pellets		Total
Coarse	49	63%	1	1%	3	4%			13	17%	2	3%	5	6%	5	6%	78
		64%		14%		38%				46%		29%		28%		25%	47%
Smoothed	15	40%	2	5%	2	5%			5	13%	2	5%	5	13%	7	19%	38
		20%		29%		25%				18%		29%		28%		35%	23%
Burnished	10	22%	4	9%	3	7%	1	2%	10	22%	3	7%	7	15%	8	17%	46
		13%		57%		38%				36%		42%		38%		40%	28%
Incised	2	67%											1	33%			3
		3%												6%			2%
Total	76	46%	7	4%	8	5%	1		28	17%	7	4%	18	11%	20	12%	165

Fig. 65d. Different types of lugs and handles.

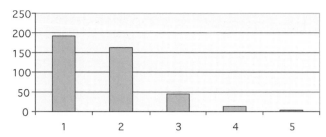

Fig. 65e. Decorated sherds. 1. Incised; 2. Ridges-bands; 3. Lugs etc; 4. Impressed and plastic; 5. Impressed.

of a particular society, they are merely suggestive of relativities.

With reference to the pottery material from Pangali, four general categories have been distinguished according to surface treatment and decoration, as no scientific analyses were conducted. In addition, the fragmentary condition of the specific material led to the classification of the shapes in three general categories: open, wide-mouthed and closed.

The pottery from Pangali is rather homogenous in fabric and consists of semi-coarse and coarse wares. A reddish clay (5/6-5/8 red 10 R Munsell) was used, with a variety of inclusions according to ware and shape. The amount and size of inclusions is rather dependent on the size of the pots and may have been functionally dictated. It is the thickness of the fabric that distinguishes shapes produced in coarse and finer clay. Some inclusions are rather big, >5mm. Even thin walled pots contain inclusions in a fair quantity. Mica seldom appears. The core is black to gray, but occurs also in several shades of brown and red according to firing procedures, turning reddish towards the surface. The varied thickness of blackened core of the Pangali pottery is due to uncontrolled firing.

A large amount of the material presents firing clouds and mottled areas, and in some instances inner and outer surfaces have different colors indicating differences in firing temperatures and atmosphere. The identification of calcium carbonate in some sherds examined[201] gives some clues about firing temperatures since decomposition starts over 750° C.[202] Moh's test provided some additional clues about hardness and firing conditions. The majority of sherds belong to the category that can be scratched with a fingernail and a lim-

ited amount was harder, especially the fine burnished ware.

It is in general a dark faced pottery ranging in shades of brown to gray and black. Very few sherds that are heavily slipped and burnished and bear plastic decoration appear with a dark red surface, and constitute a specific category. Another burnished category with dark gray/black burnished surface and carinated shapes can be distinguished, although represented by a small number of samples. In several cases, the visible marks of a burnisher with a luster imparted to grooves were identified. The phenomenon of cracked and crazed surfaces is not rare, and temper comes through the surface.

Several stages in the manufacturing process of the pots are evident, such as trimming and scraping on closed vases, or fine striations indicating dry burnishing. Lugs and other plastic elements were added separately, while in some instances the bases of pithoi were constructed from a coil added around the main body of the vase. Incisions on thin walled pots were deep with thrown up edges or shallow, according to the plastic condition of the clay. Moreover, a detailed recording of the circumference of rims showed that the majority were preserved in 5% (in relation to thin walled open vases) and in 10% (mostly coarse vases, pithoi etc).

Wall thickness was measured for almost all sherds, as to some extent it relates to vessel type, their use, and function, and is indicative of specific choices on behalf of the potters. More specifically, sherds with walls 0,4-0, 6 cm thick belong to thin-walled vases, usually burnished, and open or wide-mouthed. Medium sized walls belong to smoothed or coarser vases, some thin walled jars included. Thick walls (1,1-1,5 cm thick) belong to large pithoi and other specific types. With reference to vessel size, the majority is medium in size (14-25 rim diametre range). Very small or large vases are not the rule.

Some clues about pottery production can be mentioned. Some standardization is evident in relation to open shapes. Rounded, straight walled,

[201] with the use of a 10% dilute solution of Hydrochloric acid.
[202] Rye 1981, 33.

flaring rim, closed and some carinated bowls are common among all wares.

A distinction between smoothed and coarse vases is not always possible. Additionally, in relation to incised ware vases occurred with fine burnished surface and carefully executed decoration but also larger and coarser examples with roughly executed decoration. Large biconical and flat unperforated lugs, as well as plastic ridges, are characteristic of large pithoi, although the latter are found similarly on fine burnished vases. Raised knobs and a variety of lugs also decorated coarser wares, and smaller ones were applied for the decoration of finer pottery categories as well.

Wares and shapes.

The pottery wares from Pangali were distinguished on the criteria of surface treatment and decoration. As already mentioned, it has not been possible to conduct any scientific analysis for a better comprehension of the role and meaning of the material culture in a specific socio-temporal context. The sherds presented here characterize the main forms (typology) of the material excavated. The numbers (n. hereafter) of the sherds mentioned in the text are the same for the figures and catalogue of finds. Some additional sherds that have no number and are not included in the catalogue were also placed in the figures, in frames at the bottom of each typological category (e.g. open shapes, handles, sherds with incised decoration) in order to present minor variations of the basic forms.

Sherds with number 1-20 refer to open shapes. No differences were observed in relation to open forms present in each ware. Sherds with numbers 21-24 refer to sherds of closed bowls-open mouth vases of the fine burnished ware, numbers 25-28 to open shapes of different wares with asymmetrical rims, numbers 29-42 to sherds of the incised ware, numbers 43-46 to closed shapes, numbers 47-62 to decorated sherds of pithoi, jars and other coarse vases, numbers 63-82 to characteristic lugs and handles of all wares, numbers 83-84 to fine burnished and slipped decorated sherds, numbers 85-94 to basic base forms, and numbers 95-98 to various clay items.

Burnished ware (Pls. 21-22, Fig. 66)

Burnished ware comprises bowls and wide-mouthed vases. In most cases they are thin- walled, fine slipped and burnished. Surface colours range from variations of brown, dark red to grey/black. The fabric is semi-coarse, with sporadic inclusions. Some mica is also present.

Some wide-mouthed vases or closed bowls belong to a special variety (nos. 21-24). The majority of samples forms a short neck or represent a differentiated rim. The closest parallels of these vases are found in Limnes cave[203] but also at other sites, such as Nestor's cave,[204] and Pevkakia.[205] Few carinated shapes, mostly bowls with black burnished surface, belong to the burnished category as well.[206]

A very few sherds are heavily burnished and coated with thick dark red slip. They also bear evidence of plastic decoration (small knobs and curved ridges) (nos. 83, 84). As only two samples of body fragments were preserved, and no shape can be recognized, their relation with the socalled LN II red burnished bowls, is uncertain. Red burnished bowls have been recovered at sites slightly later than Pangali, such as Athens Agora[207] or Tharrounia cave.[208] The examples from the Agora excavations represent deep, thick walled shapes[209] that do not correspond to the Pangali fine, thin walled vases.

Bowls of various categories are very common and known from many sites in this period.[210] As previously mentioned, burnished, incised and open vases with smoothed or rough surfaces share the same shapes. Rounded and conical bowls of different types are most common, while flaring rim, straight walled, closed and carinated samples have also been recovered.

Rounded bowls and some conical ones (nos. 1, 2, 10, 11, 13, 15) are known from numerous sites,

[203] Sampson 1997, 136-136, fig. 40.
[204] Sampson 1980, fig. 18:39.
[205] Weisshaar 1989, types 72, 73.
[206] See Mavridis SPR, 279, also n.:19.
[207] Immerwahr 1971, table 68.
[208] Sampson 1993, 161, fig. 182, 183.
[209] Immerwahr 1971, 5.
[210] Pullen 1995, 7.

Fig. 66. Pangali.
Burnished wares.

among which Ayios Demetrios[211] and Limnes cave.[212] A rim fragment with flat top decorated with slashes, slightly carinated in profile (nos. 3) is reminiscent of a sample from Aghios Demetrios.[213] Other carinated profiles with or without handles (nos 16, 67) find close parallels at Aghios Demetrios.[214] Vases carrying handles below the rim and straight or curved walls belong to burnished or incised wares (nos 7, 8, and 39). They find close parallels at sites, such as Aghios Demetrios,[215] Limnes cave,[216] Nestor's cave[217] and Tharrounia cave.[218] Carinated bowls, S-shaped in profile, with differentiated rim are common at Pangali (in several varieties) (nos 17, 20). They are known from Limnes cave,[219] Aghios Demetrios,[220] Tharrounia cave,[221] Aghios Galas,[222] Emborio phases VIIII-VI,[223] Kalythies cave,[224] Pevkakia.[225]

Straight walled (nos. 6, 14) and flaring rim bowls (no. 9) have been recovered at numerous sites, such as Limnes cave,[226] Plakari in Karystos,[227] Saliagos on Antiparos,[228] Ayios Demetrios,[229] Franchthi cave,[230] Kephala,[231] Emborio,[232] Kitsos cave[233] and more. Few instances (nos. 26-28), unfortunately in a very fragmentary state, could belong to vases with asymmetrical rim, such as those found in Tharrounia cave[234] and Pevkakia.[235]

Small handles of various types, such as strap handles, tubular lugs, ledge lugs as well as plastic knobs

[211] Zachos 1987, figs. 16-17.
[212] Sampson 1997, fig. 1:8.
[213] Zachos 1987, fig.16:80.
[214] Zachos 1987, fig.20.
[215] Zachos 1987, figs. 21:87:7, 289:80, Δ:13.
[216] Sampson 1997, figs. 34:524, 569, 51, 35:431, 38:465, 302, 303, 314.
[217] Sampson 1980, figs.16:13, 19:23.
[218] Sampson 1993, figs.32:33,40, 35:106.
[219] Sampson 1997, fig.34:535, 569.
[220] Zachos 1987, fig.76:82.
[221] Sampson 1993, table 19,21, figs. 34:57, 72, 48:41.
[222] Hood 1981, fig. 27:157, 158, 162.
[223] Hood 1981, figs. 98:14a,b,c, 123:158.
[224] Sampson 1987, fig.41:433.
[225] Weisshaar 1989, type 8-9, table 98.
[226] Sampson 1997, figs. 31, 32.
[227] Keller 1982, 54, fig. 2.6:P21, P28, P29, P131.
[228] Evans, Renfrew 1968, figs. 49-52.
[229] Zachos 1987, fig. 16.274:81, 17:35/81.
[230] Vitelli 1999, 40, 58, 60, 70.
[231] Coleman 1977, 13, table 27:34.
[232] Hood 1981, fig. 94:4a,b.
[233] Lambert 1981, 310.
[234] Sampson 1993, fig. 78.
[235] Weisshaar 1989, figs. 47, 92.

Fig. 67. Pangali. Incised wares.

and mastoid protrusions belong to vases of the burnished ware.

Incised ware (Pl. 23, Fig. 67)

Incised ware represents the fine decorated pottery category of the site (nos. 29-42). The Pangali material represents the first evidence for the occurrence of this ware in this region of West Greece. Shapes are thin or medium walled. Rounded and conical bowls (nos. 29, 31, 32, 33, 34, 35, 37) as well as straight walled and flaring rim ones (no. 42 and drawings in the bottom framing), or some carinated shapes (nos. 41) occur. Closed bowls constitute another category (nos. 36, 38, and 40). Small sized bowls were found (no. 30), as well as a limited number with diameter of rim ca. 30 cm (no. 29). Lugs and handles are rare (nos. 32, 39). This observation is in accordance with the incised sherds from Prosymna,[236] while the material from Limnes cave has given no evidence of lugs related to this ware.

The Pangali incised sherds were represented in an adequate quantity. Mostly rim fragments were found.

A few samples (no. 25) could belong to open vases with asymmetrical rim such as those from Tharrounia cave[237] and Pevkakia.[238] The limited amount of published incised sherds from Drakaina

[236] Blegen 1937, fig. 627.
[237] Sampson 1993, fig. 78.
[238] Weisshaar 1989, figs. 47, 92.

cave on Kephalonia[239] does not seem close to the Pangali material.

Some vases are particularly thin walled with fine burnished surface, while others are coarser with plainer smoothed surface. The same characteristics more or less appear in Limnes cave.[240] The incised ware from East Yerogalaro, Prosymna has been considered rather coarse.[241]

Decoration quality varies in terms of the motifs' execution. Incisions are very fine and shallow indicating that they were executed after the clay had dried. Some sherds need to be observed at a specific angle for the decoration to be visible. Other samples carry decoration executed with less caution. In most of these cases, incisions have thrown up edges indicating that they were executed when the clay was still in plastic condition.

There is a great variety of motifs, which are virtually unique on each separate vase. Some standard patterns were used, but their orientation, combinations and symmetry vary (see Fig. 28 with all represented incised motifs). The majority of the motifs are rectilinear. A limited number of curvilinear ones occurred.

Such a decorative variation can be attributed to the agency of the potters and the symbolism or semantics of certain motifs or combinations of motifs. The decoration was executed in zones below the rim or generally at the upper part of the vases. Very few bases or lower parts of fine ware were identified, none with incised decoration. As indicated, the area below rim was the main decorated zone. The most usual patterns are hatched zones (horizontal, vertical or oblique), multiple chevrons, different types of hatched triangles (in row or antithetic), lines in all short of combinations and positions as parts of a larger motif, very often within the limits of borderlines. A limited number of motifs are cross-hatched. A more detailed analysis of the decoration syntax was not possible due to the fragmentary state of the material.

In the case of the Prosymna incised ware, decoration consists of friezes below the rim, divided in panels. There has been also evidence of a lower and an upper horizontal marginal line. At Klenia, the decoration is executed more freely, without the presence of such margins.[242] Fine incised ware

has been recovered at many sites of central Greece, such as Orchomenos,[243] Elateia,[244] Kitsos cave,[245] Tharrounia cave,[246] but these instances do not share similar characteristics with the incised ware from Pangali. The Prosymna incised ware has been identified as a Peloponnesian phenomenon, with parallels in Klenia, Corinth and relatively limited in other areas.[247]

The Pangali material finds close parallels in Limnes cave,[248] as well as Prosymna.[249] A limited amount of sherds was found at Aghios Demetrios,[250] together with pattern burnished ware, which is absent from Pangali. This could be indicative of an upper chronological limit of the ware in use. The best of samples of this specific ware are concentrated in the south-western part of Greece. However, its distribution remains a matter of further investigation.

Smoothed-coarse ware (Pl. 25)

Smoothed and coarse wares are described under a single category, as the quality of surface treatment is not easy to distinguish in each case, and no important differences exist in relation to shapes.

Open shapes with smoothed or coarse surface belong to bowls similar to those described in the previous two wares (nos. 1, 2 and bottom framing). Apart from this category of vases, the remainder of the shapes (mainly jars and pithoi) was represented mostly by body fragments, which made the identification of shapes a difficult task, specifically in reference to wide-mouthed and closed vases. Handles and lugs are common. Ledge and tubular lugs, strap handles, knobs and mastoid pro-

[239] Chatziotou *et al.* 1989, 55, fig. 14.
[240] Sampson 1997, 232-252.
[241] Blegen 1937, 23.
[242] Phelps 1975, 301.
[243] Kunze 1931, pl. IX.4.
[244] Weinberg 1962, pl. 62d, 7-9.
[245] Lambert 1981, pl. XLIII.
[246] Sampson 1993, 91-100.
[247] Phelps 1975, 300. Sampson 1997, 245.
[248] Sampson 1997, figs. 65-73.
[249] Phelps 1975, 300.
[250] Zachos 1987, fig. 34, table 17a.

trusions occurred. Except the usual bowl shapes, some smoothed rim fragments are very wide, and may be characterized as pans. They have thick, straight walls with rounded or differentiated rim (nos. 49, 50 and bottom framing).

The wares with smoothed and coarse surface comprise different types of jars. The limited number of rim fragments preserved permitted the reconstruction of only very few shapes, such as hole-mouthed and conical neck jars (nos 43-46), funnel neck jars[251] and jars with thick rounded rim[252] or differentiated rim (no. 46). Also some jars with straight walls occur (nos. 53, 57), as well as fragments from the shoulder of jars (no. 51). All of these closed forms are common finds at several sites of this period, such as Limnes cave[253] and Aghios Demetrios.[254]

Plastic decoration features pithoid vases (Fig. 68a-c). Coarser and larger pithoi (Pl. 26), with walls over 1 cm thick, are decorated with raised bands and cordons ovoid or squarish in section (nos. 52, 55, 57), which are occasionally combined with or form the edges of flat raised bands bearing

impressed dots (nos. 51, 58, 59), with ledge lugs (no. 61) or fingertip impressions in the form of a rope-like pattern (no. 56), and with strap handles bearing plastic decoration (no. 76). Thinner plastic bands, cordons, and ridges, half rounded in section, are commonly found in various combinations on jars, which are usually more carefully manufactured (nos. 51, 52, 54, 57). In most cases, bands and ridges are straight, with the exception of few curved ones (no. 54, Fig. 68a). In a single case a cordon is decorated with oblique slashes.[255] Since the material is very fragmentary, no safe conclusions can be drawn in reference to the decoration syntax.

Some fragments seem to belong to exceptionally large pithoi with various types of plastic decoration. They are coarse, with no special attention paid in surface treatment. To this category belongs

---

[251] Mavridis, Alisøy in FPR, fig. 13: 23.
[252] Mavridis, Alisøy 1998, fig. 12: 18.
[253] Sampson 1997, figs. 49-52.
[254] Zachos 1987, fig. 25, 26.
[255] Mavridis 2000, fig. 27.

Fig. 68b. Pangali. Jars and pithoi.

one pithos fragment with a combination of plastic rectilinear and curvilinear bands,[256] and one thick rim fragment with a single curved band bearing a spiral motif,[257] which were found during the 1995 surface survey, and two fragments of a large pithos with ledge lugs, broad raised bands decorated with impressed dots, and cordons (nos. 61, 62), which were recovered from the trial trench. They are reminiscent of an intact vase found at Sfakovouni, in Arcadia.[258]

Plastic decoration is characteristic in this period. In southern Greece it is known from sites such as Asea, Ayioritika,[259] Aghios Demetrios,[260] Limnes cave,[261] Prosymna,[262] Nestor's cave[263] in the Peloponnese, the Athenian Agora[264] and Kitsos cave[265] in Attica, Leukas[266] in the Ionian, Saliagos[267] and Kephala[268] in the Cyclades, Tharrounia cave in Euboea,[269] as well as from several sites of this period in Thessaly[270] and elsewhere.

[256] Mavridis & Alisøy 1998, fig. 12:1.
[257] Mavridis, Alisøy 1998, fig. 13:5.
[258] Spyropoulos 1996, 275.
[259] Phelps 1975, 333.
[260] Zachos 1987, figs. 26-28.
[261] Sampson 1997, figs. 59, 61.
[262] Blegen 1937, fig. 626.
[263] Sampson 1980, fig. 17.
[264] Immerwahr 1971, pl. 11:169.
[265] Lambert 1981, 351.
[266] Dörpfeld 1927, pls. 84, 85.
[267] Evans & Renfrew 1968, figs. 42, 43.
[268] Coleman 1977, 12.
[269] Sampson 1993, figs. 87, 88, 89.
[270] Gallis 1992, 74.

Fig. 68c. Pangali. Jars and pithoi.

Fig. 69a. Pangali. Lugs and handles.

Several small fragments of a coarse vessel type were found, called "strainer" due to its numerous perforations (nos. 47, 48). Two different types were distinguished. Some sherds are very brittle, not well fired and bear holes with thrown up edges indicating that they have been opened when the clay was still wet (no. 47). Their surface is rough and the exterior usually black. The second type has a smoothed surface, with perforations opened when the clay was at a leather hard stage (no. 48). The latter are also better fired and their clay is always red/reddish brown with numerous inclusions. No rim or base fragments were found.

Several similar sherds have been recovered in Limnes cave, where they were identified as deep closed vases with a flat base (occasionally with holes) and rounded rim.[271] They are also known from Aghios Demetrios,[272] where a function for liquids was proposed for the finer category and another as fire holders for the coarser ones.

Another fragment with perforations (no. 60) has very thick walls, and seems to belong to a different type due to the different surface treatment. A reconstruction of shape is difficult. It is possibly close to samples from Aghios Demetrios[273] and Kitsos cave.[274]

The coarse and smoothed wares from Pangali, with vases either undecorated or with plastic decoration, together with a group of characteristic types

Fig. 69c. Pangali. Lugs and handles.

[271] Sampson 1997, fig. 53.
[272] Zachos 1987, fig. 21:32/83, 14/82.
[273] Zachos 1987, fig. 21:32/83.
[274] Lambert 1981, fig. 244.

Fig. 69b. Pangali. Lugs and handles.

of lugs and handles, represent a most identifiable category of pottery in the Final Neolithic. A change in pottery production, consumption, use and meaning of pottery is evident during this phase.

Handles and lugs (Pl. 26)

Lugs and handles are a common characteristic of the Pangali pottery material (Fig. 69, a-c). Large strap handles (no. 76) are commonly found on coarse vases, smaller ones among the remainder of the wares (no. 72 and bottom framing). There is also a variety of buttons (no. 65 and bottom framing), and mastoid protrusions (no. 67) on burnished open vases, while larger raised ones are found on smoothed or coarse vases (nos. 63, 66). Button like protrusions are very common at most sites of the period. They are known from Alepotrypa cave, where on one occasion they have been combined with ridges and bands giving the impression of a human face,[275] Tharrounia cave,[276] Pevkakia,[277] and many other sites.

A type of a flat lug rising above the rim (tab handle) (no. 73) occurs on a burnished rounded bowl. It is well known from sites, such as Saliagos,[278] Ftelia,[279] Emborio,[280] Limnes cave,[281] and Pevkakia.[282] Tubular lugs in vertical or horizontal position are relatively uncommon (nos. 69-71). Several types of biconical (no. 82) and horned handles (nos. 75, 77-79) are found on burnished, smoothed and coarse vases[283] as well as a variety of unperforated flat lugs (ledge lugs), placed vertically or horizontally on burnished or coarser vases (nos. 74, 80, 81). They are rounded or squarish in section. All shapes of handles from Pangali occur also in Limnes cave.[284]

---

[275] Papathanasopoulos 1996, 218.

[276] Sampson 1993, fig. 115.

[277] Weisshaar 1989, figs. 48:7, 69:14.

[278] Evans & Renfrew 1968, fig. 58: 2, 3, 11, 12.

[279] Sampson 2002, fig. 111.

[280] Hood 1981, fig. 105: 8-11.

[281] Sampson 1997, fig. 56:149.

[282] Weisshaar 1989, table 39:2.

[283] See for example Saliagos Evans, Renfrew 1968, figs. 46:8-17, 58: 10, 15, 59: 4,5,8, Ftelia, Sampson 2002, figs. 105-107, 111, 112 and Pevkakia, Weisshaar 1989, 90:18.

[284] Sampson 1997, figs. 112, 116-118.

Fig. 70a. Pangali. Ring bases.

Fig. 70b. Pangali. Ring bases.

Bases (Pl. 27)

The fragments of bases were less common in comparison to rim and body fragments. They belong almost exclusively to vases with smoothed or coarse surfaces. Samples of burnished ware are very limited. No bases belonging to vases with incised decoration were found.

Flat bases predominate (nos. 85, 86), while beveled ones are also common (nos. 93, 94). A few hollowed bases (no. 92) of coarse vases were also found. Ring bases are a characteristic feature of the Pangali pottery assemblage (nos. 87-90 and bottom framing), and belong to burnished, smoothed and coarse vases (Fig. 70, a and b). No fragments belonging to the upper part of the same vases were found. It is possible that some bowl fragments, especially of the straight walled type, belong to

vases with this type of bases. They have been recovered at other sites, such as Aghios Demetrios,[285] Limnes cave,[286] Ftelia,[287] Pevkakia[288] and elsewhere. There are also samples of a conical low foot, either concave or convex in profile.[289]

A single sample belongs to a rather thin walled, coarse vase. It is a type of a double base formed by a differentiated base (possibly a high ring base) and the lower part of the main body (no. 91). It is uncertain whether it belongs to a vase with a ring base or to a special vessel type called "rechaud", which is known only from the Aegean.[290]

Other clay items (Pl. 29)

A clay artifact, which is long, rounded in section, and carries an incision at the beginning of the larger part (no. 95), could belong to the handle of a scoop,[291] or to a figurine.[292]

Several spindle whorls of different types were also recovered (nos. 96-98 and Fig. 71). They commonly occur in the sites of this period.[293] Some were burned after breakage.

Changes in pottery production and consumption

As already mentioned, changes are also evident in the use and meaning of the material culture. It has been observed that a large amount of material was deposited at these sites. It is a practice possibly connected with a re-direction of the symbolic expression.

In general, the study of all the stages from the production to the final deposition of artifacts is of

---

[285] Zachos 1987, fig. 30.

[286] Sampson 1997, fig. 58.

[287] Sampson 2002, figs. 89, 93.

[288] Weisshaar 1989, figs. 79: 19-20, 54: 13, 16, 18.

[289] n. 87-89, see also Mavridis 2000, fig. 55: 1, 2.

[290] Ftelia on Mykonos, Sampson 2002, 71-73; and Tharrounia in Euboea, Sampson 1993, fig. 90.

[291] See examples from Tharrounia cave, Sampson 1993, 178, 179; and Kitsos cave, Lambert 1981, pl. X.

[292] See examples from Pevkakia, Weisshaar 1989, fig. 66: 1, 4, 14.

[293] See the samples from Limnes cave, Sampson 1997, fig. 77.

primary importance, as expressions of changes in social strategy and ideology can be identified. Such an approach has furnished important information in reference to the role and meaning of several artifacts dated to the Aegean Neolithic and Early Bronze Age.[294] Significant regional differences as well as site-and-context distinctions were recognized, which are indicative of the material culture's changing role and meaning.

There is relatively limited information about pottery production and consumption in the Aegean Neolithic. Given the abundance of pottery in most settlements, it is logical to assume that pottery artifacts carried a range of connotations and meanings. Despite the appearance of analyses dealing with the use and production of specific shapes, wares and motifs,[295] the presence of specific strategies and choices and the occurrence of decoration elements in broader areas are still difficult to explain in many aspects.

It is generally accepted that pots were used for the display and consumption of food, drink or for storage and food preparation. Nevertheless, the symbolic meaning of these and other practices are not well figured out. With reference to the earlier Neolithic phases it has been suggested that the use of vessels was not their practical function over the fire:[296] they were not used in domestic activities, but probably related to symbolic and ceremonial spheres.[297] It has also been suggested that fine decorated pots were suitable for drinking and eating occasions where intra communal sharing and inter community hospitality were in operation.[298]

The ceramic assemblages of the second half of the 5th millennium B.C. and possibly of an even earlier date indicate certain changes in the dynamics of pottery production and consumption. It is generally believed that, during the Final Neolithic, the importance and role of decorated pottery weakened.[299] It is possible that pottery in the Final Neolithic takes part in a wider array of social and economic activities. However, the prevalence of coarse wares over fine decorated ones does not necessarily imply that the symbolic and social significance of pottery vanished, but that their earlier use and meaning has changed.

Fig. 71. Pangali. Spindle whorls.

Thus, approaches to the Final Neolithic pottery production suggestive of a decline in the ability of potters to create more elaborate vessels are not necessarily factual.[300] Another suggestion refers to changes related to the pottery manufacturers as well as their social role in the Final Neolithic.[301] The predominant idea is that pottery becomes utilitarian in function, with its main production coming into the hands of non-specialists and kept within the domestic, private sphere.[302] This relates to the phenomenon that, in contradiction to the preceding village cohesion, household autonomy appears most significant during the Final Neolithic, in combination also with an unequal accumulation of exchange tokens and hoarding of valuables indicating that such operations were channeled through elite groups.[303]

However, a close examination of pottery production of the Final Neolithic offers an alternative explanation: There is no real decline of craftsmanship, as new techniques, shapes, types of decoration etc. emerge; pottery does not loose its importance, but it is being transformed in terms of its meaning, similarly to many aspects of social and

[294] Nakou 1995, Broodbank 2000, Day & Wilson 2002, Mavridis 2002.
[295] For example Cullen 1985.
[296] Vitelli 1989, 24.
[297] Vitelli 1989, 1993b, 213-217.
[298] Halstead 1995, 17.
[299] Vitelli 1993a.
[300] Kalogirou 2003, 104.
[301] Vitelli 1993a, 252, Kalogirou 2003, 104.
[302] e.g. Vitelli 1993a, 252.
[303] Halstead 1995, 18.

economic life. Fine pottery categories, such as burnished and incised wares, have a major part in the Pangali pottery assemblage. Likewise, crusted and pattern burnished wares as well as some painted ones in some regions, still occur during the Final Neolithic.

It is during this phase and more notably during the LNIIa period that "ceramic regions" become broader as parts of a more complex social situation.[304] It seems that the use and symbolism of the Final Neolithic pottery were transformed from aspects related to regional alliance and co-operation.[305] Thus, changes in pottery forms, production, use and meaning are therefore connected to their new role and significance which is indicative of a stronger symbolic component,[306] especially in relation to the technological domain as a combination of material agency and cognition.[307] These new material manifestations refer to more general social transformations, possibly evident by new forms of elite expression and the statement of social identity in ways still not feasible in previous times.

The Pangali site as well as several cave and open-air sites such as Tharrounia,[308] Limnes,[309] Gioura,[310] Sarakenos,[311] Kitsos,[312] Leontari caves,[313] Pevkakia[314] and many more, seem related to some of the aspects previously described. The study case of the Late Neolithic Ib phase is exemplary for the recognition and examination of many social, symbolic and ideological manifestations of human existence.

Summary

Character of occupation and chronology

The opening of a trial trench at the site of Pangali brought to light a significant amount of pottery, and many other finds indicating a range of activities conducted at the site. Figurines and items of personal adornment were almost entirely absent. A similar picture was represented by the Limnes cave assemblage. A specialized or periodical usage of the latter site has been proposed.[315]

In the case of the Pangali excavation, the study

of animal bones indicates a periodical occupation of the site during early winter. This evidence is not related to specialized economic practices (pastoralism or intensive exploitation of the secondary products of animals). Most of the slaughtered animals were young in age, evidence that characterize a meat oriented economy. The bone material is dominated by sheep and goat; cattle and pig remains are also present. Wild animals were also identified (about 19% of the assemblage). Bones of wild boar (young and adult animals), fox, roe and red deer, fish, birds as well as land snails and sea shells were recovered.[316] Stone tools support the picture of the increased importance of hunting (presence of finished and unfinished points), as well as the practice of several other activities. They were produced locally; however, the preliminary stages of the operational chain are not well represented. Pre-shaped cores were brought to the site from elsewhere. The relatively few finished tools and cores recovered probably indicate that stone items were removed from the site. Radiolarite and most of the flint varieties were available in the vicinity of the site. Obsidian was frequently imported indicating exchange activities. Grinding stones and spindle whorls were also found.

In contradiction to the evidence from animal remains and stone tools, pottery does not indicate a specialized or periodical occupation of the site. All wares and shapes known from other sites were

[304] Vitelli 1999, 103.

[305] Established through the spread of wares and motifs in different sites, e.g. in the case of the shared elements of the Middle Neolithic Urfirnis, see Cullen 1985).

[306] Nakou 1995, 2.

[307] Lemonnier 1986, Dobres 2000.

[308] Sampson 1993.

[309] Sampson 1997.

[310] Sampson 1996, Mavridis in press.

[311] Sampson 1998.

[312] Lambert 1981.

[313] Karali & Mavridis (in press), Karali, Mavridis, Komazopoulou 2005.

[314] Weisshaar 1989.

[315] Sampson 1997, 273).

[316] See details in Bangsgaard & Strand Petersen this volume.

identified. The presence of storage jars, although limited in number, in addition to the wide range of activities attested (on the basis of the different artifact categories recovered), could possibly suggest that the movement of people was not great in distance. The general impression of the character of the site is not that of a specialized camp related exclusively to the movement of flocks in upland areas (see below); however further detailed research could possibly answer some of these speculations.

The Limnes cave assemblage, which is very close connected to that of Pangali, has been divided into three phases, similarly to the Pangali stratigraphy. The C-14 datings from Limnes cave correspond to ca. 500 years of occupation spanning the largest part of the second half of the 5th millennium, between ca. 4.700 and 4.200 B.C. This chronological evidence corresponds to Phase II of Tharrounia cave[317] and Phase III of Kitsos cave.[318] This evidence indicates that we are dealing with a phase that can be placed prior to the appearance of the pattern burnished ware[319] and that slightly corresponds, at its earliest part, with the last phase of the matt-painted ware (the polychrome variety). The evidence from Prosymna[320] and Gioura cave in the Northern Sporadhes[321] is also indicative of such a case. However, the stratigraphical data of these two sites are not completely clear. Therefore, the Pangali occupation can be placed at the second half of the 5th millennium B.C., and corresponds to the Late Neolithic Ib phase.

It seems that the assemblages excavated at Pangali, Kastria and to a lesser extent at Aghios Demetrios and Prosymna, represent a regional cultural complex that shares common elements with other parts of the Aegean, most of which appeared for the first time during this period. Coarse wares[322] with plastic decoration, biconical, horned and other types of ledge lugs as well as obsidian and flint arrowheads characterize the material culture of this period. The barbed/tanged and tanged points found at Pangali, have also been recovered at sites, such as Franchthi cave (phases III-I),[323] Kitsos cave[324] and many others.[325] Their recovery during surface surveys can date almost securely the phase of a location's occupation.[326] New character-

istic elements are also evident in relation to the use of space and the location of sites in the landscape (see below), which strengthen the possibility of a distinct cultural horizon at the beginning of the Aegean Final Neolithic. Some of these features could have been present even earlier however; it is during the second half of the 5th millennium B.C. that they are strongly evident.

The site of Pangali in its wider cultural context

At least for the time being, the character of the occupation at Pangali cannot be easily defined in reference to a model of a year round or seasonal occupation, or of a special purpose site. The location of the site at Pangali is typical of this phase, during which marginal environments (meaning the habitation of spots in the landscapes that were not intensively inhabited before), were colonized. Upland areas, caves as well as seascapes were preferred for habitation. For instance, it is characteristic that in the region of the Peloponnese during the period between the end of the 5th and the beginning of the 4th millennium B.C., Neolithic habitation increases, especially in caves (at 27%).[327] It is also important to stress that systematic survey programs in Mainland Greece indicate that apart from caves, open air sites are also well attested.[328]

This evidence in combination with the scarcity of extensive architectural remains has been considered as indicative of a greater emphasis on a seasonal, pastoral economy[329] together with the

---

[317] Sampson 1993, 286, table 65.
[318] Lambert 1981, 77.
[319] See the Aghios Demetrios' stratigraphy, Zachos 1987.
[320] Blegen 1937, figs. 628, 629-630.
[321] Mavridis in press.
[322] Jacobsen 1969, 271.
[323] Jacobsen 1969, 82.
[324] Lambert 1981, 13.
[325] See Diamant 1974, 223, Zachos 1987, fig. 75.
[326] e.g. Carter, Ydo, 1996, fig. 18:5.
[327] Diamant 1974.
[328] e.g. see Wells, Runnels 1999.
[329] Diamant 1974, Wickens 1986, Zachos 1987, Sampson 1993, Douzougli 1998, Dousougli, Zachos 2002.

exploitation of secondary products of domesticated animals.[330] Nevertheless, it has been admitted[331] that the use of caves and upland areas during this period does not necessarily indicate new economic practices. So far, evidence supportive of economic specialization (pastoralism) is weak. There are no data available for trade markets that could have been supplied with the products of such a specialized activity or for herds big enough to support such markets.[332]

It should be noted that the Pangali trial excavation as well as evidence from the investigation of other sites are supportive of an increase in the occurrence of spindle whorls during the Final Neolithic. In the Franchthi cave, such evidence has been interpreted as indicative of intensive exploitation of wool and possibly of the development of a local textile industry.[333] In addition, some other explanations have also been proposed in relation to evidence on the habitation of marginal environments. An environmental/economic approach suggests that the selection of sites during the Final Neolithic is due to a shift from spring fed to rain fed agriculture and the use of less demanding crops, such as legumes and barley.[334]

According to Runnels and van Andel (1987), the expansion of trade activity result in a population increase and a more dispersed settlement pattern spreading into marginal agricultural areas. It is also possible that the existence of many open air and cave sites characterizes a more settled way of life that can be traced more easily in the landscape.[335] In this respect, the increased visibility of Final Neolithic sites is connected to the absence of raids and adventures that were taking place in earlier periods, a parameter that established a feeling of security and allowed people to move freely in larger areas.[336]

Apart from the explanation finally to be accepted, it is evident that major changes take place in relation to landscape use, inter and intra site space. A consideration of these phenomena is necessary not only in relation to economic processes, but also to all aspects of social life. Since most of these sites were occupied for the first time during the Final Neolithic, it seems possible that the deliberate accumulation of material, a common practice

in the Balkan Neolithic,[337] could have played a symbolic role in making these landscapes familiar and "domesticated". It is also possible that the declaration of the human presence in the landscape, at an individual and collective level, was of primary importance. Some sites of this period can be considered as places for gathering events serving ceremonial purposes,[338] which could give another possible explanation for the deposition of considerable quantities of material in the Final Neolithic sites.

In reference to the selection of settlement location, it is important to note that, like Pangali, not all sites are distant from the sea. Some locations appear to be rather naturally fortified, while occasionally had direct access and eye contact with the sea. In later periods, at the early stages of the Early Bronze Age, low hills, very close to the sea shore, were more preferable for habitation indicating a different space use and ideology in reference to the selection of settlement location.[339] The identification of Early Helladic I material on the hill of Aghia Triada in the vicinity of Pangali[340] supports these shifts in settlement location. The occurrence of naturally protected sites, but also fortified ones[341] is another element in reference to settlement patterns of this period.[342] The possible existence of different cultural traditions at the same time (a matter that needs further documentation) could be supportive of the notion that security was the main target behind choices in settlement location.

Based on the interpretation of obsidian

---

[330] Sherratt 1981, 1982, Chapman 1982, Greenfield 1988, 2003.
[331] Demoule, Perles 1993, 399.
[332] Cherry 1988, Halstead 1990, 1996, 2000.
[333] Vitteli 1999, 103.
[334] Demoule & Perles 1993, 399.
[335] Vitteli 1999, 103.
[336] Vitelli 1999, 103.
[337] Chapman 2000.
[338] Vitelli 1999, 102.
[339] Wells, Runnels 1996, 454–455.
[340] Dietz, this volume.
[341] Aslanis 1998.
[342] With the assumption that some ditches and perimeter walls very often found to enclose Final Neolithic sites could have had such a function; see also Bailey 2001, for a symbolic meaning in the use of ditches, enclosures and walls.

exchange patterns,[343] it has also been proposed that the intensiveness of seafaring activity during the Final Neolithic has made people see that their settlements were not safe, but exposed to raids from the sea, a situation that caused a general concern for security and therefore led to the settlement of better defended sites.[344] In this respect, it is a matter of further investigation whether such new elements of intra- and inter-site space could also be related to other evidence, such as the existence of different types of open-air sites (tell and flat extended sites).

These transformations of the second half of the 5th millennium B.C. are featured also by some other aspects of economic and symbolic behavior. In more detail, in the later phases of the Neolithic and the Early Bronze Age, there is an increase in the occurrence of wild game bones. The recovery of numerous obsidian and flint points can be related to this upgraded importance of hunting. An economic interpretation has been offered in reference to this phenomenon. The process of sharing the meat between the different households of a community made hunting a non-productive activity during the earlier phases of the Neolithic, by contrast with the later phases during which the meat of wild animals was consumed within the private domain.[345] However, taking into consideration the evidence available so far for the early phases of the Final Neolithic described briefly above, a broader reasoning seems necessary. Hunting as a social and not exclusively as an economic activity can be related to a new ideological frame connected to the use of space. The colonization of marginal lands could be considered as an important arena for social power and contest of the gender roles.[346] It is possible that the symbolism of space, power, authority, social reproduction and boundaries were not only connected with the idea of the Neolithic village, its bounded space, but with the marginal and remote as well. The concept of marginal does not relate to the distant, isolated and insular. Space is a socially constructed idea, a mental product that does not always coincide with its geometric properties. In this respect, marginal landscapes share the same qualities with hunting activity, widely practiced during the Final Neolithic, since they all are ventures of the outside and signify exceptional abilities.[347]

The Aegean Final Neolithic give evidence for major changes related to the use and meaning of the material culture, inter- and intra-site space, ideology, symbolism, social relations, production and consumption strategies. The causes and consequences of these changes need to be the focus of future research.

The site of Pangali is an exemplary product of social transformations and changing ideologies in the early part of the Final Neolithic. It is one among numerous Neolithic sites in this part of Western Greece, most of which unfortunately have been poorly investigated to the present. They are evident of a fairly intense habitation pattern. Several caves on Mount Varassova were used during the Final Neolithic. The cave of Aghios Nikolaos near Astakos, which has yielded material of earlier as well as later periods,[348] is the sole site apart from Pangali that has been excavated in the area. The specific region is an exceptional case where the chronological and cultural characteristics of a period at least from the Middle Neolithic onwards can be studied in an area of continuous habitation, which offers important evidence on socio-economic patterns and the different choices of people living in the same social and natural landscape.

Catalogue

(numbers 1-20: open shapes, n. 21-24: closed bowls-open mouthed vases of fine burnished ware, n.25-28: open shapes of various wares with asymmetrical rim, n.29-42: incised ware, n. 43-46: closed forms, n. 47-62: decorated pitoid jars, various coarse vases, n. 63-82: lugs-handles, n. 83-84: fine burnished ware with plastic decoration, n. 85-94: bases, n. 95-98: various clay items.

---

[343] Demoule, Perles 1993, 383.
[344] Vitelli 1999, 102.
[345] Halstead 1999.
[346] Hamilakis 2003, 243.
[347] Hamilakis 2003, 240.
[348] Benton 1947.

Pl. 21

1. Rim to body fragment of a large conical bowl. Walls convex towards inside turned, rounded rim. Black burnished surfaces (3/1 5YR dark gray). Coarse clay with many inclusions. Black core. D 23; H 4,6; Th 0,8.

2. Rim to body fragment of a small rounded bowl. Curved walls. Inside turned, rounded rim. Worn, smoothed and slipped (out 4/8 red 10R, 5/6 yellowish red 5YR in). Coarse clay (stone gritted). Gray core. D 7,0; H 3,6; Th 0,8.

3. Rim fragment of a bowl with S-profile. Flat on top, out-turned, decorated with a row of slashes. Burnished (4/8 red 10R). Coarse clay with many inclusions. Black core. D 18; H 2,2; Th 0,8.

4. Rim fragment of a rather conical bowl, flat at top, inside turned. Burnished (2.5 /1 black 7.5 YR). Semi-coarse clay. Blurred core. D 15; H 4,0; Th 0,5 .

5. Rim to body fragment of a bowl. Thick rim, flattened at top. Thickened below rim. Burnished (4/2 brown 7.5YR). Coarse clay. Black core. D 11; H 3,2; Th 0,8.

6. Rim to body fragment of a straight sided bowl. Straight out-turned walls. Rounded rim. Burnished (3.1 7.5 YR dark gray). Semi-coarse clay. Black core. D 22; H 4,1; Th 0,8.

7. Rim fragment of a straight sided bowl. Straight walls, out-turned. Two small strap handles below inside turned, rounded rim. Slipped and smoothed (4/4 dusky red 2.5YR outside, 2.5/1 reddish black 2.5YR). Semi-coarse clay with few inclusions and mica. Gray core. D 14; H 4,5; Th 0,6.

8. Rim fragment of a rounded/closed bowl. Small strap handle below rim (triangular in section, H 1,7; W 0,7; Th 0,4). Rim squarish in section, flat on top, inside turned. Slipped and smoothed (4/4 reddish brown 5YR). Semi-coarse clay with few inclusions and mica. D 13; H 4,2; Th 0,4.

9. Rim and body fragment of a bowl. Out turned, concave walls. Out-turned rim (flaring rim bowl). Black burnished (3/1 very dark gray 5YR). Mottled brown at inside rim. Semi-coarse clay with inclusions. Gray core. D 23; H 3,5; Th 0,5.

10. Rim to body fragment of a rounded bowl. Rounded, inside turned rim. Burnished (strong brown 4/6 7.5 YR out, yellowish red 4/6 5YR in). Thin, gray core. Semi-coarse clay with inclusions and mica. D 16; H 6,6; Th 0,7.

11. Rim to body fragment of a rounded bowl. Curved walls, convex below pointed, upright rim. Burnished (4/4 brown 7.5 YR). Semi-coarse clay with sporadic inclusions. Gray core. D 15; H 4,0; Th 0,6.

12. Rim fragment of a closed bowl. Curved walls, thick inside turned rim. Smoothed (4/6 yellowish red 5YR out, 4/8 red 2.5 YR in). D 24; H 3,0; W 3,2; Th 0,9.

13. Rim to body fragment of a rounded bowl. Convex, upright walls. Rounded, inside turned rim. Smoothed (4.3 7.5YR brown). Semi-coarse clay. Gray core. D 16; H 5,6; Th 0,8.

14. Rim fragment of a bowl. Straight, upright walls. Rounded rim. Smoothed (4/6 red 7.5 YR). Semi-coarse clay with inclusions. Gray core. D 15; H 3,8; Th 0,8.

15. Rim to body fragment of a rounded/ slightly S-shaped walled bowl. Rounded rim slightly differentiated, out turned. Smoothed (4/6 red 2.5 YR). Coarse clay with inclusions and mica. Reddish core. Not well fired. D 17; H 4,3; Th 0,6-0,8.

16. Rim to body fragment of a carinated bowl. Above carination, straight walls and rounded rim. Burnished (3/2 dark brown 7.5.YR). Coarse clay with inclusions. Gray core. D -; H 4,9; W 4,8; Th 0,5.

17. Rim to body fragment of a bowl with S-profile. Rounded, out-turned rim. Fine black burnished (2/1 black 10YR). Semi-coarse clay with few inclusions. Core red. D 20; H 4,3; Th 0,4.

Pl. 22

18. Rim to body fragment of a bowl carinated below rounded rim. Fine black burnished (2/1 black 10 YR). Coarse clay with various inclusions and some mica. D 22; H 3,6; Th 0,8.

19. Rim to body fragment of a carinated bowl. Rounded, out-turned rim. Fine burnished (2/1 black 10 YR). Semi-coarse clay with sporadic inclusions. D 16; H 4,4; Th 0,7.

20. Rim to body fragment of a thin walled, S-shaped bowl. Rounded, out-turned rim. Fine burnished (5/8 red, 2.5 YR). Semi-coarse clay with sporadic inclusions. Brown core. D 13,5; H 5,2; Th 0,6.

21. Rim fragment of an wide-mouthed vase. Rounded rim. Burnished (3/2 dark brown 7.5 YR). Semi coarse clay with sporadic inclusions. Brown core. D 18, H 2,4; Th 0,7.

22. Rim to body fragment of a wide-mouthed vase. S-shaped walls, inside turned, rounded rim. Smoothed (3/2 dark brown 7.5 YR). Black core. Semi-coarse clay with few inclusions. D 18; H 4,2; Th 0,5.

23. Rim to body fragment of a wide-mouthed vase. Inside turned walls forming shoulder below rounded rim. Black burnished (2/1 black 10 YR). Semi-coarse reddish clay (4/6 red 2.5 YR). D 14; H 3,0; Th 0,4-0,5.

24. Rim to body fragment of a carinated, wide-mouthed vase. Curved, inside turned walls forming shoulder below rounded rim. Fine burnished (2/1 black 10 YR). Semi-coarse clay with inclusions and possibly grog. Gray core. D 18; H 3,0; Th 0,6.

25. Rim to body fragment of a closed bowl/ vase with asymmetric rim. Black burnished (2/1 black 10R). Semi-coarse clay with few inclusions. Gray core. Incised decoration from rim with two parallel bands filled with oblique lines. D 12; H 3,8; Th 0,4.

26. Rim to body fragment of a closed bowl/ vase with asymmetric, inside turned rim. Convex walls. Black burnished (2/1 black 10 YR). Coarse clay with. Reddish core. D 15; H 4,4; Th 0,5.

27. Rim to body fragment of a closed bowl/ S-shaped vase with asymmetrical, out-turned, differentiated rim. Semi-coarse clay with few inclusions. Fine burnished (3/1 very dark gray 5YR). Thin gray core. D 14; H 4,1; Th 0,5.

28. Rim to body fragment of a scoop (?)/ bowl with asymmetrical rim. Out-turned, curved walls. Inside turned, rounded rim. Burnished (3/1 very dark gray 5YR) mottled red on the inside (4/6 red 2.5 YR). Semi-coarse clay with fine-grained inclusions. Gray core. D 15; H 5,2; Th 0,4.

Pl. 23

29. Rim to body fragment of a rounded bowl. Convex below pointed rim. Out-turned, thick walls. Burnished (3/3 dark reddish brown 5YR). Incised decoration of a horizontal band with multiple chevrons below rim. Coarse clay with many inclusions. Black core. D 22; H 6,4; Th 1,0.

30. Rim fragment of a small rounded bowl. Rim flat at top, inside turned. Slipped and burnished (4/8 dark red 2.5YR out, 3/2 dark reddish brown 2.5 YR in). Incised decoration of one oblique and two horizontal lines below rim. Semi-coarse clay with sporadic inclusions. Gray core. D 10; H 1; Th 0,3.

31. Rim to body fragment of a rounded bowl. Rounded rim. Burnished (4.3 brown 7.5YR). Incised decoration of multiple chevrons/triangles from rim. Semi-coarse clay. Black core. H 3,8; W 3,6; Th 0,5.

32. Rim to body fragment of a rounded bowl. Curved walls. Pointed, slightly inside turned rim. Burnished (3/3 dark reddish brown 5YR). Two small knobs, squarish in section, in a vertical row below rim. On the right of knobs two small perforations. On the left part preserves incised decoration: four parallel bands, each forms angle filled with vertical and oblique lines. Semi-coarse clay with sporadic inclusions and mica. Black core. D 12; H 5,2; Th 0,8.

33. Rim to body fragment of a conical bowl. Burnished (5/6 yellowish brown 10R). Incised decoration with a vertical line and others forming triangles, attached to it. Semi-coarse clay. Gray core. D 14; H 3,2; Th 0,4.

34. Rim to body fragment of a rounded bowl. Rim rather flattened at top. Burnished (3/2 dark brown 7.5 YR). Incised decoration from rim with two oblique bands filled with oblique lines. Semi-coarse clay with sporadic inclusions. Gray core. D 15; H 3,0; Th 0,3.

35. Rim to body fragment of a conical bowl. Black burnished (2.5/1 7.5YR). Rounded, slightly inside turned rim. Incised decoration with systems of horizontal and oblique lines separated with a vertical one below rim. Semi-coarse clay. Black core. D 22; H 4,7; Th 0,5.

36. Rim fragment of a closed bowl. Curved, inside turned walls. Rounded rim. Burnished (5/3 brown 7.5YR). Incised decoration with a vertical band forming angle filled with horizontal lines. Semi-coarse clay. Gray core. D 15; H 3,8; Th 0,4.

37. Rim to body fragment of a rounded bowl. Slightly curved walls. Rounded rim. Slipped and burnished (3/1 dark gray 10YR in, 4/3 brown 7.5YR out). Incised decoration with two antithetic triangles filled with oblique lines. Semi-coarse clay with sporadic stones and some mica. Gray core. D 16; H 3,0; Th 0,3.

38. Rim to body fragment of a closed bowl. Curved walls. Rounded, inside turned rim. Burnished (3/4 dark reddish brown 2.5 YR). Incised decoration of a hatched triangle and four parallel lines. Semi-coarse clay with small, sporadic inclusions. Brown core. D -; H 2,1; W 2,9; Th 0,5.

39. Rim to body fragment of a closed bowl. Convex walls, rounded, inside turned rim. Small strap handle below rim.

Incised decoration of a triangle filled with vertical lines, also below rim. Burnished (3/2 dark brown 7.5 YR). Semi-coarse clay. Gray core. D 21; H 4,6; Th 0,9.

40. Rim to body fragment of a closed bowl. Convex, inside turned walls, rather pointed rim. Incised decoration of oblique lines from rim. Burnished (4/4 brown 7.5 YR out, 3/2 dark brown 7.5 YR in). Gray core. Semi-coarse clay with few inclusions. D 11; H 2,4; Th 0,6.

41. Rim to body fragment of a straight sided bowl (slightly S-shaped walls). Incised decoration with two horizontal rows of triangles filled with oblique lines. Burnished (3/2 dark brown 7.5 YR). Gray core. Semi-coarse clay with some inclusions. D 16; H 4; Th 0,8.

42. Rim fragment of a straight sided bowl. Out-turned walls, rounded rim. Burnished (3/1 dark grey 10 YR). Incised decoration of oblique lines (hatched triangle?) and a triangle. Semi-coarse clay with sporadic inclusions. Gray core. D 18; H 1,9; Th 0,4.

Pl. 24

43. Rim and neck fragment of a jar. Inside turned walls, rounded rim. Smoothed (4/6 red 2.5 YR). Coarse clay with copious inclusions and organic material. Gray core. D 16; H 8,5; Th 0,8.

44. Rim and neck fragment of a jar. Concave walls. Out turned, rounded rim. Smoothed (4/8 dark red 2.5 YR). Coarse clay . Gray core. D 14 ; H 8,4 ; Th 0,9.

45. Rim fragment of an open mouthed, coarse vase. Smoothed (4/6 red 2.5 YR). Coarse clay with inclusions of variable size, some mica and organic material. Gray core. D 20; H 4,0; Th 0,8.

46. Rim fragment of a wide-mouthed, coarse vase. Inside turned walls, differentiated rim forms low neck. Smoothed (4/6 red 2.5 YR). Coarse clay. Brown core. D 25; H 5,3; Th 0,9.

Pl. 25

47. Body fragment of a coarse vase (strainer?). Convex walls. Rough surfaces (5/8 red 2.5YR). Perforations opened prior to firing. Coarse, brittle clay. H 2,7; W 3,0; Th 0,6; D of aperture 0,8.

48. Body fragment of a vase with two perforations opened after (strainer?). Smoothed (3/6 dark red 2.5YR). Well fired. Coarse clay with white, brown, gray inclusions. Gray core. H 6,4; W 4,2; Th 1,2; D of aperture 0,7.

49. Rim fragment a large, possibly wide and shallow vase. Straight, thick walls. Rounded out-turned, thick rim. Smoothed (2/1 black 10 YR out, 3/1 very dark gray 5 YR in). Coarse clay with inclusions of variable size and some mica. Black core. D -; H 4,8; W 4,3; Th 1,8.

50. Rim fragment of a large, wide vessel. Very thick, straight walls and rim squarish flat at top. Rough (5/4 brown 7.5 YR). Coarse clay with inclusions and some mica. Very dark brown core. D 55; H 4,1; Th 2,0.

51. Shoulder fragment of a jar. −S shaped walls, slightly inside turned. Slipped and smoothed, worn (4/4 brown 7.5YR). Plastic decoration of a thin ridge and impressed dots. Coarse clay. Thin gray core. H 3,6; W 4,4; Th 2,1.

52. Body fragment of a jar. Straight walls. Slipped and burnished (4/8 dark red 2.5 YR). Decorated with a horizontal plastic ridge. Semi-coarse, porous clay with few inclusions and mica. Gray core. H 5,5; W 6; Th 1,0.

53. Rim and upper body fragment of a jar. Straight walls, thickened towards rim, squarish flat at the top. Smoothed (5/8 yellowish red 5 YR out, 5/6 yellowish red 5 YR in). Coarse clay with many inclusions and some mica. Blurred, red core. D –; H 7,8; W 6,2; Th 1,5-1,8.

54. Body fragment of a jar. Curved walls. Traces of slip and burnishing in and out (4/4 reddish brown 2.5YR). Decorated with a relief band forming angle. Black core. Coarse clay with white and brown inclusions. H 4,1; W 4,6; Th 0,9.

55. Body fragment of a jar. Thick walls. Smoothed (4/4 brown 7.5 YR). Decorated with straight and oblique plastic ridges. Coarse clay. Gray core. D –; H 6,4; W 6,1; Th 1,0.

56. Body fragment of a jar. Thick, slightly curved walls. Smoothed (4/4 brown 7.5 YR). Decorated with two parallel raised bands carrying fingertip impressions. Coarse clay. Black core. H 3,7; W 3,6; Th 2,2.

57. Rim and body fragment of a jar. Slightly concave walls, thick rounded rim. Smoothed (3/3 dark brown 7.5 YR). Decorated with two straight, horizontal plastic ridges. Coarse clay. Gray core. D –; H 8,8; W 3,8; Th 0,8.

58. Body fragment of a jar. Curved walls. Smoothed (5/6 red 2.5 YR). Decorated with impressed dots and a plastic cordon. Coarse clay. Gray core. H 9,8; W 5,4; Th 0,9.

59. Body fragment of a jar. Slightly curved walls. Smoothed (4/4 reddish brown 5YR). Decorated with a broad band with impressed dots. Coarse clay. Gray core. H 6.8; W 7,2; Th 1,2-1,6.

60. Body fragment of a coarse, thick walled vase. Carries small perforations along the entire preserved part. Rough (red 4/6 2.5YR in, 5/8 red 2.5YR out). Very coarse clay. Brown core. H 5,5; W 4,3; Th 2,0.

61. Body fragment of a large, coarse vase (pithos). Convex walls. Decorated with two vertical unperforated lugs and raised, wide areas-bands, cordons and impressed dots. Smoothed (4/8 red 2.5 YR). Coarse clay with many inclusions. D –; H 9,1; W 6,8; Th 1,5.

62. Body fragment of a large, coarse vase (pithos). Thick, straight walls. Decorated with raised cordons enclosing area with impressed dots. Smoothed (4/8 red, 2.5 YR). Coarse clay with many inclusions. D –; H 8,2; W 5,9; Th 1,3.

Pl. 26

63. Raised button-like protrusion. No part of the vase preserved (broken from pot, to which added from different clay lump). Smoothed (brown 4/4 7.5 YR). Coarse clay. H 1,8; W 2,5.

64. Rim fragment of a small vase. Curved walls, rounded rim. Knob below rim. Smoothed (5/8 yellowish red 5YR). Semi-

coarse clay with some inclusions. D –; H 1,9; W 1,8; Th 0,4; w. of knob 1,1; h.of knob 0,4.

65. Button-like protrusion, hollow in the middle, of a fine slipped and burnished bowl (4/8 red 2.5 YR). Curved walls. Semi-coarse clay. D –; H 2,0; W 1,1; Th 0,4.

66. Raised button-like protrusion of a rather closed vase . Burnished red outside, rough inside (4/8 red 2.5 YR). Gray core. Coarse clay. H 4,9; W 4,1; Th 0,5; button 3,2 x 2,9.

67. Rim to body fragment of a closed bowl. Pointed rim. A horizontal, un-perforated protrusion (knob) at beginning of carination. Smoothed (3/4 dark brown 7.5 YR). Coarse clay with many inclusions. Gray core. D 19; H 6,4; Th 0,7.

68. Small un-perforated lug, oval shaped. No part of the vase preserved. Smoothed (brown 4/4 7.5 YR). Coarse clay. H 1,8; W 2,5.

69. Rim fragment of a small carinated vase. Inside turned walls, pointed rim. Below rim, small tubular lug with vertical perforation. Burnished (2.5/1 black 5YR). Semi-coarse clay with some inclusions. D –; H 2,7; W 3,3; Th 0,5; w. of lug 2,3; h. of lug 1,1; D of aperture 0,8.

70. Rim to body fragment of a carinated vase. Tubular lug vertically pierced at the point of carination. Rough, worn, traces of smoothing (3/1 very dark gray 7.5 YR). Very coarse clay with inclusions and mica. H 4,6; W 3,9; Th 0,8; w. of lug 0,8; h. of lug 2,0; D of aperture 0,6.

71. Large, tubular lug, concave in the middle, of a coarse vase. (3/1 very dark gray 7.5 YR inside, reddish brown 5/4 5YR outside. Coarse clay with many inclusions. H 4,5; W 3,4; D of aperture 3,2.

72. Rim fragment of a small rounded bowl preserving part of a small strap handle (cylindrical in section) from rim. Curved walls, rounded rim. Smoothed (2.5/1 black 5YR). Gray core. Semi coarse clay with some inclusions. D –; H 2,6; W 2,7; Th 0,4.

73. Rim fragment bearing tab lug of a bowl with straight, upright walls. Rounded rim. Smoothed (3/1 very dark gray 7.5 YR outside, 5/6 red 2.5 YR inside, lug 3/4 dark brown 7.5YR). Coarse clay with many inclusions. D –; H 5,4; W 5,7 (with handle); Th 0,6.

74. Rim fragment bearing lug of a carinated bowl. Walls straight, upright towards pointed rim. Vertical flat, ear shaped, un-perforated lug from rim to carination. Smoothed (5/4 reddish brown 5YR) surfaces. Semi-coarse clay with inclusions and some mica. D 16; H 4,6; Th 0,8; max. w. of lug 2; h. of lug 3,3.

75. A small horned handle of an open burnished vase (3/3 dark brown 7.5 YR). Semi coarse clay. Gray core. D –; H 2,2; W 1,1.

76. Large strap handle of a jar with traces of plastic decorated ridges. Rough (2.5/1 black 5YR in, 3/3 dark brown 7.5YR out). Coarse clay. H 7,5; W 5,7; Th 1,5.

77. A large horned handle of a coarse vase. Smoothed (3/1 very dark grey in, 3/6 dark red 10R out). Coarse clay with many inclusions. Gray core. H 4,1; W 5,5.

78. Horned handle. Walls of vessel slightly curved. Smoothed (3/3 dark brown 7.5YR). Coarse clay. Thick black core. H 5,8; W 6,1; Th 0,8; w. of lug 4,6; h. of lug 2,2.

79. Biconical handle. No part of the vase preserved. Rather convex sides. Oval in section. Smoothed (4/4 brown 7.5YR). Coarse clay. Gray core. H 3,8; W 3,8.

80. Body fragment and lug of an open vase. Flat, trapezoidal, un-perforated protrusion (ledge lug). Slipped and smoothed (3/3 dark reddish brown 5YR out, 4/8 dark red 2.5 YR/ 3.1 very dark grey 7.5 YR in). Gray core. H 0,8; W 4,0.

81. Fragment of a flat, trapezoidal, un-perforated ledge lug of a coarse vase. Smoothed (4/6 red 2.5 YR). Coarse clay with many inclusions. Gray core. H 2,8; W 4,0.

82. Thick, biconical handle, elongated, oval in section belonging to a coarse vase. Rough (3/3 dark reddish brown 5YR). Coarse clay with many inclusions. Gray core. H 2,2; W 6,2.

83. Small body fragment of a fine slipped and burnished vase (3/6 dark red 2.5YR). Decoration of a thin, curved ridge beginning from a small knob. Semi-coarse clay with fine grained inclusions. Thin dark gray core. H 3,4; W 1,6; Th 0,6.

84. Body fragment of a "red burnished bowl". Curved walls. Slipped and burnished (3/6 dark red 10R). Well fired. Decorated with two curved, narrow ridges. Semi-coarse clay with sporadic inclusions. Thin gray core. H 2,3; W 2,2; Th 0,5.

Pl. 27

85. Bevelled base fragment of a large coarse vase. Walls flaring outwards. Slipped and smoothed (4/4 brown 7.5YR out, 4/6 red 2.5YR in). Coarse clay. Black core. D 15; H 8,5; Th 1,0.

86. Flat base fragment of a coarse vase. Slipped and polished out (4/8 dark red 2.5YR), rough in (4/6 dark yellowish brown 10R). Stone gritted clay. Gray core. D 20; H 6; Th 1,5.

87. Ring base fragment. Convex in profile. Smoothed out (4/6 red 2.5 YR), rough in (mottled 4/6 red 2.5 YR, 3/1 very dark grey 7.5 YR). Semi-coarse clay with limited inclusions and some mica. Gray core. D 11; H 4,2; W 7,2; Th 0,9.

88. Ring base fragment. Convex in profile. Smoothed (5/6 yellowish brown 10 YR). Coarse clay with some mica and inclusions. No core. D 10; H 4,8; Th 0,8-1,2.

89. Ring base fragment. Concave in profile. Smoothed (3/3 dark brown 7.5YR in, 4/8 2.5 red YR out). Coarse clay with sporadic inclusions. Red core. D 10; H 2,5; Th 1,0.

90. Ring base fragment. Concave profile. Smoothed (4/4 dark yellowish brown 10YR). Coarse clay. Black core. D 6; H 3,4; Th 0,6-1,3.

91. Ring base fragment (?). The beginning of a possibly tall base and the differentiated lower part of the vase, belonging to "rechaud" type vase ? Thin, curved walls. Smoothed (5/4 reddish brown 5YR). Gray core. D -; H 4,9; W 7,4; Th 0,6.

92. Hollowed base fragment of a coarse vase. Smoothed (5/4 reddish brown 5YR). Coarse clay with inclusions. Gray core. D -; H 3,2; W 3,6; Th 3,6.

93. Bevelled base fragment of a large, coarse vase. Concave in profile, walls, flaring outwards. Slipped out and smoothed (4/6 yellowish red 5YR out, 3/2 dark brown 7.5 YR in). Coarse clay with many inclusions. Gray core. D 20; H 6,7; Th 1,0-1,4.

94. Flat (slightly bevelled and hollowed) base fragment of a large, coarse vase. Concave walls, flaring outwards. Smoothed (5/4 reddish brown out, 3/2 dark brown 7.5 YR in). Coarse clay with coarse-grained inclusions. Gray core. D 18; H 6,8; Th 0,8-1,2.

Pl. 29

95. Figurine (?) or handle fragment. Smoothed (3/3 dark brown 7.5YR). Incision along wider part. Not well fired. Coarse clay with sporadic large inclusions. H 4,3; W 2,8; Th 1,9.

96. Spindle whorl. Smoothed (3/2 dark brown 7.5 YR), blackened due to fire exposure. Convex at upper part, flat at lower side. Coarse clay with many inclusions. H 1,4; W 5,7; Th 1,5; D of aperture 0,5.

97. Spindle whorl. Concave at lower and upper sides. Rough (4/6 yellowish red YR , 2.5/1 reddish black 2.5 YR and 4/6 red 2.5 YR). Coarse, stone gritted clay and some mica. H 4,3; W 4,1; Th 1,3; D of aperture 0,8.

Spindle whorl of the same shape (not illustrated). Broken, almost in half. Smoothed (4/6 red 2.5 YR). Burnt after breakage. Coarse clay. H 3,4; W 3,6; D of aperture 0,9.

98. Oval shaped spindle whorl. Preserved in half. Smoothed (5/8 yellowish red 5YR). Burnt after breakage. Coarse clay. H 5,3; W 5,0; D of aperture 0,9.

Spindle whorl of the same shape (not illustrated). Burned after breakage. Brittle, coarse clay. H 2,8; W 4; D of aperture 0,9.

The chipped stone assemblage and the bone material

By Lasse Sørensen[349]

Farmers herding, hunting and exchanging – a normal behaviour of Final Neolithic farmers?

Introduction

In the following the lithic and bone tool assemblages from Pangali in Aetolia will be investigated with special emphasis on raw material, technological and typological analysis, comparing this assemblage with other contemporary sites from the Aegean area. In addition the site of Pangali also sheds new light on some more general questions such as: Why did they settle there? For how long was the site settled? Was there more than one occupation on the site? What activities did the inhabitants carry out on the site? Were they traders or farmers? It is the behaviour of the Final Neolithic people and the habitants of this particular site, which is interesting and a great challenge.

Research history at Pangali

In 1996 a 2x2 m trench was excavated to bedrock, and some layers were observed together with the remains of a hearth. The layers seemed to be partly synchronic. The deposit was approx. 60 cm thick and the surface was cleaned for rocks and larger vegetation. The soil was dry sieved in a four mm mesh in order to obtain even the smallest finds. A vast quantity of sherds, lithics, bones, bone tools, sea shells and land snails as well as some spindle whorls and a fragment of a figurine were recovered from the excavation. Among the stone tools an important number of points were found, which were made of different raw materials and belonging to different types. The pottery has been analyzed and dated to the Final Neolithic phase LNIb (4.600 to 4.200 Cal. BC).[350] In the analysis from Pangali, the total amount of lithic and bone assemblages from the survey in 1995 are analyzed together with the assemblage from the 1996 excavation. The only difference between the survey and the excavation material is that, in the excavated assemblage, a larger proportion of fragmented blades and bones were found.

The chipped stone industry at Pangali

The chipped stone industry of Pangali is unique in Western Greece, but has overall similarities with other contemporary Late and Final Neolithic sites such as Dimini, Lerna, Saliagos, Ftelia, Kitsos, Skoteini (Fig. 72). This is especially true regarding the obsidian assemblage, where a systematic blade production is observed. The overall similarities in the different types of points found at Pangali indicate a typological dating in the Late and Final Neolithic. The Pangali industry differs from the Early Helladic, although there seem to be a continuity of the flint technological choices from the Final Neolithic to the Early Helladic[351] The presence of obsidian pressure flaked blades and the many simple tool types through the different layers stay the same and show the same tool tradition, and the same basic flint knapping techniques were used throughout all phases of the settlement. The chipped stone assemblage thus gives the same results as observed in the pottery assemblage, where all the layers on Pangali were interpreted as being synchronic belonging to the Final Neolithic.[352]

[349] I would like to express my thanks to Dr. L. Kolonas and Dr. Søren Dietz for permission to study the stone and bone assemblage from Pangali and to Dr. Søren Dietz for his useful comments. Furthermore, I owe many thanks to Dr. Fanis Mavridis, Stud. mag. Hege Alisoy, Stud. mag. Kjartan Langsted, Stud. mag. Claudio Casati, Stud. Mag. Niels A. Møller, Cand. mag. Pernille Bangsgaard, Cand. mag. Pernille Foss and Dr. Søren Sindbæk for completing some of the illustrations and for discussing the main themes within this article. Finally I want to express my gratitude to my fellow student hall "The Admiralty" and to Stud. mag. Lotte Andersen for checking the final version of the English text.
[350] Mavridis & Alisoy 1998, Mavridis above pp. 132-3. See also Heinemeier in Appendix 3, this volume.
[351] Above Dietz & Moschos p. 110.
[352] Mavridis above p. 117.

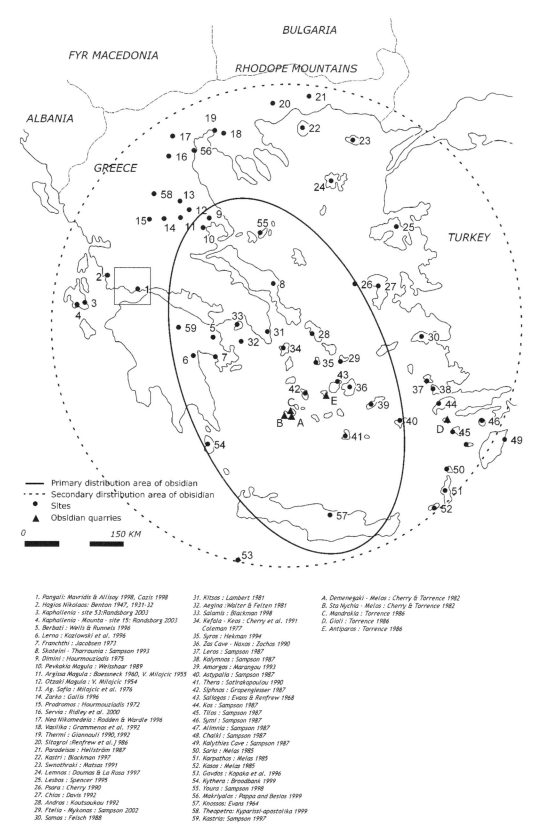

BULGARIA

FYR MACEDONIA

RHODOPE MOUNTAINS

ALBANIA

GREECE

TURKEY

- Primary distribution area of obsidian
- - - Secondary dirstribution area of obisidian
- Sites
▲ Obsidian quarries

0   150 KM

1. Pangali: Mavridis & Allisoy 1998, Cazis 1998
2. Hagios Nikolaos: Benton 1947, 1931-32
3. Kaphallenia - site 53:Randsborg 2003
4. Kaphallenia - Mounta - site 15: Randsborg 2003
5. Berbati : Wells & Runnels 1996
6. Lerna : Kozlowski et al. 1996
7. Franchthi : Jacobsen 1973
8. Skoteini - Tharrounia : Sampson 1993
9. Dimini : Hourmouziadis 1975
10. Pevkakia Magula : Weisshaar 1989
11. Argissa Magula : Boessneck 1960, V. Milojcic 1955
12. Otzaki Magula : V. Milojcic 1954
13. Ag. Sofia : Milojcic et al. 1976
14. Zarko : Gallis 1996
15. Prodromos : Hourmouziadis 1972
16. Servia : Ridley et al. 2000
17. Nea Nikomedeia : Rodden & Wardle 1996
18. Vasilika : Grammenos et al. 1992
19. Thermi : Giannouli 1990,1992
20. Sitagroi :Renfrew et al.] 986
21. Paradeisos : Hellström 1987
22. Kastri : Blackman 1997
23. Swnothraki : Matsas 1991
24. Lemnos : Doumas & La Rosa 1997
25. Lesbos : Spencer 1995
26. Psara : Cherry 1990
27. Chios : Davis 1992
28. Andras : Koutsoukou 1992
29. Ftelia - Mykonos : Sampson 2002
30. Samos : Felsch 1988

31. Kitsos : Lambert 1981
32. Aegina :Walter & Felten 1981
33. Salamis : Blackman 1998
34. Kefala - Keos : Cherry et al. 1991 Coleman 1977
35. Syros : Hekman 1994
36. Zas Cave - Naxos : Zachos 1990
37. Leros : Sampson 1987
38. Kalymnos : Sampson 1987
39. Amorgos : Marangou 1993
40. Astypalia : Sampson 1987
41. Thera : Sotirakopoulou 1990
42. Siphnos : Gropenglesser 1987
43. Saliagos : Evans & Renfrew 1968
44. Kos : Sampson 1987
45. Tilos : Sampson 1987
46. Syml : Sampson 1987
47. Alimnia : Sampson 1987
48. Chalki : Sampson 1987
49. Kalythies Cave : Sampson 1987
50. Saria : Melas 1985
51. Karpathos : Melas 1985
52. Kasos : Melas 1985
53. Gavdos : Kopaka et al. 1996
54. Kythera : Broodbank 1999
55. Youra : Sampson 1998
56. Makriyalos : Pappa and Besios 1999
57. Knossos: Evans 1964
58. Theopetra: Kyparissi-apostolika 1999
59. Kastria: Sampson 1997

A. Demenegaki - Melos : Cherry & Torrence 1982
B. Sta Nychla - Melos : Cherry & Torrence 1982
C. Mandrakla : Torrence 1986
D. Gioli : Torrence 1986
E. Antiparos : Torrence 1986

Fig. 72. Map with selected Late and Final Neolithic sites in the Aegean and the Aegean obsidian sources with the primary and secondary distribution areas indicated. Partly after Torrence 1986; Broodbank 1999; Runnels and Murray 2001. L. Sørensen and K. Langsted.

Fig. 73. Pangali. The different types of raw materials. Lower row: Marble. Second row: Radiolarite. Third row: Flint. Fourth row: Obsidian. L. Sørensen photo.

The contemporary sites, which have been well analyzed, are not many and most of them are situated in the Aegean area: Saliagos near Antiparos has been published in detail[353] and the Kitsos cave in Attica.[354] There are also comparative data from the few securely stratified multilevel sites such as the Skoteini cave in Euboea,[355] Lerna in the Argolid,[356] Makriyalos in the Pieria[357] and Ftelia on Mykonos.[358] Finally the many surveys at Keos,[359] Berbati Limnes,[360] Southern Argolid[361] and the Asea Valley[362] have produced interesting chipped stone assemblages (Fig. 72).

Local and exotic raw material studies

During the surveys and the excavation of Pangali a total amount of approx. 3.5 kg and a total of 1300 pieces were recovered. Both in weight and numbers, the radiolarite predominates followed by the flint, obsidian and marble (Figs. 73 and 74). The radiolarite is a dark red, almost chocolate coloured chert, which represents 59 % of the material. The radiolarite is mainly of a good and fine-grained quality, which was a very popular type of raw

material from Paleolithic, Mesolithic and Neolithic sites all over Greece. The flint assemblage from Pangali consists of 18 % of the whole assemblage and is dominated by a light grey colored type, which is fine and medium grained (Fig. 74). But there were also other types of flint with various colours. Most of the flint types are of local origin, but there was a light yellow fine grained core, which is imported. This type is known as honey flint, a fine, opaque, honey colored flint the provenance of which has to be settled. On the basis of geology and archaeological distribution, the regions of Epirus and Southern Albania have been suggested as probable sources.[363]

The large proportion of radiolarite and flint indicates that there was an easy access to this particular resource. Some preliminary raw material surveys, made by the author in 2004, proved that radiolarite and flint of excellent quality could have been procured locally at the beach at Kato Vasiliki or in the nearby riverbeds of the Evinos River. This indicates that these raw materials were probably procured within a radius of maximum five km. from the site. The final local material was marble constituting 2 % of the total assemblage (Fig. 74). The marble was found on the site and was the nearest raw material, but also the less desirable in quality. Nevertheless it was used for a crude flake production, which indicates a need and shortage of raw materials. It is very rare to observe marble in other Neolithic assemblages. In contrast, the exotic raw material obsidian is considered to be the best material for cutting tools. The obsidian assemblage at Pangali is the largest from hitherto published sites in Western Greece and consists of 276 pieces or 21 % of the total assemblage (Figs. 73 and 74).

[353] Evans & Renfrew 1968, 46ff.
[354] Perlès 1981, 129ff.
[355] Perlés 1993, 448ff.
[356] Kozlowski et al. 1996, 295ff.
[357] Skourtopoulou 1999, 121ff.
[358] Galanidou 2002, 317ff.
[359] Torrence 1991, 173ff.
[360] Johnson 1996, 37ff.
[361] Kardulias & Runnels 1995, 74ff.
[362] Carter 2003, 129ff.
[363] Perlès 1992a, 124f. Tringham 2003, 84ff.

Provenance of the obsidian

A grey shiny type dominates the obsidian from Pangali, which is fine grained, followed by a black shiny type (Fig. 73). During the registration it was very difficult to observe the different types of obsidian, but when the pieces were observed against a bright light it was possible to see the color differences. The obsidian found at Pangali could theoretically derive from two possible areas as the site is situated within sailing distance from both the Cycladic and the Italian obsidian sources. In order to determine the origin of the obsidian in prehistoric contexts several studies of especially the Aegean obsidian have been carried out.[364] One of the best methods used to decide the place of origin is the spectroscopic analysis for trace elements.[365] The first distinction of Aegean obsidian was based on the content of barium and zirconium in the obsidian and gave a possibility of distinguishing Aegean from Anatolian obsidian. A further and simpler distinction has been to note the appearance and to divide the obsidian by using six properties: 1) Colour in transmitted light 2) Colour in reflected light, 3) Fracture 4) Translucency 5) Transparence with internal structure and 6) Lustre.[366] These methods of determining provenance resulted in the identification of five obsidian sources in the Aegean area. Three are located on the island of Melos.[367] The remaining two are found on Antiparos and Giali (Fig. 72). The obsidian from Pangali evidently derives from Melos,[368] but it is difficult to determine from which particular source on Melos the obsidian comes, as the greyish and the black obsidian, dominating the Pangali assemblage, are both found in Demenegaki and Sta Nychia. Future raw material studies of obsidian provenance might be able to clarify this problem.

The obsidian procurement during Aegean prehistory

Some of the earliest evidences of Melian obsidian were found in Upper Paleolithic and Mesolithic context in the Franchthi Cave.[369] Obsidian was also observed at Nea Nicomedeia in Macedonia,

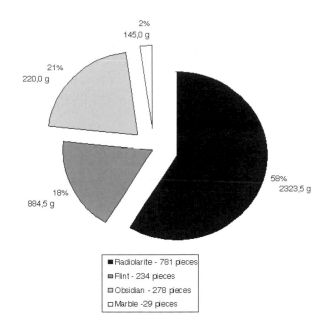

Fig. 74. Pangali. The frequency and weight of the different raw materials. L. Sørensen and C. Casati.

which has been dated to 6.220 +/- 150 Cal. BC.[370] and at Knossos dated to 6.100 +/- 180 Cal. BC. The two other obsidian sources Antiparos and Giali are regarded as secondary sources in the Neolithic Age (Fig. 72). Obsidian is found all over Greece, but there is more obsidian on prehistoric sites in Thessaly, southern Greece and the Cyclades than in sites of Western Greece. However, Melian obsidian has also been found as far west as Kephallénia and far north as Corfu and Macedonia.[371]

The obsidian from Pangali has been weighed at 220 g (Fig. 74), which is very little compared to the amount of obsidian from contemporary sites which lie near Melos such as Ftelia on Mykonos

---

[364] Torrence 1986, 95; Williams-Thorpe 1995, 217ff.

[365] Optical Emission Spectroscopy, OES.

[366] Renfrew et al. 1965, 1966, 1968.

[367] Demenegaki, Sta Nycia & Mandrakia.

[368] I am deeply indebted to Dr. V. Kilikoglou from the Laboratory of Archaeometry, N.C.S.R. "Demokritos", who investigated some of the obsidian from Pangali.

[369] Jacobsen 1973, 45ff; 1976, 76ff; Jacobsen & Farrand 1987; Perlés 1973, 72ff; 1987; Renfrew & Aspinall 1987, 257ff; fig. 72.

[370] Renfrew et al. 1965; figs. 29 & 30.

[371] Randsborg 2003, 81ff; Perlès 1990a, 24 ff.

The difference between the conceptual scheme and Les chaîne opératoire

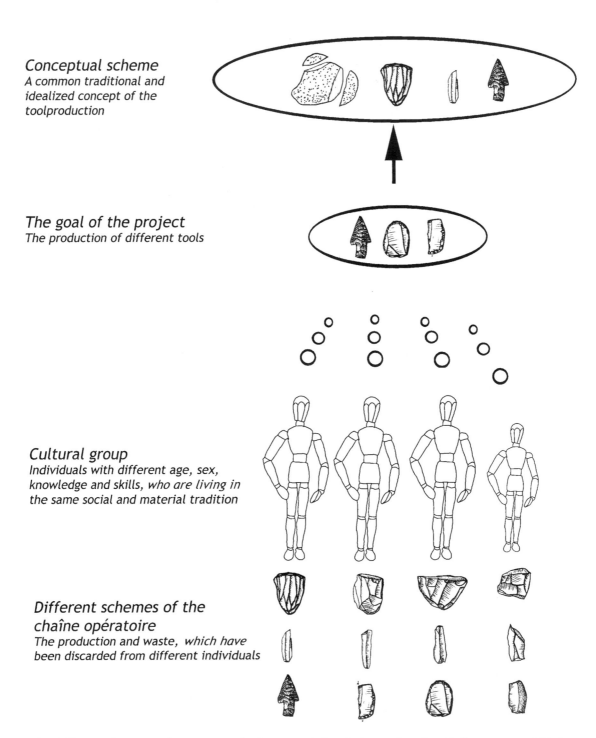

Conceptual scheme
A common traditional and idealized concept of the toolproduction

The goal of the project
The production of different tools

Cultural group
Individuals with different age, sex, knowledge and skills, who are living in the same social and material tradition

Different schemes of the chaîne opératoire
The production and waste, which have been discarded from different individuals

Fig. 75. The difference between the conceptual scheme and the chaîne opératoire. L. Sørensen and K. Langsted.

(75 km.) or Saliagos near Antiparos (60 km.). This could indicate a possible connection between distance and the amount of obsidian procured at each site.[372] At Ftelia 17,267 kilos of obsidian were recovered. Just one large obsidian core ranging in length from approx. 13 cm to 6.3 cm contains the same amount of obsidian as the whole amount found at Pangali.[373] However, a comparison between the different weights of the obsidian assemblages on different Neolithic sites would of course require that these sites have been sufficiently excavated.

Few assessments have been made in order to evaluate the amount of obsidian exchanged in different periods, but it is a general assumption that the exchange of obsidian reached its peak during the Final Neolithic and Early Bronze Age.[374] In the following Middle and Late Helladic periods the obsidian exchange declined and during the later Geometric, Archaic, Classical, Hellenistic and Roman periods obsidian was rarely observed.[375] This gives some possibilities for observing and testing different theories concerning exchange mechanisms in the Final Neolithic Age and to interpret whether the obsidian was procured directly or indirectly. Furthermore it should be possible to determine if the obsidian debitage represents the waste from a specialized activity or if it is a result of an everyday household production of obsidian tools. In order to answer these questions it is necessary to analyze the lithic assemblage in a more detailed manner by using the concept of chaîne opératoire.

Chaîne opératoire and lithic reduction

In the study of a lithic assemblage, the chaîne opératoire research provides detailed and quantifiable data on successive processes, from the procurement of raw material until the artifact is discarded, passing through all stages of manufacture and use of the different components. All these stages of the production are found on the site and it is hereby possible to identify different flint knappers, who have different skills and knowledge about flint knapping. Together with the conceptual scheme it is possible to determine why and how

the flint knappers preferred to produce a certain tool, within a common and idealized concept of the lithic production, which gives the chaîne opératoire analysis a cognitive aspect (Fig. 75).[376] The concept of chaîne opératoire makes it possible to structure the flint knappers' use of materials by placing each artifact in a technical context, and offers a methodological framework for each level of interpretation.[377]

The concept of chaîne opératoire has been used in Greece especially on Late Paleolithic assemblages from Klithi, Franchthi and Hagios Nikolaos near Kato Vasiliki,[378] involving local raw materials, which makes the chaîne opératoire analysis ideal to use. The method has many advantages when analysing a local material, because the local material is generally present in all the stages of production including raw material procurement, core production and exploitation, tool production, tool maintenance and final discard.

The problems in using this method occur when dealing with exotic raw materials such as obsidian, because the artifacts are changing hands and the conceptual context changes according to the flint knappers' knowledge and skills, which again influence the methods and techniques of knapping. When analysing the exotic material in the chaîne opératoire, the artifacts with cortex, larger flakes and larger cores are generally absent because they indicate the earlier stages of raw material acquisition, test knapping and core reduction. According to Perlès, it is necessary to take into account the uncertainties of the chaîne opératoire when dealing with different subsystems and conceptual schemes, especially where certain parts of the operational chaîne are missing, which often occurs when analyzing an obsidian assemblage. However, the method has been used successfully on the

---

[372] Renfrew 1975, 3ff; Perlés 1990a, 24ff; fig. 72.

[373] Galanidou 2002, 330, pl. I. Evans & Renfrew 1968, fig. 60.

[374] Runnels 1985, 359ff; Demoule & Perlès 1993, 393.

[375] Torrence 1986, 100ff.

[376] Perlès 1992b, 223ff; fig. 75.

[377] Inizan et al. 1999, 14ff. Dobres 2000, 167ff; fig. 76.

[378] Bailey 1997a, 1997b. Perlès 1990b. Sørensen 2004, 237ff.

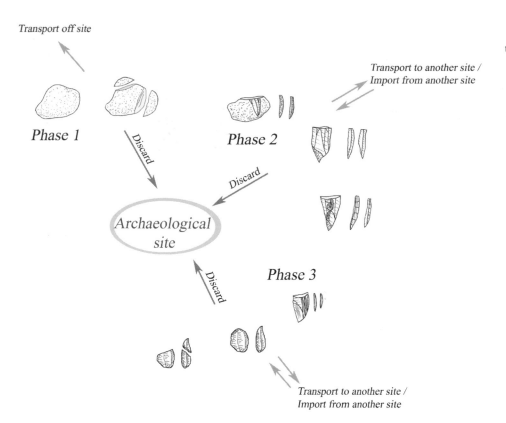

Transport off site

Phase 1

Discard

Phase 2

Transport to another site /
Import from another site

Fig. 76. Schematic illustration of a generalized reduction sequence, with the three main phases in the chaîne opératoire outlined in the article. L. Sørensen and K. Langsted.

Discard

Archaeological
site

Discard

Phase 3

Transport to another site /
Import from another site

obsidian assemblage from the Final Neolithic site Skoteini.[379] In the following, three phases in the chaîne opératoire (Figs. 76 and 78) will be the main frame in the lithic analysis, which can be narrowed down to these sequences:

Phase 1: The procurement and test knapping of the raw material, where larger flakes or blades with cortex are removed from the core.

Phase 2: The primary and secondary production sequence, with core preparation and the manufacture of blades.

Phase 3: The modification, resharpening, recycling and discarding of tools.

Pangali-edification of diagrams and presentation of knapping techniques

The debitage from Pangali gives us important information regarding the production strategies especially for the differences between local and exotic raw materials. The debitage is divided into different groups. The debitage grouping consists of the large assemblage of small and large flakes. In the second group are different kinds of blades,

microblades and fragments of blades. The third group holds the technical pieces that include hinge flakes, plunging pieces, primary blades or flakes with cortex and single or double crested blades. The fourth group has cores and the last group different kinds of tools. The different assemblages are also registered according to the amount of cortex on each artifact, because the cortex indicates which phases are present in the chaîne opératoire (Figs. 76, 77 and 78).

Finally a flint technological analysis of the assemblage has been registered, in order to observe differences in use of techniques such as hard direct, soft direct, pressure percussion or pressure flaking. Hard direct percussion is a direct blow against the raw nodule with a hammer stone made of quartz. The flakes produced from this technique are relatively thick with clear scars. The second technique is soft direct technique, which is a direct blow against the flint nodule with a soft hammer stone made of chalk or organic material e.g. antler or

---

[379] Perlès 1993, 452ff.

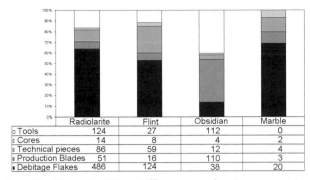

	Radiolarite	Flint	Obsidian	Marble
▢ Tools	124	27	112	0
▨ Cores	14	8	4	2
▧ Technical pieces	86	59	12	4
▨ Production Blades	51	16	110	3
▪ Debitage Flakes	486	124	38	20

Fig. 77. Pangali. The different production strategies according to each raw material. L. Sørensen and C. Casati.

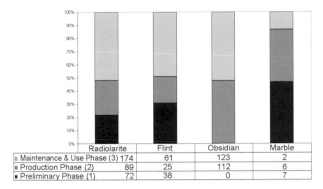

	Radiolarite	Flint	Obsidian	Marble
▢ Maintenance & Use Phase (3)	174	61	123	2
▨ Production Phase (2)	89	25	112	6
▪ Preliminary Phase (1)	72	38	0	7

Fig. 78. Pangali. The different phases in the chaîne operatoire. L. Sørensen and C. Casati.

bone. The flakes or blades produced in this technique are often thin and flat. The third technique is the pressure percussion, which is often made on points in order to make the point thin. The pressure is made in the hand with parallel retouches applied with the narrow end of a tool made of wood, antler, bone or metal, and it often produces very small and thin flakes, with almost no butt.[380]

The last technique registered in the Pangali assemblage is pressure flaking, the most difficult one to master. Pressure flaking requires the flint knapper to have particular technological skills. This technique is especially difficult to master compared to other techniques. Instead of resulting from a blow, the microblades are pressed off the core with a hard pressure using a pressure flaker. The core is fixed between the knapper's feet or can be fixed in a device made of wood. The pressure flaker is often pointed and made of antler or bone. The accuracy with which the pressure point can be positioned leads to maximum precision and standardization. This makes the recognition criteria on the cores very typical. There are four basic forms of cores, the pyramid, the bullet, the flat or the flat core with two successive debitage surfaces. The last type of cores has been recorded in the Greek Bronze Age. Pressure flaking allows high productivity and minimal waste, but requires higher technical investments than direct percussion.[381] Unfortunately it is not possible to determine which knapping technique was used on all artifacts. The amount of artifacts that could be determined from the radiolarite was 38%. For the flint assemblage it was possible to determine 44% of the artifacts. The technical diag-

nostic pieces in the obsidian assemblage were 57%, while it was only possible to determine 45% of the marble assemblage.

In many publications the chipped stone assemblage analysis is concentrated on the obsidian assemblage, which makes comparative studies difficult for the radiolarite, flint and marble assemblage. However, it is necessary to analyze the different raw materials in separate groups, because the conceptual scheme, the goal of project of the production and the actual chaîne opératoire is often not the same. Furthermore the limitations in the quality of the raw materials, often sets technical limitations for what is possible to produce in that particular material.

The radiolarite assemblage

The radiolarite artifacts are dominated by small or larger flakes amounting to 82% of the total assemblage (Fig. 77). Around 90% of these artifacts are not covered with cortex (Pl. 30). This can be interpreted to mean that some of the first phases in the chaîne opératoire are missing and that the test knapping of the raw nodules occurred where the raw material was procured (Figs. 78, 79, Pls. 30 and 31). The amount of blades in this assemblage is only 7% (Pls. 32-33), but a lot of these blades were produced into different types of tools such as scrapers or retouched pieces (Fig. 80, Pls. 34, 35

---

[380] Inizan et al. 1999. Andrefski 1998.
[381] Pelegrin 1984, 93ff; 1988, 37ff; Fig. 81.

Local raw material procurement at primary sources 100 m to 4 km from Pangali.

Larger cores was imported to Pangali and the different stages of lithic production and recycling is present on site.

Fig. 79. Pangali. Generalized reduction sequence for radiolarite, flint and marble, indicating the different phases identified at Pangali. L. Sørensen & K. Langsted.

and 36). The technical artifacts constitute 11 % of the assemblage, which indicates a larger flake and blade production on the site. The cores proved to be 2 % of the total assemblage, which also proved that a larger production took place on the site (Pls. 30 and 31). Many of the cores were totally exhausted even if they were procured locally. The tool index is 16% of the total assemblage, which is dominated by normal everyday tools such as scrapers, retouched pieces and points (Figs. 79 and 80. Pls. 34, 35, 36, 38 and 39). Often local flint was used for the production of flakes and blades of low quality (Pl. 31). This has been observed on sites far away from high quality raw material sources, often where the obsidian material is not dominant such as in Makriyalos and Sitagroi in Northern Greece.[382] However, almost every Late or Final Neolithic site in Greece has a crude flake production of a local raw material of flint, chert, jasper, quartz or radiolarite, E.g. Saliagos[383] Kitsos[384] Skoteini Cave[385] Lerna[386] and Kastria Cave.[387]

The flint technological observation of the radiolarite assemblage is dominated by the hard and the soft direct technique, which could be observed on 86% of the technical diagnostic artifacts (Fig. 81). These two techniques could be mastered by most people in the Neolithic Age. It is very common to see the raw materials from the local areas dominated by these knapping techniques. The surprise in the radiolarite assemblage was the observation on 3% of the blades, knapped by pressure flaking (Pl. 32, 9). Normally the pressure flaking is observed on blades from the obsidian assemblage, but at Pangali there seem to have been inhabitants who had the technical skills to master the pressure flaking on local raw materials. This observation is rather unusual, because pressure flaking was hardly a daily task of a farmer, but a task carried out by highly specialized flint knappers. The fact that this demanding technique was practised on local materials indicates that there were specialized flint knappers among the local inhabitants of Pangali. The last technique registered in the radiolarite assemblage was the pressure percussion with 10% of the diagnostic pieces, mainly points (Pl. 38, 1-3). The number of points indicates a specialized production of points in radiolarite for hunting purposes.

[382] Skourtopoulou 1999, 123; Tringham 2003, 81ff.

[383] Evans & Renfrew 1968, 47ff.

[384] Perlès 1981, 135ff.

[385] Perlès 1993, 452ff.

[386] Kozlowski 1996, 297ff.

[387] Karampatsoli 1997, 550; fig. 79.

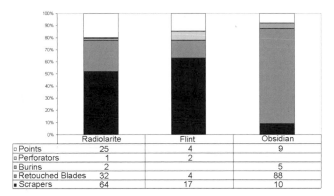

	Radiolarite	Flint	Obsidian
□ Points	25	4	9
□ Perforators	1	2	
■ Burins	2		5
■ Retouched Blades	32	4	88
■ Scrapers	64	17	10

Fig. 80. Pangali. The different tool types identified. L. Sørensen and C. Casati.

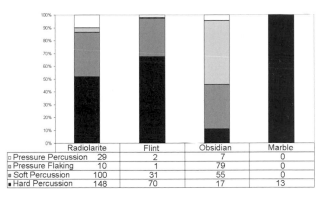

	Radiolarite	Flint	Obsidian	Marble
□ Pressure Percussion	29	2	7	0
□ Pressure Flaking	10	1	79	0
■ Soft Percussion	100	31	55	0
■ Hard Percussion	148	70	17	13

Fig. 81. Pangali. Flint technological observations L. Sørensen and C. Casati.

The flint assemblage

The flint material is dominated by flakes with 54% (Fig. 77). The number of different blades constitutes only 6% of the material, whereas the number of technological pieces is relatively high with 25% (Fig. 77, Pl. 32, 1-8). This indicates that flint knapping indeed took place at Pangali. The number of flint cores is 8 pieces, which is 3 % of the whole assemblage (Pls. 30, 4-5, 31, 1-3). The number of cores does not correspond with the high amount of flakes and technical pieces, which could be interpreted as cores being moved from the site (Fig. 79). However, one must take into account that less than one percent of the site is excavated. The tool index constitutes 12% of the total flint assemblage, dominated by scrapers, retouched pieces and points, just as in the radiolarite assemblage (Fig. 80, 7. Pl. 34, 8-10. Pl. 36, 1-5 and Pl. 38, 4 and 8). The number of artifacts without any cortex also dominates the flint assemblage with 71%. The artifacts with cortex are 29 % of the assemblage, which could be interpreted as the presence of phase one in the chaîne opératoire, but it cannot be excluded nor confirmed that some of the test knapping and decorefication did not happen on Pangali (Figs. 78 and 79). The high number of artifacts with cortex influences the interpreted chaîne opératoire phases. The first phase is represented with 30% against the radiolarite with only 20%. The second and third phase in the flint assemblage is represented with 21% and 49%, which resemble the phases from the radiolarite (Figs. 78 and 79).

The technological observations from the flint assemblage are dominated by the hard direct technique with 67%, which is high compared with the radiolarite material (Fig. 81). The second technique in the assemblage is the soft direct technique with 30%, resembling the radiolarite material. Pressure flaking is also present in the assemblage, although only represented by 1%. There was a number of blade fragments, which had many similarities with fragmented obsidian blades (Pl. 32, 1-8). It was impossible to conclude whether these blade fragments had been knapped using soft percussion or pressure flaking. It is therefore possible that the total number of blades knapped by pressure flaking could be higher than these observations indicate. The pressure percussion was also represented by 2 % which is two points (Pl. 38, 4 and 8). The production of arrowheads is not exclusively limited to one type of raw material, but to all the types. These facts indicate that the local habitants of Pangali mastered this particular technique and that the manufacture of points and preparation for hunting purposes was one of the many activities on the site.

The marble assemblage

In other publications regarding the chipped stone assemblages the marble has often been neglected, but nevertheless it is often one of the closest accessible raw materials. The quality of marble as a raw material is very coarse. However, the marble at Pangali is frequently of a fine quality, found right at the site (Figs. 78 and 79). The use of mar-

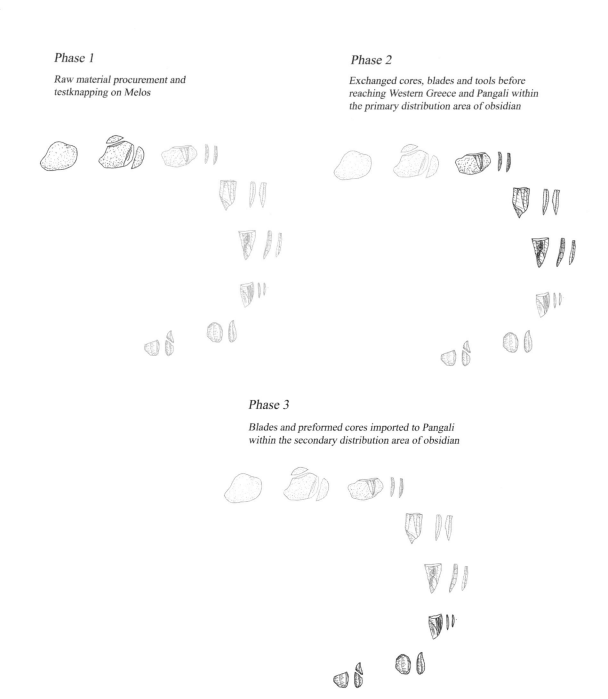

Phase 1

Raw material procurement and
testknapping on Melos

Phase 2

Exchanged cores, blades and tools before
reaching Western Greece and Pangali within
the primary distribution area of obsidian

Phase 3

Blades and preformed cores imported to Pangali
within the secondary distribution area of obsidian

Fig. 82. Generalized reduction sequences for the obsidian assemblage indicating the different stages of the obsidian exchange. L. Sørensen and K. Langsted.

ble could indicate a shortage of other raw materials at Pangali. The marble assemblage is the smallest with 29 pieces, which is dominated by 69% flakes. It is dominated by artifacts with no cortex, which proves the previous picture that the preliminary knapping of the nodules happened away from the site. However, the chaîne opératoire analysis shows that debitage from all the stages is present at the site (Fig. 81). Furthermore the mar-

ble assemblage is dominated by a hard direct technique, which is normally used in the initial phases of the chaîne opératoire (Fig. 81). No visual tools with retouche were registered in the marble assemblage, but some of the larger flakes could have been used as cutting tools. Future microwear analysis of the marble assemblage can determine if some of these flakes were actually used. The fact that 10% was blades and 14% technical pieces indicates that the habitants of Pangali probably used marble tools in the everyday household (Fig. 77).

The obsidian assemblage & exchange

The exotic obsidian from Melos showed some very different results from those of the local raw materials. Firstly the percentage of small and larger obsidian flakes consists of only 14%, whereas this group constituted over 50% in the local raw material assemblage. The second difference was the high amount of blades, with 40 % (110 pieces), which proved a concentrated use of obsidian blades compared to blades of local raw materials (Fig. 77, Pls. 30 and 33). However 96 of the obsidian blades were broken into several pieces, either deliberately or during the pressure flaking. Many of the broken blades had hinge fractures, which is a normal error when pressure flaking is used. Only 14 of the blades were complete and the average size of the blades was 4-5 cm long and 1-1.5 cm wide (Pl. 33, 18-20). Those are quite small blades compared with obsidian blades from other sites, like Saliagos,[388] Kitsos,[389] Skoteini Cave[390] or Lerna,[391] which vary from 8-10 cm to smaller ones around 3-4 cm. The size of the blades could have something to do with the different distances to the primary or secondary distribution areas (Figs. 72 and 82).

In the Pangali assemblage the majority of the obsidian blades were fragmented, perhaps because they could be used in tools, with particular shafting such as sickles, demanding that the blades were broken into smaller pieces approx. 2-3 cm in length and 1-2 cm in width. The fragmented blades express one of the most deliberate choices made on Pangali, where they tended to break the obsidian blades into fragments – so instead of one blade they got two blade fragments from one blade (Pl. 33, 7-17). This was proven by a refitted blade, which was deliberately broken by the inhabitants of Pangali (Pl. 33, 18), again indicating the importance of the obsidian blades as a cutting tool. It also proves the fact that a certain shortage of the obsidian must have occurred at Pangali. This behaviour is also observed on other sites, mostly far away from Melos such as Kitsos,[392] Skoteini Cave[393] Lerna[394] Kastria Cave,[395] Makriyalos[396] or Sitagroi.[397]

Many of the obsidian blades are perfect and have probably been made by the best flint knapper, as few technical debitage with hinge fractures, crested blades or plunging terminations have been observed. The technical pieces in the obsidian assemblage consist of only 4 %, which was very low compared with those of the local raw materials (Pl. 33, 1-3, 5). The near total absence of cortical material and preparation pieces indicates that obsidian was brought to the site in the form of initiated cores or ready made blades produced outside the habitation zone or at another site (Pl. 30, 6-8). All the blades were probably produced by highly specialized knappers (Fig. 82). This interpretation is not new and has been suggested for a number of Late and Final Neolithic assemblages such as the Kitsos assemblage,[398] Skoteini Cave,[399] Lerna,[400] Kastria[401] and Makriyalos.[402]

Only three totally exhausted obsidian cores were found from Pangali. This makes the obsidian cores extremely rare and their number is well below what would be expected from the blade production, illustrating once again that the habitants had economical awareness of the exotic material (Pl. 30, 6-8). It is probable that some of the cores were taken away for further exploitation to another site. This phenomenon has been observed on several sites dated to all the different phases in the Neolithic.[403] Normally when there are many cores at a site this could indicate some earlier phases in the chaîne opératoire, but this was

[388] Evans & Renfrew 1968, 48ff.
[389] Perlès 1981, 149ff.
[390] Perlès 1993, 453ff.
[391] Kozlowski 1996, 350-ill. 12.
[392] Perlès 1981, 210 pl. IV.
[393] Perlès 1993, 475 fig. 11.
[394] Kozlowski *et al.* 1996, 327, fig. 6.
[395] Karampatsoli 1997, 487ff.
[396] Skourtopoulou 1999, 123.
[397] Tringham 2003, 81ff.
[398] Perlès 1981, 131.
[399] Perlès 1993, 295.
[400] Kozlowski *et al.* 1996, 331.
[401] Karampatsoli 1997, 550.
[402] Skourtopoulou 1999, 123.
[403] Perlès 2001, 209, Moundrea-Agrafioti 1996, 103ff; Kozlowski *et al.* 1996, 299.

not the case in the Pangali assemblage. The scarcity of the core and trim pieces is also observed in Franchthi,[404] the Keos assemblage[405] in the Asea Valley Survey,[406] Kitsos,[407] Skoteini Cave,[408] Lerna,[409] Kastria[410] and Makriyalos.[411]

The rarity of the cores remains a puzzle, and the most obvious reason for this particular phenomenon could have something to do with the distance to the raw material source and the distribution area of the obsidian exchange (Figs. 72, 86 and 87). This hypothesis is supported by analysing the amount of cores and in particular the larger size of the obsidian cores at Saliagos[412] and Ftelia,[413] compared to other sites in Greece. The amount of obsidian imported to Saliagos and Ftelia seems to have been constant during the Late and Final Neolithic, so that the flint knappers probably had unlimited supplies of obsidian. Many of the sites near Melos such as Saliagos or Ftelia had systematic blade productions and procured the obsidian directly, whereas many of the sites on the mainland probably did not have any obsidian blade productions and procured the obsidian indirectly.[414] The consequence of an indirect obsidian procurement strategy could sometimes be a shortage of obsidian. But interestingly enough it also indicates the beginning of an exchange route between Melos to some of the Cycladic islands in connection with probable seasonal tasks or specialized trips.[415]

The procurement pattern of obsidian appears in three zones in the Late and Final Neolithic. Zone 1: A direct supply zone, within the primary distribution area at the Cyclades and coastal sites. At these sites the obsidian is present in large amounts and comprises over 95% of the lithic assemblage. Zone 2: An intermediate zone, within the primary distribution area at Thessaly, western Peloponnese, where the obsidian is exchanged indirectly through middlemen as semi-finished products in relatively large amounts, with no really fall-off effect as the distance from the source increases. Zone 3: An indirect supply at the secondary distribution area at more distant places such as western Macedonia, where obsidian is found in very smallquantities, which is illustrated by an absolute fall-off curve (Figs. 72, 81, 82 and 86). In the area

beyond western Macedonia in central and eastern Macedonia virtually no obsidian is found. Pangali is situated just outside the primary distribution area, and it can therefore contribute to the picture of the obsidian procurement pattern in western Greece, which is lacking in the analysis.[416] There are possibly three kinds of models, which would apply to the to the obsidian assemblage at Pangali, namely down the line, free-lance and directional exchange.[417] It is at present impossible to predict the fall-off pattern for the Pangali assemblage, because only a part of the site has been excavated, although a tendency towards a down the line or directional trade is most likely (Figs. 86 and 87).[418]

Technological observations in the obsidian assemblage

The flint technological registration is dominated by the demanding pressure flaking with 50 %, mainly registered on the many blades in the assemblage (Pl. 33, 4, 6, 9, 11, 12, 18-20). The pressure flaking requires a long apprenticeship and regular practice.[419] Even if the detachment of the blade is

---

[404] Perlès 1973, 80.
[405] Torrence 1991, 188.
[406] Carter 2003, 130f.
[407] Perlès 1981, 131.
[408] Perlès 1993, 295.
[409] Kozlowski *et al.* 1996, 331.
[410] Karampatsoli 1997, 550.
[411] Skourtopoulou 1999, 123.
[412] Evans & Renfrew 1968, fig. 60.
[413] Galanidou 2002, 330 pl. 1.
[414] Perlés 1990a; Perlés 2001, 207; Demoule & Perlés 1993, 396; 22ff; Torrence 1986, 219ff.
[415] Agouridis 1997, 1ff; Runnels & van Andel 1988, 95ff; Renfrew 1975, 3ff; Knapp 1985, 5ff; Figs. 86 and 87.
[416] Perlés 1990a, 24ff.
[417] Renfrew 1975, figs. 11-14; Figs. 86 and 87.
[418] The distance from Melos to Pangali varies, depending on whether the sea transportation took place along the coastline or on the open sea. The direct sea route around Peloponnese and into the Gulf of Patras is app. 480 km. whereas a route along the coastline is approx. 980 km. The approx. distance from Melos to the different sites (Figs. 86 and 87) are all calculated as the shortest distance from Melos made by direct sea or land routes.
[419] Pelegrin 1984, 1988.

not difficult in itself, strict control of the core and the reduction sequence are very important. Considering the high number of blades produced at Pangali, it seems likely that some individuals underwent this demanding apprenticeship. However, observations of the blades at Pangali prove an almost null rate of conceptual or gestural errors. These facts also indicate introduction of obsidian into the site as pre-formed cores or partly exploited cores made by external specialized knappers, because the technical debitage such as flakes with cortex, crested blades is underrepresented in the material. Even the cores, with 3 pieces are very rare in the assemblage (Pl. 30, 6-8), which indicates that there is no firm evidence of on-site production of obsidian.

The second technique most used is the soft direct percussion with 35 %, which is also observed on the blades. Only 11% of the material has been knapped with the hard direct technique, which indicates that the inhabitants on the site have knapped on the obsidian cores (Pl. 30, 7-8). Some of the larger blades have been reknapped into points by pressure percussion, making up 4% of the flint technological observations. Some of these points were also manufactured on Pangali, because some of these points are unfinished preforms (Pl. 34, 2-5). The low variability in the obsidian blade technology on Pangali implies that the blade production was carried out by very few flint knappers, which is an opposite situation to that of the material from Keos, where many flint knappers have been identified.[420]

Another important observation is the fact that 96% of the obsidian assemblage was not covered by cortex, which is far higher than the local raw materials. These percentages have great influence on the interpreted chaîne opératoire phases present in the obsidian assemblage. The initial phases in the obsidian chaîne opératoire are totally absent, whereas the unretouched blades are distributed in phase 2 and the finished or reknapped tools are placed in phase 3 (Figs. 78 and 82, Pls. 33 and 37). At contemporary settlements in Southern Greece 100 km from Melos, another chaîne opératoire has been observed in which all the phases are present

such as Saliagos[421] or Ftelia.[422] At contemporary sites further away from Melos at Kitsos,[423] Franchthi,[424] Lerna[425] the primary decortification pieces are rare but every stage of the lithic reduction, from larger flakes with cortex to larger blades and finished tools are present on these sites (Fig. 86). This does not seem to be the case at Pangali and other sites situated at great distance from Melos.[426]

The obsidian at Pangali appears to have been indirectly procured from Melos in the form of slightly decortified nodules, preformed cores or larger flakes. When the obsidian reached Pangali it had already gone through many hands (Fig. 82). At Pangali the obsidian blades were probably broken into pieces. At present it is uncertain if an actual minor blade production occurs on Pangali, indicated by the many hinge fractures seen on the obsidian blade fragments and because of the technical difficulties in handling the pressure flaking. However there were some good flint knappers at Pangali, as proven by some of the blades made in the local raw materials. In general, the blade production at Pangali could be interpreted as a specialized skill, made by middlemen, because pressure flaking also occurs in the local material. Although it is rare, it proves the fact that the locals at Pangali also mastered this technical difficult skill of producing straight blades. This observation is quite rare, which puts the flint knappers at Pangali in a special position. Maybe the flint knappers at Pangali had a specialized production of obsidian blades or perhaps they redistributed already finished blades or pre-made cores and exchanged these goods further on to other sites. To prove an actual production centre at Pangali is at present difficult. It is necessary to take soil samples of the cultural layer. If there are small obsidian flakes in the assemblage it would indicate an actual knapping place on the

---

[420] Torrence 1991, 173ff; Fig. 81.
[421] Evans & Renfrew 1968, 46ff.
[422] Galanidou 2002, 317ff.
[423] Perlès 1981, 133ff.
[424] Perlès 1973, 80ff; 1990b, 2ff.
[425] Kozlowski *et al.* 1996, 331ff.
[426] Tringham 2003, 82f; Perlés 1990a, 24ff.

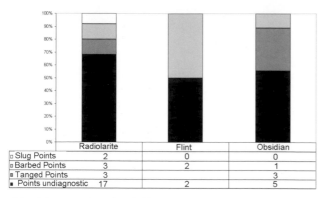

	Radiolarite	Flint	Obsidian
▢ Slug Points	2	0	0
▢ Barbed Points	3	2	1
▪ Tanged Points	3		3
▪ Points undiagnostic	17	2	5

Fig. 83. Pangali. The different point types identified. L. Sørensen & K. Langsted.

site. However, flintknapping and tool maintenance took place at Pangali, which is observed on the many tools in the lithic assemblage.

Tool types at Pangali

A total amount of 263 tools was registered, which is 20% of the total assemblage (Figs. 80 and 83). The tool assemblage was dominated by 47% of retouched blades, which indicates that many of the blades were indeed re-knapped into tools. The total obsidian assemblage had a very high tool index of 41%, dominated by the retouched blades, which is not very surprising, as obsidian is an excellent raw material often used as cutting tools (Fig. 80, Pls. 33 and 37). Some of these blades could be used as knives or as sickles. The demand for this particular tool type must have been high, even though many of the blade fragments at Pangali seem to be unused. No detailed study of microwear traces has yet been conducted on the Pangali material. However, the frequent presence of edge damage and retouche along the obsidian blade edges is an indication of intensive blade use. Blades with fresh edges, lacking any substantial traces of wear, could also have invisible traces of use wear.[427] The other predominant tool type with 35 % includes the different types of end or side scrapers (Pls. 35, 36 and 37). The most robust blades were selected and re-knapped into retouched pieces, which also included end-scrapers, notches, perforators and burins (Pls. 34, 35 and 36). Some of the scrapers revealed frequent traces of intensive use, such as the bluntness of working

edges on some end scrapers. The sizes of the scrapers were very different, from large ones (5-8 cm) often made in radiolarite to small thumbnail scrapers (2-3 cm) in obsidian (Pls. 35 and 37). Similar thumbnail scrapers are also observed in the Final Neolithic assemblage from the Asea Valley survey.[428] Finally, some burins, perforators and splintered pieces were registered amounting to only 4 % of the tool assemblage (Pl. 34).

The range of retouched tool types represented on Pangali matches that already known from other Late and Final Neolithic settlements in Greece such as Saliagos[429] Franchthi,[430] Kitsos,[431] Keos,[432] Skoteini Cave[433] and Lerna.[434] However, the Greek Late and Final Neolithic assemblages pose difficult typological problems, because there are very few standardized tool forms, especially when arrowheads are lacking in the material. This has caused some problems in the typological dating of the chipped stone assemblage from different recent surveys, such as Keos,[435] Southern Argolid,[436] Berbati-Limnes,[437] Makriyalos Project[438] Kephallénia[439] and the Asea Valley survey,[440] which was forced to characterize the period simply as consisting of large numbers of retouched flakes and blades, without diagnostic types. However, at Pangali 38 points was registered, which were 15% of the total tool assemblage (Figs. 83 and 84, Pls. 38 and 39).

The point assemblage at Pangali

The 38 points from the Pangali assemblage were divided into 4 main categories: 1.undiagnostic

---

[427] Jensen 1994.
[428] Carter 2003, 147.
[429] Evans & Renfrew 1968, 46ff.
[430] Perlès 1973, 78ff.
[431] Perlès 1981, 133ff.
[432] Coleman 1977, 7ff.
[433] Perlès 1993, 51ff.
[434] Kozlowski et al. 1996, 319ff.
[435] Torrence 1991, 173ff.
[436] Kardulias & Runnels 1995, 74ff.
[437] Runnels 1996, 40ff.
[438] Pappa & Besios 1999, 108ff.
[439] Randsborg 2003, 81ff.
[440] Forsèn & Forsèn 2003.

points. 2.tanged points. 3.barbed points. 4.slugs (Fig. 83, Pl. 38). Furthermore the points were divided into a finished and an unfinished group. 63% of the points were unfinished, which includes all the preforms or the points discarded at an early stage (Fig. 84, Pl. 39). Only 26% (12) of the points were diagnostically determined (Pl. 38). The Pangali point assemblage was divided into two sub-categories, dominated equally by 16% tanged points and 16% barbed points. These artifacts were produced by means of pressure percussion and are made up of two parts. The body, which is pointed, triangular or almond shaped, is approx. 2/3 of the length of the point, and the tang. Sometimes the tang is only suggested and sometimes it is very clearly defined and varies in morphology and thickness. The tanged points are mostly symmetrical in section. They are subdivided into simply tanged points and tanged barbed points.

The tanged and barbed points were produced by pressure percussion, mastered by the inhabitants at Pangali (Fig. 83. Pls. 38 and 39). The production of a point began by the creation of notches at the place where the body and the tang of the point meet. Sometimes the blade provided advantages with a flat dorsal side, which was used to shape the point with pressure percussion. The retouche was used only on the dorsal face, while on the ventral face the retouche was limited to the tip and the tang. Most of the points were made in radiolarite, but there seem to be no prefered raw material for the production of points. The habitants at Pangali used whatever raw material there was available. One of the more rare type of points was the slug, of which we have only 2 diagnostic specimens and one possible preliminary work (Pl. 38, 9-10 and Pl. 39, 7).

The 3 different types of points from Pangali have been observed on many Late and especially Final Neolithic sites on the mainland and on the Cyclades such as Saliagos on Antiparos,[441] Kephala on Kea,[442] Paoura on Kea,[443] the cave of Zas on Naxos,[444] Kitsos in Attica,[445] Ftelia on Mykonos,[446] Lerna in Argolid,[447] Skoteini Cave at Tharrounia,[448] Asea Valley survey[449], Keos[450] and Southern Argolid.[451] Especially the point assemblages at Saliagos and Ftelia have many similarities with the point assemblage at Pangali. Also the

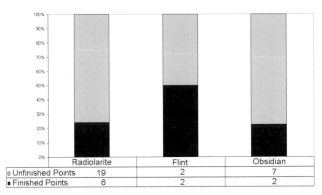

Fig. 84. Pangali. The amount of unfinished points. L. Sørensen & K. Langsted.

	Radiolarite	Flint	Obsidian
Unfinished Points	19	2	7
Finished Points	6	2	2

many pre-forms of the points occur at Saliagos.[452] Some of these arrowheads were actually used for hunting, proven by a fragmented point, which had visual signs of macro wear traces, because of the hinge terminating bending fracture (Pl. 38, 5). Two other arrowheads had a snap fracture.[453] During the Final Neolithic Pangali was probably one of these sites in which the hunt was prepared, proven by the many preformed points (Pl. 39). After the hunt some of the animals were brought back to the site and especially the hide must have been processed on the site, proven by the many scrapers and different bone needles found there.

Typological dating of selected artifacts

The diagnostic arrowheads from Pangali have many parallels from numerous Final Neolithic sites especially in the South and Central Aegean Final Neolithic context, including Saliagos, Franchthi,

---

[441] Evans & Renfrew 1968.
[442] Coleman 1977.
[443] Coleman 1977.
[444] Zachos 1999.
[445] Lambert 1981.
[446] Galanidou 2002.
[447] Kozlowski et al. 1996.
[448] Perlès 1993.
[449] Carter 2003, 147.
[450] Torrence 1991.
[451] Kardulias & Runnels 1995, 90.
[452] Evans & Renfrew 1968.
[453] Pl. 38, 6-7; Fischer et al. 1984, 23.

Kitsos, Pevkakia-Magula, Skoteini, Lerna, and Ftelia.[454] This Final Neolithic dating of the Pangali assemblage corresponds to the dating of the pottery assemblage. However, what sets Pangali apart from the Aegean Late and Final Neolithic sites is the absence of the bifacially retouched flakes termed "ovates".[455] Similar leaf shaped and triangular forms in flint are known from other Late or Final Neolithic contexts at Franchthi,[456] Kitsos.[457] This could have a chronological impact on the typological dating of the Pangali assemblage, because the ovates are not observed in the Kitsos layer IV, nor at Ftelia.[458]

The majority of the artifacts from Pangali thus belongs typologically to the beginning of the Final Neolithic. However, one of the points could be interpreted either as a pre-formed slug or a hollow-based arrow head (Pl. 38, 11). If it is a hollow-shaped arrowhead, then the Pangali assemblage has been mixed with Early Bronze Age material. After the beginning of the Early Bronze Age the tanged points were replaced with a hollow-based type, which has a special importance for understanding the chronological succession of prehistoric arrowheads in Greece.[459] However, at Lerna there have been registered tanged points until the Middle Helladic, which confuses the typological framework.[460] At Pangali there are also other indications of an Early Bronze Age dating from one of the obsidian core fragments (Pl. 30, 6). This particular core could be interpreted as a parallel epipedal flat core, which belongs to the Early Bronze Age.[461] This observation fits with the preliminary excavation report from Pangali[462] stating that there was pottery, which could be dated to the Early Bronze Age. These facts do not necessarily prove a continuity of the site into the Early Helladic, especially because the obsidian blades from Pangali had a width of above 1 cm and a thickness of above 0.35 cm, fitting with a Final Neolithic date. The Final Neolithic blades are generally both thicker and wider than the blades from the Bronze Age.[463] The overall dating of the lithic assemblage from Pangali points thus to the Final Neolithic. Furthermore, the bone tool assemblage also points to a dating within the Final Neolithic.

Bone tools

This particular assemblage is dominated by finished and fragmented products, 15 organic tools in total, which have been discarded after use (Pls. 40-42). 14 out of 15 specimens are made on long bones and 1 on antler parts (Pl. 41). Based on morpho-functional criteria, such as shape, the active edge of the implements, and the degree of modification of used raw material, the tools from Pangali have been classified into different categories such as pointed implements, transverse edge implements and needles. Because of the proximity to the sea, the absence of fishing hooks is noticeable. But we know for a fact that they fished, and brought the fish to the site, as fish bones were found there.[464]

Aspects of bone tool production

The aspects of the bone tool production and the reduction procedures are still recognizable on some of the artifacts from Pangali. The most common procedure is the transverse division of longitudinal bones and division of long bones, aimed at the removal of bone or antler portions and the extraction of appropriate blanks for further manufacturing and shaping. These techniques are rather time-consuming and were performed with great accuracy involving the bilateral grooving and lengthwise splitting of bones as well as grooving and splitting techniques for removal of shaft parts from the long bones.[465] All have been document-

[454] Evans & Renfrew 1968, 56ff; Perlès 1973, 82; Perlès 1981, 175ff; Weisshaar 1989, Taf. XVIII; Perlès 1993, Kozlowski et al.1996, 350ff.
[455] Evans & Renfrew 1968, 31.
[456] Perlès 1973, pl. 17b.
[457] Perlès 1981, pl. VII, 7, 8.
[458] Lambert 1969, 960, fig. 10.; Perlès 1973, fig. 31.3; Galanidou 2002, 322.
[459] Runnels 1985, 371ff; Carter 2003, 150f.
[460] Runnels 1985, 386.
[461] Inizan et al. 1999, 79.
[462] Cazis 1998, 280.
[463] Runnels 1985, 357ff.
[464] Bangsgaard this vol.
[465] Phoca-Cosmetatou 2002, 221ff.

ed in the artifacts from Pangali (Pl. 40, 6, 8-12 and Pl. 42). The techniques involved indicate either that most of the tools from Pangali were items of a planned production, which could have taken place at the site, or that it could have been a production imported from another site. This last hypothesis is mainly supported by the lack of bone waste from the production of these particular tools. In the bone tool assemblage there is a correlation between the anatomical parts used as raw material in the bone manufacturing. This has been observed on many other Late and Final Neolithic sites such as Dimini, Pevkakia, Makri and Kastria.[466]

Pointed, chisel and socketed tools

The most common tool is a perforating tool made on a split metarcarsus or carpus with the distal end of the splitted bone polished. In the Pangali material one pointed tool on the metapodialis (Pl. 40, 8) and three pointed tools with a split distal metapodial were registered (Pl. 40, 10-12). This technique is observed on many Neolithic sites in Greece,[467] Thessalie,[468] Saliagos,[469] Sitagroi[470] and Kitsos.[471] The particular bone-tool type dominates many assemblages in Greece. Two pointed tools all made of long bones with a groove and splitter method have been found (Pl. 40, 9 and Pl. 42). All of these have parallels within the Late and Final Neolithic tool assemblage and similar pointed tools have been observed in Kastria,[472] Northern Greece,[473] Thessalie,[474] Saliagos,[475] Sitagroi,[476] Tharrounia[477] and Kitsos.[478] The use wear analysis made on the pointed tools from Kastria proves that these particular tools were used mainly as perforators of thin leather and in addition for a hard material.[479] Furthermore there were also many fragments of small polished needles, especially around the fireplace in stratum 3 and 3a. Until now, two examples of needles have been registered, one of them having been burned, which also indicates that they have been found close to a fireplace (Pl. 40, 3).

There were also registered parts of a composite tool. It was made of antler, which had been intensively treated by grinding and polishing (Pl. 41).

The socketed antler beam was perforated and still retained its shaft hole, which also indicates the use of this tool as some sort of axe for wood working. Similar socketed antler beams have been observed in other Late and Final Neolithic assemblages such as Kastria[480] and Dimini,[481] Pevkakia-Magula[482] and Sitagroi.[483] An elaborated bone artifact with indications of four holes in a rib bone was also registered (Pl. 40, 1). In terms of use this piece could be for scraping, gouging and polishing. An alternative explanation of this object could be that of a device on a cloth. A similar artifact has also been observed in the Sitagroi assemblage. Here the first interpretation of the use has been suggested.[484]

The second most dominant tool type in the Pangali assemblage was four examples of chisel tools with rounded ends (Pl. 40, 4, 5, 7 and Pl. 42). The rounding at the tip may be a result of heavy use. This particular tool also has many parallels in other Late and Final Neolithic sites such as Northern Greece,[485] Thessaly,[486] Sitagroi[487] and Kitsos.[488] Finally a small fragment of a split rib bone, which had been polished, was registered in the bone assemblage (Pl. 40, 2). This tool type has

[466] Moundrea-Agrafioti 1981; Stratouli 1997, 551; 1998; 2000, 322f.

[467] Stratouli 1998.

[468] Moundrea-Agrafioti 1981.

[469] Evans & Renfrew 1968, 66ff.

[470] Elster 2003.

[471] Leroy-Prost 1981, 241ff.

[472] Stratouli 1997, 550; fig106:1 & 109:3.

[473] Stratouli 1998.

[474] Moundrea-Agrafioti 1981.

[475] Evans & Renfrew 1968, 66ff.

[476] Elster 2003.

[477] Sampson 1992, 85.

[478] Leroy-Prost 1981, 241ff.

[479] Stratouli 1997, 550.

[480] Stratouli 1997, 551 – fig. 107.

[481] Stratouli 1998, Tafel 35.

[482] Stratouli 1998, Tafel 41.

[483] Elster 2003, 47.

[484] Elster 2003, 44 – fig. 2.7.

[485] Stratouli 1998.

[486] Moundrea-Agrafioti 1981.

[487] Elster 2003, 45f.

[488] Leroy-Prost 1981.

Phase	Site	Site type	Sheep	Sheep /goat	Goat	Pig	Cow	Manage meat of sheep and goat
Final Neolithic	Pangali	Cave	10%	62%	6%	17%	5%	Meat strategy
Final Neolithic	Ftelia	Open air	9%	69%	6%	6%	6%	Meat strategy
Final Neolithic	Kalythies	Cave	45%	-	42%	6%	7%	Meat strategy
Final Neolithic	Skoteini	Cave	40%	-	32%	24%	4%	Meat strategy
Final Neolithic	Zas	Cave	41%	-	52%	6%	1%	Meat strategy
Final Neolithic	Kefala	Open air	39%	-	44%	9%	8%	-
Final Neolithic	Pevkakia	Open air	34%	-	17%	28%	22%	-
Final Neolithic	Sitagroi II	Open air	43%	-	9%	17%	30%	-

Fig. 85. Pangali. The amount of sheep, goats, pigs and cows on comparable Final Neolithic cave and open air sites. L. Sørensen. Partly after Halstead 1996.

also been observed in Dimini,[489] Pevkakia Magula,[490] and in Saliagos.[491]

In the bone assemblage a large quantity of organic tools was registered around the nearby fireplace, which measured approx. 1.5 m. in diameter. It is possible that many activities involving the pointed bone tools took place around this fireplace. All the bone tools in total indicate a large activity zone, in which the perforation of materials such as hides could have been an impotant activity. However, the relatively small number of bone tools identified at Pangali, combined with their restricted forms and functions, suggests that the tools did not serve a wide range of purposes. It is probable that the inhabitants of Pangali used the site periodically and for short periods of time. Pangali was probably settled for so long, that certain social, symbolic and economically activities occurred on the site. This is supported by the evidence from a number of findings from the deposits such as decorated pottery, cooking pottery, local and exotic raw materials, a bone assem-

blage indicating specialized herding of sheep and goat with a meat subsistence strategy (Fig. 85). Finally a human skeletal remain was found, which could imply that the site was inhabited so long that people died here and were buried on the site. However, further excavations might enlighten issues of the social-symbolic significance at Pangali.

Concluding remarks and perspectives

Pangali is so far one of the only Final Neolithic sites in Western Greece with a large research potential. The site was settled during the Final Neolithic phase LNIb ca. 4.600 – 4.200 Cal. B.C. The site has many topographical advantages as an observation point, lying near a natural harbour,

[489] Moundrea-Agrafioti 1981, pl. 28.
[490] Stratouli 1998, pl. 42, 43.
[491] Evans & Renfrew 1968, fig. 80, 8-10.

Fig. 86 (opposite page). The amount of obsidian found at selected Late and Final Neolithic sites in Greece. Partly after Perlés 1990a, table 4. A: Raw nodules. B: Preliminary preparation of the core. C: Core with removed cortex and primary blades. D: Pre-formed core. E: Blade or flake cores. F: Exhausted cores. The approx. distance from Melos to the different sites in (Figs. 86 and 87) are all calculated to be the shortest distance from Melos. L. Sørensen. Abbreviations:
Adtm: Approximately distance to Melos
Pocoo: Proportion of cortex on the obsidian
Aoroc: Amount of reduction on the cores

ion	Site	Phase	AdtM	Amount of obsidian	Pocoo	Aorotc	References
tern edonia	Sitagroi	LN/FN	500 km	1%	non	No cores	Tringham 2003, 81ff
	Nea Nicomedeia	LN	460 km	Represented but rare	–	–	Rodden 1962; 1964
	Makriyalos II	LN	450 km	5%	non	E/F	Skourtopoulou 1999, 122ff
	Mégalonissi	FN	450 km	Well represented but not dominant	–	–	Fotiadis 1987
	Galanis	FN	450 km	Well represented but not dominant	–	–	Perlès 1990a
	Servia	LN	440 km	Represented but not dominant		–	Ridley & Wardle 1979; Watson 1984
lias	Pangali	FN	480 km	21%	1%	E/F	This Vol.
	Hagios Nikolaos	LN	480 km	Non dominant	–	–	Benton 1947
hellonia	Site 53	LN/FN	450 km	Non dominant	–	E/F	Randsborg 2002
saly	Theopetra	LN	500 km	1%	Non	E/F	Kyparissi-Apostolika 1999, 148
	Agia Sofia	LN	380 km	79%	2%	D/E	Milojcic et al. 1976; Perlès 1990a
	Pirgos	LN/FN	330 km	86%	–	–	Perlès 1990a
	Dimini	LN	320 km	84.5%	5%	C/D	Moundrea-Agrafioti 1981
	Agios Pétros	LN	290 km	69%	9%	–	Moundrea-Agrafioti 1981; Efstratiou 1985
tral Greece	Antre Corycien	LN	260 km	Well represented but not dominant	–	–	Perlès 1981
	Élatée	LN	230 km	Dominant	–	–	Weinberg 1962
	Étreusis	LN	200 km	Dominant	–	–	Perlès 1990a
rounia ponnese/ lid	Skoteini	LN/FN	200 km	95%	> 5%	C/D	Perlès 1993, 451ff
	Agios Dimitrios	FN	280 km	87%	7%	–	Perlès 1990a
	Kastria	LN/FN	300 km	54%	> 5%	D/E	Sampson 1997, 550
	Asea	LN/FN	200 km	Dominant	–	–	Holmberg 1944
	Corinth	LN	180 km	Dominant	–	–	Lavezzi 1978; Perlès 1990a
	Kouphovouno	LN/FN	180 km	> 90%	Rare	–	Renard 1989
	Lerna II	LN/FN	180 km	92%	Rare	D	Kozlowski et al. 1996, 324ff
	Franchthi - I	LN	140 km	52%	17%	A/B	Perlès 1990a
	Franchthi - II	LN	140 km	81%	16.5%	A/B	Perlès 1990a
	Franchthi - III	LN	140 km	94%	17.5%	B	Perlès 1990a
	Franchthi - I	FN	140 km	89%	3%	D	Perlès 1990a
	Franchthi - II	FN	140 km	80%	21%	D	Perlès 1990a
a	Néa Makri	LN	150 km	Dominant	–	–	Perlès 1990a
	Kitsos	LN/FN	120 km	97.5%	6%	B/C	Perlès 1990a
ades	Knossos	LN	180 km	13%	–	–	Evans 1964; Perlès 1990a
	Ftelia	LN/FN	125 km	99%	Rare	B/C	Galanidou 2002, 318ff
	Mavrispilia	LN	110 km	99%	19%		Belmont & Renfrew 1984; Torrence 1986; Perlès 1990a
	Anavolousa	LN	110 km	99%	7%		Belmont & Renfrew 1984; Torrence 1986; Perlès 1990a
	Praoura	FN	100 km	99%	–	–	Coleman 1977; Perlès 1990a
	Zas Cave	LN	100 km	98%	Present	D/E	Zachos 1999, 158
	Kefala	FN	95 km	99%		A	Coleman 1977; Perlès 1990a
	Saliagos	LN	70 km	99%	–	A/B	Evans & Renfrew 1968; Torrence 1986; Perlès 1990a
	Vouni	LN	70 km	99%	–	–	Evans & Renfrew 1968; Perlès 1990a
	Agrilia	LN	Melos	100%	–	A	Perlès 1990a

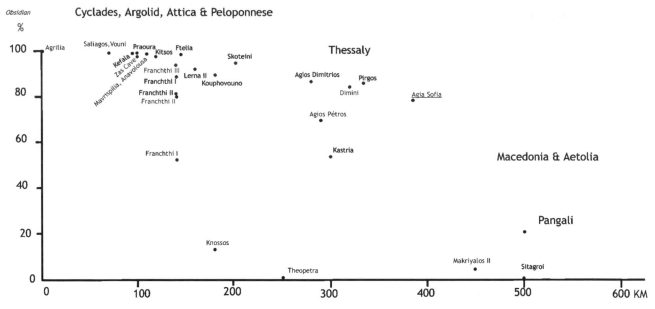

Fig. 87 Selected Late and Final Neolithic sites with their percentage of obsidian found at the sites compared with the distance to Melos, indicating two different falls off patterns: 1. A down the line exchange and 2. A directional trade. Sites in grey scale are dated to the Late Neolithic and sites in black scale are dated to the Final Neolithic. The approx. distance from Melos to the different sites in (Figs. 86 and 87) are all calculated to be the shortest distance from Melos. K. Langsted and L. Sørensen.

with a view to the Gulf of Patras. Furthermore the site had access to fresh water resources from Mount Varassova and finally the site is lying on a transportation route, where obsidian and other goods could have been exchanged from the coastal area to the inland regions on the river Evinos. The finds from Pangali proved to have many similarities with other Final Neolithic sites. The pottery assemblage was dominated by coarse ware although some fine ware was also registered. The lithic assemblage was dominated by local raw material, but imported obsidian was present in the material, which indicates extensive local contacts with other cultural groups in the area. The obsidian was probably imported to the site from Melos through middlemen as proven by the chaîne opératoire analysis. An actual production of obsidian blades on the site has not yet been confirmed, because there is no firm evidence of an on-site production. However, we can not conclude that this particular production did not take place in the region near the site. The archaeological material at Pangali gives only a small insight into the lithic and bone assemblage. The study of the pottery, lithic

and bone assemblages is an ongoing process, which could benefit from a future excavation as many new questions arise from this material.

Pangali has many similarities with other Final Neolithic sites regarding topographical position, seasonal habitation, lithic assemblages, imported artifacts, tool manufacture and bone assemblage. Do we face the same problems when it comes to the interpretation and function of these sites? Let me refer to the title of this article, where I have asked the question: "Farmers herding, hunting and exchanging – a normal behaviour of Final Neolithic farmers?" It is a rather important question to all Final Neolithic sites, which moves into marginal and coastal areas. When the Pangali assemblage is compared to other contemporary sites, the answer to the question must be yes! It is a normal behaviour, because many of these features are observed both at Pangali and other Final Neolithic cave sites. At Pangali the following observations has been made:

1. During the Final Neolithic Pangali was a preparation site for hunting wild game, because of the many points and pre-formed points in the lith-

ic assemblage. Hunting in the region encouraged social and political relations between local cultural groups.

2. The seasonal aspects of the bone assemblage indicated that Pangali was repeatedly settled during fall or winter for a couple of seasons, which is indicated by the thick cultural layers at the site.

3. The bone material showed that hunting was an integrated part of the subsistence, even if breeding and herding of goat and sheep was the basic occupation. The kill-off-patterns of the sheep and goats indicate a meat strategy, slaughtering the male infant, juvenile and sub adults.[492]

4. Pressure percussion and pressure flaking were observed on both local and exotic raw material, which indicates that the local habitants mastered this technique as well as the middlemen, who conducted the indirect exchange of the obsidian. The high technical skill suggests an obsidian production made by local and regional craftsmen.

5. The finds from Pangali also indicate that the site could have been used for religious purposes, because a figurine has been found.

6. Finally a human skull was found in the layers, indicating that some of the inhabitants were actually buried on the site.

Pangali is one of the first settlements in Western Greece prove a possible local distribution of obsidian, which leads to an increasing development of local as well as exotic sea routes. Pangali was probably inhabited by semi farmers, who had specialized in seasonal exchange of obsidian and other goods, besides being normal peasants. The development of a fixed transportation route and the increasing exchange of obsidian lead to an established route, which became important when metal and other exotic goods was traded during the following Helladic periods. Especially the obsidian exchange may have stimulated an already known sea route, which later societies could benefit from.

---

[492] See the contribution by Pernille Bangsgaard in this vol. p 162.

The animal bones from Pangali

By Pernille Bangsgaard

The faunal remains from Pangali include all the bones found during the excavation season of 1996, where a test trench measuring 2 by 2 meters was excavated down to bedrock located approximately 1 meter below the surface. The soil was dry-sieved with a mask-size in the range from 3 to 6 mm. The material was analysed in 2004 at the Wiener Laboratory, at the American School of Classical Studies in Athens, using the comparative collection and other facilities available there.[493]

The faunal remains from Pangali includes 1371 fragments (1800.9 grams) of which 395 fragments (978.2 grams) have been identified to species or family, leaving 976 fragments (822.7 grams) as unidentified. The identified material includes at least 13 different species (Table 1). It was relatively well preserved, but suffered from some surface damage mainly due to root etching, making the identification of cut-marks difficult. The material is limited in number and furthermore represents a very limited area of the entire site. The distribution and connected interpretation should thus be considered with some caution, as it may not be representative for the site as a whole.

Domesticated mammals

The domesticated mammals are by far the most dominating group of animals at the site

	Number	Weight
Pig, *Sus domesticus*	35	164.4
Cattle, *Bos taurus*	12	209.0
Goat, *Capra hircus*	23	88.8
Sheep, *Ovis aries*	15	18.7
Goat/sheep, *Capra/Ovis sp.*	140	304.2

Domesticated pig, *Sus scofa*

35 fragments were identified as deriving from domesticated pig. They represent the entire body, although it would appear that the small compact bones of the feet are slightly underrepresented.

The only information available for time of death comes from the fused/non-fused bones (Table 2) as no mandibles were found at the site. The bones indicate that pigs were butchered at a young age, as the only fused fragment found is the proximal end of metapodium (fused before birth). The conclusion therefore is that pigs were butchered before the age of 12 months at the latest and possibly earlier. Included in the fused/non fused material are three fragments from bones that were categorized as belonging to the foetal-pullus age group. All were visible larger than the stillborn found in the collection and would therefore most likely be pullus. No evidence of the cause of death was identified. Due to the age distribution of the pigs, a limited amount of material was available for measurements and therefore a number of fragments not yet fully fused were also measured (Table 3). This is probably the main reason for the fact that five of the six measurements from Pangali are slightly smaller than measurements from other contemporary Greek sites, such as the cave of Skoteini[494] and Platia Magoula Zarkou.[495] All measurements taken of the Pangali material were taken according to the guidelines described by von den Driesch (1979).

Cattle, *Bos taurus*

Domesticated cattle were also found at the site, although in limited amounts as cattle are only represented by 12 fragments. Evidence for the time of death for cattle is available only by information from fused/non-fused bones (Table 4). Once more the amount of information is very limited (5 fragments). However, the results indicate that the bones originate from more that one individual and the fragments suggest various times of death. A none-fused distal metapodium suggests a time of death before the age of 11/2 year and most of the other evidence suggests a time of death around the

---

[493] I would like to thank Dr. Sherry Fox and everybody at the Wiener laboratory, for the gracious help and warm co-operation I received during my stay there.

[494] Kotjabopoulou *et al.* 1993.

[495] Becker 1991.

age of 3 years. Additionally a single fused vertebrae was also identified (suggested time of fusion is around the age of 7-9 years)

None of the fragments identified as being from cattle could be measured.

Goat/sheep, *Capra/Ovis sp.*

Goat and sheep is by far the most common group of all in the fauna found at Pangali. The two species collectively representing at least 45% of the entire collection, additionally the small ruminate group (96 fragments) are probably also mainly to be identified as goat/sheep, which means that as much as 69% of the identified faunal material were from sheep/goat. The material was identified as either goat or sheep when possible. The identification was primarily based on the criteria described by Boessneck (1964) and Prummel *et al.* (1985) and here goat dominates 3:2. No mandibles with teeth were found and therefore information regarding time of death was available only from the fused/non-fused bones (Table 5). It was decided to combine the data from sheep and goat as the preliminary analysis suggested that no significant difference existed between the two species. This means that the probable period of fusion had to be expanded in order to incorporate the period of fusion as defined for each of the two species. However, this disadvantage was considered as insignificant compared to the creation of a much larger amount of data, and therefore a more reliable result.

The information obtained suggests that the main period of butchering was around the age of one year or slightly before. A few animals reached an age above 3-4 years and these were most likely kept for breeding. Included in the group of non-fused bones is a number of fragments identified as belonging to the pullus-foetal age category. Comparison with a stillborn in the collection revealed a variation in size as both smaller and larger individuals were identified. Therefore most of these were probably not a result of butchering but more likely a product of natural causes resulting in miscarriages. The conclusion of the time of death data must be that the animals were most likely pri-marily bred and kept as a meat supplier. However, the age of butchering is below the point of optimal meat gain compared to food intake (generally at the age of 2-3 years). This discrepancy could be caused by such factors as amount and availability of food during the winter.[496]

Measurements were taken when possible for all fragments that could be identified as either sheep or goat (Tables 6 and 7). These were compatible with measurements taken from contemporary Greek sites such as the cave of Skoteini[497] and Platia Magoula Zarkou.[498] The majority of the Pangali measurements had a tendency to be in the lower range of the other measurements. The exception to this rule is one first and third phalange from goat. The pattern of size range is most likely due to the rather low amount of material and the pronounced male-female size difference found in sheep and goat.[499]

Wild mammals

A number of wild mammals have been found at Pangali. All these species have been identified before at other archaeological excavations in Greece, including the cave of Skoteini,[500] Platia Mogoula Zarkou,[501] Sitagroi and Achelleion.[502] These species are still present in mainland Greece today.[503] It is worth noting that at Pangali the wild game account for approximately 19% of the identified faunal material. This is higher than any other Final Neolithic site, indicating that hunting and fishing played a more significant role here than at other sites of the period.

	Number	Weight
Wild pig, *Sus scofa*	6	54.6
Roe deer, *Capreolus capreolus*	18	24.1

[496] Payne 1973.
[497] Kotjabopoulou *et al.* 1993.
[498] Becker 1991.
[499] Zeder 1999.
[500] Kotjabopoulou *et al.* 1993.
[501] Becker 1991.
[502] Bökönyi 1986 and 1989.
[503] Mitchell-Jones *et al.* 1999.

Deer. *Cervus sp.*	2	39.1
Fox, *Vulpes vulpes*	4	9.8
Wild cat, *Felis silvestris*	9	3.6
Hare, *Lepus europaeus*	11	4.3

Wild boar, *Sus scofa*

A few fragments were identified as coming from wild boar and not from domesticated pig. Some of these fragments could be measured (Table 8) and these are compatible with measurements taken for wild and not domesticated pig from other contemporary sites in Greece.[504] Additionally all the fragments identified as wild boar are clearly larger and more robust than their domesticated counterparts at Pangali.

Among the fragments two measurements of phalanges are worth mentioning. When compared to contemporary wild boars from Platia Magoula Zarkou[505] and the cave of Skoteini,[506] the Pangali phalanges are of similar length although in the higher range, whereas they are more robust as the width are significantly higher both proximal and distal. Although it may be tempting to link this difference to the myth of the Kalydonian boar mentioned by Homer, 2 phalanges hardly constitute an adequate proof for larger or more robust wild boars in this region of Greece. All fragments were identified as fused thereby indicating a general time of death above the age of 1-2 years.

Roe deer, *Capreolus capreolus*

The dominating species of the hunted game of Pangali is the roe deer, the smallest of the deer found in Greece today. A total of 18 fragments were identified including 8 teeth. Due to the large number of loose teeth the MNI remains low at 2 individuals. Additionally two antler fragments were identified only to deer. These may be from either roe deer or red deer and the last is the most likely candidate due to the size of the fragments. However, as the fragments are worked, the species cannot be established with certainty. The modification consists of a smoothing of the entire outer surface, which blurs the structure of the antler. A single measurement was taken from a humerus,

when compared to measurements from other contemporary sites such as Sitagroi[507] and the cave of Skoteini the Pangali specimen is significantly smaller. The limited amount of information available for the time of death suggests that the roe deer was killed around the age of 1-2 years. However, due to the amount of statistic material no conclusion concerning the general hunting pattern of roe deer can be made.

Additionally red fox, wild cat and hare were also found at Pangali. A few measurements were taken for these species (Table 10-13). However, the material available for comparison is limited and therefore only red fox could be compared directly to measurements from the contemporary site of Sitagroi[508] and these were within the same size range.

Birds, *Aves sp.* and fish, *Pieces sp.*

	Number	Weight
Pigeon, *Columbidae sp.*	4	1.5
Crow and allies, *Corvidae sp.*	1	0.5
Unidentified bird, *Aves sp.*	9	2.2

	Number	Weight
Porgies and sea breams, *Sparidae sp.*	2	1.0
Mullets, *Mugillidae sp.*	2	0.3
Unknown fish. *Pieces sp.*	6	1.6

A small number of fish and birds are represented at the site, accounting for 6, 2 % of the total number of identified bones. Wet sieving may have produced an even greater number of fragments, as this would have allowed for a smaller mesh-size. Any possible difference would naturally depend entirely upon the size of fish and birds eaten at the site.

The bird and fish bones have only been identified to family mainly due to the general difficulties in distinguishing between various species and for

---

[504] Kotjabopoulou *et al.* 1993 and Becker 1986 and 1991.
[505] Becker 1991.
[506] Kotjabopoulou 1993.
[507] Bökönyi *et al.* 1986.
[508] Bökönyi 1986.

both the birds and the fish there are several species of each family found in Greece. The comparative collection used did not have a complete range of these species found in the area today, making identification very difficult. However, the identification achieved so far suggest no significant surprises as all families are represented by at least one species in the Mediterranean and in Greece today.

It is perhaps worth noting that although fish and bird fragments are generally considered as being significantly more fragile compared to mammal fragments, the fish and bird fragments have non the less survived at Pangali despite the general weathering and surface damage displayed by the faunal material. Therefore the conclusion must be that the site has much potential for expanding the knowledge of faunal remains from Final Neolithic open-air sites in Greece in general and for this area of Greece in particular.

Conclusion

The analysis of the faunal remains from Pangali is based on 1371 fragments of which 395 have been classified to species or families. The excavation consists of a single test trench and therefore the amount of faunal remains is restricted and originates from a limited area of the site. As stated earlier these circumstances influence the reliability of the result and the interpretation of the site as a hole.

Generally the results fit well within the framework of the period and are compatible with faunal remains found at contemporary sites throughout Greece. However, some differences were identified and will be described briefly. Pangali display a higher percentage of sheep and goat and a lower percentage of cattle and pig compared to the other sites. Additionally the percentage of wild animals is significantly higher suggesting more emphasis on hunting at Pangali. These differences could be influenced by several factors such as difference in the economic base of the sites, availability of domesticated and wild animals, difference in settlement pattern, environment differences or simply a coincidence due to the low amount of material from Pangali.

The domesticated mammals are most numerous in the collection and among these sheep/goat dominates, pigs are common, but also cattle was found here. The wild species include wild pig, roe deer, red fox, wild cat, hare and a few fish and bird bones. Due to the small amount of material most of the secondary analysis such as size and age distribution are inconclusive or must be treated with some caution. However, for sheep/goat and pig the age distribution does suggests that the majority was killed around or before the age of 1 year. This is a rather low age of butchering especially for sheep/goat and could suggest problems in obtaining winter food or other limitations that made butchering necessary before the point of optimal weight gain. More information of this sort both for these and other species would assist in giving more detailed information regarding the use of both domesticated and wild animals in this early period.

The site has proven to hold much potential with rich amounts of finds, faunal and otherwise especially due to the low number of Final Neolithic sites from this area of Greece. Additional excavation at the site would give important new and more detailed information about the site itself and to the body of evidence from the Final Neolithic period in general.[509]

---

[509] In addition to the faunal material found at the site a fragmented part of parietale from a human skull was found during cleaning of the test trench. The sutures are clearly visible and were not fully fused at the time of death indicating an individual in the age category of juvenile or young adult.

Table 1: Pangali. The distribution of faunal remains

	Domesticated pig *Sus domesticus*	Wild pig *Sus scofa*	Cattle *Bos taurus*	Goat *Capra hircus*	Sheep *Ovis aries*	Goat/sheep *Capra hircus/ Ovis aries*	Roe deer *Capreolus capreolus*	Deer *Cervus sp.*	Small ruminate	Red fox *Vulpes vulpes*	Wild cat *Felis silvestris*	Hare *Lepus europeaus*	Pigeon *Columba sp.*	Crow *Corvus sp.*	Bird *Aves sp.*	Fish *Pieces sp.*	Unidentified
Cranium	1	–	–	2	–	9	1	2	–	1	1	–	–	–	–	2	1
Mandible	–	–	–	–	–	4	–	–	13	1	–	1	–	–	–	–	–
Loose teeth	9	–	1	8	4	43	12	–	28	–	–	2	–	–	–	–	2
Vertebrae	2	–	3	–	–	6	–	–	8	–	–	–	–	–	–	8	1
Ribs	4	–	2	–	–	1	–	–	36	–	–	–	–	–	–	–	56
Coracoid	–	–	–	–	–	–	–	–	–	–	–	–	–	–	1	–	1
Scapula	2	–	1	1	–	1	–	–	7	–	–	–	–	–	–	–	1
Humerus	3	–	–	1	–	5	1	–	–	–	–	1	2	–	–	–	–
Radius	1	–	–	1	–	8	2	–	–	–	–	–	–	–	–	–	–
Ulna	1	–	–	–	–	3	–	–	–	1	–	–	2	1	–	–	–
Pelvis	–	–	–	–	–	3	–	–	2	–	–	–	–	–	–	–	–
Femur	2	–	1	–	–	3	1	–	2	–	–	–	–	–	–	–	1
Tibia	3	–	2	–	–	7	–	–	–	–	–	–	–	–	1	–	1
Patella	–	–	–	–	–	1	–	–	–	–	1	–	–	–	–	–	–
Carpal/tarsal	1	1	–	1	3	13	–	–	–	1	1	1	–	–	–	–	–
Metacarpal/tarsal	1	2	1	3	1	22	1	–	–	–	5	4	–	–	1	–	1
Phalanges	5	3	1	6	7	11	–	–	–	–	1	2	–	–	–	–	–
Unidentified	–	–	–	–	–	–	–	–	–	–	–	–	–	–	6	–	912
Total	35	6	12	23	15	140	18	2	96	4	9	11	4	1	9	10	976
% of identified	8.9	1.5	3.0	5.8	3.8	35.4	4.6	0.5	24.3	1.0	2.3	2.8	1.1	0.3	2.3	2.5	–
Total weight (in g)	164.4	54.6	209.0	88.8	18.7	304.2	24.10	39.1	50.3	9.8	3.6	4.3	1.5	0.5	2.2	2.9	822.7

Table 2: Pangali. The distribution of fused and non-fused bones for domesticated pig.

Bone	Fused	Non-fused	Time of fusion
Scapula, distal	–	2	12 months
Humerus, distal	–	2*	12–18 months
Radius, proximal	–	1*	12 months
Ulna, proximal	–	1	36–42 months
Metapodium. proximal	2	–	Before birth
Metapodium, distal	–	2	24–27 months
Proximal phalanges	–	2	24 months
Medial phalanges	–	2	12 months

Information regarding the time of fusion was obtained from Reitz *et al.* 1999, 76.
*: 2 humerus and 1 radius were categorised in the foetal-pullus age.

Table 3: Pangali. Measurements for the pig bones (in mm).

Bone	n	Measurements		$\overline{X}$
Ulna				
DPA	1	30.61★		30.61
BPC	1	18.08★		18.08
Femur				
Bd	1	43.30		43.30
Proximal Phalanges				
Bd	1	12.46★		12.46
Medial Phalanges				
Bd	2	10.18★	10.80★	10.49

★: One end of the bone is non-fused.

Table 4: Pangali. The distribution of fused and non-fused bones for cattle.

Bone	Fused	Non-fused	Time of Fusion
Vertebrae	1	–	84-108 months
Femur, proximal	–	1	42 months
Tibia, distal	1	–	24-30 months
Metapodium, distal	–	1	24-36 months
Medial phalanges	–	1	18-24 months

Information regarding the time of fusion was obtained from Reitz *et al.* 1999:76

Table 5: Pangali. The distribution of fused and non-fused bones for sheep/goat.

Bone	Fused	Non-fused	Time of fusion
Vertebrae	–	2	48-60 months
Scapula, distal	2	–	4-10 months
Humerus, proximal	–	2★	23-84 months
Humerus, distal	1	4★	6-13 months
Radius, proximal	1	3★	4-10 months
Radius, distal	–	6★	33-84 months
Ulna, proximal	–	2★	24-84 months
Femur, proximal	–	1	24-84 months
Femur, distal	–	1	23-60 months
Tibia, distal	1	3★	15-24 months
Calcaneus	1	3★	23-60 months
Metapodium, proximal	6	–	Before birth
Metapodium, distal	3	19★	18-36 months
Proximal phalanges	6	11★	6-16 months
Medial phalanges	3	2	9-16 months

Information regarding the time of fusion was obtained from Reitz *et al.* 1999, 76
★: 2 humerus, 3 radius, 3 tibia, 1 ulna, 2 calcaneus, 6 metapodiums and 1 proximal phalange, were categorised in the foetal-pullus age.

Table 6: Pangali. Measurements for the sheep bones (in mm)

Bones	N	Measurements				$\overline{X}$
Metacarpal						
Bp	1	19.45				19.45
Proximal Phalanges						
GLpe	2	28.34	31.48			29.91
Bp	2	10.09	10.91	10.50		
Bd	4	8.24	9.67★	9.82★	9.95★	9.42
Medial Phalanges						
Gl	2	16.80	17.90			17.35
Bp	2	9.85	11.01			10.43
Bd	3	7.07★	8.17	8.67		7.97

★: One end of the bone is non-fused.

Table 7: Pangali. Measurements for the goat bones (in mm)

Bone	n	Measurements			$\overline{X}$
Astragalus					
GLl	1	25.77			25.77
GLm	1	23.84			23.84
Dl	1	13.65			13.65
Metacarpal					
Bp	2	18.95★	19.06★		19.01
Dp	2	12.50★	12.51★		12.51
Metatarsal					
Bd	1	22.66			22.66
Dd	1	14.95			14.95
Proximal Phalanges					
GLpe	1	40.54			40.54
Bp	1	15.41			15.41
Bd	3	10.63	11.28★	15.41	12.44
Medial Phalanges					
GL	1	21.27			21.27
Bp	1	9.80			9.80
Bd	1	7.87			7.87
Distal Phalanges					
DLS	1	33.35			33.35
Ld	1	26.18			26.18
MBS	1	5.21			5.21

Table 8: Pangali. Measurements for the wild pig bones (in mm)

Bone	n	Measurements		$\overline{X}$
Metacarpal IV				
Bp	2	21.42	23.03	22.23
Proximal Phalanges				
GLpe	1	43.27		43.27
Bp	1	26.12		26.12
Bd	1	20.38		20.38
Medial Phalanges				
GL	1	28.63		28.63
Bp	1	21.44		21.44
Bd	1	19.30		19.30

Table 9: Pangali. The distribution of fused and non-fused bones for roe deer.

Bone	Fused	Non-fused	Time of fusion
Humerus, distal	1	–	5-6 months
Radius, distal	2	–	?-2 months
Metapodium, distal	–	1	18-22 months

Information regarding the time of fusion was obtained from Noe-Nygaard , 1987

Table 10: Pangali. Measurements for the roe deer bones (in mm)

Bone	n	Measurements
Humerus		
Bd	1	22.20

Table 11: Pangali. Measurements for the red fox bones (in mm)

Bone	n	Measurements
Cranium		
8	1	58.27
9	1	53.15
10	1	26.41
11	1	32.10
12	1	27.05
13L	1	15.33
13W	1	5.71
14	1	13.71
19	1	14.35
20	1	11.30

Table 12: Pangali. Measurements for the wild cat bones (in mm)

Bone	n	Measurements
Patella		
GL	1	14.99
GB	1	9.01
Proximal Phalanges		
GL	1	19.91
Bp	1	6.11
Bd	1	4.86

Table 13: Pangali. Measurements for the hare bones (in mm)

Bone	n	Measurements		$\overline{X}$
Astragalus				
GL	1	15.20		15.20
Proximal Phalanges				
GL	2	19.94	22.76	21.35
Bp	2	6.05	6.15	6.10
Bd	2	4.72	4.89	4.81

Appendix 1

Shellfish in the stratigraphical context of Final Neolithic and Bronze Age supplemented by ^{14}C dating.

Kaj Strand Petersen[510]

Introduction

The frequency table 1 presented in Petersen 2004 was constructed on the basis of molluscs sampled at Aghia Triada from the outset of the project in 1995 until 2000 covering the strata from the Bronze Age through the Archaic up to the Classical/Hellenistic. Now the Final Neolithic material of molluscs from Pangali west of the fishing town Kato Vassiliki together with the samples from 2001, are included.

In the present paper the Final Neolithic shellfish will be considered together with the Bronze Age material divided into the archaeological five substages: EHI/1; EHI/2; MHIII; LHI and LHIII.

Considering the frequency, this is counted on the basis of occurrence or not in each bag (in TPR, 537 bags with shellfish were recorded). Together with this the total number of specimens are given for each substage marked by A – F on Table 1 and 2, $^{\text{N of frequency}}$(N of specimens). In this way it is possible to follow the trend of evolution in the occurrence of species in question. The order of bags listed in the catalogue Figs. 94a-c within each substage is also in stratigraphical order (the youngest material has the oldest collection date).

The survey

In the material of molluscan species from Chalkis within the Bronze Age nine species have been recorded out of the 22 species (*Patella* spp and Trochidae counted as two "Shellfish spp" in the frequency table 1 in TPR covering the time interval from the Bronze Age to Classical/Hellenistic. The nine species are: *Cerastoderma glaucum*, *Cerithium vulgatum*, *Hexaples trunculus*, *Pinna nobilis*, *Patella spp*, *Spondylus gaederopus*, *Tapes decussatus*, *Ostrea edulis* and *Glycymeris glycymeris*.

From the Neolithic six species have been recorded (see catalogue of shells below Fig 94a) with the total dominance of *Patella* spp. These species are only no. 5 in frequency, where *Cerastoderma glaucum* is an easy first. This species is not occurring in the Neolithic material of 6 bags. The same is nearly true for EHI-early with *Patella* spp on ^{5}(30) and *Cerastoderma* on ^{1}(1).In the EHI late the two shellfish representing the epi- and the infauna are near to equal ^{8}(14) to ^{7}(19) respectively. Regarding the sum of A+B+C (Fig. 94) it appears that *Patella* spp with ^{16}(96) are dominating the *Cerastoderma* with only ^{8}(20). Compared to the very low occurrence during the Late Neolithic and EHI-early it must be that the change took place during the EHI-late.

The implication of these figures is that the epifauna forms on rocky coast were gathered more than the shallow infauna species from sandy shores which are found with low frequency and in low numbers during the Late Neolithic and EHI-early. Considering the Final Neolithic samples from Pangali, which are shown on Fig. 94a, only one infauna element has been recorded (*Pinna nobilis*), while *Patella* spp has been found in 52 specimens

[510] ksp@geus.dk

Fig. 88. The tiny *Columbella rustica* which might have been used as charms in the Late Neolithic (Bag no. 10/07/96).

Fig. 89. *Hexaples trunculus*, one of the finds from Late Neolithic with special hole on the last whorl possibly chipped off for extraction of the colour yielding hypobranchial glan (Bag no. 19/07/96).

and in three of the bags taken from Pangali with shells [3](52).

When comparing the Final Neolithic material with the oldest of the Bronze Age EHI-early it appears that we have nearly the same occurrence of species except for the find of a single shell of *Cerastoderma glaucum* within an equal number of bags taken.

However, from the Final Neolithic, we do have records of some other species not meet with in the younger material: *Columbella rustica, Jubinus striatus* and some *Alvania* like species, all of them far from the size of being edible; but might have been used as charms – especially *Columbella rustica* (Fig. 88).

In TPR, *Hexaples truncatulus* is mentioned as

having an inferior meat compared to that of the purple dye *Murex* and also produce a purple dye of lesser quality. In two of the specimens found from the Final Neolithic at Pangali, *Hexaples trunculus* is found with special hole on the last whorl like a shipped off for extraction of the colour yielding hypobranchial glan (Fig. 89) as shown also in Delamotte & Vardala-Theodorou (2001, p. 31).

In this way one might venture upon the idea that purple dye production started already in the Final Neolithic. The founder of Stoicism, the "Phöniker Zenon, hatte", according to Capelle (1933), "bevor er selbst eine "Schule" eröffnete mehr als zwanzig Jahre in Athen, wohin er eines Tages als seefahrender Kaufmann, der phönikischen Purpur einführen wollte". This happended in the last part of the 4. centery BC. Phoenicia can only be traced back to around 1000 BC. – so our finds of holes made for extraction of the glan in *Hexaples* from Pangali are well beyond the time of the Phoenicians.

Hexaples is rather common in MHIII, [12](18) Fig. 94b, and will be studied in the younger material as found in other places in the Mediterranean basin (Reese 1987, 201-6) in order to see if those holes for extracting the glan are present in the younger material. *Tapes decussatus* is recorded from the MHIII Fig. 94b with [5](7). This is another representative of the infauna form but burrowing deeper (TPR table 1). Further comments upon this will be given considering the whole material from the ancient Chalkis in a later publication.

From the catalogue of shells it appears that the younger deposits MHIII have the dominating frequency of *Cerastoderma glaucum* with [19](66) and *Patella* spp only [2](3). The only potential influence by epifauna elements is seen in the occurrence of *Hexaples*. The total dominating rôle of the infauna forms is to appear in the "deposits" from LHI and LHIII where we have *Cerastoderma* in [3](15) and [7](36) respectively and only few *Hexaples*.

Theis information points to a new situation with both sandy and rocky shores in this area, which means that a natural change has taken place in the older Bronze Age EHI/2 and is characterized by development of sandy shores making the habitat for the infauna molluscan species. But still we have the epifauna forms in the samples from the ancient Chalkis showing that people still searched for the species living attached to the rocks like Oysters as Patroclus figured it in his song in the Iliad XVI, 854-63 "...Diving for Oysters..." quoted in total in Petersen (2004) (TPR).

The shore-line changes in Late Holocene

The geological background for changes in the shore region might be seen in the rising sea-level in the latest part of the Holocene as argued by Pirazzoli (1976); Petersen (2000) and Petersen & Hoch (2005). Pirazzoli (1976) in his survey from Western Mediterranean bases his argument of rising sea-level on the finds of roman piscina now laying under water, which lead to the conclusion that eustatic rise has been around 0.5 m since Roman Times.

Petersen (2000) bases the idea of sea-level rise on the progration of the little delta at Kato Vasiliki and studies of bioerosion, as figured in Petersen (2000 (SPR), fig. 54. Further more the relative sea-level curve from West Greenland, presented from the

6 cm

Fig. 90. The large *Patella caerulea* recorded from the Late Neolithic Pangali material. (bag no. 17/07/96).

area around Sisimiut (Petersen & Hoch 2005), shows a steady rise during the last 2000 – 3000 years.

The record of *Patella* spp from the Neolithic

As shellfish the *Patella* spp have been counted as one, however, the many finds from the Neolithic deserve to be given further comments. Three *Patella* spp have been found: *Patella caerulea*, *Patella ulyssiponensis* and *Patella lusitanica*. The three species have a size range from 20 – 55 mm, with *P. lusitanica* as the smallest laying between 20 – 45 mm and *P. caerulea* as the largest. This is also true for the specimens found at Pangali, where *P. caerulea* even is recorded with a length of 60 mm (Fig. 90). Also today all three species are found in the Mediterranean and further out in the Atlantic, however, *P. lusitanica*, as the species name says also off Portugal (Lusitania, an ancient region and Roman province in the Iberian Peninsula, corresponding largely to modern Portugal).

Considering the limpets as shellfish in the present days cuisine they are normally eaten raw, however, some Greeks make a soup with them – but the results are not such as to warrant the marketing of limpets (Davidson 2002). From the North Atlantic

Fig. 91. Limpets used as pendant at the National Archaeological Museum in Athens.

they have been recorded from the middens (Køkkenmøddinger) i.e. the Stone Age settlement at Skara Brae in Orkney (Davidson 2003), where also more modern tones are heard about the limpet:

And should the strongest arm endeavour
The limpet from its rock to sever
`Tis seen its loved support to clasp,
With such tenacity of grasp,
We wonder that such strength should dwell
In such a small and simple shell.

But the limpet has also been used for pendant (Fig. 91). Then the topmost part of this "chapeau chinois" has been lost – not by the agency of man but in nature by the waves along shore (Fig. 92).

The geological implication of the ^{14}C dates

In Petersen 2000 (SPR) it was shown that marine deposits were not located on the eastern side of the hill of Aghia Triada, but only on the western side. Here marine strata were found in three places proving the existence of a small bay, see Fig. 93, F.B. These marine sediments were characterised by molluscs such as *Conus, Bittium* and *Gibbula* which facilitated AMS-datings of the sediments. According to the datings so far obtained by this method, the small bay existed in 3270-3040 BC (AAR-4348) and in 1820-1650 BC (AAR-4347).

The samples of molluscs from the oldest layers of Tx72, near the area now known to have been a

Fig. 92. Cormorant chick "hiding" among the Patella shells in the shore region on the island of Colonsay in the Hebrides. Here many of the Limpets (*Patella vulgata*) are seen with hole in the topmost part.

small bay, have also been dated by the AMS method. All of these datings point to the Bronze Age: 1830-1760 BC (AAR-4586), 1800-1620 BC (AAR-4588) and 1580-1440 BC (AAR-4587). In other words they derive from a period in which the area west of the trench formed a small bay. The two datings from Pangali of *Patella* sp (AAR-9670) and charcoal (AAR-9671) confirm the expected Final Neolithic age and show that the calculated ozean reservoir age (approx. 400 years) is good also for this part of the Mediterranean Sea (see Heinemeier appendix 3).

Conclusion

From the catalogue of shells it is seen that of the 22 species listed after frequency nine have been found in the time interval from Late Neolithic to LHIII.

Fig. 93. Air photo over the Chalkis area with Aghia Triada (HT) east of the small fishing town of Kato Vassiliki (K.V.) with the former Bay (F.B.) in between. The area is situated between the mountains Varassova (V) and Klokova (KL). R.C. stands for rocky coast and S.B. sandy beach.

Here four belong to the infauna, which became the dominant group in the younger part, MHIII to LHIII (D+E+F), with *Cerastoderma glaucum* on a frequency and N of specimens on[29](117) compared to *Patella* spp within the same period on [2](3) as seen in the catalogue.

The younger finds – up to Hellenistic time – not treated in this book – have another 13 species to occur, most of them with a lesser frequency, but still with nine epifauna forms. So we still have the epifauna elements present from the places around the ancient Chalkis.

The main result of the present study on molluscs – shellfish – is the demonstration of an environmental change with rising sea-level occurring during the EHI – late, which is the background for the recorded drawback for the epifaunal elements represented first and foremost by the three *Patella* spp. Furthermore it appears that *Hexaples* has been handled for the particular purpose to extract the colour yielding hypobranchial glan. This points to an earlier use of the purple dye – long before the Phoenicians.

Table 1. Molluscan species Listed after Frequency — Bags in time

Bags in time	Cerastoderma glaucum	Cerithium vulgatum	Hexaples trunculus	Pinna nobilis	Patella spp.	Spondylus gaederopus	Tonna galea	Tapes decussatus	Ocenebra erinaceus	Mactra glauca	Venus verricosa	Ostrea edulis	Trochidae	Glycymeris glycymeris	Pecten jacobaeus	Bolinus brandaris	Conus ventricosus	Callista chione	Aporrhais pespelicani	Arca noae	Dosinia lupinus	Luria lurida	Others
A) Late Neolithic Ib:																							
Pangali 10.07.97		1																					X1
Pangali 15.07.96						2																	X1
Pangali 15.07.96			1																				X1
Pangali 17.07.96		1	1		5																		
Pangali 18.07.96			1	1	28									1									
Pangali 19.07.96			1	1	19	1																	
B) EH I/1 (EH I-early)	2(2)	4(4)	2(2)	3(52)	2(3)									1(1)									
Tx43/4b/1263/98	1																						
Tx43/4b/1604/98					1																		
Tx43/4b/1612/98			1		22																		X2
Tx43/4b/1703/98		2			4																		
Tx43/4b/1780/98				1	2																		X1
Tx43/5/1616/98					1																		
C) EH I/2 (EH I-late)	1(1)	1(2)	1(1)	1(1)	5(30)																		
Tx43/3/1259/98	10	2																					
Tx43/3a/1260/98		1			1																		
Tx43/3c/1273/98					1																		
Tx43/3c/1275/98			1																				
Tx43/3d/1431/98		1			2																		
Tx43/3d/1774/98	1																						
Tx43/4/1436/98					2																		
Tx43/4/1437/98																							X3
Tx43/4/1773/98		1			5																		
Tx20/3/-					1																		
Tx20/3/216/-	1																						
Tx20/3d/389/-					1																		
Tx20/4a/387/-					1																		
N27/AFU/3354/99	2	1																					
N27/AFU/3274/99	2																						
N27/AFU/3291/99	2	3																					
N27/AFU/3282/99	1			1																			
	7(19)	6(9)	1(1)	1(1)	8(14)																		
A) + B) + C)	8(20)	9(13)	6(6)	4(4)	16(96)	2(3)								1(1)									

Table 1.
X1 = *Helix pomatia*
X2 = *Gibbula sp.*
X3 = *Monodonta turbinata*

Fig. 94a. Catalogue of shellfish from Pangali and Aghia Triada.

Table 2.

Bags in time	Cerastoderma glaucum	Cerithium vulgatum	Hexaplex trunculus	Pinna nobilis	Patella spp.	Spondylus gaederopus	Tonna galea	Tapes decussatus	Ocenebra erinaceus	Mactra glauca	Venus verricosa	Ostrea edulis	Trochidae	Glycymeris glycymeris	Pecten jacobaeus	Bolinus brandaris	Conus ventricosus	Callista chione	Aporrhais pespelicani	Arca noae	Dosinia lupinus	Luria lurida	Others
D) MHIII																							
Tx72/10/1684/98	2																						
Tx72/11/1699/98	1		1																				
Tx72/11/1843/98						1																	X1
Tx70/5a/1828/98	3																						
Tx70/5a/1830/98	1																						
Tx70/5a/1837/98	2					1																	
Tx70/6/1833/98		1																					
Tx70/6/1835/98	1																						
Tx70/6/1838			1																				
Tx72/11/1845/98	1	1										1											
Tx72/12/1847/98			2	2	1																		
Tx72/13/1850/98	2		2	2				1															
Tx72/13/1851/98			1																				
Tx72/13/1854/98		1	3																				X4
K29/7b/4953/01	1	1						1															
K29/7b/4944/01	9		1																				
K29/7b/4939/01	3		1																				
K29/7e/4940/01	2	1																					
K29/7e/4943/01	7		1																				
K29/7e/4938/01	2		1																				
K29/8e/4962/01	2							1															
K29/8e/4945/01	11							2															
K29/8e/4961/01	1	1										1											
K29/9b/4978/01	13		3	2				2															
K29/10b/4983/01	2	2	1																				
(D subtotal)	19(66)	7(8)	12(18)	2(4)	2(3)	2(2)		5(7)				2(2)											
E) LH I																							
Tx70/5/1798/98	4					1																	
Tx70/5/1799/98	1																						
Tx70/5/1822/98	10																						
(E subtotal)	3(15)					1(1)																	
F) LHIII																							
K27/6b/4811/01	2																						
K27/6b/4819/01	1	1																					
K28/9a/4832/01	10		1								1												
K28/AHF/4863/01	2																						
K28/9 2p/4824/01	9	4	2																				
K29/7b/4858/01	1																						
K29/7d/4928/01	11	1	1																				
(F subtotal)	7(36)	3(6)	3(4)									1(4)											
D) + E) + F)	29(117)	10(14)	15(22)	2(4)	2(3)	4(4)		5(7)				2(2)											
A) + B) + C) + D) + E) + F)	37(137)	19(27)	21(28)	6(8)	18(99)	6(7)		5(7)		1(1)	3(6)		1(1)										

X1 = Helix pomatia
X4 = Lyonsia sp.

Fig. 94b. Catalogue of shellfish from Pangali and Aghia Triada.

Appendix 2

The animal bones from Aghia Triada

By Pernille Bangsgaard

The faunal remains analysed are the complete collection of animal bones found at Aghia Triada during the Danish-Greek excavation campaign from 1995 to 2001. The material was analysed in Greece at the Wiener laboratory, The American School of Classical Studies in Athens, using the comparative collection and other facilities available here.[511] The work was sponsored by the Consul General Gösta Enboms foundation and the Danish Institute at Athens.

The collection includes 3694 fragments (28155 grams) of which 1718 fragments (21648 grams) have been identified to family or species, leaving 1976 fragments (6507 grams) unidentified (Table 1). The faunal material is generally well preserved, although it does display some post-depositional damage including surface damage due to root etching, which could effect the detection of cut-marks and other human induced modifications. However, more significantly is the probable bias due to the lack of sieving. The material contains very few fish bones, which seems rather atypical for a site located near the sea. Furthermore and perhaps more telling is the systematic lack of small compact bones, such as the carpal and tarsal bones and phalanges, found among most of the identified mammals. This includes all the medium sized mammals such as sheep and goat and also pig. With the study of Payne in mind, it should thus be assumed that some distortion of the result has occurred and thus the percentage of large mammals such as cattle is inflated and that the smaller birds, mammals and especially fish are underrepresented.[512]

Domesticated mammals

The domesticated animals are by far the largest group of bones in the collection, perhaps not a surprising fact for a historical site like Aghia Triada.

	Number	Weight
Pig, *Sus domesticus*	276	2668.1
Cattle, *Bos taurus*	379	10942.0
Horse/donkey, *Equus* sp.	37	1106.5
Large ruminate, *Bos/Equus* sp.	54	358.3
Goat, *Capra hircus*	99	1042.0
Sheep, *Ovis aries*	68	680.1
Goat/sheep, *Capra/Ovis* sp.	435	2923.8
Dog, *Canis familiaris*	46	369.3

Pig, *Sus domesticus*

276 fragments were identified as coming from *Sus* sp. From this group, 39 of the fragments could be measured (Table 2) and these measurements are comparable to the range of measurements from domesticated pig from other Greek sites, such as Kastanas and Platia Magoula Zarkou.[513] All measurements taken for the Aghia Triada material were taken according to measurements described by von den Dreisch (1979).

The majority of the fragments can be securely identified as domesticated pig and not wild pig, due to size and morphology. It was therefore decided to treat the majority of the *Sus* sp. fragments as a single group of domesticated pig. However, it cannot be completely excluded that

---

[511] I would like to thank Dr. Sherry Fox and everybody at the Wiener laboratory, for the gracious help and warm co-operation I received during my stay there.
[512] Payne 1972, 1975.
[513] Becker 1986 and 1991.

the material does not contain a few fragments of juvenile wild pig bones, as wild pig is present in the area and have also been found in small numbers at the site (see below).

Death distribution for the Pangali faunal material is preferably based on information obtained from mandibles. However, due to the small amount of material generating a low number of mandibles, information from fused/non-fused bones had to be used as well in order to obtain as much information as possible for each species. The age distribution for pig is slightly different from the other domesticated mammals. For most of the species a specific period of butchering could be identified; however, the domesticated pig mandibles indicate a more widespread period of butchering within the first two years. This tendency can be seen by the relative evenly distributed age categories (Table 3). Above the age of 2 years the only available information is obtained from non-fused/fused bones (Table 4). The evidence suggest that only a small number of the pigs lived longer than three years and these were most likely kept for breeding purposes. For the period before the age of three, the evidence obtained from fused/non-fused bones also suggests a broad period of butchering, where the pigs appear to have been killed continually, perhaps as fresh meat was needed. However, there is a tendency for a more intense period of butchering around the age of 1 year.

Included in the time of death distribution is a small group of ten fragments, which were identified as belonging to the age category of foetal-pullus. All were compared to a stillborn individual in the collection and all were slightly larger. This leaves two possible interpretations; either the small piglets died of natural causes around or shortly after the time of birth and were consequently thrown out or the piglets were butchered shortly after birth for human consumption. However, as no butchering marks or other evidence for cause of death have been found, no conclusion should be made at present.

21 fragments had modifications that could be identified as being human made. These modifications mainly consisted of cut-marks of varying types relating to the process of butchering. Most of the marks are related to the initial dismembering of the carcass such as the separation of leg and body, the division of the front leg or hind leg into two sections. All marks are generally shallow cuts, single or multiple. They are located on the diaphysis or on the epiphysis at a transverse angle to the axis of the long bone and often with a fracture located nearby. Additionally two marks are related to the filleting of the front leg.[514]

Cattle, *Bos taurus*

As mentioned earlier the importance of cattle is probably slightly inflated due to the lack of sieving. However, the faunal remains identified as cattle represent a significant part of the complete collection (22 % of the identified material). This tendency is even more pronounced when the weight of the fragments are considered (approximately 50% of the identified material). So although the weight of the bone fragments is not directly linked to the meat yield per animal, it does give a better indication of the probable importance of each species as a meat supplier, thereby indicating the significance of cattle at Aghia Triada.

Only three of the mandibles identified as being from cattle could be used for time of death estimation. Two mandibles indicated a time of death above three years and one mandible indicated a time of death of two to three years.[515] This is an extremely limited amount of information for estimating age distribution. However, the amount of data is considerable higher when information from fused/non-fused bones is included in the analysis (Table 5). The result indicates that a small percentage of the cattle were butchered at a slightly younger age than two years. However, the majority was butchered at a more mature age. This could indicate that cattle were also used as a draught animals and were therefore killed at a substantially older age than most of the other domesticated animals. This is supported by the find of 2 proximal phalanges that display clear signs of exos-

---

[514] Based on Binford 1981 and Bangsgaard 2001.
[515] Estimates are based on Hillson 1986.

toses around the joints, a phenomenon that could have been caused by physical stress and old age, although it cannot be excluded that other factors such as an infection could also have affected this process.[516] The production of milk may also have served as a reason for butchering the cattle at a later date. However, the lack of any bones from young calves appears to contradict this explanation.

Some fragments were found to have modifications that could be identified as human made. The majority of these were regular cut-marks related to the butchering process. These marks are generally of the same morphological types as are found for pig. However, they display a greater variation in position and orientation, and therefore also a greater variation in function. The majority of the marks are still related to the process of dismembering, whereby the body is separated into various sections such as head, neck, lower and upper body, and also front leg and hind leg. The legs have additionally been separated into at least two sections. Furthermore a few marks located on the phalanges appear to be related to the process of skinning and finally a few marks relating to filleting were identified.

A number of fragments were so complete that it was possible to measure them (Table 6). These measurements were subsequently compared to measurements from sites such as Kastanas and Platia Magoula Zarkou.[517] The measurements from Aghia Triada are compatible with the others, with a slight tendency for a position in the lower range. However, it should be mentioned that a single proximal phalanx is significantly larger in all measurements. It is therefore possible that this bone could originate from an aurochs, *Bos primigenius*. However, the surface and general appearance of the bone does clearly indicate that it originates from an older and most likely senile individual and therefore it is also plausible that the bone is from a very large domesticated male.

Horse/donkey, *Equus sp.*

A total of 37 fragments were identified to *Equus* sp. and the initial analysis suggested an identification of either horse or donkey. Due to the difficul-

ties in distinguishing these two, the metapodiums from Aghia Triada were measured and compared to measurements from donkey and horse of the period.[518] The result could indicate that both species were found here. However, with such a limited number of measurements, the result must be considered inconclusive.

Although a few loose teeth were found the data does not give further information concerning age, therefore only information from fused and non-fused bones will be considered here (Table 7). The distribution clearly suggests that the horses or donkeys were not butchered until they were at least fully-grown and probably even older. This is perhaps not a surprising fact as horse or donkey often served primarily as a beast of burden and therefore was butchered at a later age when they no longer served their primary function.

Among the fragments identified as equid were five fragments that had human induced modifications (2 radius. 1 ulna. 1 tibia and 1 metacarpal). The cut-marks on the metacarpal are consistent with skinning. However, all other cut-marks are consistent with marks left during dismembering and filleting. This does suggest that although these animals may have served the function of beast of burden, they were eventually eaten.

Goat and sheep, *Capra/Ovis sp.*

The commonest of the domesticated animals are the group of sheep and goat, with 602 fragments (5005.9 gram). 30% of this material could be identified as either sheep or goat according to the criteria described mainly by Boessneck, but other authors were also used.[519] Within the identified group goat predominates 3:2.

A number of mandibles from sheep and goat revealed information regarding time of death. These mandibles were combined in a single table as the initial study revealed no significant difference in

---

[516] Baker 1980.
[517] Becker 1986, 1991.
[518] Becker 1986.
[519] Boessneck *et al.* 1964, Prummel *et al.* 1986, Payne 1985 & Halstead *et al.* 2002.

the distribution between the two species. The result indicates that the majority was butchered either in their 2nd year or survived above the age of 4 years (Table 10). The later is probably a product of increased butchering due to old age, failing birth rates or low productivity of milk. The high mortality frequency at the age of 2-3 years indicates that the animals were kept primarily for meat production, as animals at that age had reached the point of optimal weight gain in relation to food intake.[520] The age distribution from the mandibles is supported by the data retrieved from the fused/non-fused bones (Tables 9, 11 and 12). Although the evidence is less clear, it does also suggest a main butchering period around the age of 2-3 years, with some animals living beyond the age of 4 years.

Six fragments of bones identified as being from sheep or goat has been categorised as belong to the pullus-foetal age category (Table 9). The majority of the fragments appears to be in the category of foetal as they are smaller or of similar size as the stillborn found in the collection at the Wiener Laboratory. This would suggest that the bones are most likely from stillborn individuals and not from individuals intentionally butchered at a very young age.

When possible fragments were measured although only those that had been identified as either sheep or goat (Tables 13 and 14). These measurements were compared to similar measurements from the sites of Kastanas and Platia Magoula Zarkou[521] and they are for the most part similar in range and average. The difference is greatest when only a few measurements are available, whereas the distributions are similar when a large number of measurements is available. Furthermore the observed differences are not evenly distributed, as part of the Aghia Triada measurements are in the lower range of the distributions from the other sites, whereas others are in the upper range. Therefore it must be assumed that the observed differences between Pangali and other sites are most likely the combined product of sample size and the pronounced male-female difference found in sheep and goat.[522]

Among the fragments identified as sheep or goat

were also a number of fragments that had been modified by human hand. The type and position of these butchering marks are similar to the others observed for pig and cattle and represents mainly the dismembering process but also marks related to skinning were found. Additionally 3 marks found on vertebrae are related to the carving of the tenderloin.

A number of modifications cannot be related to the process of butchering, but they must nevertheless still be considered as modified by human hand. This group include six complete astragali identified as being from sheep, goat or sheep/goat. The modification is characterised by wear located on a single or up to four sides of the bone. The wear consists of a smoothed surface that in some instances have completely removed the exterior wall of the bone, leaving the inner cancellous bone exposed. No lines or indentations of any kind are visible under the microscope or otherwise. This could suggest that they were thrown or rubbed against a relatively elastic surface that would not bruise the bone with small indentations such as skin or sand. Combined with their relatively small size, it seems unlikely that the astragali found use as a tool. However, the pattern of modification found here appears to be consistent with a function of gaming pieces. The use of astragali for various games is well known for Greece in antiquity and evidence for this comes from written sources, sculptures and faunal remains.[523]

Dog, Canis domesticus

46 fragments were identified as coming from domesticated dog. The fragments represent all parts of the body, although the small compact bones of the extremities are underrepresented. The distribution of fused and non-fused bones has been registered (Table 15) and it clearly suggests mainly fully grown dogs above the age of 2 years, with a

---

[520] Payne 1973.
[521] Becker 1986 and 1991.
[522] Zeder 1999.
[523] Rohlfs 1963.

single bone suggesting that an individual died before the age of 1 year.

A single fragment displays a clear cut-mark, of a type associated with dismembering and not skinning. The bone fragment is the distal half of a radius and the mark is a transverse chop located on the anterior surface of the bone immediately above the articulated surface. The chop has completely severed part of the distal articulated surface from the rest of the bone. Whether or not the dog was eaten or whether it was dismembered for some other purpose is impossible to determine from the find of a single cut-mark. However, is should be noted that similar cut-marks have been recorded at other Greek sites.[524] Whatever the purpose the dismembering of dogs served, it does not appear to be an isolated phenomenon found only at Aghia Triada.

Wild animals

	Number	Weight
Wild boar, *Sus scofa*	3	124.7
Red deer, *Cervus elephus*	19	263.1
Roe deer, *Capreolus capreolus*	3	57.30
Fox, *Vulpes vulpes*	5	20.8
Beech marten, *Martes foina*	2	5.9
Hare, *Lepus europaeus*	2	5.5
Vole, *Microtus* sp.	1	0.1
Turtle, *Testudo* sp.	55	147.7

Wild pig, *Sus scofa*

Three fragments were positively identified as being from wild pig. One is a fifth metacarpal and the two other fragments are a large fragment of occipitale, partly black burnt, and a pelvis fragment. Although only the metacarpal and pelvis fragment could be measured (Table 17), all were visibly larger than the rest of the Sus sp. fragments. The measurement of the fifth metacarpal could be compared to measurements from Kastanas[525] and are within the range recorded there. Furthermore comparison with a modern large wild pig from the collection at the Zoological Museum in Copenhagen indicates that these bones originate from a large wild individual.

Red deer and roe deer, *Cervus elephus* and *Capreolus capreolus*

The most common of the wild mammals is the deer, as 19 fragments were identified as being from red deer, *Cervus elephus* and additionally three fragments were identified as coming from roe deer, *Capreolus capreolus*. Their presence is perhaps not very surprising as both species are found in the area today. Furthermore both species have been found at several Neolithic and Bronze age sites, where red deer is one of the most common wild mammals. Included in the Aghia Triada material are two fragments of red deer antler, which display signs of having been worked. One bears clear signs of having been sawn in two, while the entire surface of the other fragment has been smoothed.

Red fox, *Vulpes vulpes*

The red fox, Vulpes vulpes is represented at Aghia Triada by five fragments. The red fox along with the marten are the only wild carnivores represented at the site suggesting that they played a minor role in the economy of the site, whether it was as a supplier of meat or more likely as a supplier of skin or fur.

Beech marten, *Martes foina*

Two fragments were identified as coming from marten. Due to the similarity in size and morphology it cannot be ruled out purely on morphological grounds that the bones are not from the pine marten, *Martes martes*. Today the pine marten is not found in Greece except in the far north of the mainland and none are reported from archaeological excavation.[526] It must therefore be considered as most likely that the bones are from a beech marten. However, it should be noted that the identification is purely on zoogeographical grounds.

---

[524] Snyder *et al.* 2003.
[525] Becker 1986.
[526] Yannouli 2003.

Vole, *Microtus sp.*

A single mandible from a small rodent was found at Aghia Triada. The fragment was identified as being from a vole, *Microtus* sp. However, no secure identification to species was possible due to a lack of comparative skeletons from some of the various voles found in Greece today.[527] The bone was found relatively close to the surface and it is therefore possible that the fragments originate from a vole of a more recent date.

Turtle, *Testudo sp.*

The majority of the 55 fragments identified as coming from some species of turtle are fragments from the carapace and only one fragment is from a non-fused humerus. This distribution combined with a lack of comparative material made further identification impossible. The main part of the fragments is from a single find (F99-5070), which is a concentration of 30 *Testudo* sp. fragments, indicating that they are from a single individual, although only some of the fragments could be connected. Furthermore, as with the vole mandible, the location of the turtle concentration close to the surface could suggest that they are from a turtle of a more recent date.

Birds, *Aves sp.*

	Number	Weight
Chicken, Gallus domesticus	8	10.5
Unknown bird. Aves sp.	14	14.2

Chicken, *Gallus domesticus*

8 fragments were positively identified as being from domesticated chicken. The fragments represent bones from both front and hind leg. Included among the fragments is also a scapula with exostoses around the articulated surface. All the fragments were found in the upper loci and no secure dating has been made for any of these. Therefore it cannot be excluded that the chicken bones are of a relatively recent date. However, it should be noted that finds from other sites suggest that chick-

en were found in parts of Greece as early as the Bronze Age.[528]

Fish, *Pisces sp.*

	Number	Weight
Porgies and sea bream, *Sparidae* sp.	1	1.6
Shark, *Notidanoidei* sp.	1	2.8
Unknown fish, *Pisces* sp.	1	2.6

Only three fragments were identified as coming from fish. However, as mentioned earlier it is very likely that a number of fragments were overlooked during the excavation, as *pisces* sp. fragments are often fragile and relatively small in size.

The three fragments found represent at least two species and all fragments are of a size that made discovery by hand possible. The unidentified fragment is a vertebra that has chewing marks probably from a dog. The majority of the original surface is partially or completely gone making identification impossible. The two other fragments include a dentary fragment from a porgy or sea bream of a significant age, as the fragment appears to come from an individual with a length of around 0.5 meter or more. Finally the last fragment is a vertebra identified as coming from a relatively large shark. Due to a lack of comparative material and the number of shark species found in the Mediterranean Sea no further identification could be made.[529]

Conclusion

The faunal analysis of the material from Aghia Triada is based on 3694 fragments (28155 grams), of which 1718 fragments (21648 grams) were identified and the material represented at least 15 species. The domesticated animals clearly dominate and sheep/goat is the most common of these, although also pig and cattle played an important role. Additionally dog, horse or donkey and chick-

---

[527] Mitchell-Jones *et al.* 1999.
[528] West *et al.* 1988.
[529] Whitehead *et al.* 1984.

en are also represented at the site. A number of wild species was also identified, although in small number; these include red deer, roe deer, wild pig, fox, hare, turtle and a few fish. The distribution of wild animals does not indicate any major climate difference, as all species are all found in the area today.

The distribution seen at Aghia Triada does in many respects resemble collections from other Greek sites of the period (Becker 1986 and 1991. Yannouli 2003). The main part of the minor differences that does exist, especially pertaining to the lack of fish and small mammal and bird species, is likely caused by the lack of sieving.

The material appears to be consistent with that generated from normal household consumption, where a variety of domesticated animals were kept primarily for their meat but where some additional products were utilised such as skin, possibly milk or wool. Cattle and horse or donkey were probably also utilised as beasts of burden. The wild mammals represent a supplement that were utilised when the opportunity arose, although they obviously only played a minor role in the economic structure of the site. Additionally fishing was probably also carried out on some scale. The evidence therefore indicates a community where a broad based farming production was the main supplier of meat and protein, but where the surrounding area was utilised for some additional products by hunting and fishing.

Table 1: The distribution of faunal remains found at Aghia Triada.

	Pig *Sus s. domesticus*	Wild pig *Sus scofa*	Cattle *Bos taurus*	Horse/donkey *Equus caballus/asinus*	Large ruminate *Bos/Equus sp.*	Goat *Capra hircus*	Sheep *Ovis aries*	Goat/sheep *Capra hircus/Ovis aries*	Red deer *Cervus elephus*	Roe deer *Capreolus capreolus*	Small ruminate *Ovis/Capra/Cervus sp.*	Dog *Canis familiaris*	Fox *Vulpes vulpes*	Beech marten *Martes foina*	Hare *Lepus europeaus*	Vole *Microtus sp.*	Turtle *Testudo sp.*	Bird *Aves sp.*	Fish *Pisces sp.*	Unidentified
Cranium	12	1	11	–	–	19	5	17	3	–	1	10	–	–	–	–	–	–	1	33
Mandible	33	–	21	4	–	8	4	33	–	1	10	9	1	1	–	1	–	–	–	9
Loose teeth	59	–	78	10	8	11	1	145	3	–	46	6	–	–	–	–	–	–	–	1
Vertebrae	9	–	17	2	3	4	–	19	–	–	7	2	–	–	–	–	–	–	2	28
Ribs	22	–	8	–	38	–	–	6	–	–	79	2	–	–	–	–	–	–	–	–
Scapula	15	–	17	–	1	3	–	12	3	–	21	1	–	–	–	–	–	1	–	1
Humerus	37	–	30	1	–	12	15	19	1	2	7	2	–	–	1	–	–	3	–	1
Radius	16	–	11	3	–	6	7	37	3	–	16	2	–	–	–	–	1	1	–	–
Ulna	11	–	12	2	–	3	1	10	–	–	1	1	–	–	–	–	–	4	–	–
Pelvis	12	1	24	2	–	2	3	11	1	–	–	2	–	–	–	–	–	–	–	1
Femur	6	–	10	1	–	1	–	13	–	–	7	3	2	1	–	–	–	2	–	2
Tibia	14	–	20	3	–	2	–	54	2	–	9	2	2	–	1	–	–	4	–	1
Fibula	1	–	–	–	–	–	–	–	–	–	–	–	–	–	–	–	–	–	–	–
Patella	–	–	–	–	–	–	–	–	–	–	–	–	–	–	–	–	–	–	–	–
Carpal/tarsal	5	–	29	–	–	12	15	14	1	–	2	–	–	–	–	–	–	–	–	–
Metacarpal/tarsal	22	1	58	7	1	8	10	40	2	–	4	4	–	–	–	–	–	5	–	–
Phalanges	4	–	33	2		8	7	5	1	–	–	–	–	–	–	–	–	–	–	–
Unidentified	–	–	–	–	–	–	–	–	–	–	–	–	–	–	–	–	54	2	–	1899
Total	275	3	379	37	54	99	68	435	19	3	210	46	5	2	2	1	55	22	3	1976
% of identified	16.0	0.2	22.1	2.2	3.1	5.8	4.0	25.3	1.1	0.2	12.2	2.7	0.3	0.1	0.1	0.1	3.2	1.3	0.2	
Total weight (in gr)	2668.1	124.7	10942.0	1106.5	358.3	1402.0	680.1	2923.8	263.1	57.30	541.0	369.3	20.8	5.9	5.5	0.1	147.7	24.7	7.0	6507.0

Table 2: Mandibles from domesticated pig, *Sus domesticus*

Stage	Number	Presumed age
Stage 1	2	4–8 months
Stage 2	4	7–13 months
Stage 3	2	12–16 months
Stage 4	3	16–22 months
Stage 5	5	Older than 22 months

(Information regarding the time of eruption was obtained from Hillson 1986)

Table 3 : The distribution of fused and non-fused bones for domesticated pig, *Sus domesticus*.

Bone	Fused	Non-fused	Time of fusion
Vertebrae	3	3	48–84 months
Scapula, distal	6	1	12 months
Humerus, proximal	1	2	42 months
Humerus, distal	5	16★	12–18 months
Radius, proximal	3	5★	12 months
Radius, distal	–	7★	42 months
Ulna, proximal	1	1	36–42 months
Ulna, distal	–	2	36–42 months
Femur, proximal	1	1	42 months
Femur, distal	1	2	42 months
Tibia, proximal	–	7★	42 months
Tibia, distal	1	4	24 months
Fibula, distal	–	1	30 months
Calcanceus	–	2	24–36 months
Metapodium, proximal	18	–	Before birth
Metapodium, distal	6	8★	24–27 months
Proximal Phalanges	2	1	24 months

★:1 metapodium, 1 pelvis, 2 humerus, 2 tibia and 4 radius in the age category of foetal-pullus. (Information regarding the time of fusion was obtained from, Reitz *et al.* 1999).

Table 4: The distribution of fused and non-fused bones for cattle, *Bos taurus*.

Bone	Fused	Non-fused	Time of fusion
Vertebrae	3	3	84–108 months
Scapula, distal	7	2	7–10 months
Humerus, proximal	–	1	42–48 months
Humerus, distal	12	3	12–18 months
Radius, proximal	4	–	12–18 months
Radius, distal	1	–	42–48 months
Ulna, proximal	2	4	42–48 months
Femur proximal	1	1	42 months
Femur, distal	1	–	42–48 months
Tibia, proximal	1	–	42–48 months
Tibia, distal	10	1	24–30 months
Calcaneus	3	5	36–42 months
Metapodium, proximal	23	–	Before birth
Metapodium, distal	10	4	24–36 months
Proximal Phalanges	16	–	18–24 months
Medial Phalanges	7	–	18–24 months

(Information regarding the time of fusion was obtained from Reitz *et al.* 1999, 76)

Table 5: The distribution of fused and non-fused bones for, *Equus* sp.

Bone	Fused	Non-fused	Time of Fusion
Vertebrae	–	1	
Humerus, proximal	–	1	36-42 months
Radius, proximal	1	–	15-18 months
Radius, distal	2	–	42 months
Ulna, proximal	1	–	42 months
Pelvis	1	–	52-60 months
Femur proximal	–	1	36-42 months
Metapodium, proximal	2	–	Before birth
Metapodium, distal	2	–	15-18 months
Proximal Phalanges	2	–	13-15 months

(Information regarding the time of fusion was obtained from Silver 1971)

Table 6: The distribution of fused and non-fused bones for sheep/goat, *Ovis/Capra* sp.

Bone	Fused	Non-fused	Time of Fusion
Vertebrae	4	7	48-60 months
Humerus, proximal	1	–	36-48 months
Humerus, distal	5	2	3-13 months
Radius, proximal	2	3★	4-9 months
Radius, distal	1	5★	36-60 months
Ulna, proximal		2	36-60 months
Femur proximal	3	5	30-42 months
Femur, distal	–	1	36-48 months
Tibia, proximal	2	1	(24 months)
Tibia, distal	18	6	15-24 months
Calcaneus	1	1	23-60 months
Metapodium, proximal	17	1★	Before birth
Metapodium, distal	5	2★	18-36 months
Proximal Phalanges	3	–	6-24 months

★:1 metapodium, 2 scapula and 3 radius in the age category of foetal-pullus. (Information regarding the time of fusion was obtained from Reitz *et al.* 1999, 76)

Table 7: Mandibles from sheep/goat, *Ovis/Capra* sp.

Stage	Number	Presumed age
Stage C	4	6-12 moths
Stage D	5	1-2 years
Stage E	10	2-3 years
Stage F	1	3-4 years
Stage F-G	5	3-6 years
Stage G	3	4-6 years
Stage G-H	12	4-8 years

(Information regarding the time of eruption and wear was obtained from Payne 1973)

Table 8: The distribution of fused and non-fused bones for goat, *Capra hircus*.

Bone	Fused	Non-fused	Time of Fusion
Vertebrae	1	1	
Humerus, distal	7	3	11–13 months
Radius, proximal	6	–	4–9 months
Ulna, proximal	2	1	24–84 months
Femur proximal	1	–	23–84 months
Tibia, proximal	2	–	23–60 months
Metapodium, proximal	6	–	Before birth
Metapodium, distal	3	1	23–36 months
P. Phalanges	5	2	11–15 months

(Information regarding the time of fusion was obtained from Reitz *et al.* 1999, 76)

Table 9: The distribution of fused and non-fused bones for sheep, *Ovis aries*.

Bone	Fused	Non-fused	Time of Fusion
Humerus, distal	9	3	3–10 months
Radius, proximal	5	–	3–10 months
Radius, distal	1	–	36–42 months
Ulna, proximal	1	–	36–42 months
Metapodium, proximal	7	–	Before birth
Metapodium, distal	2	2	18–28 months
Proximal Phalanges	6	–	6–16 months

(Information regarding the time of fusion was obtained from Reitz *et al.* 1999, 76)

Table 10: The distribution of fused and non-fused bones for dog, *Canis familiaris*.

Bone	Fused	Non-fused	Time of Fusion
Vertebrae	2	–	20–24 months
Scapula, distal	1	–	6–7 months
Humerus, distal	1	–	8–9 months
Radius, distal	2	–	11–12 months
Ulna, proximal	–	1	9–10 months
Femur proximal	1	–	18 months
Tibia, proximal	1	–	18 months
Metapodium, proximal	2	–	Before birth
Metapodium, distal	1	–	8–10 months

(Information regarding the time of fusion was obtained from Silver 1971, for the vertebrae from Schmid 1972)

Table 11: The distribution of faunal material found at Aghia Triada, from the EHI period

	Pig *Sus doemsticus*	Cattle *Bos taurus*	Goat *Capra hircus*	Goat/sheep *Capra hircus/ Ovis aries*	Shark *Notidanoidei* sp.	Unidentified
Cranium	2	–	–	1	–	–
Mandible	2	–	–	2	–	2
Loose teeth	5	7	–	12	–	–
Vertebrae	–	2	–	1	1	–
Ribs	–	–	–	3	–	–
Scapula	1	1	–	–	–	–
Humerus	2	2	1	1	–	–
Radius	3	–	1	3	–	–
Ulna	3	–	1	–	–	–
Pelvis	2	–	–	–	–	–
Femur	–	–	–	–	–	–
Tibia	–	–	–	2	–	–
Patella	–	–	–	–	–	–
Carpal/tarsal	–	–	–	–	–	–
Metacarpal/tarsal	3	–	1	1	–	–
Phalanges	–	–	1	1	–	–
Unidentified	–	–	–	–	–	75
Total	23	12	5	27	1	77
Total weight (in g)	237.7	376.1	34.7	77.5	2.8	240.8

Table 12: The distribution of faunal material found at Aghia Triada, from the MH and LH periods

	Domesticated pig *Sus domesticus*	Wild pig *Sus scofa*	Cattle *Bos taurus*	Goat *Capra hircus*	Sheep *Ovis aries*	Goat/sheep *Capra hircus/ Ovis aries*	Dog *Canis domesticus*	Unidentified
Cranium	–	–	–	–	–	3	–	1
Mandible	5	–	2	–	–	2	1	–
Loose teeth	1	–	7	–	–	5	2	–
Vertebrae	–	–	2	–	–	–	–	–
Ribs	–	–	1	–	–	4	–	–
Scapula	2	–	1	1	–	1	–	–
Humerus	2	–	–	1	–	–	–	–
Radius	1	–	–	1	–	6	–	–
Ulna	–	–	1	–	–	1	–	–
Pelvis	–	1	–	–	1	–	–	–
Femur	–	–	1	–	1	1	–	1
Tibia	1	–	–	–	–	1	–	–
Patella	–	–	–	–	–	–	–	–
Carpal/tarsal	–	–	–	–	–	–	–	–
Metacarpal/tarsal	1	–	3	–	1	1	–	–
Phalanges	–	–	2	–	–	–	–	–
Unidentified	–	–	–	–	–	–	–	87
Total	13	1	20	3	3	25	3	89
Total weight (in g)	171.5	41.2	711.8	26.7	45.6	144.8	14.0	266.8

Table 13: Measurements for the pig, *Sus s. domesticus* bones (in mm)

Bone	N	Measurements			$\overline{\text{X}}$
Mandible					
8	2	61.36	62.34		61.85
10L	3	28.27	29.83	31.23	29.78
10W	3	13.73	14.11	15.13	14.32
Scapula					
GLP	3	28.91	30.49	35.71	31.70
LG	3	24.39	25.13	31.89	27.14
BG	2	19.86	24.59		22.23
SLC	2	19.16	21.17		20.17
Humerus					
Bd	2	33.74	36.09		34.92
BT	3	27.70	29.29	29.82	28.94
Radius					
Bp	2	25.20	27.31		26.26
Ulna					
BPC	1	24.41			24.41
Pelvis					
LA	1	35.47			35.47
LAR	2	29.23	29.29		29.26
Femur					
Bd	1	40.14			40.14
Tibia					
Dd	1	23.84			23.84
Astragalus					
GLl	1	37.38			37.38
GLm	1	34.99			34.99
Calcaneus					
GB	1	18.88★			18.88
Metacarpal III					
Bp	3	10.78★	14.12	14.30★	13.07
Metacarpal IV					
GL	1	64.07			64.07
Bd	1	15.24			15.24
Metatarsal II					
GL	1	70.42			70.42
Metatarsal III					
GL	1	63.63			63.63
Bp	3	14.33	14.74	15.40	14.82
B	1	10.98			10.98
Bd	2	13.65	14.92		14.29
Metatarsal IV					
Bp	2	13.11	13.52		13.32
Proximal Phalanges					
Bp	2	13.82	14.41★		14.12
Distal Phalanges					
DLS	1	14.42			14.42
Ld	1	13.47			13.47
MBS	1	7.90			7.90

Table 15: Measurements for the horse/donkey, *Equus* sp. bones (in mm)

Bone	N	M
Mandible		
9L	1	31.37
9W	1	14.34
10L	1	27.72
10W	1	14.87
11L	1	29.98
11W	1	15.07
Ulna		
SDO	1	33.48
Pelvis		
LA	1	45.55
LAR	1	39.57
Metacarpal		
Bp	1	36.20
Bd	1	44.28
Metatarsal		
Dp	1	26,46
Bd	1	31.67
Proximal Phalanges		
GL	1	80.88
Bp	1	51.88
Bd	1	45.34

★: One end of the bone is non-fused or fusing.

Table 14: Measurements for the cattle, *Bos taurus* bones (in mm)

Bone	N	Measurements					$\overline{X}$
Scapula							
BG	1	37.52					37.52
Radius							
Bd	1	72.08					72.08
BFd	1	54.96					54.96
Ulna							
BPC	1	37.78					37.78
Femur							
DC	1	38.06					38.06
Tibia							
Bd	5	50.60	50.66	58.19	59.10	60.62	55.63
Dd	4	38.40	42.82	43.87	47.17		42.39
Astragalus							
GLl	5	52.84	53.55	56.46	63.81	65.49	58.43
GLm	7	49.21	52.48	54.43	55.75	59.39	
				60.93	61.19		56.20
Dl	7	28.58	28.63	30.50	33.24		
			35.82	36.20	37.62		32.94
Dm	3	28.68	29.73	32.45			30.29
Bd	5	32.85	38.44	40.64	42.31	45.58	39.96
Metacarpal							
Bp	3	51.10	52.63	58.42			54.05
Dp	3	28.57	31.00	34.69			31.42
Bd	1	53.55					53.55
Dd	1	27.97					27.97
Metatarsal							
Bp	3	42.69	46.76	50.34			46.60
Dp	2	40.01	40.39				40.20
Bd	3	45.07	52.16	54.14			50.46
Dd	2	24.83	29.41				27.12
Proximal Phalanges							
Glpe	12	44.86	51.76	53.41	54.08		
		56.32	57.87	59.51	60.46		
		61.24	61.30	66.10	70.72		58.14
Bp	12	21.53	24.20	24.85	27.24		
		27.30	28.00	28.89	29.17		
		30.76	30.88	31.65	34.16		28.22
Bd	11	23.76	25.26	225.76	26.35		
		26.63	26.88	27.52	27.71		
		28.67	30.82	33.38			27.52
Medial Phalanges							
GL	3	38.15	49.04				43.94
Bp	2	33.57	34.83				34.20
Bd	1	24.66					24.66
Distal Phalange							
DLS	4	49.89	59.36	66.86	67.62		60.93
Ld	3	43.73	46.50	54.06			48.10
MBS	4	14.35	18.35	21.23	24.46		19.60

Table 16: Measurements for the goat, *Capra hircus* bones (in mm)

Bone	n	Measurements					X̄
Cornus							
41	2	20.83	28.62				24.73
42	4	14.80	19.49	21.46	27.49		20.81
Scapula							
BG	1	24.41					24.41
Humerus							
Bd	3	26.83	33.50	34.95			31.76
Radius							
BP	5	29.19	29.26	31.29	31.64	35.85	31.45
BFp	4	28.25	28.85	30.28	35.08		30.62
Ulna							
DPA	2	24.32	25.71★				25.02
SDO	1	21.34					21.34
BPC	1	22.61★					22.61
Pelvis							
LA	1	31.44					31.44
LAR	1	24.74					24.74
Femur							
Bp	1	42,90					42.90
Tibia							
Bp	2	37,27	38,41				37.84
Astragalus							
GLl	8	25.45	26.79	29.08	29.88		
		30.03	30.17	30.25	32.14		29.08
GLm	9	23.66	25.02	26.73	26.79	27.24	
		27.68	28.24	29.13	29.57		27.12
Dl	10	13.41	14.73	14.87	15.14	15.27	
		15.51	15.80	16.65	17.09	17.56	15.59
Bd	7	16.32	17.34	18.67	19.51		
		19.53	19.71	19.76			18.69
Calcaneus							
GL	1	61.36					61.36
GB	1	21.83					21.83
Metacarpal							
GL	1	108.50					108.50
Bp	4	23.22	26.35	27.06	28.79		26.36
Dp	4	16.52	16.56	18.86	19.53		17.87
Bd	4	25.34	25.70	27.05	27.67		26.44
Dd	2	15.82	16.90				16.36
Metatarsal							
Bp	2	19.19★	19.61				19.40
Dp	1	18.39					18.39
Proximal Phalanges							
Glpe	4	37.44	39.44	39.95	40.76		39.40
Bp	4	12.59	12.86	13.72	14.04		13.30
Bd	8	10.30	10.34★	11.40★	12.38		
		13.29	13.38	14.23	16.36		12.71

★: One end of the bone is non-fused or fusing.

Table 17: Measurements for the sheep, *Ovis aries* bones (in mm)

Bone	n	Measurements					$\overline{X}$
Humerus							
Bd	5	28.94	30.04	31.30	33.40	34.40	31.62
Radius							
BP	4	26.24	27.66	33.05	34.98		30.48
BFp	4	24.15	26.88	30.56	31.92		28.38
Bd	1	29.56					29.56
BFd	1	25.94					25.94
Astragalus							
GLl	12	27.66	28.01	28.25	28.54		
		28.77	30.18	30.52	30.67		
		30.82	31.39	31.99	32.58		29.95
GLm	11	26.52	26.60	26.67	27.00		
		27.18	27.35	27.97	28.20		
		28.65	28.81	29.67			27.69
Dl	10	14.58	15.02	15.37	15.48	15.52	
		15.71	15.76	17.16	17.25	17.48	16.04
Bd	8	17.73	17.76	18.08	18.41		
		19.38	19.49	19.97	20.55		18.92
Metacarpal							
Bp	4	23.84	23.88	24.50	25.26		24.37
Dp	4	17.30	17.37	17.38	18.41		17.62
Metatarsal							
Bp	4	18.46	20.83	20.97	21.12		20.35
Dp	3	18.73	19.85	20.69			19.76
Bd	2	23,49	23.58				23.54
Proximal Phalanges							
Glpe	4	33.11	34.51	36.45	41.52		36.40
Bp	4	11.77	11.88	13.17	13.98		12.70
Bd	5	10.24	10.47	11.42	12.26	14.13	11.70
Medial Phalanges							
,GL	1	25,.72					25.72
Bp	1	13.39					13.39
Bd	1	10.08					10.08

Table 18: Measurements for the dog, *Canis familiaris* bones (in mm)

Bone	N	Measurements		$\overline{X}$
Cranium				
16	1	17.05		17.05
18L	1	19.11		19.11
18GB	1	10.49		10.49
20L	1	12.64		12.64
20W	1	15.49		15.49
21L	1	10.49		10.49
21W	1	10.11		10.11
41	2	41.55	41.58	41.57
Mandible				
5	1	91.72		91.72
6	1	97.75		97.75
7	1	65.75		65.75
8	1	61.98		61.98
9	2	55.78	63.32	59.55
10	1	27.41		27.41
11	1	33.84		33.84
12	2	28.58	32.73	30.66
13L	2	17.18	19.10	18.40
13W	2	6.63	7.54	7.23
14	2	17.24	18.73	17.99
17	1	9.23	9.23	
19	2	16.41	18.04	17.23
20	2	14.07	14.76	14.42
21	2	33.79	36.59	35.19
Radius				
Bd	1	23.52		23.52
Ulna				
DPA	1	20.78		20.78
SDO	1	14.27		14.27
Tibia				
Bp	1	32.14		32.14
Metacarpal II				
GL	1	51.19		51.19
Bd	1	7.65		7.65

Table 19: Measurements for the red deer, *Cervus elephus* bones (in mm)

Bone	n	M
Scapula		
SLC	1	25.11
BG	1	27.70
Radius		
Bd	1	49.21
BFd	1	43.02
Proximal phalanges		
Bd	1	16.84★

★: One end of the bone is non-fused or fusing.

Table 20: Measurements for the fox, *Vulpes vulpes* bones (in mm)

Bone	n	M
Mandible		
9	1	54.23
10	1	37.52
12	1	26.15
14	1	18.48

Table 21: Measurements for the beech marten, *Martes foina* (in mm)

Bone	n	M
Mandible		
13L	1	12.47
13W	1	6.00
Femur		
Bd	1	12.72

Table 22: Measurements for the hare, *Lepus europus* (in mm)

Bone	n	M
Mandible		
13L	1	12.47
13W	1	6.00
Femur		
Bd	1	12.72
Bone	n	M
Tibia		
Bp	1	18.87

Table 23: Measurements for the chicken, *Gallus gallus domesticus* (in mm)

Bone	n	M
Femur		
Bd	1	15.31
Dd	1	14.17
Tibia		
GL	1	98.57
La	1	94.52
Dip	1	17.57
Bd	1	10.65
Dd	1	10.55
Metatarsus		
Bp	1	13.94

Appendix 3

Radiocarbon dates on shell fish from Chalkis Aitolias

By Jan Heinemeier[530]

A total of 8 shells have been radiocarbon dated by means of the AMS (Accelerator Mass Spectrometry) technique, which allows measurement of samples containing less than 1 milligram of carbon. Also, one charcoal sample has been dated to provide a terrestrial date as a reference for the marine shell dates.

Table 1 lists the conventional ^{14}C age BP (Before Present = AD 1950), which has been corrected for isotopic fractionation by normalizing to a standard value of δ^{13}C of -25‰ VPDB in accordance with international convention.[531] Because carbon residence times in the ocean are longer than for atmospheric CO_2, marine organisms will have higher ^{14}C ages than contemporaneous terrestrial organisms. The difference is called the marine reservoir age, which is of the order of 400 years for large parts of the world oceans, but because of deviations from this value it is necessary to establish local values to make the necessary marine reservoir corrections to the measured ^{14}C ages.

For the Eastern Mediterranean, Reimer and McCormac (2002) have provided a compilation of reservoir ages based on 'pre-bomb' shells collected live before 1950 when atmospheric nuclear bomb tests started to disturb the atmospheric ^{14}C content. The average excess reservoir age for the Eastern Mediterranean is $\Delta R = 53$ years and the second data column in Table 1 gives the corrected ages after subtraction of a total reservoir age of 453 years for all the samples, except the last one (AAR-9671), which is a terrestrial charcoal sample found at the Pangali site in close association with a shell (AAR-9670). After reservoir correction of the shell age, this marine/terrestrial sample pair has

very similar ^{14}C ages, 5552 BP and 5530 BP, respectively. This excellent agreement constitutes a very useful test of the validity of the reservoir correction.

Because of variations in the atmospheric ^{14}C content through time, radiocarbon dates need to be calibrated to give meaningful calendar dates. The latest terrestrial calibration curve, IntCal04, has been established based on tree rings,[532] and the corresponding marine calibration curve, Marine04, has been constructed from the terrestrial curve by world ocean model calculations, which take into account the much slower variations in the oceanic ^{14}C content, resulting in a much smoother curve.[533] One single marine calibration curve is assumed to represent all oceans, but with local offsets described by the ΔR parameter.

A radiocarbon date is not a single, fixed number like a historical calendar date. Due to its nature as the result of a physical measurement of a sample's residual ^{14}C content, it has an experimental uncertainty of a statistical nature, described by the ± figure given in the date column of Table 1 and a corresponding probability distribution of likely true ages.

The probability distribution in the calibrated

[530] AMS ^{14}C Dating Centre
Department of Physics and Astronomy
University of Aarhus
DK-8000 Aarhus C
Denmark
www.c14.dk
jh@phys.au.dk
[531] Stuiver and Pollach 1977.
[532] Reimer et al. 2004.
[533] Stuiver and Braziunas 1993; Hughen et al. 2004.

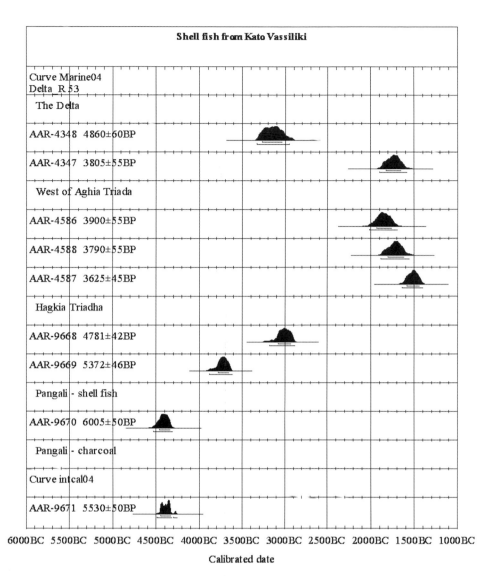

Fig. 95. Plot of the probability distributions in the calibrated ages of the series of marine shells and one terrestrial charcoal sample. The principles of terrestrial and marine ^{14}C calibration are explained in the text. The excellent agreement between the ages of the two associated samples, shell and charcoal, at the bottom of the plot illustrates the successful reservoir correction of the marine ^{14}C date of the shell.

(true) calendar age is shown in Fig. 95 for each sample. The most likely true calendar age expressed in year BC is the position of the peak in each distribution. The marine samples have been calculated with the marine curve and $\Delta R = 53$, whereas the last sample, the charcoal sample, has been calculated from the terrestrial calibration curve. As mentioned above, the marine curve is model based and errors may occur, especially when the curve is applied to areas far from the open world oceans. However, it is a very satisfac-

tory test of the present calibrated results that the distributions for the shell/charcoal pair (two bottom samples in Fig. 95) are nearly identical as they should be. In fact, as seen in data column 3 of table 1, the calibrated age intervals of these two samples, corresponding to one standard deviation in the measurement (68% probability), are 4460 − 4340 BC and 4450 − 4330 BC, respectively, i.e. same width (120 years) and the centre values (4400 BC and 4390 BC) only 10 years apart!

Table 1. 14C dates on shells from the Chalkis Aitolias project

Lab. No.	Sample	Species	^{14}C Age BP	^{14}C Age BP★ Res. Corr. 453y	Calibrated age (BC)		δ^{13}C (‰) (VPDB)
AAR–4348	Kato Vasiliki, 17/07/97 XI	*Cerithium sp.*	4860 ± 60	4407	3270	–3040	1.20
AAR–4347	Kato Vasiliki, 17/07/97 VII	*Gibbula sp.*	3805 ± 55	3352	1820	–1650	0.60
AAR–4586	Kato Vasiliki, Tx72/11, bag 1699	*Cerastoderma glaucum*	3900 ± 55	3447	1930	–1760	–8.00
AAR–4588	Kato Vasiliki, Tx72/13, bag 1850	*Cerastoderma glaucum*	3790 ± 55	3337	1800	–1620	–1.20
AAR–4587	Kato Vasiliki, Tx72/12, bag 1847	*Trynculiopsis truncatus*	3625 ± 45	3172	1580	–1440	0.00
AAR–9668	Aghia Triada, Tx43/4b, bag 1780	*Patella caerulea*	4781 ± 42	4328	3080	–2930	1.00
AAR–9669	Aghia Triada, Tx43/4b, bag 1703	*Cerithium vulgatum*	5372 ± 46	4919	3780	–3660	1.10
AAR–9670	Pangali TR1/STR 2/4.p	*Patella sp.*	6005 ± 50	5552	4460	–4340	2.28
AAR–9671	Pangali TR1/STR 3/5.-6.p	charcoal	5530 ± 50		4450	–4330	–25.57

^{14}C age BP★ is the reservoir corrected ^{14}C age BP (Before Present = 1950); it is calculated from the conventional ^{14}C age by subtracting a reservoir age of 453 years (Reimer and McCormac 2002).

The calibrated age interval in calendar years BC corresponding to 1 standard deviation in the measured conventional ^{14}C age has been calculated from the marine model (Stuiver and Braziunas 1993) with the probability method using the Oxcal V. 3.10 calibration programme (Bronk Ramsey 1995) with the marine calibration curve marine04 (Hugen et al. 2004). The charcoal sample has been calibrated using the standard terrestrial calibration curve, IntCal04 (Reimer et al. 2004).

In the catalogue (pp. 86–97) the stratified material from the deep trenches in TX72 has been systematically treated according to the number system of excavated strata (Fig. 38). In the list of 14C dates above table 1 the terminology of "true" strata (Fig. 37), however, has been mixed up with the terminology of excavated strata. This problem gives rise to the following list of concordance:

Terminology table 1	Excavated strata (catalogue pp. 86–97)	Calibrated age (BC)
AAR–4587 Tx 72/12	STR 10	1580–1440
AAR–4588 Tx 72/13	STR 11	1800–1620
AAR–4586 Tx72/11	STR 13 +	1930–1760

Summary

By Søren Dietz and Ioannis Moschos

The small fishing village of Kato Vasiliki is situated near the coast in a valley plain between the two large karstic lime stone mountains of Varassova and Klokova (respectively 914 m and 1037 m above sea level). The small mound of Aghia Triada, a geologically younger phenomenon from the Middle Eocene, formed by cohesive conglomerates, shales and sandstones, lies as a small island, approximately 30 metre high in the delta east of the village of Kato Vasiliki. The delta itself consists of fertile soil stretching inland to the bed of the Evinos River. The narrow valley opens to the west between the northern termination of mount Varassova and the Evinos river towards the area of ancient Kalydon; towards the east, however, access to the Makynia/Naupaktos area is blocked by the rough massif of mount Klokova. The area itself is thus very much dependant on the sea and the western connections. 14C dates confirm that a bay (the harbour of Chalkis) was situated immediately to the west of the Aghia Triada hill during prehistoric times (datings around 3.000 BC and 1.800 BC)

Final Neolithic

An impressive quantity of pottery, stone, animal bones and marine shells was recovered from the small, 2x2 m, trial trench on a sloping plateau with the modern name Pangali on the east side of the Varassova mountain. The trench was excavated in three horizons, but no distinct stratigraphical layers were documented and no structural remains were observed though a fire place was found at the bottom of the trench. Pangali is an open air habitation close to a shelter. Towards the south a narrow gorge connects the site with the sea. The characteristic pottery, coarse wares with plastic decoration and biconical, horned and other types of ledge

lugs in combination with obsidian and flint arrow heads places the site chronologically in the earlier part of the Final Neolithic, in the phase termed LNIb, in the second half of the 5th Millenium B.C. – the dating neatly supported by 14C datings from the site of Pangali itself. The site is especially closely connected with the Limnes cave assemblage near Kalavrita on the northern Peloponnese but also to Ayios Demetrios in Elis and Prosymna in the Argolid.

Among the domesticated animals, sheep and goat predominated, constituting around 70 % of the bones recovered. Goat was probably more important than sheep. Next to goat and sheep, pig was most important among domesticated animals followed by cattle. Bones of wild animals made up almost 20 % of the total amount of animal bones recovered which is significantly more than on other contemporary sites. Among the wild animal bones, those of roe deer are by far the most common, but bones of wild boar (of extraordinary size), red fox, wildcat and hare were also identified. Hunting of birds and fishing probably was more important than directly indicated by the small amount of bones collected.

Patella was by far the predominant species among the shellfish found on Pangali indicating that the coast at that time was rocky. The sandy shores were probably not created until the 2nd phase of the EHI (see also below). *Columbella rustica* might have been used for charms.

The local red/brown radiolarite was the main lithic used for tools followed by local flint and a fair amount of imported obsidian from Melos. The fact that no cores were found and that flakes and blades were not produced on the site indicates that the first stages of the obsidian tool production were performed in other places. Besides an astonishing number of points and pre-formed points, knifes, sickles, end-scrapers, notches, perforators and burins were found. Various tools made of animal bones were also produced on the site.

It is suggested that the habitation on Pangali, from the second half of the 5th Mill. B.C., served as a seasonal camp, with periodical use during fall and early winter. The repeated use of the site is concluded from the extraordinarily rich deposits and is not attested through stratigraphical observations of succeeding floor levels. The main occupation was the herding and breeding of goat and sheep but in addition pigs and cattle were kept. The fact that sheep, goat and pigs were butchered in the age of 12 months or earlier leaves the impression of a butchering station where only a few animals were kept to the age of 3 to 4 years for breeding purposes. Game and birds were hunted during the season and tools for the hunt produced on the site. Pottery for daily use in the characteristic style of the period was also produced locally. In the near by sea below the site, fishing was performed and shellfish were collected on the rocky coast. Sørensen considers that the "semi-farmers" of Pangali in addition specialized in seasonal exchange of obsidian for the larger environment.

Early Helladic

When the first Early Helladic settlers came to the area around 3.000 B.C. they chose another environmental zone for their settlement than the hilly slopes of Varassova, where the Final Neolithic people lived for a time of the year. The low mound of Aghia Triada where they settled on the top, projected right out in the sea with a small bay on the west side. During the first phase of occupation the *Patella* still predominated in the collected shellfish indicating that the shore line was rocky as in Neolithic times. With slightly less than 50 % of the domesticated animals goat and sheep were still predominating if not to the same degree as earlier. Pigs outnumbered cattle in ratio two to one. The numbers for animal bones are based on a statistically small material and include both phases of the EHI. That fish bones are not recorded from Aghia Triada is probably due to the fact that the soil was not dry-sieved as it was on Pangali, but on the low

mound at the beach a close symbiosis between man and sea was probably practised. In contrast to the Neolithic habitation on the terrace of Varassova, the site on the Aghia Triada is considered a permanent farmer household (even if very little is preserved) taking advantages of the fertile hinterland in the delta supplemented by fishing and collecting shellfish.

The coarse pottery in the early phase is first of all locally made with open bowls, with more or less incurving rims and often burnished, being the dominant shapes. The repertoire undoubtedly reflects the fact that the deposit is placed near a fire place. The shapes correspond to contemporary pottery from for instance Eutresis (IV), Vouliagmeni and Kephalari in the Argolid with the addition of typical local features and preferences. Obsidian outnumbers radiolarite and flint in the lithic assemblage but the material is smaller and the variation of tools is much more restricted. It is characteristic that no points (for hunting) are recorded in this material.

In the later part of EHI a radical change in recorded types of shellfish occurs as the *Cerastoderma glaucum* now becomes the predominant species as it remains for the rest of Antiquity. As said before this is an indication of a change in environment. During the approximately 300 years of EHI,[534] the coast line changes from a more or less rocky coast to sandy shores or a mixture between the two.

In the pottery repertoire, carinated sections are now found on the shallow bowls (as in Eutresis V) and some of the vessels have raised bases in contrast to the exclusively flat bases on pottery from the first phase. 25 to 30 % of the vessels are still burnished, more red burnished than black.

Early Helladic materials and levels are found both on the top of Aghia Triada and in the lower levels in the area west of the mound. Here the identification mainly rests on T-rim bowls with raised band and finger impressions of a more advanced character than in the EHI layers. It

---

[534] Dating EHI between 3.100/3.000 and 2.650 B.C. See Cullen 2001, 106 after Manning 1993.

should be noted, however, that the material is either small and insignificant or scattered from surface collections. No sauceboats were identified. Even if some activities in the EHII period might thus be suggested both on the Aghia Triada mound and from the area to the west of the hill, there are no indications of a substantial EHII settlement to succeed the well defined EHI habitation on the mound.

The MH and LH periods

As for the Middle Helladic period it is interesting to observe the presence of elements (even if they are not numerous) deriving from the early part of the period. A "Minyan" bowl with high swung handles from the Aghia Triada and Lustrous painted pottery from the area west of the mound. Lustrous painted pottery in the Middle Helladic period is usually thought to have been inspired from Crete at the beginning of the MH period with a distribution covering the eastern areas of the Peloponnese and Mainland Greece. This kind of pottery is especially abundant in southern Peloponnese and Kythera. Lustrous painted pottery is usually more abundantly at hand during the earlier phases of the MH than towards the transition to LHI.[535] The traces are faint but it is nevertheless interesting to note that this early wave of Cretan influence even reached the Northwestern regions of Greece. An estimation of the character of this influence has to await excavations of more sites from this period in the region.

The majority of the pottery from the MHIIIB/LHIA horizons is closed shaped vessels in local, hard fabric. Characteristic are jars with flat, oblique rims and cups, close shaped bowls or jars with S-shaped profile and thin rim. The holemouth and vertical triangular handles indicate connections with Central Greece and Northwestern Peloponnese. Some jars with MP patterns and a krater with a "hawk beak rim" point to a date within the general frame of MHIIIB/LHIA in argive terminology.

The information given by the C14 dates[536] give rise to some comments. According to the pottery all strata should be dated to the later part of the

MH period or the early LH I (LHIA). A dating of layer Tx72/13 to around 1700 BC corresponds to the dating of this layer in MMIII/LHIA (high chronology).

Quite a few shapes in the small LHIB deposit in the shallow land west of the mound point towards the NE Peloponnese and a LHIB date. Of specific interest are the two semiglobular cups (FS211) with lustrous paint and a cup with "wish bone" handle on the rim with close parallels from Pagona in Patras opposite Chalkis in Achaea and Thermon in inland Aitolia.

The pottery from the LHIII horizons is all of Late IIIC/early submycenaean date. It is of considerable importance that the socalled "local Geometric" class of pottery well-known from the Iron Age levels in Thermon and the construction and use of megaron B is now, for the first time, shown to be present already in LHIIIC times.

The majority of the tools in the MH/LH layers are made of radiolarite and flint while obsidian is only present in MHIIIB/LHIA. Very few tools are identified. As for the animals it seems as if compared to the situation in EHI cattle, replaced pigs as the more important food recource, with sheep/goat still being the most usual if slightly decreasing in importance. Further research is necessary in order to decide whether the cattle/pigs ratio is the result of different ecological niches or reflects a general tendency at the time. *Cerastodermus* were the preferred shellfish in the menu indicating that sandy beaches were present in the 2nd Mill. BC in Chalkis Aitolias.

---

[535] For instance in Argos. Philippa-Touchais 2003, 3 and 4, n. 13.

[536] See Fig. 95 nos. **AAR-4586** (Tx72/11 (STR 13 +) 1930-1760), **AAR-4588** (Tx72/13 (STR 11) 1800-1620) and **AAR-4587** (Tx 72/12 (STR 10) 1580-1440). Se note above p. 198.

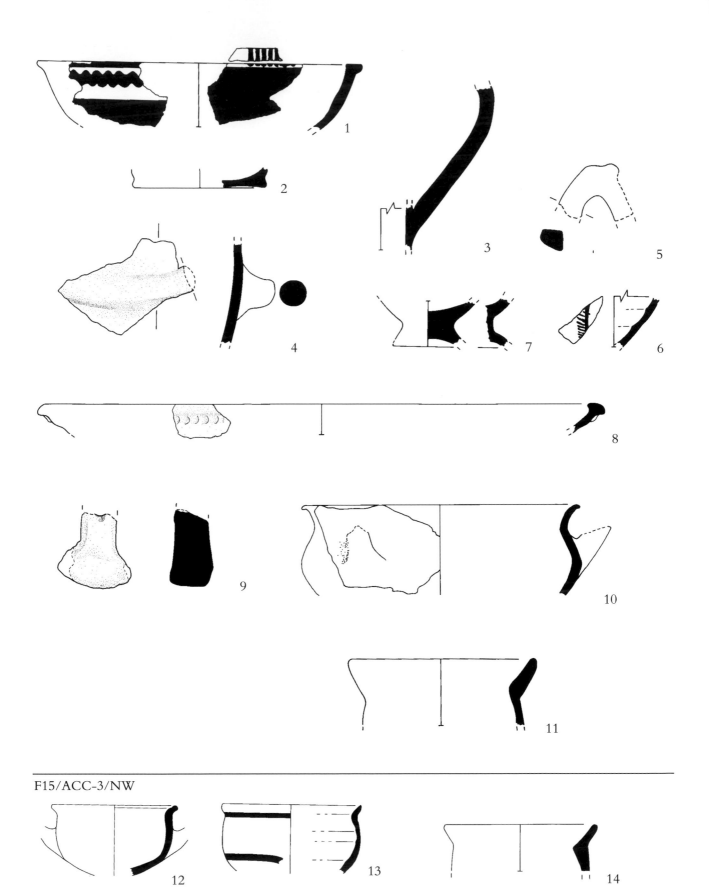

Pl. 1. Aghia Triada. Survey 1995. Selected finds and pottery from F15/AAC-3/NW. 1:3.

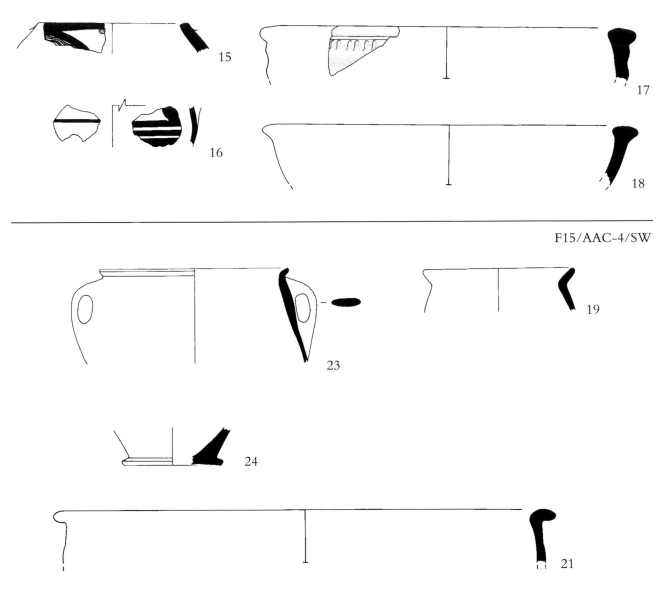

Pl. 2. Aghia Triada. Pottery from F15/AAC-3/SW and F15/AAC-4/SW. 1:3.

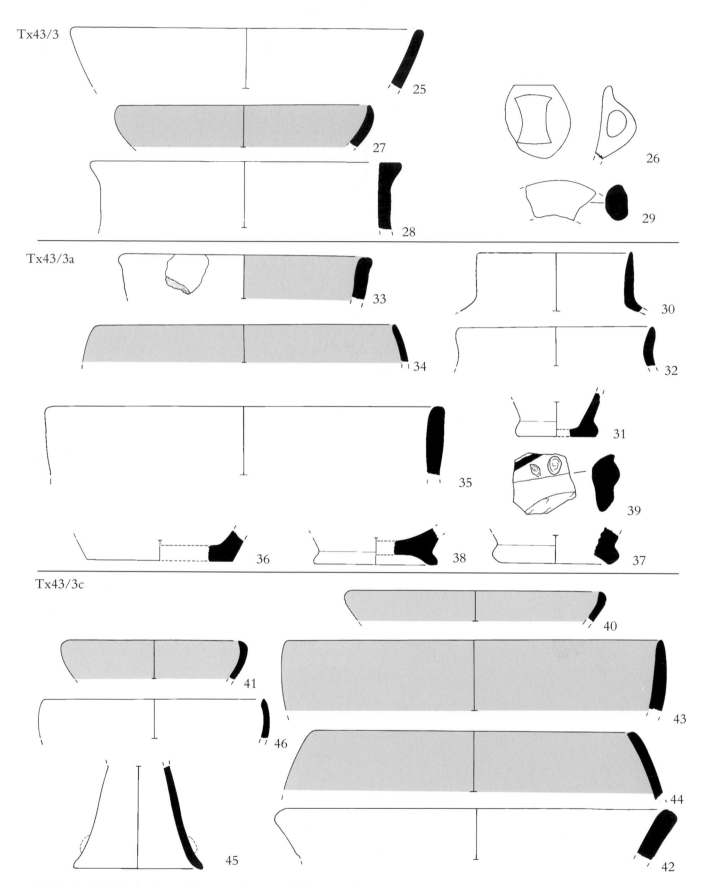

Pl. 3. Aghia Triada, Area I. Pottery from Tx43/3, 3a and 3c. 1:3.

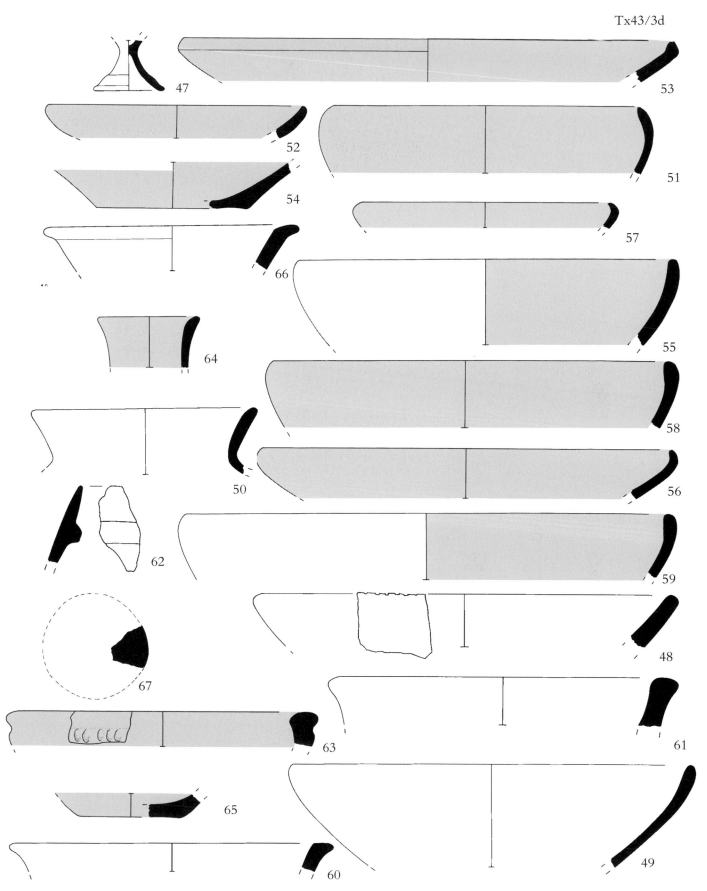

Pl. 4. Aghia Triada, Area I. Pottery from Tx43/3d. 1:3.

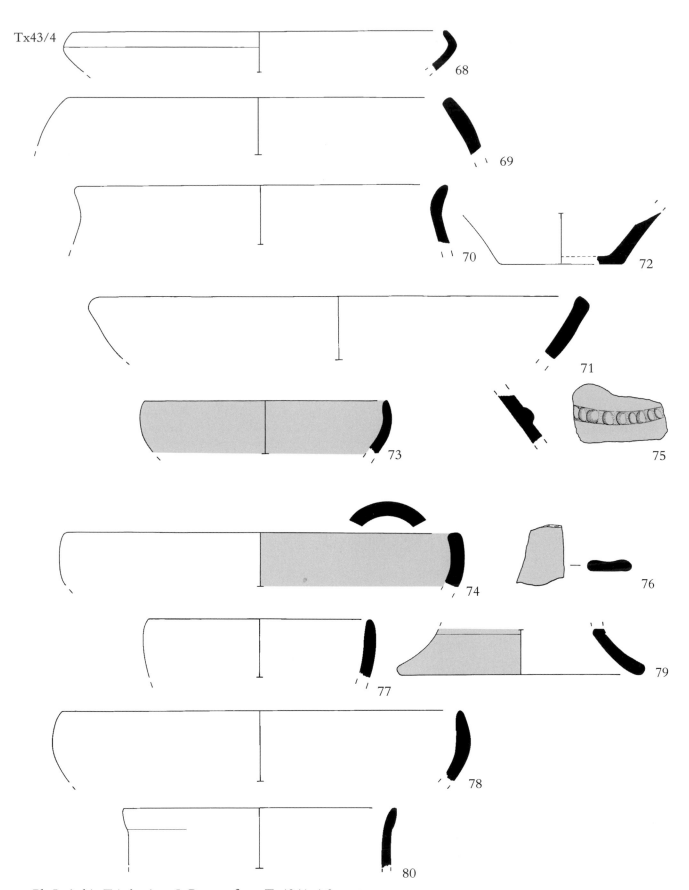

Tx43/4

Pl. 5. Aghia Triada, Area I. Pottery from Tx43/4. 1:3.

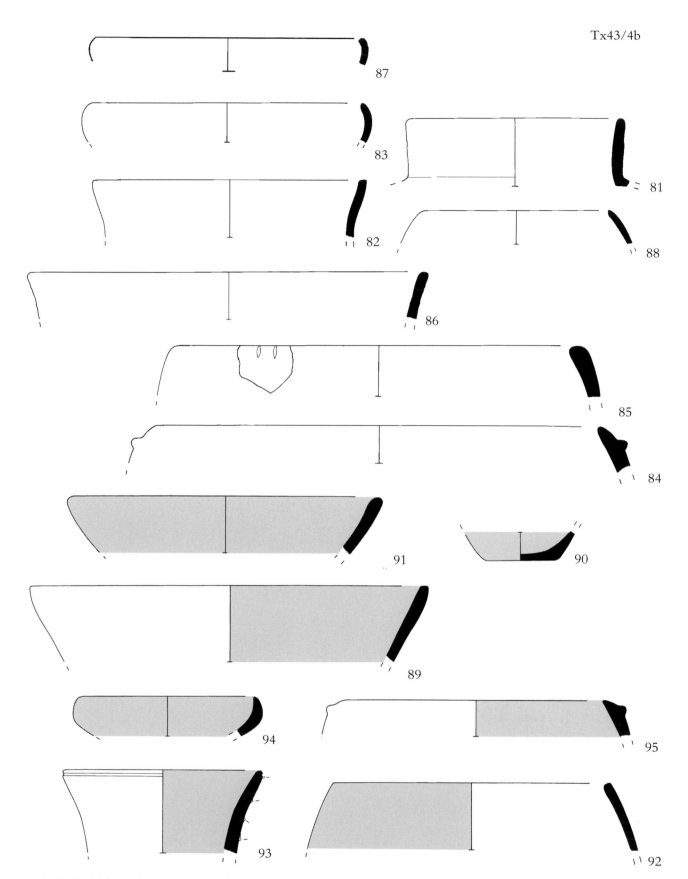

Pl. 6. Aghia Triada, Area I. Pottery from Tx43/4b. 1:3.

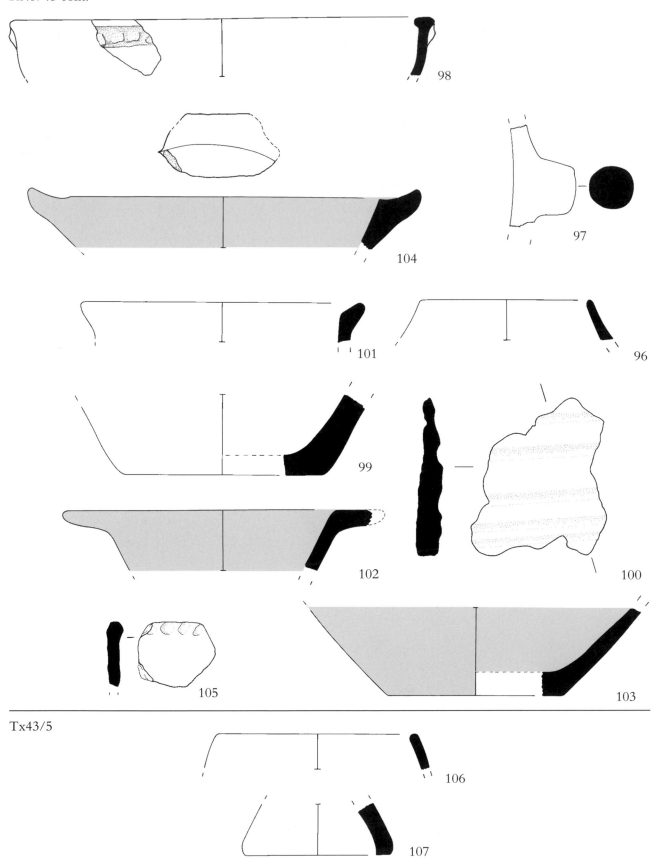

Tx43/5

Pl. 7. Aghia Triada, Area I. Pottery from Tx43/4b (continued) and Tx43/5. 1:3.

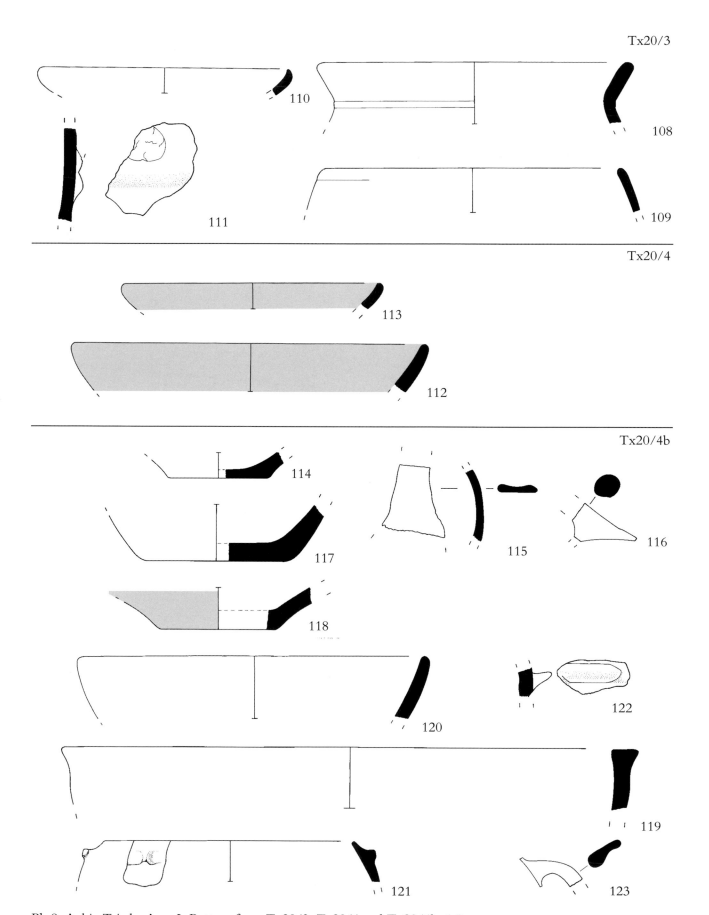

Pl. 8. Aghia Triada, Area I. Pottery from Tx20/3, Tx20/4 and Tx20/4b. 1:3.

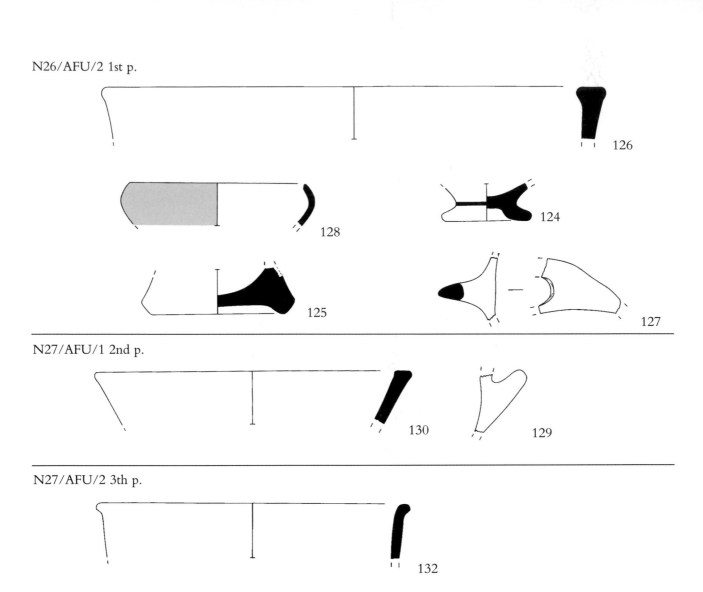

N26/AFU/2 1st p.

126

128

124

125

127

N27/AFU/1 2nd p.

130

129

N27/AFU/2 3th p.

132

131

133

Pl. 9. Aghia Triada, Area I. Pottery from N26 and N27. 1:3.

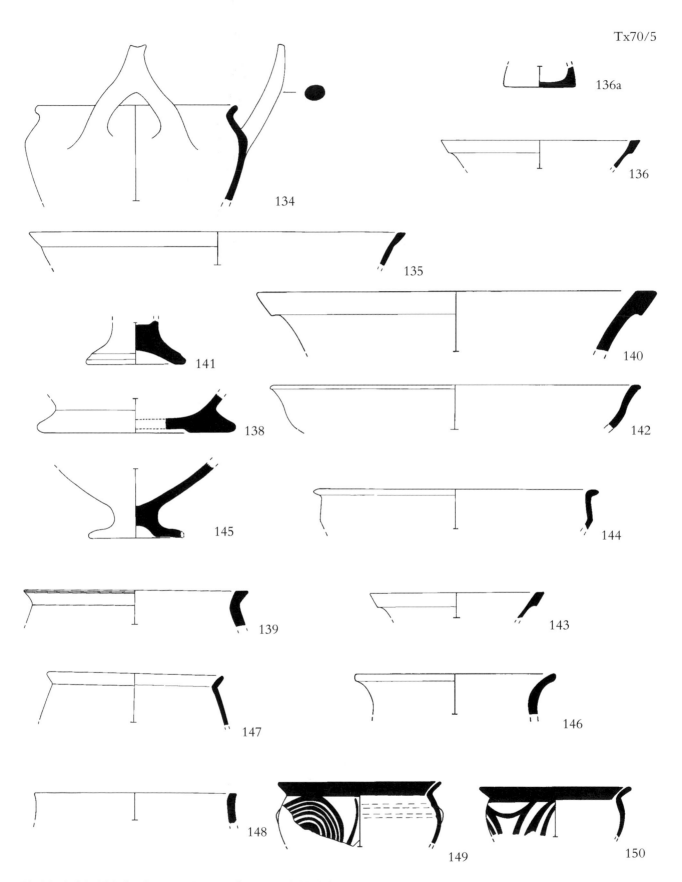

134
136a
136
135
141
140
138
142
145
144
139
143
147
146
148
149
150

Pl. 10. Aghia Triada, Area II. Pottery from Tx70/5. 1:3.

Tx70/5a

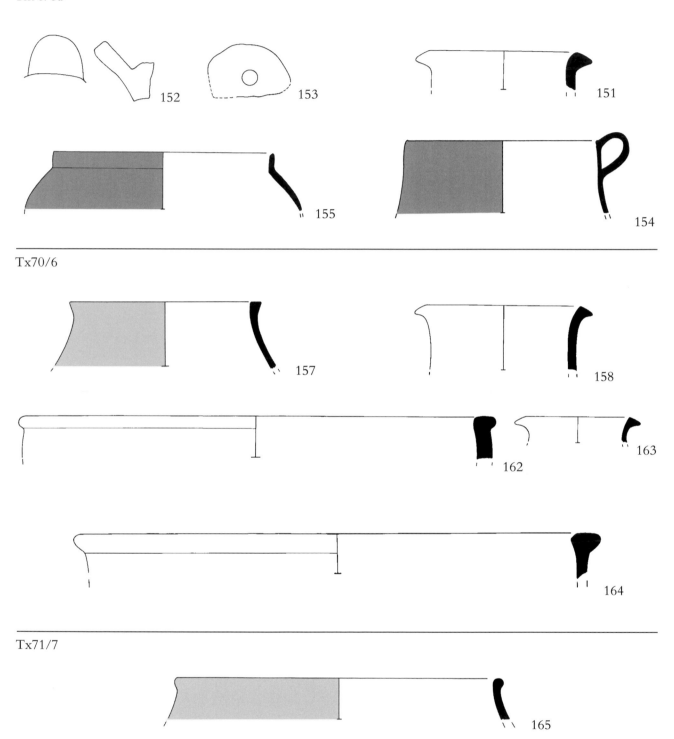

152 153 151

155 154

Tx70/6

157 158

162 163

164

Tx71/7

165

Pl. 11. Aghia Triada, Area II. Pottery from Tx70/5a, Tx70/6 and Tx71/7. 1:3.

212

Tx72/ARA/1

Tx72/ARA/2

Tx72/11

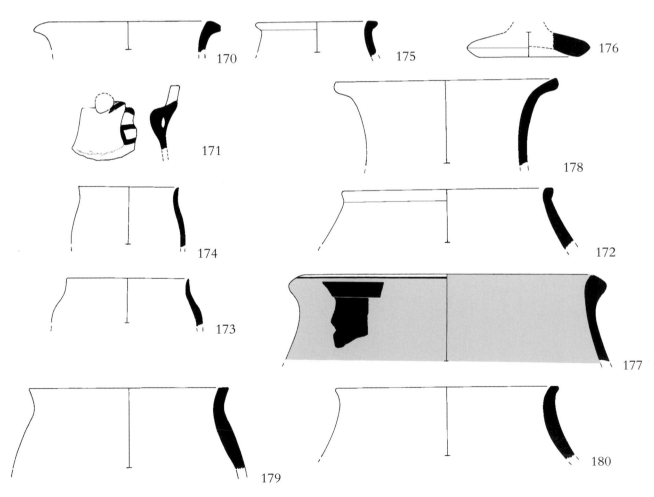

Pl. 12. Aghia Triada, Area II. Pottery from Tx72/ARA/1, Tx72/ARA/2 and Tx72/11. 1:3.

213

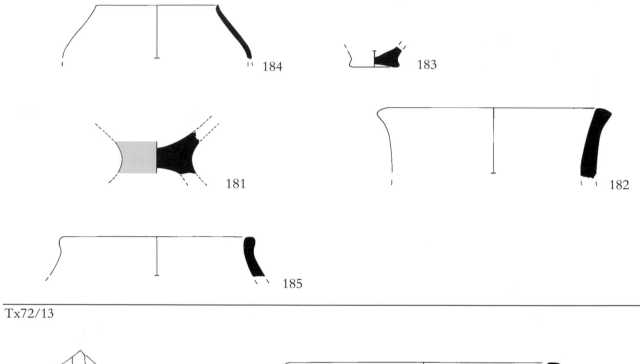

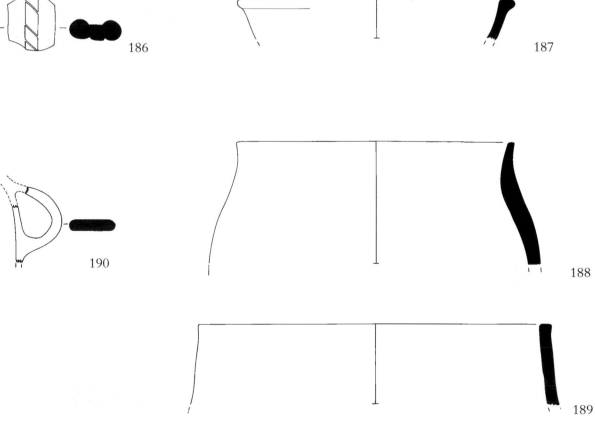

Pl. 13. Aghia Triada, Area II. Pottery from Tx72/12 and Tx72/13. 1:3.

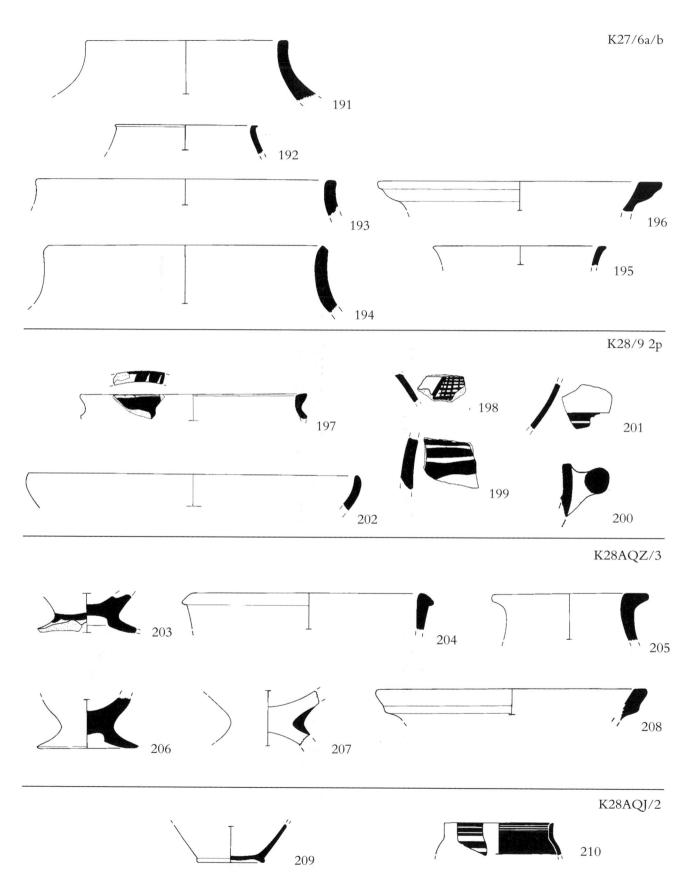

191

192

193

196

195

194

197

198

201

199

200

202

203

204

205

206

207

208

209

210

Pl. 14. Aghia Triada, Area II. Pottery from K27/6a and b, K28/9 2p, K28 AQZ/3 and K28/AQJ/2. 1:3.

K29/7b 1p

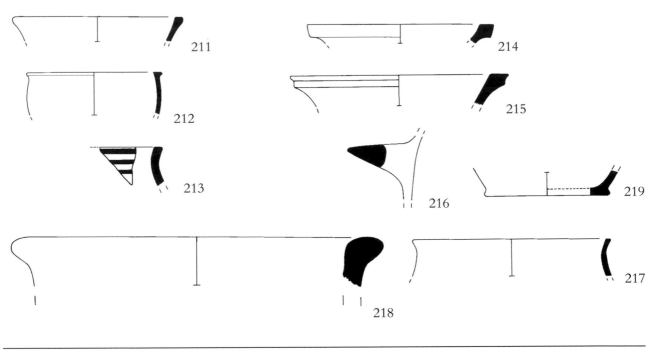

211

214

212

215

213

216

219

218

217

K29/7e 2p

220

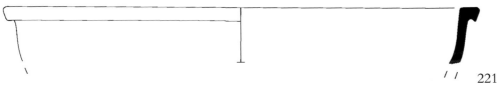

221

K29/7e 3p

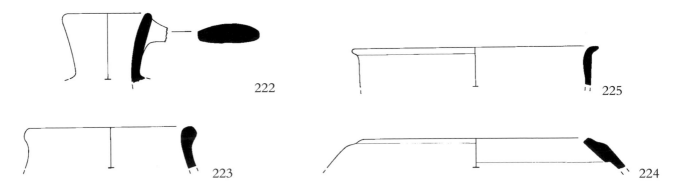

222

225

223

224

Pl. 15. Aghia Triada, Area II. Pottery from K29/7b 1p, K29/7e 2p and K29/7e 3p. 1:3.

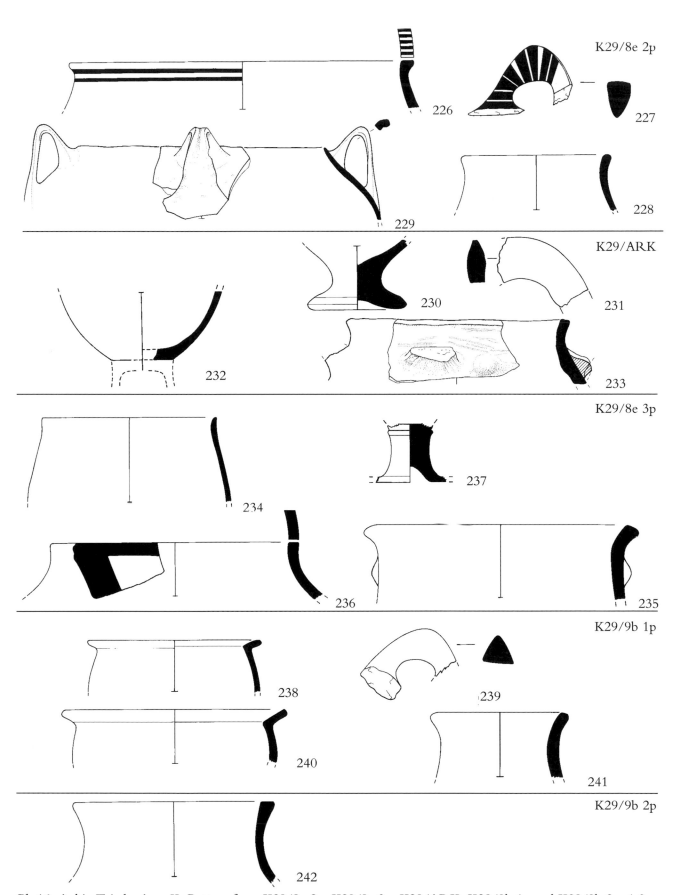

K29/8e 2p

226

227

228

229

K29/ARK

230

231

232

233

K29/8e 3p

234

237

236

235

K29/9b 1p

238

239

240

241

K29/9b 2p

242

Pl. 16. Aghia Triada, Area II. Pottery from K29/8e 2p, K29/8e 3p, K29/ARK, K29/9b 1p and K29/9b 2p. 1:3.

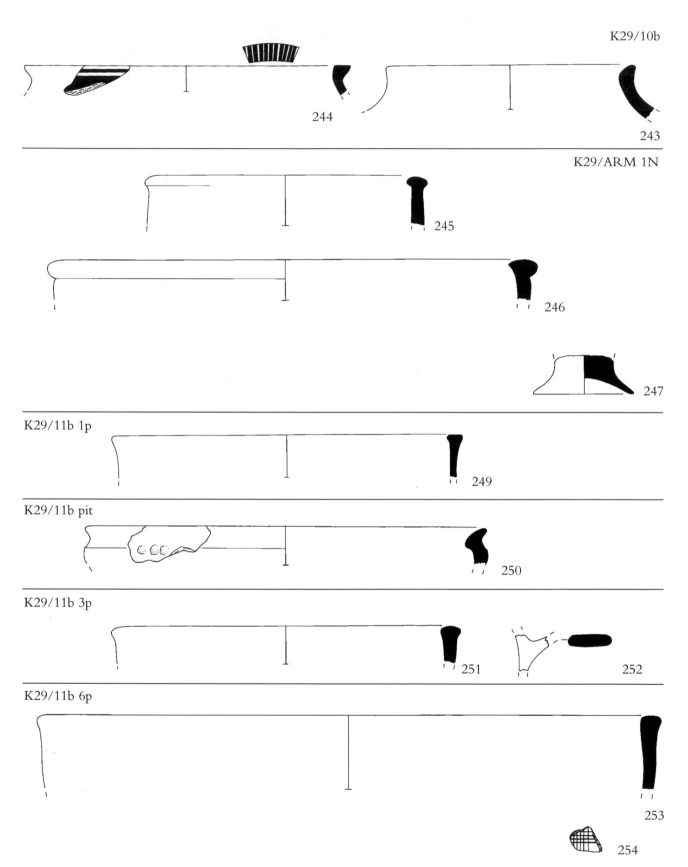

Pl. 17. Aghia Triada, Area II. Pottery from K29/10b, K29/ARM 1N, K29/11b 1p, K29/11b pit, K29/11b 3p and K29/11b 6p. 1:3.

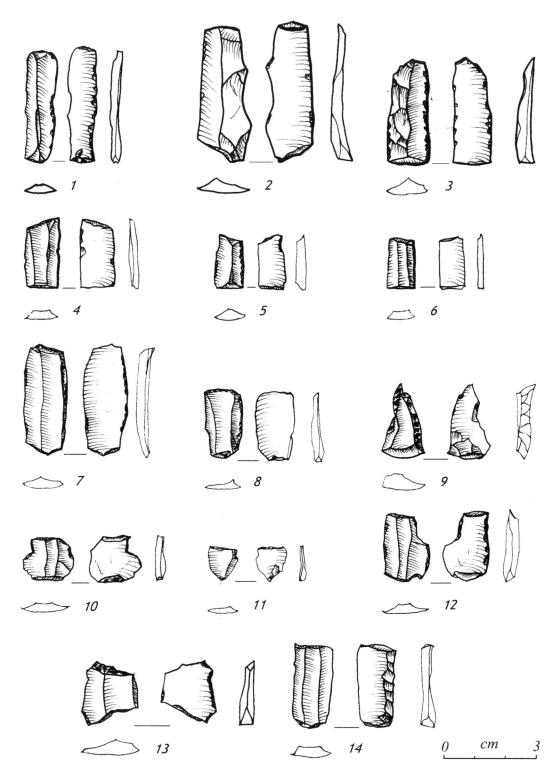

Pl. 18. Drawings of selected flaked-tools from EH I. 1-7. Sickle fragments. 8 & 13. End scrapers. 9. Perforator. 10-12 & 14. Blade fragments with retouche. Raw materials: Obsidian (1-6, 10-13). Flint (7). Radiolarite (8 & 14). Marble (9). Drawings L. Sørensen.

No. 1 = Catalogue nr. 3. No. 2 = Catalogue nr. 13. No. 3 = Catalogue nr. 20. No. 4 = Catalogue nr. 29. No. 5 = Catalogue nr. 28. No. 6 = Catalogue nr. 28. No. 7 = Catalogue nr. 5. No. 8 = Catalogue nr. 8. No. 9 = Catalogue nr. 10. No. 10 = Catalogue nr. 24. No. 11 = Catalogue nr. 19. No. 12 = Catalogue nr. 29. No. 13 = Catalogue nr. 16. No. 14 = Catalogue nr. 23.

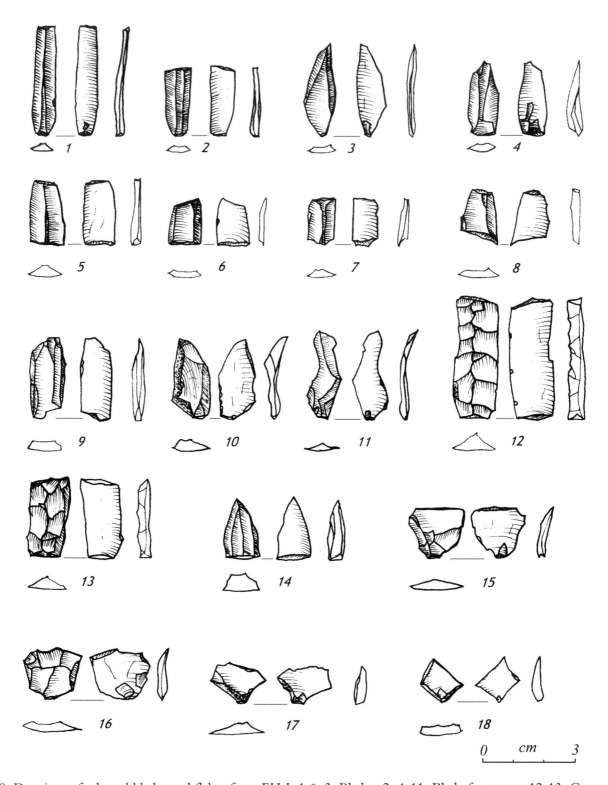

Pl. 19. Drawings of selected blades and flakes from EH I. 1 & 3. Blades. 2, 4-11. Blade fragments. 12-13. Crested blades. 14-18. Flakes. Raw materials: Obsidian (1-18). Drawings L. Sørensen.
No. 1 = Catalogue nr. 14. No. 2 = Catalogue nr. Find. nr. 1274. No. 3 = Catalogue nr. 12. No. 4 = Catalogue nr. 26. No. 5 = Catalogue nr. 9. No. 6 = Catalogue nr. 24. No. 7 = Catalogue nr. 24. No. 8 = Catalogue nr. 29. No. 9 = Catalogue nr. 24. No. 10 = Catalogue nr. 24. No. 11 = Catalogue nr. 17. No. 12 = Catalogue nr. 15. No. 13 = Catalogue nr. 18a. No. 14 = Catalogue nr. 29. No. 15 = Catalogue nr. 27. No. 16 = Catalogue nr. 24. No. 17 = Catalogue nr. 21. No. 18 = Catalogue nr. 24.

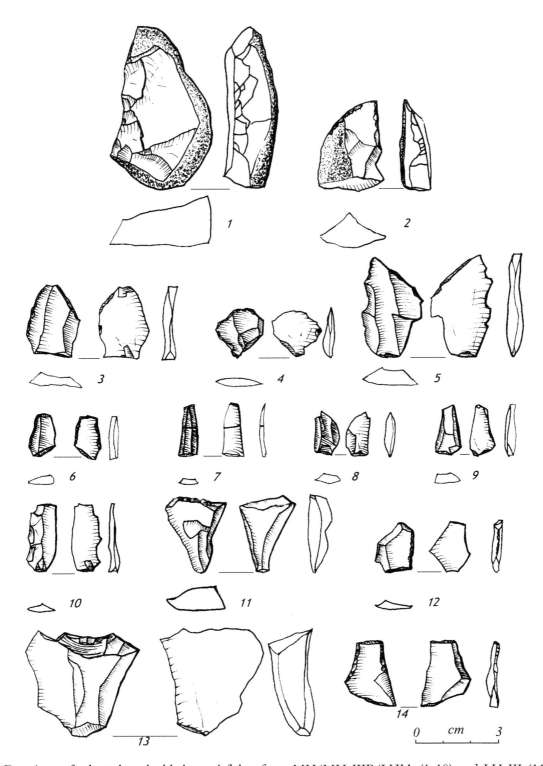

Pl. 20. Drawings of selected tools, blades and flakes from MH/MH IIIB/LHIA (1-10) and LH III (11-14). 1-2. Scrapers. 3, 5, 12 & 14. Flakes with retouche. 4, 11 & 13. End scrapers. 6. Blades with retouche. 7. Blade fragment. 8-9. Flakes. 10. Crested blade. Raw materials: Obsidian (5, 7-10). Flint (1-2, 4, 6, 11 & 13). Radiolarite (3, 12 & 14). Drawings L. Sørensen.

No. 1 = Catalogue nr. 70. No. 2 = Catalogue nr. 69. No. 3 = Catalogue nr. 42. No. 4 = Catalogue nr. 46. No. 5 = Catalogue nr. 46. No. 6 = Catalogue nr. 48. No. 7 = Catalogue nr. 47. No. 8 = Catalogue nr. 48. No. 9 = Catalogue nr. 46. No. 10 = Catalogue nr. 36. No. 11 = Catalogue nr. 63. No. 12 = Catalogue nr. 60. No. 13 = Catalogue nr. 57. No. 14 = Catalogue nr. 55.

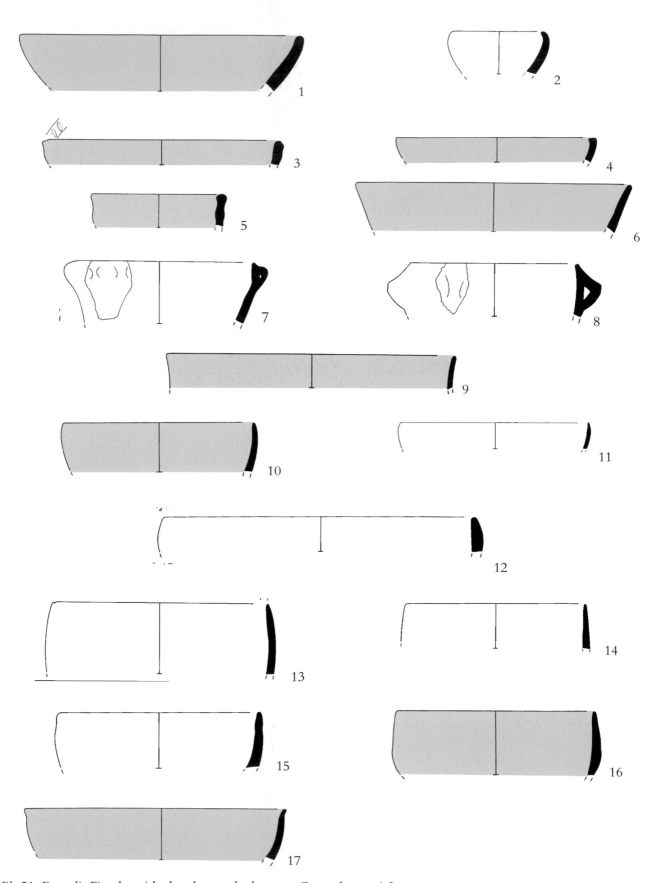

Pl. 21. Pangali. Fine burnished and smoothed wares. Open shapes. 1:3.

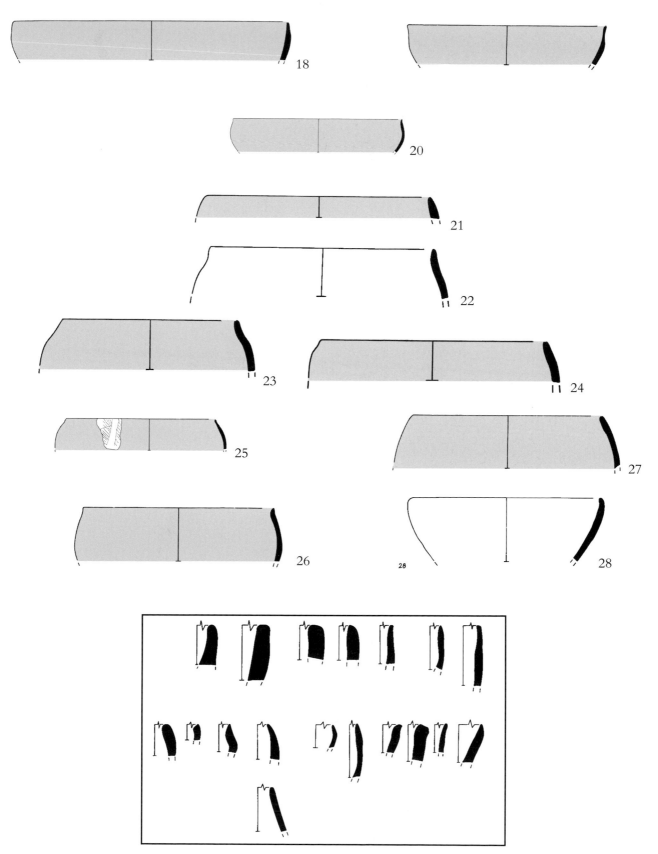

Pl. 22. Pangali. Fine burnished and smoothed wares. Open shapes (18-20) and open mouthed closed shapes (21-24). Open shapes with asymmetrical rim (25-28). 1:3.

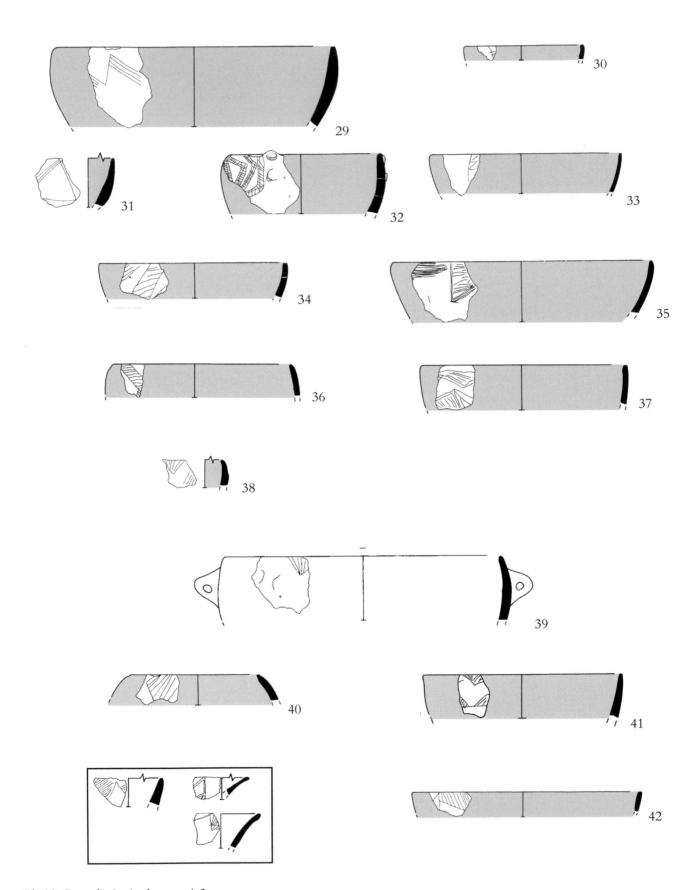

Pl. 23. Pangali. Incised ware. 1:3.

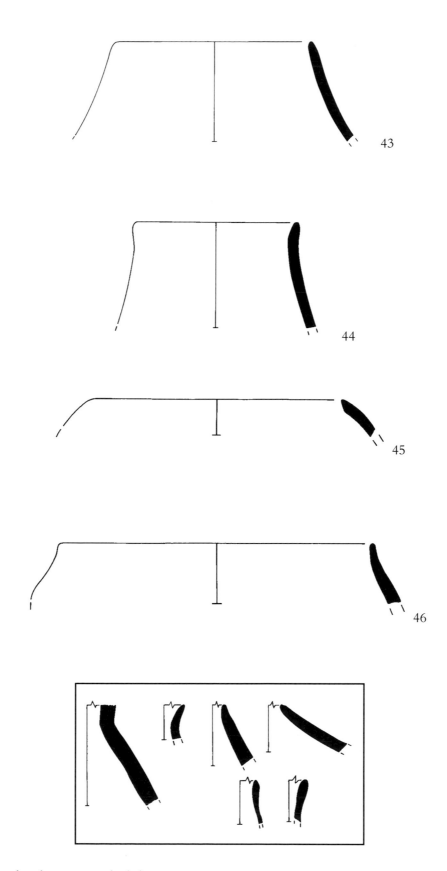

Pl. 24. Pangali. Closed and open mouthed shapes.

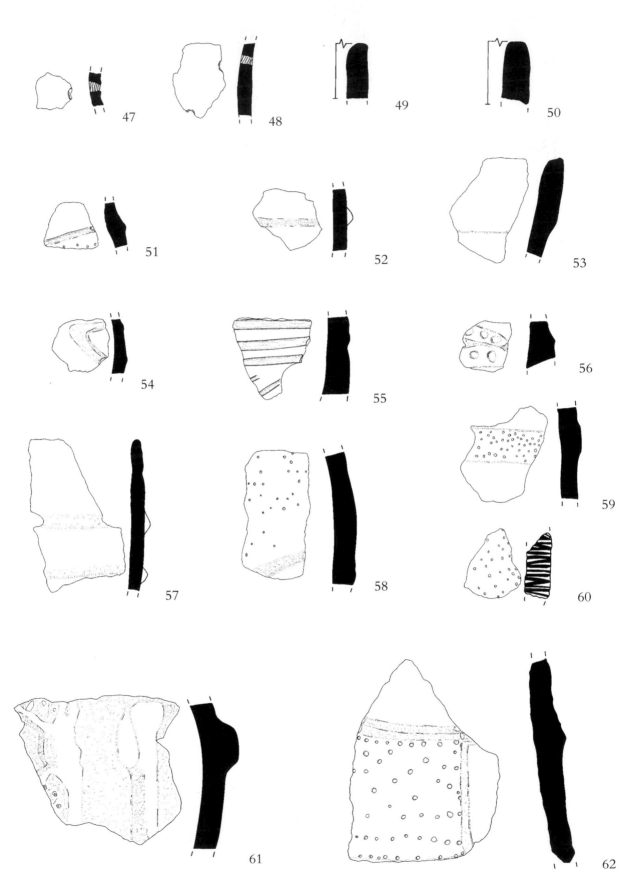

Pl. 25. Pangali. Coarse wares. 1:3.

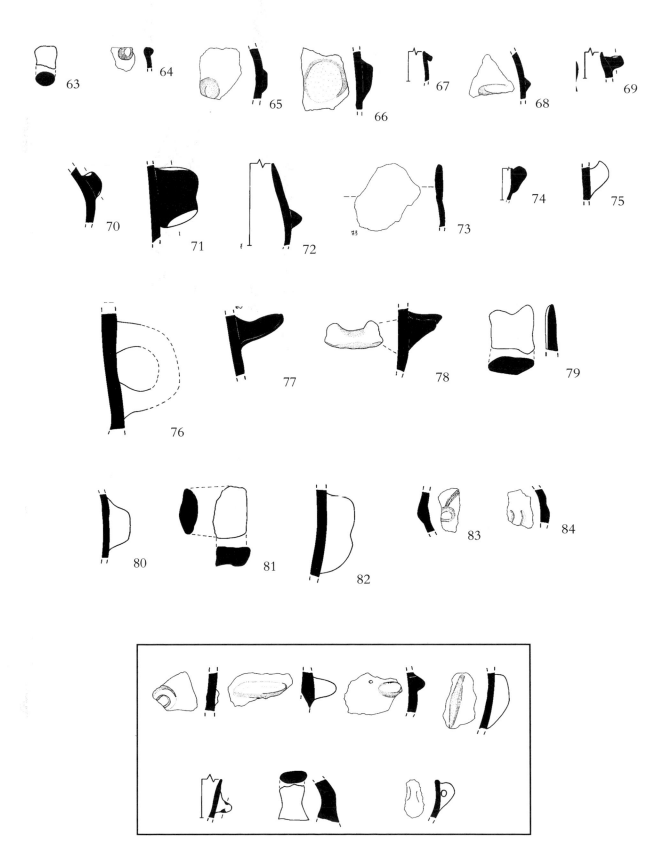

Pl. 26. Pangali. Lugs and handles (63–82) and fine burnished ware with plastic decoration (83–84). 1:3.

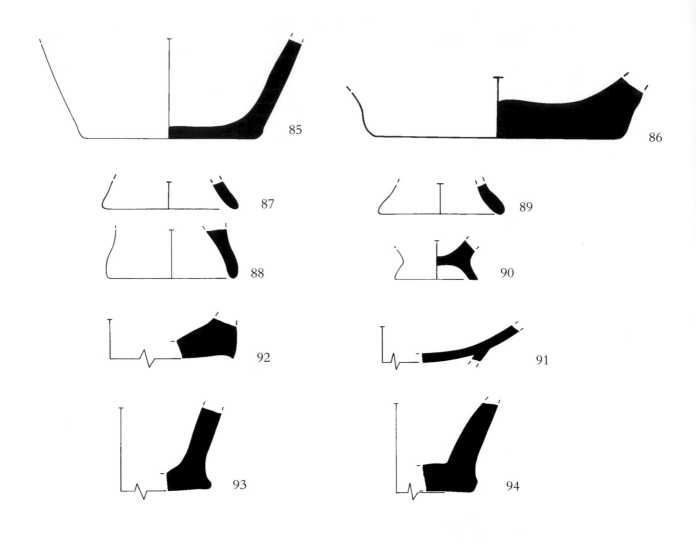

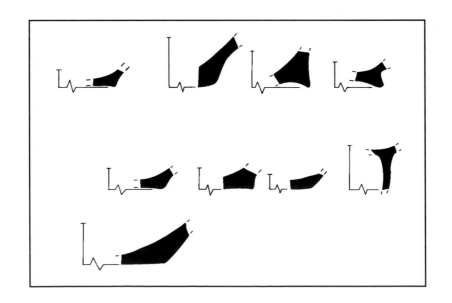

Pl. 27. Pangali. Bases. 1:3.

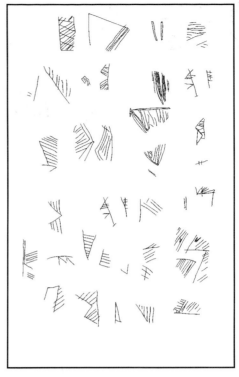

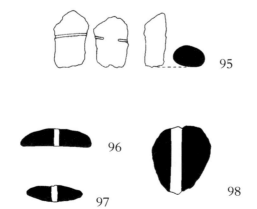

Pl. 28. Pangali. Motifs of incised ware. 1:3.
Pl. 29. Pangali. Various clay items. 1:3

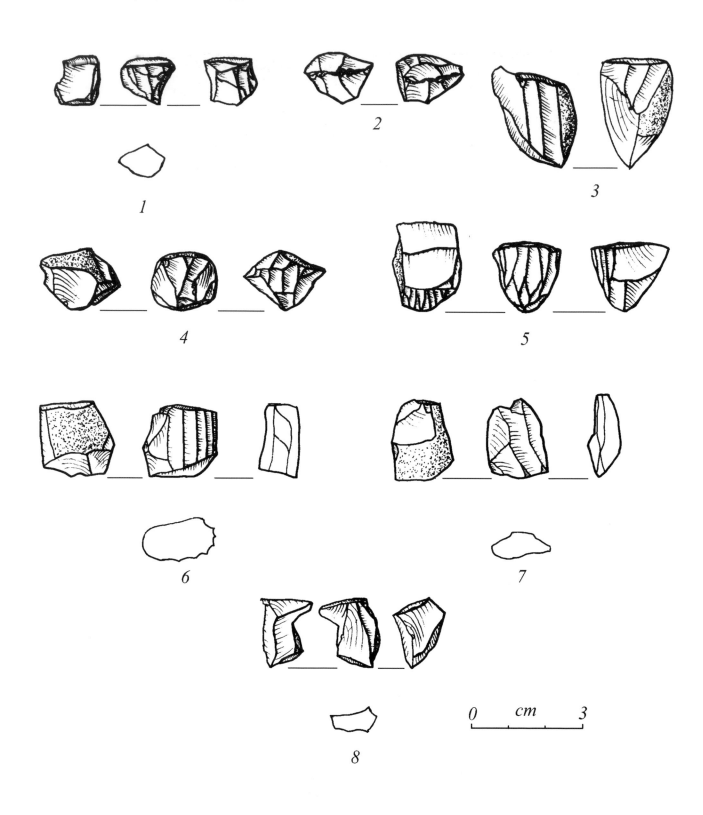

Pl. 30. Pangali. Drawings of small flake and blade cores. 1, 2, 4: Flake cores. 3: Blade core. 5: Microblade core. 6: Blade core. 7-8: Totally exhausted flake cores. Raw materials: radiolarite (1-3), flint (4-5), obsidian (6-8). C. Casati (graphic) and L. Sørensen (drawing).

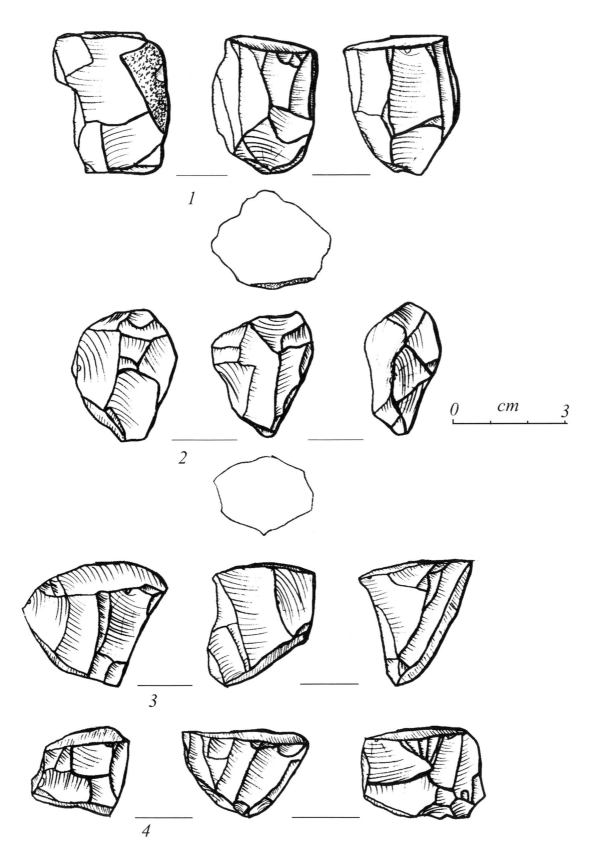

Pl. 31. Pangali. Drawings of selected larger flake cores. 1-4: Larger flake cores. Raw materials: flint (1-3), radiolarite (4). C. Casati (graphic) and L. Sørensen (drawing).

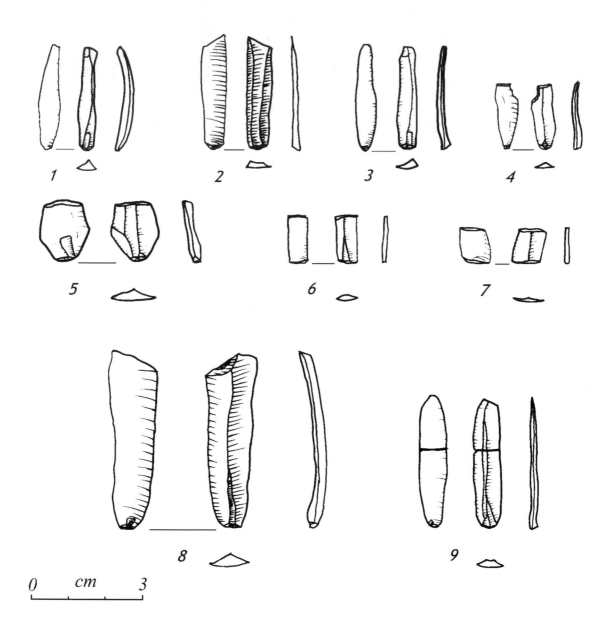

Pl. 32. Pangali. Drawings of selected microblades and blades from Pangali. 1–4: Microblades. 5: Fragmented blade. 6–7: Fragmented microblades. 8: Blade. 9: Refitted microblade. Raw materials: flint (1–8), radiolarite (9). C. Casati (graphics) and L. Sørensen (drawings).

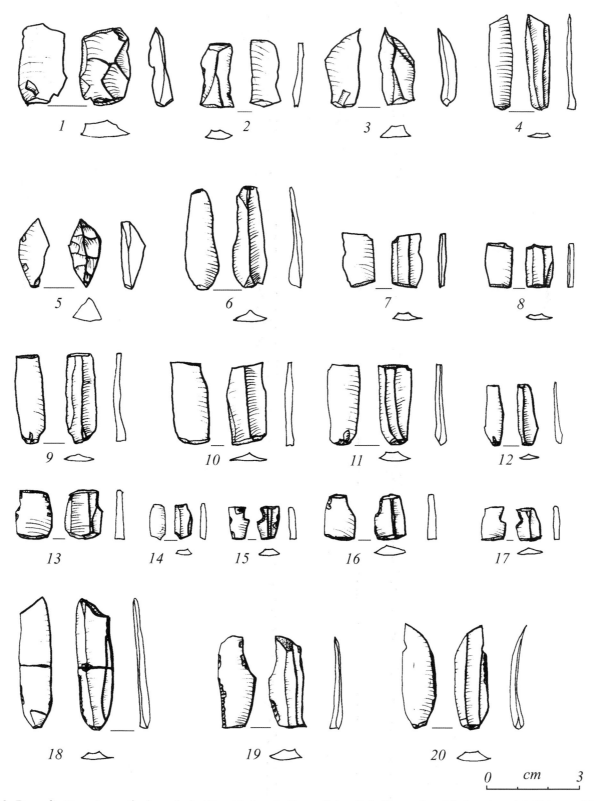

Pl. 33. Pangali. Drawings of selected obsidian blades. 1: Front flake. 2-3: Secondary blades. 4 and 6: Primary blade. 5: Crested blade. 7, 8 and 10: Fragmented median blades. 9 and 11: Fragmented proximal blades. 12: Fragmented proximal microblade. 13-17: Fragmented blades with retouche. 18: Refitted blade, which was broken intentionally. 19-20: Blades with retouche, possible knives or sickle elements. Raw materials: obsidian (1-20). C. Casati (graphic) and L. Sørensen (drawing).

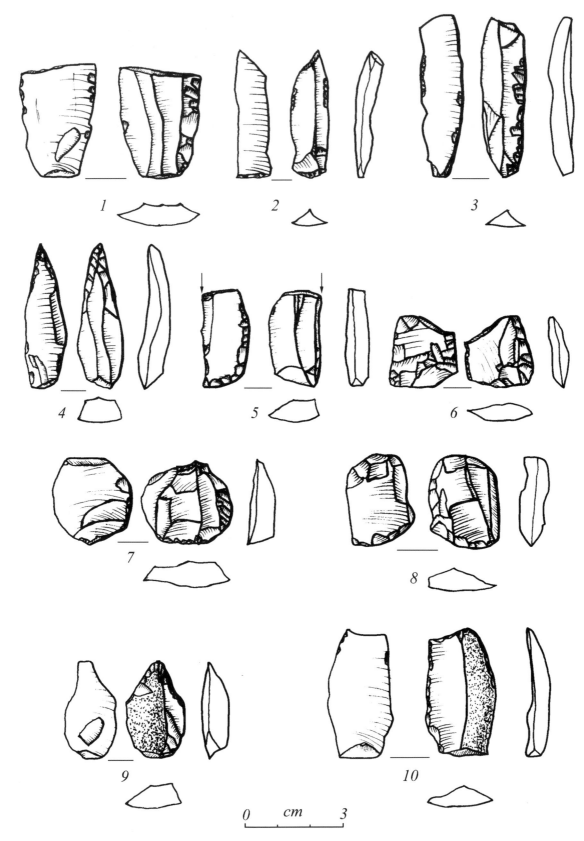

Pl. 34. Pangali. Drawings of selected artifacts. 1 and 10: Flakes with retouche. 2-3: Knives or sickle elements. 4 and 9: Perforators. 5: Burin. 6-8: Splintered pieces. Raw materials: radiolarite (1-7), flint (8-10). C. Casati (graphic) and L. Sørensen (drawings).

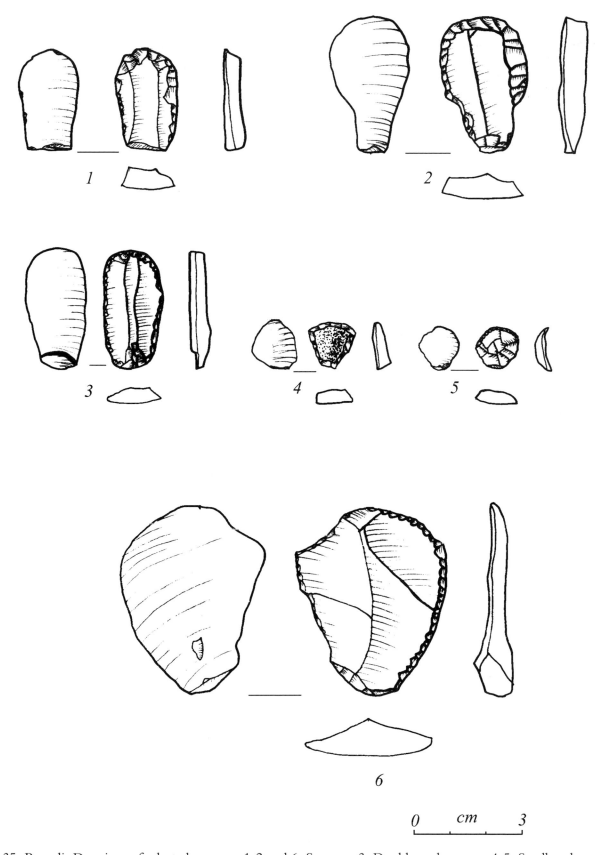

Pl. 35. Pangali. Drawings of selected scrapers. 1–2 and 6: Scrapers. 3: Double end scraper. 4–5: Small end scrapers. Raw material: radiolarite (1–6). C. Casati (graphic) and L. Sørensen (drawings).

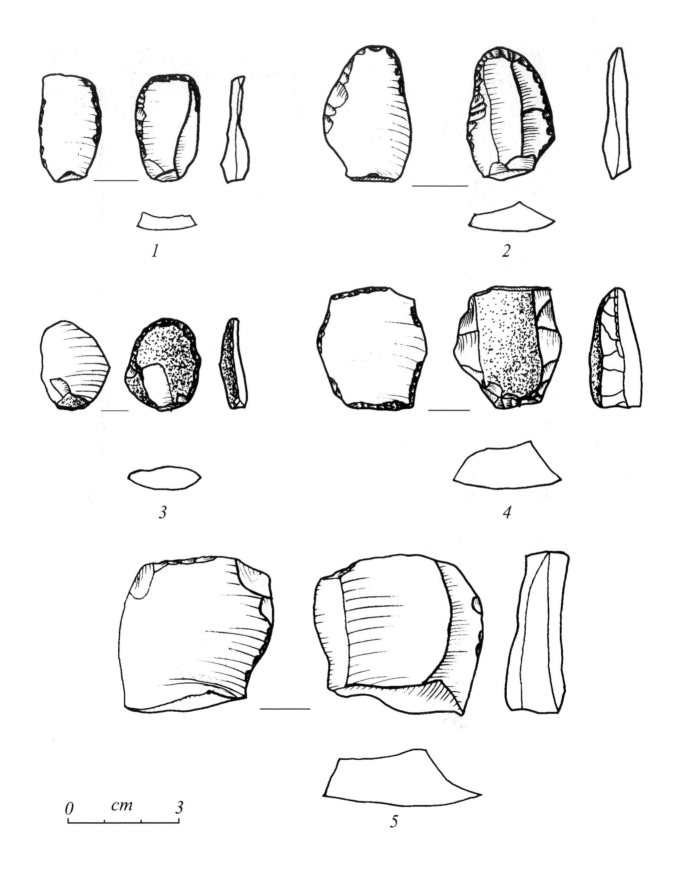

1

2

3

4

0 cm 3

5

Pl. 36. Pangali. Drawings of selected scrapers. 1–5: End scrapers. Raw material: flint (1–5). C. Casati (graphic) and L. Sørensen (drawings).

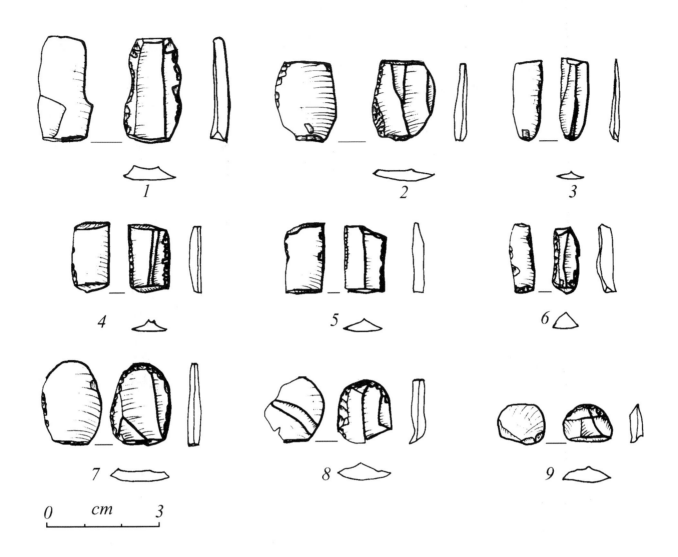

Pl. 37. Pangali. Drawings of selected obsidian artifacts. 1-6: Blade fragments with retouche, possible knives or sickle elements. 7-9: Small scrapers. Raw material: obsidian (1-9). C. Casati (graphic) and L. Sørensen (drawings).

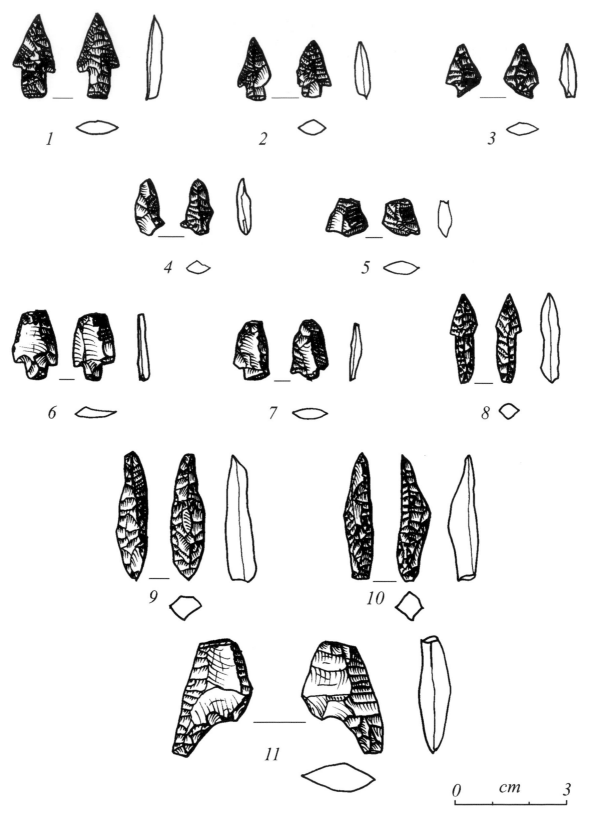

Pl. 38. Pangali. Drawings of selected points. 1-4: Tanged barbed points. 5: Tanged barbed point with hinge terminating bending fracture. 6-7: Tanged points with snap fractures. 8: Tanged point. 9-10: Slugs. 11: Preformed slug or a hollow based arrow head. Raw material: radiolarite (1-3, 9-11), flint (4, 8), obsidian (5, 6, 7). C. Casati (graphic) and L. Sørensen (drawings).

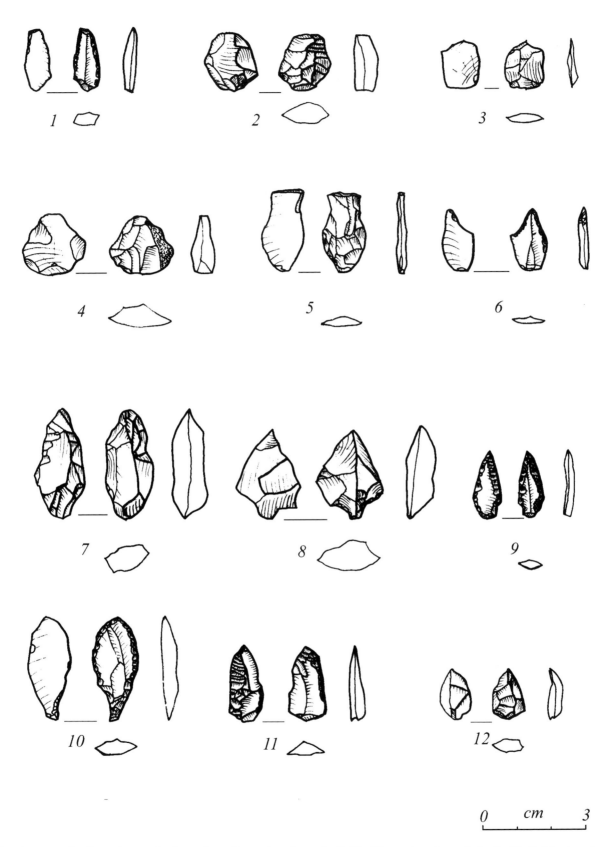

Pl. 39. Pangali. Drawings of selected preformed points. 1, 9-12: Tanged points. 2-6, 8: Unfinished points. 7: Unfinished slug. Raw material: radiolarite (1, 7-12), flint (6), obsidian (2-5). C. Casati (graphic) and L. Sørensen (drawings).

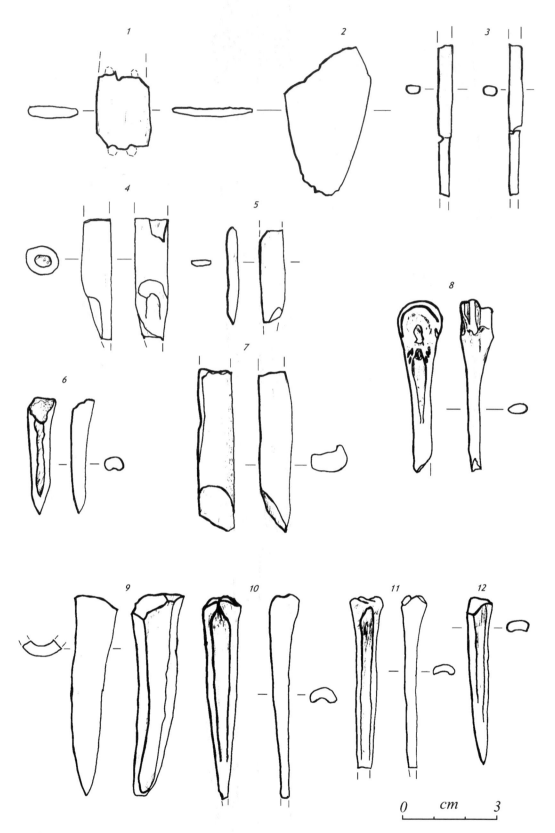

Pl. 40. Pangali. Drawings of bone tools. 1: Elaborated bone artifact with four holes. 2: Split and polished rib bone. 3: Two fragments of polished needles. 4, 5 and 7: Chisel tools with rounded ends. 6 and 9: Pointed tools made by groove and splitter method. 8: Pointed tool made of the metapodialis. 10-12: Pointed tools with a split distal meta-podial. Graphic by C. Casati. Drawings by L. Sørensen and Anne Hooton.

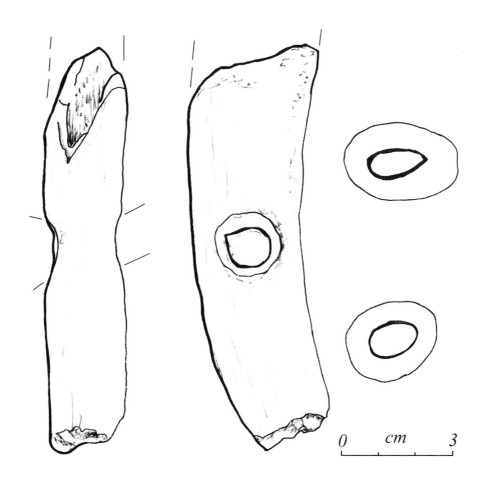

Pl. 41. Pangali. Drawing of a socketed antler beam with a shaft hole. Drawing by L. Sørensen and Anne Hooton.